LABOUR AND NATIONALITY IN SOVIET CENTRAL ASIA

LABOUR AND NATIONALITY
IN SOVIET CENTRAL ASIA

An Uneasy Compromise

Nancy Lubin

Princeton University Press
Princeton, New Jersey

Published by Princeton University Press,
41 William Street, Princeton, New Jersey 08540

Printed in Hong Kong

Library of Congress Cataloging in Publication Data

Lubin, Nancy.
    Labour and nationality in Soviet Central Asia.

    Bibliography: p.
    Includes index.
    1. Labor supply—Uzbek S.S.R.   2. Discrimination in
employment—Uzbek S.S.R.   3. Ethnology—Uzbek S.S.R.
I. Title.
HD5797.U9L83   1984   331.6'0958'7   83–26913
ISBN 0–691–07674–X

Contents

Foreword

Murray Feshbach

In the spate of books about the USSR, and of regional aspects in particular, few have been written by a political scientist-cum-economist-cum-ethnographer as is this book by Dr Nancy Lubin. Having studied as a postgraduate student at Oxford under the supervision of Mr Michael Kaser, she adds her reading of the basic materials as well as a one-year experience of daily life, conversations and research in the region under study.

Nowhere is this special access made more clear than her recounting of the source materials used for this book, ranging from field research to emigré interviews, to interviews with Soviet officials, scholars and factory managers, to site visits, to review of over thirty dissertations and to personal contacts. Thus the basis for writing on this topic depends on a wide, even unprecedented range of sources. The book would be valuable for that alone. But it is valuable for many other reasons related to the topics under discussion.

Starting with the demographic and economic background, and always conscious of the nationality aspects of each factor and/or issue, Dr Lubin provides us with a unique view and insight into the actual practice of labour hiring, its distribution and payment, as well as ethnic considerations within each category. As such, in contrast to many prior evaluations, she elicits serious consideration to her findings which are contrary to many interpretations received by myself and others.

Thus sources of tension, *versus* actual patterns of life and/or policies which diffuse these tensions, are depicted throughout the book. Tensions ensue from considerations of language, religion, customs and traditions, yet Dr Lubin asserts that the true picture lies in their containment.

After discussions and presentations of basic data on population trends and labour force distributions by activity, some of the nationality data are displayed for Uzbeks within industry, enterprises and occupations. Much of this material is very useful and new. For example, the low proportion of Uzbeks in machinery and chemical plants contrasts sharply with the proportions in light and food industry plants. Explanations related to urban residence of non-Uzbeks can be utilised only up to a point; herein Lubin also provides documentation and discussion of the underlying choices made by the indigenous population to seek employment in less modern industry. These choices are made on the basis of other criteria related to economic opportunities in household consumption and second economy operations.

New materials on ethnic composition of educational institutions, especially at the higher levels, confirm patterns of traditional choices reflecting agricultural, educational, or light and food industrial occupational training noted in earlier times.

Part II, Chapters 5 to 8, contains the core of her argument. The argument lies not in standard statements about discrimination against the local nationalities in hiring, job assignment and locational choices. Rather, Lubin argues that the indigenous population seeks to avoid many of the seemingly preferable jobs because of alternative choices or preferences. For this argument she adduces materials not previously cited or known in the West such as dissertations, discussions with individuals and observations made during her year of study in the region. In conclusion, she finds that the usual interpretation of discrimination against the locals, population pressures and lack of urbanisation are more the consequence of different criteria by the native populations than hitherto credited or discerned. Evidence from interviews, for example, is cited to underscore reverse discrimination against Russians rather than preferred admission practices in higher educational institutions of Uzbekistan: 'if an Uzbek cannot study here, where else can he go' is noted by one respondent. Unique data on applicants *versus* admissions – for both sexes and for women alone, for all nationalities and for indigenous populations – are provided for a large array of higher educational institutions; these data underscore the point of pro-nationality admissions to Uzbeks. Fascinating information on bribe differentials paid by Jews, Russians and Uzbeks, in descending order as listed, show conscious unofficial affirmative action in favour of native applicants. Even choices of nationality designation for children of mixed nationality marriages demonstrate the felt advantage of choosing the native nationality rather than Russian, the otherwise preferred choice in the RSFSR.

Lubin uses information on incomes to underscore her explanation of why individual natives choose one job or another, not because of outside discrimination but because of income possibilities. Thus, after consideration of the official tier of public-sector earnings, she examines the private-sector source of income from illegal as well as legal sources and uses this material to demonstrate why seemingly contrary patterns emerge. They emerge not from the exclusion of Uzbeks from preferred jobs, but because of the conscious choice of jobs by Uzbeks depending on income possibilities. One of her major sources, the book by Davletov, published in Tashkent in 1978, cites some eighty variations of possible embezzlement of funds from industrial enterprises alone. A systematisation of these variations fall into six major categories: (i) type and character of enterprise activity; (ii) conditions of activity, or flow of inputs and outputs; (iii) production connections; (iv) rules and regulations; (v) opportunity; and (vi) surrounding circumstances (location, demand for product, etc.). Undoubtedly agricultural and service sectors provide variants on the theme. A systematic study such as that by Davletov, as described by Lubin, implies that such considerations are widespread and that the public practises them on a wide scale. Dr Lubin also considers different consumption patterns between nationalities as hiding real income differentials with Western (read Russian) standards not applicable to the Uzbeks, and that actually they consider themselves to be better off than otherwise noted by observers.

Chapter 7 is devoted to an examination of cultural differences between Uzbeks and other nationalities, and the reasons for retention of culturally based choices. These choices lead to persistence of preferences for rural residence and associated occupations. Citation of survey material found in a doctoral dissertation on attitudes among Uzbeks and Russians is examined to demonstrate the persistence of attitudinal differentials, even if some are not too disparate between the two nationalities. Transformation of attitudes into different forms are cited from another study to allege reinforcement of past attitudes rather than their weakening. These sources are then examined in light of cultural policies and the labour force, and of cultural attitudes towards occupational choices by each nationality rather than central control.

In the concluding chapter, Lubin utilises the materials analysed in the previous chapters to argue that there is less tension due to economic issues than thought otherwise, and that their choice as to job, official salary scales and location are due to background differentials and not to discrimination. None the less, negative attitudes towards

Russians exist among the native population because of other criteria or perceptions. Among the major issues which could lead to an increase in tensions would be serious interruptions or cessation of possibilities to earn income from the second economy, a potential consequence of the Andropov drive on discipline and corruption. Only in combination with other language, religious and cultural issues could tensions rise to a system-level problem. None the less, the current balance is found by Dr Lubin to prevent major travails for the system maintainers of Moscow.

The text, in its structure, materials and analysis, together with the unusual statistical information found in the appendices, make the Lubin contribution an important addition to the still limited but significant literature on nationality, and cultural and economic aspects of Soviet society.

Preface

Demographic and economic change in the USSR, and the rise of Islamic consciousness throughout the Muslim world, have drawn a great deal of attention recently to developments in Soviet Central Asia. Demographic and economic trends suggest that a growing proportion of the USSR's total population, military conscripts and civilian labour force will be of Muslim heritage in the near future and will be concentrated in the less-developed southern tier of the country. The growth of ethnic, national and Islamic identity in the USSR has imbued this trend with new political implications.

Because of these concerns, much has been written about the possible growth of manpower and nationality tensions within the predominantly Muslim regions of the Soviet Union, and a great deal of speculation has taken place as to what these strains might hold for the future of the USSR. Remarkably little on-the-ground research, however, has been carried out by Western scholars, and thus tremendous gaps in our knowledge remain.

The following study is meant to be but one contribution in the attempt to fill some of these gaps. It was carried out largely during a one-year stay in Uzbekistan, USSR, and was designed to investigate many of the assumptions observers have made concerning the interplay of manpower and nationality questions within Soviet Central Asia. With a growth in manpower surpluses, Russian dominance of certain sectors or jobs and increasing educational attainment among the indigenous nationalities, for example, to what extent might nationality pressures be growing there? What factors might be contributing to these pressures, and what factors mitigating them? Ultimately, what kinds of challenges might this situation pose for Moscow, and what might it imply in terms of ethnic and political trends within Soviet Central Asia and the USSR as a whole?

These questions will undoubtedly pose serious challenges for Moscow in the near future. But as the book suggests, the answers are not straightforward, and the sources of stability or unrest suggested by labour problems in Soviet Central Asia might be quite different from what one might normally expect to find. While the conclusions outlined in this book are by no means definitive, they are intended to place the main elements of the manpower problem in Soviet Central Asia in a somewhat broader perspective, by examining factors often overlooked in Western analyses; and by so doing, they are intended to suggest alternative ways of interpreting a complex situation in a region growing in economic, political and strategic importance. It is hoped that the present study will encourage more research in a field which is so important to the future of the USSR and yet still so little understood.

Terms regarding 'nationality' and 'ethnicity' used throughout the book, as well as data sources, should probably be clarified from the outset. As mentioned below, while technical differences exist between 'nationality', 'ethnicity', a 'people', an '*ethnos*', etc., these different kinds of loyalties and allegiances are varied and complex in Soviet Central Asia, with the lines between them often indeterminate and vague. Scholars refer alternately to an Uzbek 'nationality' as well as to an Uzbek or Tadzhik 'ethnic group' or 'people', and often refer to Islamic 'national', 'religious' and 'cultural' identities interchangeably. Competing and complementary identities in Central Asia – such as 'Islamic', 'Eastern', 'Pan Turkic' and 'Asian' – have been discussed in various degrees and ways, with various identities used in juxtaposition.[1]

Without entering into an analysis of the different types and strengths of identities in Soviet Central Asia, this book treats the concept of 'nationality' in its broadest sense, i.e. as simply a psychological phenomenon or emotional attitude by which one group sees itself as unique and distinct from other groups. As Rupert Emerson, a scholar of Asian and African nationalism, noted in the 1960s, 'The simplest statement that can be made about a nation is that it is a body of people who feel they are a nation; and it may be that when all the fine-spun analysis is concluded, this will be the ultimate statement as well.'[2] Like family, religion or clan, 'national identity' is considered here as a composite of all of the above divisions. It is considered a basic object of loyalty stemming from a common heritage, tradition, language, consciousness of common experience or from another perhaps vague, but none the less potent emotional force.

For this reason, this book concentrates on the broad distinction between the 'indigenous' and 'non-indigenous' nationalities in Soviet Asia, or the 'Asians' as opposed to the 'Europeans' or 'Slavs'. Vast differences exist, of course, among the nationalities within each grouping, as among the various indigenous nationalities, or between, say, Russians and Ukrainians in Uzbekistan. But in a general political sense, the Asians and Europeans in Uzbekistan can be classified into two relatively distinct groups on the basis of both physical as well as cultural and experiential differences. As an Uzbek scholar notes for his own definitional purposes, 'the local nationalities are close to the Uzbeks by spiritual affinity, just as the nationalities which migrated from European parts of the USSR are close to the Russians'.[3] This book refers to the indigenous nationalities variously as 'natives', 'local nationalities', 'Asians' and 'indigenous nationality groups', and to their opposite numbers as 'Europeans' or 'Slavs'. Where just Uzbeks, Russians or another individual nationality is meant, the distinction is specified.

As for data and information, a note on sources is due. Problems of data collection in the study of Soviet affairs are familiar to anyone who has studied Soviet politics or economics. Problems of data availability are particularly acute with regard to labour and nationality problems. Because Soviet officials view these as such sensitive matters, few statistics are published and even fewer are deemed fit for foreign consumption.

In addition to a general paucity of data on labour and nationality problems, available data are at best fregmentary and contradictory. Discrepancies often occur between official sources of information. Official sources are often contradicted by other, less official sources of information. And both of these problems are compounded by definitional changes and various usages of identical terms by different authors. Terms such as 'labour force', 'labour reserves' and 'labour resources', for example, are often used interchangeably by Soviet authors, even though technically each has its own distinct meaning. When distinctions are made, many authors define each term differently, leading to vast statistical disparities among them. Moreover, changes between censuses sometimes occur, as a result of changes in administrative territorial delineations within the republics, or simply because of improved reporting methods.

Compounding the problem of data availability and analysis is the

Soviet process of data collection itself. Distortions occur at every stage of the data collection process in the USSR, perhaps particularly with regard to labour and nationality topics. Several enterprise directors whom I interviewed in Central Asia, for example, admitted to exaggerating the reported number of Asians employed in their plants on government forms. Just as enterprise production records may be fudged or falsified in order to conform to the directives or policies of the Soviet government, so too are labour force statistics altered to conform to what all directors understand to be the objectives of the central leadership. In the case of Central Asia, data are commonly distorted to imply higher rates of participation of the indigenous nationalities. It can safely be assumed that even the statistics that Soviet authorities in Moscow receive on labour force participation by nationality are not necessarily a valid reflection of reality. One can only assume when reading many Soviet sources, therefore, that the data simply paint the best possible picture from an official point of view.

Finally, information on cultural and attitudinal questions is also particularly difficult to acquire. Analyses of attitudes and cultures, of course, are difficult under any circumstances in any area of the world. The task, however, is particularly difficult in the USSR, where sociological surveys are scarce and where survey data, when available, often appear suspiciously biased. In Central Asia, moreover, interviews are often particularly unreliable, because of the defence mechanisms of the local inhabitants themselves. Fearful that their customs and traditions will appear 'backward' and 'barbaric' to foreign visitors – just as they have been labelled by the Russians up north – the indigenous nationalities often respond to questions in ways which depend more on what they perceive one would like to hear than on reality. In other words, answers to questions often depend simply on how the question is asked.

Bearing these handicaps in mind, the research for this book was based on a wide variety of sources. In addition to primary and secondary sources in Russian and Uzbek (including newspapers and journals acquired while in Soviet Asia), research was based primarily on one year's field work at Tashkent University, Uzbekistan, during 1978–9; a subsequent three-week visit to Central Asia in August–September 1981; and interviews with forty *émigrés* from the Soviet Union who reside in New York, Miami and Dallas. Research activities in Soviet Central Asia included ten months' study at the Population Laboratory of Tashkent University; field research in over thirty cities and towns in Uzbekistan, Kirgizia, Tadzhikistan and Turkmenistan; a total of over sixty interviews with local government officials, scholars, economic planners, factory managers and demographers in these cities and towns; participation in several local conferences and meetings on population and economic issues; visits to over twenty-five factories, organisations and collective farms on both an official and informal basis; analysis of thirty dissertations written in Uzbekistan on labour and nationality questions there; and extended personal contact living with local families throughout Central Asia. In addition, a total of seven weeks were spent in Moscow and Leningrad in 1979 and 1981, researching and interviewing at organisations also concerned with Central Asian manpower. Taken together, it was hoped that all these sources would provide a general framework for evaluating what questions need to be asked, and how the answers to them can begin to be approached. As mentioned above, it is hoped that the present study will encourage more research in a field which is vital to the future of the USSR, and yet still so little understood.

For the purpose of this book, the Library of Congress transliteration system has been used for all translations from Russian to English; for translations from Uzbek, I have adopted the system generally accepted by American scholars.[4] American definitions rather than British or European have been used for all numerical designations, such as 'billion'. Finally, it should be noted that while information not readily available to Westerners has been endnoted fairly extensively, it was necessary in several instances to exclude endnotes, to avoid compromising certain individual sources who wished not to be cited. Information that is not noted should be assumed to have come through private communication to the author.

The number of people who have assisted me in this project is simply too large to list, and I hope I will be excused for not mentioning them all individually. None the less, I would like to thank especially Michael Kaser, the supervisor of my doctoral work at St Antony's College, Oxford University; Archie Brown, also of St Antony's College, Oxford; and Murray Feshbach, Senior Research Scholar at the Kennedy Institute of Ethics, Georgetown University. Their guidance and support from the project's very inception, and their continuous insights as the project progressed, were essential contributions to whatever virtues this book may have, and I seriously doubt whether I would have completed the work had it not been for their care and encouragement. I also owe an enormous debt of gratitude to James Critchlow, of the Board for International Broadcasting, Washington, DC; Rosemarie Crisostomo, analyst at the Foreign Demographic Analysis Division, US Bureau of the Census; and Walker and Mary Connor for the inordinate amount of time and energy they also devoted to this project; their critical advice and support throughout the project were simply invaluable.

In addition, I would like to thank numerous other scholars who assisted me at different stages of the research and writing. Several specialists at the US Department of State were especially helpful in their criticisms of the full manuscript at its later stages: consistently long discussions with Paul Goble helped to focus several of the ideas in this manuscript in a way which I could not have done alone; I also greatly appreciate the support of specialists in the Office of Long Range Assessment and Research under the supervision of Eric Willenz and Dallas Lloyd. Other scholars who commented on or assisted with individual chapters of the book and to whom I also owe a large debt of gratitude include Joseph Berliner, Donald Carlisle, Richard Dobson, William Fierman, Susan Lightbody-Goodman, Gregory Grossman, Thomas Krantz, Gail Lapidus, Robert Martin, Gur Ofer, Theodore Postol, Irwin Selnick, Richard Stites, Tadeuz Swetachowski and Michael Telson.

During the year I spent in Uzbekistan, the staffs of the International Research and Exchanges Board and the US Embassy in Moscow could not have been more helpful. Without the constant support of Barbara Allen, Pat and Bill Kushlis, Edward McGaffegan and Sharon Miles of the US Embassy when I was thousands of miles away from Moscow – indeed, without the consistently strong support of the Embassy and Consular staffs generally – I can safely say that my year in Uzbekistan would well have been much more difficult. The staff of IREX certainly facilitated my entry into, and my work once within, the USSR. Finally, I would also like to thank Ambassador and Mrs Sutherland of the United Kingdom, my guardians while I was in England and presently stationed in the British Embassy in Moscow. Both specialists on the USSR, they made my return to the West not only a warm and welcome one, but enormously profitable as they helped to refine the fresh insights gained from Uzbekistan before these could be lost.

On the financial side, I am grateful to the American Association of University Women (AAUW); the International Research and Exchanges Board (IREX); Britain's National Association of Slavic and

East European Studies (NASEES); the Office of Long Range Assessment and Research, Bureau of Intelligence and Research, US Department of State (INR/LAR); St Antony's College and the Faculty of Social Studies, Oxford University; and the Russian Institute, Columbia University, for providing the financial and often other assistance necessary to carry out various stages of the research and writing. Among Soviets in the USSR and abroad, I would like to thank the many officials, academicians, friends, dissidents and *émigrés* who helped in essential ways. For administrative and typing assistance, the long, 'last-minute' hours contributed by Dottie Richroath and Janet Rouamba were invaluable for completing the project on time. And finally, special thanks must be extended to my parents, family and friends who experienced all of the ups and downs with me but were never lacking in support. The views expressed in this book, of course, are my sole responsibility.

NANCY LUBIN

Glossary

atlas	national dress worn by Central Asian women
blat	connections, influence or 'pull' in the Soviet system
chaikhona	teahouse
chapan	type of coat worn by Central Asian men
chernorabochie	lowest-skilled workers
Doktor Nauk	a higher doctorate (than the Ph.D. equivalent, *Kandidat Nauk*)
doppi	type of skullcap worn by Central Asian males and females
FZU	*fabrichno zavodskoe uchilishche*, or schools for factory/plant apprenticeships
gorod khlebnyi	literally, 'bread city'; reference to city where food is in plentiful supply
kalym	bride-price
Kandidat Nauk	Ph.D.
khudzhum	assault in the mid-1920s in Soviet Central Asia against female seclusion
kolkhoz	collective farm
korenizatsiia	'nativisation'
medresseh	religious school
Minpros	*Ministerstvo Prosveshcheniia*, Ministry of Education
Minvuz	*Ministerstvo Vysshogo i Srednego Spetsial'nogo Obrazovaniia*, Ministry of Higher and Specialised Secondary Education
nechernozem	non-black earth zone; a major land-reclamation scheme in the RSFSR
OBKhSS	*Otdel' Bor'by Khishcheniiami Sotsialisticheskoi Sobstvennosti*, special economic police

oblast'	province; administrative division in the USSR
Obispolkom	*oblast'* executive committee
orgnabor	organised recruitment of labour
parandja	veil
PTU	*Professional'noe tekhnicheskoe uchilishche*, Professional Technical Institute
rabochie mesta	workplaces
rabochie na storone	hired workers
raion	region; administrative division of the USSR
rastsvet	'flourishing'
RSFSR	Russian Soviet Federated Socialist Republic
samizdat	underground literature
sblizhenie	coming together, rapprochement
slianiia	assimilation, merging
sovkhoz	state farm
ShUMPy	*Shkoly ucheba massovykh professii*, schools for the apprenticeship of mass professions
stavka	shift
tandoor	clay oven
TashPI	Tashkent Pedagogical Institute
tekhnikum	technical school
TIERRT	Tashkent Institute for Engineers of Railway Transport
TsSU	*Tsentral'noe Statisticheskoe Upravlenie*, Central Statistical Administration
tvorog	farmer cheese
VUZ	*Vyshee uchebnoe zavedenie*, higher educational establishment
zakonomernost'	regularity, conformity with a law

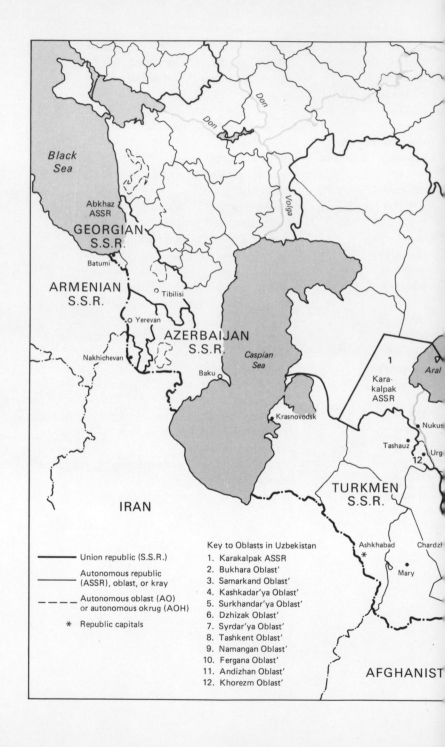

Black
Sea

Abkhaz
ASSR

GEORGIAN
S.S.R.

Batumi

ARMENIAN
S.S.R.

○ Tibilisi

○ Yerevan

AZERBAIJAN
S.S.R.

Nakhichevan

Caspian
Sea

Baku ○

Don

Don

Don

Volga

1

Kara-
kalpak
ASSR

Aral

Nukus

Krasnovodsk

Tashauz

Urg

12

TURKMEN
S.S.R.

IRAN

Ashkhabad

Chardzh

*

Mary

AFGHANIST

Key to Oblasts in Uzbekistan

——— Union republic (S.S.R.)

——— Autonomous republic
(ASSR), oblast, or kray

– – – Autonomous oblast (AO)
or autonomous okrug (AOH)

* Republic capitals

1. Karakalpak ASSR
2. Bukhara Oblast'
3. Samarkand Oblast'
4. Kashkadar'ya Oblast'
5. Surkhandar'ya Oblast'
6. Dzhizak Oblast'
7. Syrdar'ya Oblast'
8. Tashkent Oblast'
9. Namangan Oblast'
10. Fergana Oblast'
11. Andizhan Oblast'
12. Khorezm Oblast'

Introduction

From Alexander the Great, to Chingis Khan, to Tamerlane, one tends to associate the importance of Central Asia with a romantic, dramatic past. Lying at the meeting-place of East and West, Central Asia was the location of spectacular economic, cultural and political achievements attained centuries ago. Agriculture was well advanced; trade was extensive; and great centres of education, art, architecture, poetry, religion and scientific thought developed and flourished. With the sixteenth century, however – as European merchants turned their attention towards the New World, and as oceans became a more important mode of transporting goods – Central Asia's importance greatly declined. In the eyes of many, Central Asia remained stuck in its past, and slowly lost its glory, power and relevance as the rest of the world entered the modern age. For the past century, it seemed to lie not only on the geographical fringes of Russia and the USSR, but on the fringes of Russian and Soviet society as well. It was a living relic of a long-lost glory, for the most part ignoring, and ignored by the rest of the world.

The past few years, however, have seen an enormous resurgence of attention on the Soviet Asian region, because of the political and strategic role which the area has begun to play in a modern, global context. Almost suddenly, the USSR's Central Asian region has become a crucial factor in Soviet foreign and domestic affairs. The December 1979 invasion and continued Soviet presence in Afghanistan have highlighted its importance in Soviet foreign policy. Bordered by the Middle East, Soviet Asia has become a geographic springboard for Soviet involvement, political and military, in the nations on its southern flank. Tashkent now provides an excellent base for interaction in that part of the world. And in addition to their regional proximity, ethnic similarities with the populations across the border make the Central Asian people strategically important as well. Both before and after the 1979 invasion, for example, Soviet Asians were sent to Afghanistan as economic and political advisors; and thousands of Afghan students and professional workers have been sent to schools, summer camps or to other joint projects in Soviet Central Asia. Since the invasion, speeches from Soviet Islamic leaders have been broadcast repeatedly to Afghanistan, emphasising the common heritage which the inhabitants of the two countries share and urging support for the Soviet-installed Karmal regime. Moscow is similarly employing Central Asians to strengthen ties with other peoples on its southern borders.

In a more general foreign policy sense, Soviet Central Asia serves as a showcase for what Communism can achieve in lesser-developed countries throughout the world, and also provides the USSR with opportunities for furthering its designs in the Muslim and Asian worlds as a whole. Central Asians have served as Soviet ambassadors, advisors and other personnel throughout the Middle East, propagating the notion that the Soviet Union shares a common past with those countries and thus a common interest with them. The Soviet Asian region, moreover, is frequently included in the itinerary of officials who visit the USSR from other less developed countries throughout the world.

With regard to the Soviet domestic situation, there are also several reasons why Soviet Central Asia has been attracting more of the world's attention. Probably foremost among them is the demographic question. With average annual growth rates throughout the 1970s ranging between 3.1 and 3.5 per cent per year, the Asian population of the Soviet Union is growing more than four times as fast as the USSR's ethnic Russian population.[1] This means that within thirty or forty years there will be as many Central Asians entering the workforce as there will be ethnic Russians; and because of the low mobility of the Soviet Asian population, it also means that a growing proportion of the Soviet labour force will be concentrated in the southern tier of the country.

In purely strategic terms, moreover, while the Russians have long taken for granted their dominance in the military, by the year 2000, at least one fifth of the USSR's 18 year-olds will come from the four Central Asian republics. (The Russian republic's potential supply of 18 year-old males will drop to 44 per cent of the total number of 18 year-olds in the year 2000, as against 56 per cent in 1970). It has been suggested that the nationalities with a Muslim heritage will account for one third of the military conscript pool by the year 2000.[2] At a time when the Soviet Union is expecting a severe labour shortage in the near future; when this labour shortage will be particularly acute in the European parts of the USSR and in Siberia and the Far East; and when evidence of ethnic tension already exists within the Soviet army; this rapid population growth of the Soviet Central Asians is assuming even greater significance than the numbers alone would suggest.

Finally, Soviet Central Asia is also gaining prominence in the world's eyes because of its natural resources. Although a large portion of the area is classified as either desert or mountain, Central Asia has been playing an increasingly significant role in the overall USSR economy as a major supplier of cotton, fruits, vegetables and other foodstuffs, non-ferrous and rare metals, and energy resources. Aside from accounting for more than 90 per cent of the Soviet production of cotton fibre, for the past few years, Central Asia has accounted for more than one-quarter of Soviet natural gas production,[3] one quarter of Soviet copper production, and according to one Soviet specialist in Moscow, Uzbekistan and Turkmenistan alone may now account for as much as 50 per cent of the USSR's gold output. While Western estimates are generally more conservative, they, too, point out the importance of Central Asia in gold extraction. According to a 1979 report of Consolidated Gold Fields Ltd, Uzbekistan's Muruntau complex, with an estimated gold production of eighty tons per year, was at that time the largest gold-mine in the world;[4] my own data indicate that Uzbekistan alone has at least five other deposits currently being worked. The fact that the price of gold on the world-market rose fourteenfold between 1971 and 1981, and that energy has equally become a more important economic variable, means that the relative importance of Central Asia in the Soviet economy is also becoming that much greater.

In the light of the region's renewed importance, then, how the Central Asians think and feel is becoming a crucial concern for Moscow. If the Soviet Asians are indeed loyal citizens with allegiances to Moscow, they provide enormous opportunities and represent a substantial asset in many aspects of Soviet domestic and foreign affairs. If, on the other hand, animosity toward Moscow, or a sense of nationalism and separateness is strong, then they represent an extremely grave challenge to the central authorities in vital economic and political arenas. Today, therefore, it is particularly important to analyse what the area itself is like, and what the main sources of tension there may be.

The question of what Soviet Central Asia in fact 'is like', however, has become the focus of some controversy. While Central Asia is traditionally a Muslim area with a language, tradition and culture vastly different from that of the Russians, observers disagree as to just how 'Muslim', 'Turkic' and 'pro-' or 'anti-Soviet' the Soviet Central Asians may be today, and how restive they may become in the near future. One area where this question has become particularly controversial is in manpower utilisation. As illustrated below, the indigenous nationalities in Central Asia predominate among the population not working in the national economy and among the population employed in the lower-paid jobs and sectors. Many Western observers argue that this situation is imbued with enormous political implications, as indigenous Central Asians would no doubt like to alter what must be regarded as their second-class status; but the political implications are more complex and unclear. Is the manpower situation in Soviet Central Asia the result of discrimination against the Central Asians, or of Central Asian preferences? How rapidly has it been changing? Does it pose a threat to Moscow, or perhaps, as some scholars in Moscow would argue, an opportunity? These questions form the focus of this book. Before discussing these manpower issues, however, it is useful to briefly discuss some background for Soviet Central Asia and related issues of religion, language and culture.

BACKGROUND

The four republics of Uzbekistan, Kirgizia, Turkmenistan and Tadzhikistan which together comprise Soviet Central Asia[5] occupy an area approximately 13 million square kilometres, characterised by tremendous fluctuations in altitude, terrain and climate. Bordered by Chinese Sinkiang to the East, Afghanistan and Iran to the South, the Caspian Sea to the west and European Russia and Kazakhstan to the north, the land of Soviet Central Asia is austere. Most of it consists of barren or grassy steppes and vast expanses of desert which extend to high plateaus and mountain chains. Altitudes range from well below sea-level in some regions north and east of the Caspian Sea, to one of the highest mountain masses in the world. Wide temperature fluctuations characterise the mostly dry, arid climate.

Before the 1917 Revolution, Islam formed the basis of life in Central Asia, whose people were more akin to the neighbouring Persians and Turks than to the Russians of the north. Life was organised around the tribe or clan, and traditional occupations centred on sedentary pursuits of the oasis – agriculture, commerce, artisan trades – or nomadic pastoralism. Even the Russian domination of the late nineteenth century did little substantially to alter local village life. The total Russian population living in Central Asia at the turn of the century was small, comprising only about 2 per cent of the Central Asian population; and the lives of the Russians and Asians rarely overlapped. National identity was unknown among the indigenous populations, as loyalties rarely extended beyond the family, tribe or clan.

After the Revolution, however, the Bolshevik government strove not only to rule the area, but thoroughly to transform the region and its people. It faced an almost entirely rural and Muslim population which had a 1 per cent literacy rate; a Persian (in the case of the Tadzhiks) or Turkic (in the case of most of the other major Central Asian peoples) language completely unrelated to Russian; and strong economic, social and political traditions and institutions totally alien to the Russian heritage. In the face of these obstacles, the revolutionaries set out to eradicate religion, educate the population, make Russian the *lingua franca*, introduce modern industry, and supplant local traditions with Soviet mores and ways. The explicit aim was voluntary integration of the Central Asians into the newly-created Soviet state.

Original policies toward these ends marked a compromise between the Party's aim for absolute unity and centralisation, and its recognition that the pursuit of such aims could unleash ethnic or tribal loyalties into a potent political force. The new Soviet policies therefore stressed elements of both change and continuity. With the object of ultimately eradicating ethnic differences, Soviet planners simultaneously catered to local desires, using both carrot and stick and intentionally ambiguous policies to impose change over an entire society. In other words, since nationalism was viewed mainly as a response to past oppression, Lenin's policies were designed to overcome any fear of potential Russian domination by sometimes catering to national or local consciousness. Coupled with policies fostering social and economic development, this 'dialectical' route was expected to allay suspicions and to convince the local nationalities that it was indeed in their direct interest to remain within the larger state. Thus, the promise of self-determination in the new Soviet constitution was designed 'dialectically' to lessen secessionist sentiment among the smaller nationalities. The encouragement of the local languages was to allay fears and make the message of assimilation more acceptable – which, in turn, was to lead to voluntary surrender of the national languages and narrow

national identities for a larger Soviet identity. In short, a 'flourishing of
nations' was to lead to their eventual 'coming together', or 'rapproche-
ment', which was ultimately to lead to their 'merging' or assimilation:
rastsvet was to lead to *sblizhenie* was to lead to *slianie*. Although there
may have been some retreat in their pursuit of *slianie*, present Soviet
leaders have basically remained faithful to the notion of *sblizhenie* and
to Lenin's original practical approach.[6]

Thus, over the past sixty years, large numbers of Russians and Slavs
have entered the region, bringing Soviet policies, culture and attitudes
with them. In just a short span of time, economic development in
Central Asia was spectacular, and the corresponding social transformations, dramatic. A large scale industrialisation drive was begun,
while Soviet-style buildings and homes were erected in many urban
and rural areas alike. Uzbekistan's literacy rate rose from about 1 per
cent of the population (aged 9–49) to about 99 per cent. And while the
alphabet of the local Asian languages was changed twice, the local
people also were pressed to learn a new language, Russian. On the
other hand, other aspects of Central Asian culture were allowed,
within certain limits, to persist, or 'flower'. Today, Soviet Central Asia
is an amalgam of over 100 nationalities and ethnic groups, with Slavs
accounting for about 15 per cent of the population, and Central
Asians, most of the remainder.

The result of these transformations has made the Central Asians and
their republics a dual blend of two worlds. Today, after decades of
exceptionally rapid economic development, several of Central Asia's
cities are regarded as large urban centres to rival those almost anywhere in the USSR. Tashkent – the fourth largest city in the USSR in
terms of population size, the third largest in terms of territory – is
considered a major government and cultural centre housing some of
the Soviet Union's largest factories and institutes. Yet the long dusty
roads of these cities dotted with small adobe homes built, as in most
Muslim areas, without windows or doors looking onto the street; the
old men on donkeys competing with buses and trolleys on the city's
main thoroughfares; the young Uzbek boys grazing their sheep in the
university park – everything in the physical appearance of Soviet
Central Asia's cities suggests that they are not 'modern industrial
centres' in any familiar sense of the term, but rather, that elements of
an ancient past persist, indeed still remain strong.

This duality is mirrored in the self-perceptions and ethnic identity of
Central Asia's inhabitants. Professional attainment particularly
among the indigenous nationalities, for instance, has risen remarkably
over the past sixty years; yet it is not at all unusual for an Uzbek

professor at a Tashkent institute to teach five hours of classes on modern theories of economic development in the morning, and then to don his traditional '*chapan*,' or Central Asian coat, and barter lambs, pomegranates or tomatoes in the local market in the afternoon, just as his ancestors did centuries ago (see Chapter 7). Local teenagers in the smaller cities of the Fergana Valley may spend one evening celebrating a wedding or circumcision strictly according to traditional and religious rules, and then spend the next evening dancing Western rock and roll in Andizhan's local discothèque, or studying for exams on scientific atheism.

In other words, distinctions between ancient and modern, religious and secular, or Asian and European are no longer as clearly defined as they were just a few decades ago, and the same applies to individual identity. Today, a local person can be an 'Uzbek', a 'Tadzhik' or any one of the other Central Asian nationalities in Uzbekistan without necessarily being a Muslim believer. He might consider himself first as a 'Soviet citizen' and only then as a member of an 'Uzbek' or 'Central Asian' nation. He might consider himself as an Asian first, with his identity as part of the Soviet Union only secondary or incidental. Or just as easily, he might be both at the same time: it is not at all uncommon to run across the self-proclaimed 'Soviet internationalist' and atheist who, full of conviction, renounces religion and nationalist distinctions daily, but who simultaneously insists upon observing certain 'traditions' which are nothing less than pure Islamic rites. In Soviet Central Asia this duality pervades every aspect of life.

RELIGION

In terms of religion, for example, Soviet and Western estimates on the number of Muslim believers in Soviet Central Asia range from about 5 per cent of the area to about 65 per cent. In interviews with the Mufti Babakhan, chairman of the Muslim Religious Board for Central Asia and Kazakhstan until his death in 1982; his son, the present Mufti and chairman; the deputy chairman of the Muslim Religious Board, Sheikh Abdulgani Abdullayev, and students at the Tashkent Theological Seminary, I was told emphatically that the number of believers in Uzbekistan was around 60–70 per cent of the total population. In interviews with local economists, academics and government officials, I was told equally emphatically that the proportion was not above 5–6 per cent.

But the biggest problem in evaluating the place of religion in Soviet

Central Asian life – and the reason for the exceptionally wide range of estimates – is the whole question of what in fact constitutes a 'believer'. The Communist Party member who has renounced religion all his life, but who on his deathbed demands a religious burial – is he a 'believer'? The high school student who, in equal measures, has memorised both sections of the Koran and slogans of atheist propaganda – is he a 'believer'? And the student of the local *medresseh* (religious school), whose loyalty to the Soviet regime had to be confirmed even before his acceptance to the school, and who thoroughly believes that religion, first and foremost, must serve the needs of the State – is he any more truly a 'believer'?

While formally anti-religious, the Soviet government has been determined to prove that there is 'freedom of worship' in the USSR, so it officially keeps some mosques running and the mullahs well-paid. This policy works both to provide a safety valve for religious feelings in the area itself, and to court the favour of Muslim nations throughout the world. In Uzbekistan alone there are sixty-five registered mosques and as many as 3000 active mullahs and other Muslim clerics. For almost forty years the Muslim Religious Board for Central Asia and Kazakhstan has been 'actively working to enhance all aspects of religious affairs' and has been publishing a monthly journal hailing the vigour of religious life in Central Asia. The Mufti Babakhan meets with literally hundreds of foreigners every year; and, like the delegations which assembled in Dushanbe (1979), in Tashkent (1980), and several smaller subsequent international delegations to Central Asia to mark the beginning of the fifteenth century of the Islamic calendar, there are also at least five or six international conferences and meetings on religious affairs held in Soviet Central Asia annually.

The Soviet Muslims working or participating in any of these organisations, however, are all carefully screened for political reliability. And even while the Soviet government has apparently been encouraging the practice of Islam with one hand, it has been intensifying its efforts to stamp out religion as 'an evil of the past' with the other hand. (This, of course, accounts for the lower estimates of religious affiliation, since to estimate otherwise would be an acknowledgement of defeat in their anti-religious campaign.) Thus, for example, almost at the same time that publication of the journal *Muslims of the Soviet East* was begun, compulsory courses on scientific atheism were also introduced into all institutes of higher learning. As any tourist can note today, signs deriding religion as the 'opium of the masses' dot the walls of museums, schools and other public buildings, and in Soviet Asia, atheist propaganda now pervades all educational establishments. As part of one's coursework, for example, a high-school student must write an essay on the topic: 'My Relationship towards Religious Holidays and towards Religion Itself'. In several personal interviews it became clear that if the response is anything but anti-religious, the student is kept after school for consultation and asked to rewrite the essay. There may also be repercussions later when he or she is applying for a job.

Finally, even those who may officially practice religion are limited in their ability to so so. Only about thirty Soviet citizens each year are permitted to make the pilgrimage to Mecca, and official religious schools in Soviet Asia devote only a minor amount of time to the actual study of religion. In the four-year curriculum of the Tashkent Higher School of Islam, one of the two theological seminaries in Central Asia, twenty-eight subjects are studied. Only six of them, however, (about 1400 hours) are on religious subjects, while twenty-two (3800 hours) are devoted to 'Soviet Sciences' and six hours each week are spent on Russian language study. Local inhabitants commonly note, moreover, that 'the Soviet government always schedules the best TV programmes during religious holidays – ostensibly to lure youth away from meaningless religious ceremonies' towards more secular pursuits.

Partly as a response to these ambivalent policies, the extent of 'underground religion' has apparently grown over the past several years. Particularly in smaller villages, one often finds explicitly illegal 'underground *medressehs*' or unofficial 'conversation circles' where a mullah or other religious figure presides over discussions of religious ideas with the young. Around the time that I was in Uzbekistan, about twenty-eight secondary students periodically gathered in Ganiabad for religious instruction at that village's 'underground' *medresseh*. Elsewhere, as in Namangan and Kokand, unofficial 'conversation circles' with a similar level of attendance met weekly. Several Western scholars have also referred to the possible renaissance of certain Sufi orders in Uzbekistan and other Muslim parts of the USSR, although it would be difficult to judge just how much of this is a reflection of a real growth in the strength and attractiveness of these orders among residents, and how much is due simply to the fact that our awareness of them has grown.[7] At the same time, however, one cannot underestimate the success which Soviet policies have had among other segments of Central Asia's population: as often as one hears stories about illegal religious gatherings, one will also hear stories such as that of a Muslim father who tried to raise his son to believe in Allah – and whose son subsequently renounced all his father's teachings and ran off to study at the Kuibyshev Technological Institute.

In the light of all of these factors, it is extremely difficult to get an accurate indication of just how strong religious feeling is in Soviet Central Asia. Quite by accident, however, I came across an unpublished study written by an Uzbek academic in 1975 which tried to measure how strong religion is among Uzbek youth.[8] The author interviewed over 2300 young people (aged 14–30 years old) in Uzbekistan, and divided them into seven groups: 'militant atheists', 'ordinary atheists', 'non-believers', 'followers of religious traditions', 'vacillators', 'ordinary believers', and 'staunch believers'. As most such surveys which have reached the West, this study found that the vast majority of his respondents fell into the middle categories, exhibiting some personal religious sense but little belief in God. On the basis of the 2300 interviews, he concluded that almost all Uzbek youth feel religious marriage ceremonies and circumcision are essential; most participate in Muslim festivals and holidays, and many often visit 'holy places', whether out of their own volition or because of parental pressure. He also found, however, that probably only a very small number believe in or have any conception of Allah, and few know the contents of the Koran.

In other words, the religious situation in Soviet Central Asia has been marked by an ambiguous official policy, whereby what officials say with one breath they contradict with the next, and this ambiguity has been reflected in the population's behaviour. Today most Soviet Central Asians, young and old alike, conduct their daily lives somewhere in the hazy area between officially-sanctioned and illegal or officially-disapproved religious practices. Religious policies have been difficult to implement: a teacher confided, 'I finished the institute a long time ago. Honestly speaking, I just don't know how to conduct atheist propaganda work, especially during lessons.' Instead of eradicating religion, the policies more often than not have simply institutionalised duplicity: 'I pray on my own, at home. If I were to frequent a mosque, it wouldn't be good for my job'. But however ambiguous the results, Soviet policies have at least kept the issue of religion alive. A little Uzbek boy, successfully imbued with atheist ideas, seemed to illustrate the resulting concern and confusion over this situation: 'In school we fight against religion. Why does the mullah act freely in our village, and nobody touches him? It seems to me we should put him in jail'.

LANGUAGE

The place of language is similar to that of religion. Even though many Central Asians speak hardly a word of Russian, they have begun to send their children to Russian-language schools. Typical of more and more Soviet Asian parents, they feel a knowledge of Russian is the only way to get ahead in this world. Children will need Russian to get a good job, so they might as well start when they are young. The 1979 census indicated a rise in the number of Russian-speakers in Uzbekistan of about five million people in only nine years, from 14.5 per cent of the native population in 1970 to 49.3 per cent in 1979.[9]

At the same time, however, young and old alike in Central Asia are using their local languages more often at their places of work and in daily life than they did even ten or fifteen years ago. Part of the reason for the wider use of the local language, of course, is simply the ease of speaking one's native tongue as compared with a learned language. But Soviet officials seem to be concerned that part of the reason may represent a deliberate political statement as well. As one young Uzbek communist described, in the late 1970s a meeting was called of the Uzbek Komsomol Central Committee to discuss plans for issuing a new Komsomol journal. Almost immediately the question arose concerning the language in which the journal should be written. According to the young communist, the debate became very heated, even though, as he explained, the journal could very easily have been published half in Russian and half in Uzbek. The debate ended in a stalemate, and publication of the journal never began. Apparently, these debates occur frequently, at all levels of government and Party work.

In the light of this new assertion, rather than diminution in the use of the local languages, the past few years have seen a stepped-up campaign on the part of the Soviet government to spread further the use of Russian as the *lingua franca*. Throughout the 1970s, a number of conferences were organised, and resolutions passed, to increase Russian language training and use in the non-Russian republics. In October, 1978 the USSR Council of Ministers passed a resolution entitled 'On measures for Further Improving the Study and Teaching of the Russian Language in the Union Republics'. The number of hours that Asians were required to study Russian in schools was increased, while the number of hours a Russian had to study the local language was reduced. These measures were followed by a nationwide conference held in Tashkent in May, 1979 entitled *The Russian Language – The Language of Friendship and Co-operation of the Peoples of the USSR.* The proposals emerging from this conference included intensifying Russian-language training at all levels of education, and introducing Russian training in kindergartens and nurseries. The 1980s have seen a continuing series of conferences and increasingly stringent measures to promote the use of Russian as well.

None the less, these new measures have been accompanied by policies on the part of the local organisations which seem to encourage, or at least perpetuate the use of local languages. Every year, more and more items of Western and Soviet literature are translated into the native languages in all the Asian republics and local printing-houses are publishing increasing numbers of newspapers, and journals in the local dialects. The past few years saw the emergence of the first multi-volume encyclopedia in the Uzbek language, as well as several volumes of encyclopedias and the first medical, legal and general educational textbooks in Uzbek, Tadzhik, Turkmen and Kirgiz. In short, more Central Asians are learning, and voluntarily using, Russian. But paradoxically, the growing mastery of Russian among the Asian population has been accompanied – sometimes deliberately, sometimes not – by a new assertiveness of the local, native tongues.

TRADITION AND CULTURE

Other aspects of tradition and culture occupy a similarly ambiguous place in Central Asian society, as seen through Central Asia's architecture, dress, literature or the arts as a whole. Architecturally, most of Soviet Central Asia's urban areas are a mixture of modern multi-storey apartment or office buildings and buildings reflecting the long dominance of Islam. Remains of some of the most impressive Islamic monuments in the world dominate several of Central Asia's major cities – most notably Samarkand, Bukhara, Khiva and Kokand – with active reconstruction work a large part of Soviet architectural efforts. Alongside, however, lie European-style meeting-rooms and parks, dotted with modern Soviet sculpture. Traditional homes in urban areas – one-storey adobe structures built in traditional patterns – border new regions where apartments furnished with more 'modern' Soviet appliances and furniture are the norm.

Dress and other customs among local inhabitants also reflect the same duality. The *parandja*, or veil traditionally worn among women in Central Asia has all but disappeared. In many of the region's smaller cities and towns, however, women still cover themselves with shawls from head to toe before going out onto the street. Indigenous Central Asians often admire Western items and often complement their native dress with European suits, shoes or jewellery. None the less, they still more commonly wear the traditional *atlas, duppi* or *chapan* (a national Central Asian dress for women, skullcap or type of Central Asian coat), in urban and rural areas alike. Indeed, one urban Uzbek woman was thrilled when I gave her a western skirt and sweater for her birthday. She complemented the outfit, however, with traditional Uzbek pants worn underneath – either in the conviction that it looked prettier, or in the conviction that it simply was more proper for a woman not to display her legs. The same mixture holds true for other customs: while *kalym*, or brideprice, has been outlawed in Soviet Asia, the traditional exchange of 'gifts' before marriage is not altogether dissimilar. Rites and ceremonies – births, circumcisions, marriages, funerals – still closely adhere to the dictates of tradition.

Finally, the arts in Central Asia reflect the same duality. Literature, films and plays in Central Asia appear in both Russian and the local languages, on both local and Soviet themes, and foreign films are imported from both the East and West. During the 1978–9 school year, films from Italy, France, the US and India played in the theatres of Uzbekistan, Tadzhikistan and Kirgizia, and joint film projects were under way or had recently been completed with India, Afghanistan and the United States.[10] Evenings of traditional folk music and dance alternate with western ballet in local theatres, and literature in Central Asia also combines the two worlds. As an article in a local Uzbek newspaper pointed out, the infusion of 'international characteristics' into Uzbek literature still does not imply that national differences have greatly narrowed.[11]

In the light of this situation, the 1970s have witnessed a stepped-up campaign to diminish 'cultural hangovers' as well as strictly religious or linguistic ones. Soviet planners recently adopted a policy to demolish most of Tashkent's old city, planning to let only a small part remain as a museum. Despite great resistance on the part of local inhabitants, they have begun to move residents from the old city of Tashkent to apartment buildings in the new part of town. Similarly, planners often encourage western dress at work, and strong censorship controls have been imposed on Central Asian literature just as they have been elsewhere in the USSR. At the same time, however, Soviet planners also deliberately construct many new buildings in Central Asia to reflect traditional 'Asian style'. Intricate woodwork and Islamic designs ornament the entry-ways, walls and ceilings of a vast number of public buildings throughout Central Asia. The formation of native music or dance ensembles receives official encouragement and the 1960s and 1970s have seen the rehabilitation of several indigenous Central Asian writers and poets, such as Abdulla Qadiry, Fitrat, Batu and Cholpan.[12]

Again, therefore, ambiguous policies have been reflected in ambiguous behaviour. Many Central Asian writers are content to write on Soviet themes – and quite avidly do so – knowing that this is the key to success in the USSR, and perhaps often believing what they write. At the same time, the 1970s and early 1980s have seen increased attempts on the part of the indigenous nationalities to return to classical forms of music, art and poetry – for example, to reassert the value of folk art, epics or miniature painting. Recent articles in the local press have contained appeals for a return to boys' dancing, while many indigenous literary scholars and historians have become more practised at circumventing censorship controls to assert their indigenous cultures.

In short, religion, language and the persistence of tradition and culture are indicative of a strong retention of ethnic identity in Soviet Asia, but not in the clear-cut sense in which one tends to view them in the West. Most of Central Asia's population has never made a conscious decision either to believe in Allah or to disavow him, either to assert one's native tongue or to speak Russian. Because Soviet policy seemingly encourages all these things simultaneously, therefore, the issues of language, culture and religion – while certainly alive, and sometimes even volatile – none the less remain vague to many Central Asians, who in large part unconsciously have accommodated themselves to an ambiguous kind of existence.

In a directly political sense, the ambiguity of the above situation illustrates that the social and political transformations which occurred in Soviet Central Asia have been affected only in part. As the Basmachi and other rebellions, the *khudzhum** and the purges all suggest, moreover, they have not been effected without conflict and tension. In general, the upheavals which Soviet social policies entailed led to tremendous dislocations in a way of life which had remained

---

*Term used to designate the head-on assault against female seclusion in Soviet Central Asia in the mid to late 1920s. See G. Massell, *The Surrogate Proletariat*, (Princeton, NJ: Princeton University Press, 1974) pp. 226–40.

relatively unchanged for centuries. Today, therefore, religion, language, customs and tradition – while they have undeniably changed – have all become the source of tension in Soviet Central Asia, and could prove to be the foci of immense political unrest. As political issues, however, they are also being diffused and contained, and overt nationalist demands or demonstrations over these issues in Central Asia appear infrequently.

MODERNISATION AND THE WORKFORCE

One area where this duality persists but may not be so readily contained is in modernisation and the creation of an indigenous labour force. Almost daily, it seems, one hears in Soviet Asia the same history lecture, praising the growth of skilled native cadres and emphasising how this is but another success indicator of Soviet development policy. One is constantly reminded that before Soviet rule was established in Central Asia in the early 1920s, there were few, if any, skilled indigenous personnel, no local cadres. Initially this necessitated importing workers and trained personnel from other parts of the USSR. Between 1939 and 1940, for example, 85 per cent of the new additions to Uzbekistan's industrial labour force came from outside the Central Asian region.[13]

But special efforts were made to train a skilled labour force among the local nationalities of the republics. The number of people with a higher education in Soviet Central Asia grew from four per thousand population in 1939, to thirty-five per thousand in 1970. Today, at least half of Central Asia's workers and employees are indigenous, and Asians comprise more than 80 per cent of the students in institutes of higher learning in the Central Asian republics.[14]

The frequency with which one hears this same lecture in Moscow and Central Asia underlines the importance which officials place on increasing the number of native cadres. What these officials never go on to say, however, is that their success in promoting native cadres has not led to an equal distribution of the Central Asian labour force by nationality, and has not necessarily led to an 'internationalisation' of the Uzbek workforce. Instead, after sixty years of Soviet development policies, the Soviet Asians today are still under-represented in the labour force relative to their proportion in the total and working-age populations, and are still overwhelmingly concentrated in agriculture and in the non-industrial and non-technical sectors and occupations.

In other words, while modernisation has occurred rapidly in Soviet Central Asia, the local nationalities have been only partly included in that modernisation process, and manpower use in Soviet Central Asia illustrates the same duality as do the issues of language, culture and religion. Present economic and demographic trends, however, suggest, that labour issues could increasingly become a potent source of tension in terms of nationality politics in general.

Four aspects of labour use are important in any analysis of manpower and nationality questions in Soviet Central Asia. First, because of high natural growth rates and resistance to migration among the indigenous populations, an apparent labour surplus is growing in Soviet Asia and is expected to grow even more rapidly beginning in the 1990s. The indigenous nationalities, moreover, comprise the bulk of the republics' populations not working in the socialised economy, and as surpluses grow, this trend can be expected to continue. Throughout the 1970s, for example, close to one million people in Uzbekistan alone, almost entirely of the indigenous nationalities, were not working in the socialised economy and were not students – that is, they were either not working or were working exclusively in the private sector without remuneration from the State. In the coming years, analysts expect this number to grow, with an increasingly large proportion comprised mainly of indigenous Central Asians.

Second, among the labour force employed in social production in Central Asia, Central Asians predominate in the least modernised sectors of the economy (agriculture and the service sectors), while Slavs are disproportionately represented in the more industrial and technical jobs and sectors (skilled and unskilled). Within industry, Russians predominate in the heavy industrial sectors, while the indigenous nationalities are mainly in light industries and food. And by occupation, Central Asians tend to dominate the highest, most visible positions throughout the economy, or else the lowest-skilled jobs and occupations outside the production process – truck-drivers, guards or other low-level service personnel. If labour surpluses are growing for the region as a whole, this shortfall of jobs is found particularly in the sectors and jobs where the indigenous nationalities predominate, while the Russian-dominated sectors are experiencing manpower shortages.

In terms of location, the third important aspect of manpower use is that Central Asians are concentrated in labour-surplus areas of the republic (rural areas and small towns with little industrial activity), while Slavs tend to dominate the labour-short regions (the capital cities and new industrial small towns). Again, because of differential rates of population growth and migration among the different nationalities, locational imbalances are widening as well. And finally, the fourth aspect is that rather than alleviating these problems, educational and other Soviet policies have done little to alter the situation. While many policies have been implemented in Central Asia to restructure manpower use there, their effects to date have been minimal.

By themselves, the data would suggest severe nationality and social repercussions in Soviet Asia. The existence of a small, more modernised group of non-indigenous Slavic outsiders in Central Asia is normally assumed to spell growing political tension there. On the basis of the above situation, many Western observers have concluded that the Slavs comprise a privileged élite in Soviet Central Asia; that they enjoy better incomes and greater opportunities for working in choice occupations; and that as disparities widen, the indigenous nationalities will become increasingly discontent with occupying a second-class status in their own republics.

While there undoubtedly is some truth in these assumptions, however, other factors are playing a role which make the political implications often quite different. While the indigenous nationalities may have entered Central Asia's more modern sectors, they have not necessarily adopted the values associated with that process. Instead, while a modern social and economic structure has been formally imposed on Central Asia, an informal, and more traditional structure still prevails in both economic and social life. In most cases, it is this latter, informal system which governs an individual's real income, and determines the development of social values and norms among the population as a whole. Although official data might suggest otherwise, therefore, for the most part the Slavs in Central Asia do *not* comprise a privileged élite, nor do they necessarily have access to the highest incomes, benefits or prestige. Instead, the labour situation is an outgrowth of other factors, economic and social, which go beyond questions of Slavic discrimination or superiority alone, and which undoubtedly alter the nationality relations implicit in the labour situation. This book therefore focuses on these factors to determine in what ways nationality tensions are being aggravated by the labour situation in Soviet Central Asia and, conversely, in what ways they are being contained.

The analysis focuses on Uzbekistan and is divided into two parts. Part I discusses the four aspects of labour use themselves – that is, the nationality distribution of Uzbekistan's labour force by size, sector and location, and the effects of Soviet policies to date. Part II discusses the political implications of the labour situation along nationality lines. Especially with regard to Part II, it should be stressed that the book attempts to provide as broad a gauge as possible of labour and nationality issues in Uzbekistan. For this reason, it does not focus on any one particular group, such as the leadership or intelligentsia, as an independent variable, and does not focus on questions such as the power, authority or political discontent of élite groups in particular.[15] Instead, an attempt is made to draw a broad picture of which nationalities in Uzbekistan work where, which factors contribute to determining occupational distribution, and what some of the political implications might be across a broad spectrum of economic and social groups.

In Part I, Chapter 1 discusses overall population growth in Uzbekistan and, briefly, the degree to which general economic growth there has kept pace with that population rise over the past few decades. Since it would be impossible to discuss the possibility of potentially-severe labour problems and how they may relate to broader nationality questions without first discussing general demographic trends and economic development, the inclusion of a chapter on these subjects seemed essential. While each of these topics is important, however, – and indeed could be the subject of a book in its own right – the purpose here is simply to provide a broad framework within which to evaluate more specific problems of labour utilisation. Chapter 1, therefore, discusses only broad trends on the inter-relationship of population and economic growth in Uzbekistan, as a background for understanding the kinds of strains which may be growing as a result of Uzbekistan's efforts to absorb an increasingly large labour pool.

More time is devoted in this chapter to demographic rather than economic questions for two reasons. First, of course, a grasp of general demographic trends is essential for understanding the future size and composition (by sex and nationality) of the labour force in Uzbekistan. Secondly, demographic trends, more so than economic, have become the subject of an immense amount of controversy – a controversy in which the arguments are so substantially different, that each would imply very different conclusions with regard to the future labour situation. Some scholars, for example, have argued that Uzbekistan's birthrate and rate of natural growth will undergo a sharp decline over the next few years, and others, that the local nationalities will begin a substantial out-migration from that republic to other parts of the

USSR. These projections, of course, would have a quite different impact on the size and composition of Uzbekistan's labour force in the 1980s and 1990s than would the equally well-documented projections to the contrary: that the republican birthrate and rate of natural growth instead may actually increase over the next few years, while out-migration from Uzbekistan will remain unchanged or decline. Since the material which I was able to collect during a year of research in Uzbekistan may provide some new insight into many of these arguments, a somewhat more lengthy discussion of demographic issues seemed merited in order to present a clearer picture of what Uzbekistan's labour force might look like in the near future. On the other hand, a large body of material has emerged during the past few years on economic development and present economic trends in different regions of the USSR.[16] In order not to be led too far afield from the main points, therefore, only a brief sketch of some of the more basic issues and how they affect the different nationalities in Uzbekistan is presented.

Chapter 2 concentrates on questions of utilising Uzbekistan's labour force as a whole. It focuses on changes in the size and composition of Uzbekistan's working-age population, and on ways in which this population is being absorbed in the economy, in general and by nationality. As mentioned above, many scholars have referred to a rapidly growing labour surplus in Uzbekistan, and have cited the growing number of non-working Central Asians as an indication that labour surpluses may have severe political as well as economic ramifications. Chapter 2 discusses these issues, both in terms of the non-working population and in terms of 'underemployment'. While ostensibly 'unemployment' does not exist in the USSR, changes in the dynamics of labour force participation suggest that labour surpluses may nevertheless be a growing problem. An analysis of changes in the magnitude of three key indicators over the past two decades, therefore – a growth in the proportion of the working-age population not working in the national economy and not studying; in the proportion working solely in household and private subsidiary work; and in underemployment as demonstrated by changes in labour productivity, overmanning, time-use, etc. – may give some indication of the degree to which Uzbekistan may or may not be facing a growing problem of surplus manpower, especially among the indigenous nationalities. Chapter 3 discusses essentially the same issues by sector and location – that is, the dislocations in certain sectors and geographical areas of Uzbekistan in terms of manpower supply, and how these may be related to nationality issues as well. Finally, Chapter 4 discusses the effects Soviet policies have had in substantially altering the situation and prospects for the future.

Part II analyses the implications of the labour situation along nationality lines, and the potential impact which a growing labour surplus and imbalances in Uzbekistan's economy may have on nationality relations and on ethnic and political unrest. By themselves, the trends suggested in Part I suggest an extremely tension-ridden political situation. Particularly during the 1960s and 1970s, Uzbekistan's economy seems to have weakened in its ability to support a rapidly-growing working-age population seeking jobs and other opportunities. As Chapters 2 and 3 underline, moreover, this potential unused labour pool is increasingly Asian in composition. The political implications of these trends would appear to be enormous.

None the less, other factors must be taken into account before drawing these kinds of political conclusions. It may be true that Uzbeks predominate in the non-working and non-studying population of Uzbekistan or that they comprise the vast majority of those employed in household and private subsidiary activity. Other factors, however – such as real differences in incomes between the private and socialised sectors (official and otherwise); different values and professional aspirations among the various nationalities; actual versus perceived opportunities, and differing traditions and cultures among the different nationality groups – also play a tremendous role in alleviating and altering the kind of nationality tensions implicit in that employment situation. In other words, there are often strong economic and social reasons why Asians predominate in certain locations or sectors of the economy, and why the situation cannot always be interpreted within the political framework which has generally been applied to it.

Chapter 5, therefore, analyses hiring practices and preferences for different kinds of work among the different nationality groups in Uzbekistan. Chapter 6 analyses incomes – both official and estimated real incomes – among different sectors of the labour force and among the working and 'non-working' (in social production) populations in Uzbekistan. Chapter 7 discusses the role of culture and traditions, of different standards and aspirations among the nationalities in determining behaviour in the labour force. Finally, Chapter 8 summarises these arguments and outlines their political implications. Because of the enormous complexities of Soviet Central Asian society, sources of potential political or ethnic unrest associated with the manpower situation there are extremely complex, and may be quite different from those which the data alone might suggest.

Because of Soviet Central Asia's diversity, it would be difficult to discuss these isssues comprehensively with regard to all four of the republics. As a Soviet scholar writes:

Despite the fact that the republics of Central Asia have much in common in their economic development ... each one of them is also characterized by a series of particularities connected with natural conditions and resources, the ethnic composition of the population, the level of economic development, labor habits of the population, its magnitude, etc.[17]

This book, therefore, focuses on Uzbekistan, since of the four republics, it is the largest and probably the most significant for the USSR economically, demographically and politically. Today, Uzbekistan is the third most populous republic in the Soviet Union, and Uzbeks comprise the most numerous of the USSR's Muslim peoples: Uzbeks, comprised almost 30 per cent of the total number of Soviet citizens of Muslim origin as of the early 1980s. Uzbekistan alone is expected to account for 45 per cent of the new entrants to the Soviet labour force by the end of the century – more than any other Muslim republic. And if Central Asia as a whole is growing in economic importance for the USSR, Uzbekistan's role in Central Asia is vital: in 1979, Uzbekistan accounted for more than one third of the territory of Soviet Central Asia, and about two thirds of the total amount of irrigated land in Central Asia, the total and urban populations of the Central Asian republics, total industrial personnel, and industrial and agricultural production.[18] Partly for its prominence in other realms, Uzbekistan also seems to have emerged as a possible political centre for the Central Asian region, and Uzbeks, perhaps the leading group among all Muslims in the USSR.[19] Since this book discusses the interaction of political and economic factors in Soviet Central Asia, Uzbekistan was considered the most appropriate republic on which to focus. It should be kept in mind, however, that the issues discussed often apply to the other three Soviet Asian republics, often with only minor modifications.

The combination of economic and nationality pressures as they exist in Soviet Asia would prove a challenge to any modern regime, East or West. As nationality awareness grows in Central Asia, so, too, do complex problems of economic development and modernisation. As discussed below, however, the nature and effects of such challenges in Soviet Asia may be quite different from those in other parts of the world. As Walker Connor has written, '. . . it is ironic that a society predicated upon an ideology which predicts the withering away of both state and nationality should find that each of them has grown immensely in power since the October Revolution'.[20] It is perhaps especially ironic that a region which had experienced neither 'nationhood' nor a 'modern' labour force when it was incorporated into the Soviet state should now find precisely those two elements of its society posing serious challenges to the present Soviet leadership.

Part I

The Setting: Nationality and Labour

1 Demography and Economics

Beginning in the 1960s, two fundamental changes began to occur in the size and composition of Uzbekistan's population: the total population began to swell, and the local nationalities began to comprise a growing proportion of the total population. These changes were due to a high rate of natural growth and low mobility among the indigenous populations, and to a lower fertility level and declining mobility among the Slavs. Although in the late 1970s fertility among the indigenous nationalities began to decline, this decline has nòt been rapid enough to alter existing population trends. By the early 1980s, therefore, the existing demographic structure in Uzbekistan suggested that this pattern of overall population growth would continue at least for the near future.

The first change, more rapid growth of the total population, was in sharp contrast to events occurring in other parts of the USSR. At a time when most of the USSR was feeling the effects of two world wars, collectivisation, the purges and other 'demographic catastrophes' and was undergoing a severe decline in its rate of population growth, Uzbekistan's population, in a demographic sense, was largely untouched by these events. Instead, the age and sex structure remained favourable to continued high levels of fertility while the death rate declined, and Uzbekistan's population began to grow at its most rapid rate since the onset of Soviet power. Thus, throughout the 1960s and 1970s, the total population of Uzbekistan grew almost three times faster than it had during the previous two decades. While the republic's population had risen by 28 per cent over the twenty-year period 1939–59 (from 6.3 million to 8.1 million people), it rose by almost 90

25

per cent over the next twenty-year period, from 8.1 million people in 1959 to 15.4 million in 1979. This represented a level of growth more than three times the average for the USSR as a whole: from 1959 to 1970 and from 1970 to 1979, the population of the USSR rose by about 16 per cent and 9 per cent respectively; in Uzbekistan, the rise was by 45 per cent and 30 per cent.

The second change, concerning Uzbekistan's ethnic composition, was perhaps more pronounced. Rather than merely an acceleration of previous trends, it represented a direct reversal of a pattern which had remained constant in Uzbekistan throughout the previous four decades. As mentioned above, Uzbekistan's population numerically has always been dominated by Asians. But while the Slavs had comprised a consistently growing share of that population from the early 1920s until the 1959 census, their proportion now began to decline. Russians grew steadily from less than 2 per cent of Uzbekistan's total population in 1917, to 13.5 per cent in 1959. From the 1960s on, however, their share fell steadily to 10.8 per cent in 1979. A similar decline occurred for all Uzbekistan's non-indigenous nationalities, while the proportion of Uzbeks rose from about 62 per cent to 69 per cent over the same twenty-year period (Table 1.1).

This change in nationality composition was a result of the rapid decline in the growth rates of the Europeans as opposed to the continued high growth rates of the Asians. Until 1959, the growth rate among the Russians in Uzbekistan had been high; between 1926 and 1959, the Russian population grew at a rate even higher than that of the local Uzbeks. But from 1959 to 1970 and from 1970 to 1979, the Russian population in Uzbekistan increased by only 35 per cent and 13 per cent respectively, while the Uzbek population grew by 53 per cent and 37 per cent. Put more starkly, while Uzbekistan's total population grew by 90 per cent over the twenty-year period, 1959–79, the Uzbek component more than doubled, while the Russian component grew by barely half.[2]

NATURAL GROWTH

Of the two main sources of population change – natural growth and migration – the first, natural growth, has undoubtedly been the main reason for these changes in Uzbekistan's population size and composition. Although the death rate in Uzbekistan underwent a sharp decline soon after the advent of Soviet rule, the birth rate remained high. From

TABLE 1.1 Nationality Composition of Uzbekistan, 1959, 1970 and 1979

	Number of given nationality (thousands)			Nationality as percentage of total			1970 as percentage of 1959	1979 as percentage of 1970
	1959	1970	1979	1959	1970	1979		
Uzbeks	5 038	7 725	10 569	62.1	65.5	68.7	153	137
Karakalpaks	168	230	298	2.1	2.0	1.9	137	130
Russians	1 092	1 473	1 666	13.5	12.5	10.8	135	113
Tatars	445	574	649	5.5	4.9	4.2	129	113
Kazakhs	343	476	620	4.2	4.0	4.0	139	130
Tadzhiks	331	449	595	3.8	3.8	3.9	144	133
Koreans	138	148	163	1.7	1.3	1.1	107	110
Ukrainians	88	112	114	1.1	0.9	0.7	127	102
Kirgiz	93	111	142	1.1	0.9	0.9	119	128
Jews	94	103	100	1.2	0.9	0.6	104	97
Turkmen	55	71	92	0.7	0.6	0.6	129	130
Other*	254	328	381	3.0	2.7	2.6	129	116

* Other nationalities include Belorussians, Azerbaijanis, Armenians, Georgians, Bashkir, Uighurs, Moldavians, Chuvash, Ocetians, peoples of Dagestan and gypsies.

SOURCE cclumns 1, 2, 4, 5 TsSU, *Narodnoe khoziaistvo Uzbekskoi SSR za 60 let Sovetskoi vlasti* (Tashkent: Uzbekistan, 1977),

cclumns 3, 6 'Vsesoiuznaia perepis' naselenia, 1979', *Vestnik Statistiki*, no. 9, 1980, p. 61.

1950–79, the birth rate for the USSR as a whole declined by about one third, and natural growth, by over half; total fertility declined substantially, from 2.9 to 2.3. By contrast, despite some fluctuation throughout the thirty-seven-year period, Uzbekistan's birth rate in 1977 was approximately the same level as it had been in 1940, and even higher than it had been in the early 1950s (Table 1.2). Total fertility in Uzbekistan, while reaching a peak during the 1960s, was approximately the same level in 1979 as it had been in 1959.[3]

TABLE 1.2   *Vital statistics for Uzbekistan, 1940–81 (per thousand population)*

Year	Birth rate	Death rate	Natural growth
1940	33.8	13.2	20.6
1950	30.9	8.8	22.1
1960	39.8	6.0	33.8
1965	34.7	5.9	28.8
1970	33.6	5.5	28.1
1975	34.2	7.2	27.0
1976	35.0	7.1	27.9
1977	33.4	7.1	26.3
1978	33.9	6.9	27.0
1979	34.4	7.0	27.4
1980	33.8	7.4	26.4
1981	34.9	7.2	27.7

SOURCE   TsSU, *Narodnoe khoziaistvo Uzbekskoi SSR v 1981 godu* (Tashkent: Uzbekistan, 1982) p. 11; 1950 and 1960 from T. V. Riabushkin (ed.), *Naselenie soiuznykh respublik* (Moscow: Statistika, 1977) p. 102.

Gross statistics, moreover, conceal vast disparities in natural growth among the different nationalities. As mentioned above, this continued high fertility has been exhibited particularly among the indigenous nationalities, which accounts for the ethnic shift in Uzbekistan's population. While the birth rate for Uzbekistan as a whole was high, in 1970 it was more than twice as high among the Uzbeks as it was among the Russians, and significantly higher among the Asian populations than among the Slavs as a whole (Table 1.3). Similarly, as Table 1.3 illustrates, the decline in fertility that occurred in Uzbekistan between 1959 and 1970 occurred largely among the European nationalities living there – that is, among precisely those nationality groups with the

TABLE 1.3   Changes in the crude birth rate by nationality, Uzbekistan, 1959–70

Nationality	Birth rate 1959	Birth rate 1970	1970 as percentage of 1959	Percentage Increase/Decline 1959–70
Russians	23.7	19.3	81.0	−19.0
Ukrainians	26.0	23.0	88.4	−11.6
Belorussians	34.4	25.1	73.0	−27.0
Kazakhs	34.3	36.9	107.6	+7.6
Uzbeks	41.7	39.2	94.0	−6.0
Tadzhiks	38.2	34.3	89.8	−10.2
Kirgiz	29.4	31.6	107.5	+7.5
Turkmen	32.1	32.8	102.2	+2.2
Karakalpaks	39.1	33.5	85.7	−14.3
Other	36.0	22.8	63.3	−36.7
Total	37.0	33.5	90.5	−9.5

SOURCE   Computed from Mulliadzhanov, I. R. Naselenie Uzbekskoi SSR (Tashkent: Uzbekistan, 1973) p. 117.

lowest birth rates in the first place. For example, the birth rates among the Russians and Belorussians living in Uzbekistan declined by 19 and 27 per cent respectively, between 1959 and 1970, falling from about 24 to 19 per thousand among the Russians and from 34 to 25 per thousand among the Belorussians in the eleven-year period. These figures contrast markedly with the 6 per cent decline among the Uzbeks, or with the 10 per cent decline among the Tadzhiks residing in Uzbekistan, whose birth rates fell only slightly, from 41 to 39 per thousand and from 38 to 34 per thousand respectively. The birth rate among the Kazakhs, Kirgiz and Turkmen populations living in Uzbekistan, while already high in 1959, actually rose, by as much as 8 per cent over the same period. Thus, between 1959 and 1970, Uzbekistan's European population exhibited large declines in population reproduction from an already comparatively low level, while the Asian populations were characterised by more moderate declines, relatively stable rates, or even by slight rises. By the 1970s, it appeared that natural growth alone, if not substantially balanced by migration, would perpetuate both rapid population expansion and substantial changes in Uzbekistan's ethnic composition for some time to come.

Unfortunately, similar data on population growth by nationality are not as comprehensive for the 1970s, and have not been published following the 1979 census. None the less, fragmentary data reveal that throughout the 1970s, fertility remained high in Uzbekistan, and remained particularly high among the indigenous nationalities. Another series of nationality-related crude birth rates, for example, illustrates the vast differentials between the Slavic and Central Asian nationalities which continued well into the 1970s. According to these data, the annual crude birth rate among Uzbeks in the USSR averaged approximately 45 per thousand during the 1960s, and dropped to an average annual rate of 40.8 per thousand in the period 1970–8; among the other Central Asian nationalities, the rates were comparable. Among Russians, on the other hand, the corresponding drop was from 19.0 to 16.5 per thousand, levels similar to those among the Slavic nationalities as a whole (Table 1.4). According to these statistics, therefore, the Uzbek birth rate throughout the 1970s was almost 2.5 times higher than that of the Russians, and had declined more slowly than the Russian birth rate by comparison with the preceding decade: if the Uzbek birth rate showed a decline of slightly under 10 per cent,

TABLE 1.4   *Average annual crude birth rate by nationality, USSR 1959–69 and 1970–8, (per thousand population)*

Nationality	1959–69	1970–8
Russians	19.0	16.5
Ukrainians	15.8	14.0
Belorussians	19.2	13.1
Kazakhs	41.2	30.6
Uzbeks	45.2	40.8
Tadzhiks	45.2	41.9
Kirgiz	44.0	38.4
Turkmen	45.6	39.5
Moldavians	24.7	19.3
Estonians	12.3	12.8
Latvians	12.3	12.4
Lithuanians	20.6	16.8
Armenians	28.4	22.5
Azeris	43.7	31.7
Georgians	24.0	18.4

SOURCE   Feshbach, M. 'Trends in the Soviet Muslim Population – Demographic Aspects', *The Soviet Economy in the 1980s*; *Problems and Prospects*, Part 2, Selected Papers submitted to the Joint Economic Committee, US Congress, 31 December 1982, (Washington, DC: Government Printing Office, 1983) p. 304.

the Russian birth rate declined by over 13 per cent. Perhaps because of the differences in methodology used to derive these figures,[4] the nationality differences implicit in these estimates are uniformly higher than those in Table 1.3. Analysed together, however, the two sets of data underline two crucial facts: that by the end of the 1970s Central Asian birth rates in the USSR still remained very high, and wide disparities between Slavic and Asian birth rates had not significantly diminished.

While helpful in assessing overall population growth trends, birth rates, of course, are only one indicator of fertility, and certainly not an unambiguous one. Even if fertility were to remain constant, for example, changes in the age structure or significant improvements in health care could alter the birth rate significantly. Other indicators such as family size and actual fertility rates, however – albeit also imperfect – have also suggested continued high fertility among the indigenous nationalities. In 1979, for example, the average family size in Uzbekistan was 5.5 people, a rise from 4.6 people in 1959. Among Uzbeks, however, the average family size was 6.2 people, and more than 43 per cent of all Uzbek families were comprised of seven or more members.[5] Among Russians, the average family size was about half that of the Uzbeks, and only 1 per cent of all Russian families contained seven or more members (Table 1.5). Total fertility rates in

TABLE 1.5 *Family size by nationality, USSR, 1979 (number of families, in thousands)*

Number of People in Family	Uzbeks		Russians		USSR Average	
	Number	*Percentage*	*Number*	*Percentage*	*Number*	*Percentage*
Two	164	9.1	11 031	33.5	19 664	29.7
Three	172	9.5	10 662	32.4	19 128	28.8
Four	217	12.0	7 592	23.1	15 239	23.0
Five	228	12.7	2 534	7.7	6 312	9.5
Six	239	13.3	758	2.3	2 741	4.1
Seven or more	780	43.2	343	1.0	3 224	4.9
Total number of families	1 802	100.0	32 920	100.0	66 307	100.0
Average family size	6.2		3.2		3.5	

NOTE Percentages may not add up to 100 due to rounding.

SOURCE 'Vsesoiznaia perepis' naseleniia' *Vestnik Statistiki*, no. 11, 1981, p. 57.

Uzbekistan, moreover, were also still high in the 1970s; at 4.9, 1979–80, Uzbekistan's total fertility rate was the same level as it had been in 1958–9[6] (Table 1.7, below).

These data are not meant to suggest, of course, that fertility in Uzbekistan has remained totally static or will not decline more dramatically in the future. During the last two years of the 1970s and into the 1980s, fertility rates for Uzbekistan did go down (Table 1.7); and factors normally associated in Western demographic theory with fertility declines – such as a decline in infant mortality, urbanisation, greater female participation in the labour force, changing attitudes among the young, and increased government intervention in direct population policy – will probably lead to continued fertility decline in the future. In terms of overall population dynamics, however, the main question is the *rate* of that decline. What these figures are intended to illustrate is that fertility declines in Uzbekistan occurred only after a rise in the mid-1970s, and the emphasis on having many children still remains strong – especially among the indigenous nationalities. While a decline in infant mortality, a rise in urbanisation or attitudinal change have all occurred in Uzbekistan, none has occurred significantly enough to offset present population trends. Uzbekistan's present population structure suggests that population growth will remain high for some time to come.

In terms of infant mortality, for example, while the death rate in Uzbekistan has declined substantially since the early 1900s, recent articles suggest that the past two decades may have seen an upswing in Uzbekistan's mortality rate, especially in infant mortality. Between 1971 and 1975, infant mortality for the USSR as a whole rose by one third, to a level twice as high as the US rate. Adjusting for discrepancies with the US definition, estimated infant mortality for the USSR in 1979 was 39 or 40 deaths per thousand population aged 0–1 – more than three times the US rate of 12.9. And recent articles suggest that infant mortality may be at a particularly high level in the Central Asian republics. While some of this rise, especially in Central Asia, must be attributed to improved statistical reporting, infant mortality in the late 1970s and early 1980s was high in Central Asia, reportedly as high as 90 per thousand in Tadzhikistan, 1977.[7] Soviet writers have continually referred to declines in infant mortality as significant reasons for declines in fertility, since parents then become 'soundly convinced that even a single child will survive them',[8] and hence the perceived necessity to have large numbers of children becomes diminished. Given the continued high rate of infant mortality in Central Asia, however, what the same demographer refers to as 'one of the very strong incentives for having a relatively large number of children' may not, in fact, have totally disappeared.

Similarly, urbanisation is exerting a more marginal impact upon the total republican level of population reproduction in Uzbekistan than overall urban-rural statistics might suggest. Unarguably, urbanisation has been rapid in Uzbekistan. Uzbekistan's urban population more than quintupled in fifty years, growing from 1.0 million people in 1926 to 5.5 million in 1976. The urban share of Uzbekistan's total population grew from 24 per cent to 39 per cent over the same period; in 1980, Uzbekistan was 41.2 per cent urban. And as elsewhere, urbanisation can be expected to reduce fertility levels. As a Soviet demographer in Moscow, A. Ia. Kvasha writes:

Having moved to the city, young people come upon new living conditions and, very importantly, upon surroundings where other, somewhat different standards of demographic behavior govern. In these conditions, migrants generally transfer over to an 'urban type' of reproductive behavior.[9]

None the less, as Kvasha continues: 'The major question lies in how rapidly this process is occurring'. Despite the gross republican statistics cited above, urbanisation today is occurring slowly in Uzbekistan among the Asian populations. In 1959, Uzbeks comprised only 36 per cent of Uzbekistan's urban population, and in 1970, only 41 per cent. Given the large size of the Uzbek population, moreover, the proportion of the Uzbek population which these figures represented was even smaller: in 1959, only 21.8 per cent of all Uzbeks lived in urban areas; eleven years later, that proportion had risen only three percentage points, to 24.9 per cent.[10]

Most of this urban growth in Uzbekistan, moreover, has been due to natural increase or reclassification rather than migration, suggesting that much of the newly-urban population in Uzbekistan has not been as deeply 'urbanised' as the data would imply. Between 1959 and 1970, natural increase contributed 52 per cent of the urban growth in Uzbekistan; reclassification, 16 per cent and net in-migration, only 32 per cent.[11] Of the in-migrants to Uzbekistan's urban areas, the majority have been non-indigenous: between 1959 and 1970, as much as 90 per cent came from outside Uzbekistan, and only 10 per cent of the migrants came from Uzbekistan's rural areas; and a similar situation persists today.[12] Of the in-migrants from the countryside, moreover,

representatives of the indigenous nationalities have occupied a relatively small proportion. According to one local scholar, Uzbek men
comprised only 37 per cent of all migrants from the countryside to the
city in Uzbekistan; Uzbek women, only 19 per cent of the total number
of female migrants.

Throughout the 1970s, moreover, mobility did not significantly
increase, leaving migration levels in Uzbekistan far below the Soviet
average. Whereas in the RSFSR in 1973 twenty-six out of every
thousand rural inhabitants migrated to the cities, in Uzbekistan the
ratio was only four per thousand.[13] Whereas in the RSFSR about twice
as many people left the rural areas as were provided by natural
increase, in Uzbekistan the outflow was only one tenth of natural
increase.

In other words, while gross statistics indicate a rapid growth of cities
in Uzbekistan during the years of Soviet power, urbanisation is still
occurring relatively slowly in Uzbekistan and particularly among the
indigenous nationalities. Among the indigenous nationalities,
moreover, it is occurring largely as a result of reclassification rather
than as a result of their increased mobility. This, in turn, suggests that
even as they become more urban, the local inhabitants are not dramatically transforming their way of life as much as one might expect from
the demographic data. Particularly in places which have been reclas-
sified from rural to urban during the past fifty years, the indigenous
inhabitants often live in the same traditional homes and conduct their
lives in the same manner as they did fifty years ago. Only the size of the
population and the amount of industry within the locale has grown,
and often the industry is located away from the residential areas where
the village population resides. Often, therefore, 'reclassification' barely affects the lives of the populations located there, and the effect on
native fertility among newly 'urban' inhabitants is much more gradual
than urbanisation statistics might suggest.

Finally, it must be noted that the reasons for the high birth rate in
Uzbekistan go beyond such questions of demographic transition or
urbanisation alone. Of equal importance, fertility in Uzbekistan is
important in a way which deeply affects an Uzbek's perception of his or
her place in the world. The reasons for high birth rates are far more
integral a part of the Uzbek character than the sense of kinship or
family survival alone. Just as professional attainment greatly determines a person's 'standing' in Western society – largely determining
the way one is viewed by others, as well as the way in which one views
oneself – so does the size of one's family largely determine social

standing in the Central Asian milieu. Quantity of offspring is still an important measure of 'success' in Central Asia, determining one's stature as an individual contributing to the welfare of the 'clan'. As in other parts of the Muslim world, large families are still very closely associated in the Uzbek mind with honour, respect, virility and self-esteem. The 'traditional respect of neighbours towards the mother with many children'; the 'honour and respect accorded him who has many sons'; the 'basic love of many children' are all common themes which one hears repeated constantly, by people at all relative levels of urbanisation and professional standing. They are themes which pervade Uzbek daily life, and often dominate local thought and habits.[14]

For all these reasons, it would be fallacious to assume that attitudes towards large families, or the value placed on having many children, may have weakened dramatically in Uzbekistan, even if that weakening has not been reflected in more dramatic demographic statistics. Aside from actual family size, Soviet.surveys suggest that *ideal* family size among Asian women in Uzbekistan has barely declined over the past decade. Instead, as late as 1978 Ata Mirzaev noted,

High birth rate indicators are connected with national traditions of having many children ... One must not forget that the nationality level of the birth rate is formed in the family, mainly under the influence of traditional views on number of children in the family.[15]

While there are indications that ideal family size may now be declining, that decline has been slight. Studies in the early to mid-1970s indicated that desired family size among women of the local nationalities in Uzbekistan remained at an average of about 7–8 people per family – as against 2–3 among women of the non-Asian nationalities[16] (Table 1.6). Even today, the first question with which any Uzbek greets another after some prolonged absence – whether he be a peasant or First Party Secretary – is still how many children the other has: the higher the number of children, the higher the honour accorded the respondent and his or her family. Conversely, any suggestions of impotence or sterility are widely regarded as a shame and a sin. Even the most 'Sovietised' of Uzbek officials whom I met made little effort to conceal his amazement, confusion or disapproval over the fact that I – at the time, 24 years old – had still not had 'even one child'. And as late as 1979, many Central Asians would quote me their age-old slogan: '*Balali oy – bazar; balasiz oy – mazar*' – 'A house with children is a bazaar; a house without children, a graveyard.'

TABLE 1.6 *Distribution of women by ideal number of children in USSR and selected republics in 1970, and by nationality, 1972*

	Percentage of Women Naming Ideal Number of Children								Average Ideal Number of Children
	0	1	2	3	4	5	6 and over	Total	
USSR (1970)	0.4	1.5	41.0	39.4	11.7	2.9	3.1	100	2.89
By Republic (1970)									
RSFSR	0.5	1.7	45.5	39.6	9.2	2.5	1.0	100	2.69
UzSSR	0.4	0.1	20.8	26.9	19.5	6.9	25.4	100	4.55
By nationality (1972)									
Russians	2.9	24.9	52.0	14.2	3.5	1.5	1.0	100	2.0
Uzbeks	1.2	1.5	5.4	7.1	13.0	13.0	58.8	100	6.26

SOURCE lines 1–3: Ubaidullaeva, R. A. 'Regional'nykh problemy ...', doctoral dissertation, Tashkent, 1974, p. 281. lines 4–5: Based on 1972 national survey by the USSR Central Stat Administration, of 347 314 women aged 18–59, discussed in Belova, V. A. et al., *Skol'ko detei budet v sovetskoi sem'ie* (Moscow; Statistika, 1977).

With regard to attitudinal changes among Uzbekistan's youth, most Soviet studies on ideal family size have generally included all age groups – a fact which certain scholars argue undoubtedly conceals perhaps major changes in the younger age-groups as compared with the older. Indeed, Soviet scholars, for their part, have begun to call for more studies particularly on age-specific fertility patterns, in order to determine the degree to which such generational changes may be occurring. And there were signs among my peers in Tashkent that they were expecting to have smaller families once married.

Again, however, the question is one of the rate of attitudinal change. From the few comprehensive studies that are available, it seems that for most of the republic today, the attitudes of Uzbekistan's youth towards reproduction have not changed enough to offset significantly the population trends for the near future. Despite a possible trend toward later marriages, young marriages still predominate among the majority of the indigenous nationalities in Uzbekistan.[17] Similarly, the average age of women bearing children did not rise substantially during the 1970s, as one might have expected concurrently with modernisation and the apparent rise in the educational and professional status of women in Uzbekistan (see Chapter 4). Instead, fertility among younger women, especially in the 15–29 year-old range, was higher in the mid-seventies than it had been approximately thirteen years earlier. The largest difference, in fact, was among the 20–24 year-olds, among whom fertility had risen from 209.9 births per thousand women of that age group in 1958/59 to 297.0 in 1975/76. During the latter part of the 1970s, most age-specific fertility rates in Uzbekistan began to decline, but that decline was greatest in the older age-groups, and fertility among 20–29 year-old women has remained very high (Table 1.7).[18]

In short, native fertility and attitudes toward family-size have remained high, even among Uzbekistan's youth, and disparities with the Russian population have remained wide. There has not been a severe enough decline in either ideal or actual population indicators to offset significantly near-term population trends.[19]

In the light of these factors, during the past decade Soviet policy-makers have increased their efforts to encourage smaller families in Uzbekistan through direct population policy intervention. Soviet policy-makers boast that contraception is more readily available today than ever before. A small 'propaganda campaign' was recently launched to reduce average family-size in Uzbekistan to an 'ideal' six people within the next ten to twelve years. And as illustrated even at

TABLE 1.7   Age-specific fertility rates, Uzbekistan (number of births per thousand women of given age-group)

Year	TFR	15–49	15–19	20–24	25–29	30–34	35–39	40–44	45–49
1958–9	5.044	158.8	38.3	209.9	240.7	206.0	178.6	96.8	38.4
1965–6	5.564	165.3	30.2	252.8	270.2	238.1	181.3	99.2	41.0
1971–2	5.841	163.0	45.4	275.0	284.6	247.7	198.5	93.7	23.3
1972–3	5.669	156.0	39.9	280.0	287.6	234.1	187.0	87.6	17.6
1973–4	5.706	156.8	39.9	290.0	295.4	230.3	183.2	86.4	15.9
1974–5	5.679	156.8	40.1	295.6	300.6	222.7	177.4	82.7	16.6
1975–6	5.660	157.1	39.1	297.0	301.3	225.2	170.6	82.0	16.8
1976–7	5.482	154.0	37.8	290.6	293.6	224.1	157.5	78.0	14.9
1977–8	5.247	150.6	37.2	282.4	286.3	216.9	141.3	71.9	13.4
1978–9	5.096	149.6	35.4	277.3	281.7	210.7	134.7	66.9	12.5
1979–80	4.905	148.9	35.3	276.9	271.8	202.5	122.7	60.4	11.4

SOURCE   R. Crisostomo, unpublished tables prepared for the Foreign Demographic Analysis Division, US Bureau of the Census, Washington, DC, 1982. Data for 1958–9 to 1977–8 confirmed in Aliakberov, N. M. 'Analiz sovremennykh tendentsii v rozhdaemosti v Srednei Azii' Regional'nye Demograficheskie issledovania (Tashkent: Minvuz, 1978) p. 21.

the all-Union level, enormous attention recently has been turned towards 'propagandising demographic knowledge', 'moulding the population's attitude toward problems of childbirth which meet society's interests', and towards 'intensifying educational work' and 'preparing youth for family life'.[20] In Uzbekistan, for example, a third, expanded edition of a book on marriage and the family – one of the only books of its kind to be published in Uzbekistan – appeared in Uzbek bookstores in 1979. Entitled *What You Should Know Before and During Marriage*, it offers a frank discussion of physiological and medical questions concerning sexual relations, while simultaneously trying to instil 'a correct understanding of the formation and the development of the individual, of norms of behaviour in interrelationships between male and female'.[21] As the book notes:

With the centuries, persistent, dangerous habits and survivals of the past continue to interfere with the introduction of Communist morals and of healthy sexual relations in daily life . . . Survivals of the old morality are still alive in the most intimate sector of human relationships – in questions of love and family relations[22]

The book sets out to eradicate the 'backward' and 'inflexible' 'sexual ethic' in Uzbekistan, to 'change and rebuild inter-relationships between man and woman' and to 'create a new and healthy domestic life' among Uzbekistan's population.

These efforts, however, have had little impact on altering fertility patterns among Uzbekistan's indigenous populations, or in narrowing differentials among the nationality groups. Contraceptives – of generally poor quality in the USSR – are even more poorly distributed in the Uzbek republic than elsewhere in the USSR, and are rarely used by either Russians or Uzbeks. While there has been talk of expanding family planning and 'consultation' services in general, they have been developed on only the most rudimentary level; they are almost totally absent in the countryside, where birth rates are highest; and they have been strongly resisted by the indigenous nationalities on principle. As elsewhere in the USSR, abortion is the main form of birth control in Uzbekistan; but while abortions are readily available – and the incidence of abortion in Uzbekistan is surprisingly high – they occur almost entirely among women of the European nationalities.[23] Indeed, several medical personnel remarked to me that it is common practice for doctors to perform upwards of three, four or five abortions per week for Russian women in Uzbekistan, while performing virtually none on Uzbek women. Sex education apparently is only beginning to be taught in Uzbek schools, and on a very rudimentary level.[24] By consequence, few locals have actively joined the bandwagon to bring the republican average family-size down to six people, and family planning among Uzbekistan's indigenous nationalities largely depends on 'what Allah wills'.

Today, there is no doubt that demographic trends have attracted increasing attention and concern from Soviet central planners. At the 25th Party Congress, Brezhnev called for an 'effective demographic policy' to counter unfavourable demographic trends, of which trends in Central Asia were certainly a key part. Five years later, at the 26th Party Congress, several new and sweeping demographic policies were announced, with more than nine billion roubles to be spent on them. In 1981, policies were approved which provided for increased paid maternity leaves and child-support grants up to the fourth child, and foresaw preferential housing for families with children, partial-working-days for women, and an expansion of pre-school institutions and paid leaves for women to care for sick children. The fact that most of these measures were applied first in the non-Asian, low-fertility areas of the USSR and only eventually to Central Asia – and the fact that larger incentives were offered for the first four children, and thus were aimed at lower fertility groups – suggests that direct nationality as well as regional concerns were in mind. In addition, Soviet planners have also become more verbal recently in proposing policies which differentiate by both region and nationality, ostensibly to raise fertility in Slavic areas, while, if only indirectly, aiming to limit it in Central Asia. As a leading Soviet demographer, T. Riabushkin, noted in 1982:

> Aspects of population reproduction are differentiated in various regions of the country, i.e., contrasts exist in all aspects of population movement. In accordance with these contrasts, it is obvious that demographic policy must likewise be differentiated ... Some scholars have come out against a regional demographic policy, since this supposedly can imply an infringement upon the rights of individual nationalities, or upon the rights of the inhabitants of individual regions, etc. In our view, this is absolutely not so. For example, at the present time, in our opinion, it is essential to carry out a policy of encouraging a higher birth rate in those republics where it is still low. Special measures are also essential in struggling against infant mortality in those regions where it is still comparatively high.[25]

In terms of population dynamics *within* Uzbekistan, however, these policies and policy debates promise to have little impact in changing present population trends in the near term. As the 1981 demographic measures illustrate, most Soviet discussions concerning demographic policy have focused on regional policies for the USSR as a whole, and have generally concentrated on raising fertility in labour deficit areas. Beyond broad calls for the formulation of a comprehensive and concrete set of demographic measures for the USSR as a whole, no comprehensive policy has emerged *within* Uzbekistan during the past decade, either to lower indigenous fertility, or to raise that of the Europeans residing there. By consequence, all evidence from the 1970s suggests that within Uzbekistan itself, success in either aim has been minimal. Despite the literature, few Russians in Uzbekistan desire more than three children, while the indigenous Central Asians continue to desire two or three times that amount.

This is not to suggest, of course, that the effects of modernisation or increased urbanisation, changing attitudes among the younger generation, or population policies of the Soviet government will not have an impact on lowering birth rates in the future. What it does suggest is that

none of these factors has had enough of an impact on fertility over the
past decade to shape population dynamics significantly in the near
future. Instead, deep-seated values and traditions regarding the family
have remained strong among Uzbekistan's indigenous population.
Because of traditional attitudes, the indigenous populations have a
substantially higher rate of growth compared with the European
populations living in their midst, keeping both the total republican
birth rate high and nationality differences wide.

MIGRATION

A secondary reason for these changes in the size and composition of
Uzbekistan's population has been the role of migration. While the
native birth rate was exceedingly high during the years following the
Revolution, the growth of the European population in Uzbekistan
initially kept pace largely as a result of in-migration. In the 1920s and
1930s, waves of Europeans were sent or migrated to Uzbekistan, to
quell resistance to the new Soviet rule, to build and staff new schools
and new cultural and political institutions, or to begin industrialisation
and collectivisation for better exploitation of the republic's natural and
agricultural resources. The evacuation of factories and personnel from
other parts of the USSR to Uzbekistan during World War Two gave
this growth new impetus. The first four decades of Soviet rule, therefore, saw an influx of thousands of people per year, almost entirely
Slavs coming in response to lucrative offers of jobs which the unskilled
native population could not or would not fill. At the same time, there
was extremely little out-migration on the part of any of the local
nationalities. Thus, since levels of both migration to Uzbekistan and
fertility within Uzbekistan were high, the total population of all of the
nationality groups within that republic grew rapidly through the 1950s.

Beginning with the 1950s and 1960s, however, the importance of
migration in Uzbekistan's population growth began to diminish. The
local populations remained relatively immobile, retaining, if not increasing their high rates of natural growth but still exhibiting practical-
ly no out-migration from their republic. The level of in-migration to
Uzbekistan from Slavic areas for the most part remained steady or
declined, in either case lagging behind rates of natural growth. Thus,
whereas migration had accounted for more than 42 per cent of
Uzbekistan's total population growth from 1939–59, from 1959–70 it
accounted for only about 10 percent, and from 1971–6, only about 4
per cent (Table 1.8).

TABLE 1.8 *Growth of Uzbekistan's population due to natural growth and migration 1939–70, in thousands*

	Indigenous	Non-Indigenous	Total	Percentage
Population, 17 Jan 1939	5 133	1 204	6 336	
Population, 15 Jan 1959	6 039	2 067	8 106	
Total Growth, 1939–59	907	863	1 770	100.0
Due to Natural Growth	907	115	1 022	57.7
Due to Migration from other republics	—	748	748	42.3
Population, 15 Jan 1970	9 255	2 705	11 960	
Total Growth, 1959–70	3 216	638	3 854	100.0
Due to Natural Growth	3 216	218	3 434	89.1
Due to Migration	—	420	420	10.9

SOURCE Ubaidullaeva, R. A. 'Regional'nye problemy razmeshcheniia i effektivnost' ispol'zovaniia trudovykh resursov v Uzbekskoi SSR', unpublished doctoral dissertation, Tashkent, 1974, p. 30.

During the 1960s the level of in-migration fluctuated widely, mainly due to circumstances within Uzbekistan itself. The 1966 earthquake in Tashkent entailed bringing thousands of people from other parts of the USSR to help reconstruct the city and other affected areas of Uzbekistan. The opening of new factories and new lands during the earlier part of that decade also attracted large numbers of migrants from other parts of the USSR, particularly from Siberia and the Far East. Again, however, there was little out-migration among the indigenous populations, and during the early 1970s the level of migration stabilised at a positive balance of about 30 000 people, mainly non-Asian, per year.[26]

Despite Soviet writings to the contrary, inter-republican migration to and from Uzbekistan during the past ten to fifteen years has remained low, and has remained largely a European phenomenon. Recent articles in the Soviet press have implied increased movement on the part of the Asian nationalities to other parts of the Soviet Union – in response to labour needs in the non black earth zone, (*nechernozem*, a land reclamation scheme in the RSFSR), to work on the Baikal–Amur Railroad (BAM), or to participate in agricultural projects in Siberia and other regions surrounding Moscow. Some scholars have referred to the establishment of 'trusts' of Asian workers, to provide greater labour inputs for labour-shortage areas of the USSR. In September, 1978 *Komsomolets Uzbekistana* stated that the first contingent of young people from Uzbekistan to arrive in the non black earth zone consisted of 1200 people, and more groups were being planned; as of 1979, there were an estimated 3500 people in the nechernozem who had migrated from Uzbekistan.[27] Articles in the press tend to suggest that with increasing participation of Central Asians in economic projects and educational and military training in other parts of the Soviet Union, out-migration from Central Asia should rise as well.

These same articles, however, have also suggested two crucial additional points: that the main proportion of these out-migrants to economic projects in other parts of the USSR continues to be Slavics, and that the Asians who are migrating to other areas of the USSR return to Uzbekistan within a very short period of time. In 1980, for example, indigenous Central Asians constituted only 11 per cent of all workers who had migrated from Central Asia and Kazakhstan and were working on the Baikal–Amur Railway; and they constituted less than 1 per cent of the total number of workers there.[28] According to other sources, morover substantial problems exist with recruits from Uzbekistan in the non black earth zone, with many Uzbeks staying only 15–30 days before returning home to their native republic. This was confirmed in interviews at the Institute of Ethnography in Moscow (1979 and 1981).

Although no gross data have been published on the numbers of military conscripts or students who opt not to return to Uzbekistan following service in other parts of the country, both of these factors will undoubtedly raise mobility among the local nationalities to some degree. None the less, all the young recruits or students serving or studying in a non-Asian republic whom I had the opportunity to interview desired to return home as soon as their tour of duty or study was terminated. These interviewees included military recruits who had just returned from serving in a non-Asian republic; several who were on home leave; and several Uzbek students who were studying in Leningrad and Moscow, whom I interviewed while doing research there. Throughout the 1970s, Uzbeks represented less than one-tenth of the total volume of inter-republican migration in their republic, and played a negligible role in the volume of migration with non-Asian republics.

1979 census results and a Western report make this point more clearly. In 1959, 42 000 Uzbeks were living outside Central Asia and Kazakhstan; by 1979, this number had grown to only 91 000, out of a total of about 12.5 million Uzbeks in the territory of the USSR as a whole. As Feshbach notes, these numbers indicate extremely low levels of migration among Uzbeks: assuming, 'as unrealistic as is the proposition', that none of this increment of 47 000 was due to births among those living outside the area during the entire twenty years Feshbach writes – assuming instead that the increment was due solely to out-migrants from the south – 'the resulting average is miniscule in the extreme, especially when considering that the entire Uzbek population grew by over 320 000 per year over the same period'.[29] Especially in the light of low levels of rural to urban migration within Uzbekistan (already described), most Soviet specialists whom I interviewed in the USSR felt that a significant shift in numbers of indigenous nationalities migrating out of Uzbekistan is not forthcoming for some time to come. Until such a time as mobility *within* the republic rises, they suggest, they would support Feshbach's conclusion that Uzbeks 'are just not moving at all out of the region'.

On the other side of the coin, several scholars have cited a recent migration of Slavs from Uzbekistan. Reversing a fairly consistent pattern of net in-migration to Uzbekistan during the 1960s and 1970s, the past two years (1981 and 1982) apparently for the first time saw a net out-migration of Slavs – whether this movement was a response to labour needs in other parts of the USSR, or a result of other social or political pressures. The report of the 26th Party Congress stressed the necessity of reversing these trends; it explicitly called for involving the Central Asian population more directly in developing new territories in the European parts of the USSR. [30] In the absence of any explicit programmes as to how this should be done, however, most scholars, Soviet as well as Western, have noted only the limited effectiveness of Soviet policies designed to encourage such migration. External migration to and from Uzbekistan, organised and otherwise, has remained largely a non-indigenous phenomenon, and inter-republican mobility among the indigenous populations has shown little sign of increasing.[31]

In summary, long-standing conservative traditional and family values have kept the birth rate of the indigenous nationalities high, causing total population growth in Uzbekistan to remain high even while European birth rates there have fallen. External migration, moreover – because of the decline in its magnitude – no longer significantly affects total population growth in Uzbekistan; it has become significant mainly in so far as it may affect Uzbekistan's nationality distribution. During the 1970s, Europeans continued to migrate into Uzbekistan, but not in sufficient numbers to retain their share of the republic's total population; by the early 1980s, it appeared that they had begun to migrate out of Uzbekistan. By consequence,

Uzbekistan's population today is younger, more equally divided between the sexes, and more homogeneously Asian than it was even twenty years ago.

DEMOGRAPHIC PROSPECTS

Particularly in the last few years, projections of fertility and migration in Uzbekistan have become the focus of much controversy. Some scholars contend that tradition and culture will remain strong enough in Uzbekistan to keep native birth rates high and mobility low, at least to the end of the century. Others contend that, despite the persistence of certain aspects of culture and tradition, Uzbekistan's birth rate will undergo a substantial decline in the very near future, and geographical mobility will rise. Citing processes already in motion, for example, (more women entering the labour force or becoming educated, increased urbanisation, modernisation, etc.), some scholars consider that a sharp decline in the indigenous birth rate is probable over the next few years which will be severe enough to offset future population trends significantly. Others have suggested that Uzbeks will soon begin to migrate out of Uzbekistan in greater numbers, and at a level at least great enough to have a profound effect on the size and composition of that republic's population in the very near future.[32]

While there is always great uncertainty in predicting future population dynamics in any locale, both attitudinal factors and the existing demographic structure of the population suggest that a sharp fertility decline or large scale out-migration of the indigenous populations from Uzbekistan are doubtful at least before the end of the century. As illustrated, attitudinal changes are occurring but slowly in Uzbekistan, and so far have been apparent only in the very largest cities. As Ata Mirzaev, Chief of the Population Laboratory at Tashkent University, writes:

We feel that the transition of the indigenous population of the republics of Central Asia from a high birth rate to a medium or, even more, to a low level will proceed very slowly. Towards the end of the twentieth century, it will be able to assume an intensive character only in a highly urbanised milieu, such as the capital centers and some large cities of Central Asia.

Even if one assumes that the entire urban population of Central Asia will enter into a regime of a middle or low birth rate, half of the population (the rural population) will continue to be oriented towards having many children. We must remember that in the year 2000, a population greater than the entire population of Central Asia today will be residing in rural areas alone.[33]

Yet even if attitudes were to change in the near future, the age, sex and nationality structures of Uzbekistan would by themselves perpetuate high population reproduction for some time to come. As illustrated above, Uzbekistan's population has been growing younger over the past two decades, so that a larger proportion of it falls into the lower age-groups today than even ten or twenty years ago. Whereas slightly under 38 per cent of the republic's population was aged 0–14 in 1959, that proportion was 45 per cent in 1970. In 1970, about one third of Uzbekistan's population was aged 0–10, and almost half, aged 0–15. In 1979, almost 30 per cent of Uzbekistan's population was estimated to be between the ages of 0 and 9, as opposed to 14.8 per cent in the RSFSR.[34] Moreover, as a result of steady rises throughout the 1960s of both the gross and net reproduction rates, the number of women in the child-bearing ages has been growing more rapidly than Uzbekistan's population as a whole. By 1990, the proportion of women in the child-bearing ages is expected to be almost double the 1970 figure, and by the year 2000, 269 per cent of that level. By the same reasoning, then, even should the birth rate fall among women in the child-bearing ages, that decline, too, would be offset by their growth in numbers. Thus, even if fertility rates were to decline, a drop in the number of births per thousand women of child-bearing age would be partly offset by the 'demographic momentum' set in motion, or by the greater number of women in the child-bearing ages relative to the population as a whole.

Furthermore, of that younger population, an already disproportionate and growing share is of the indigenous nationalities, whose birth rates, as illustrated above, even among the younger populations, are substantially higher than those of the European nationalities. While Uzbeks comprised less than 66 per cent of the republic's population in 1970, they comprised almost 75 per cent of all children born in that year, that is, Uzbeks living in Uzbekistan were reproducing themselves about 9 per cent faster than their proportion in the general population. Conversely, while the proportion of Russians in the total population was 12.5 per cent, Russians accounted for only 7 per cent of all children born. A comparison with the 1959 census indicates that the gap is only widening. And the sex structure among Uzbeks is also more favourable for population reproduction than among Uzbekistan's Russian population.[35] Thus, even should the birth rate begin to decline among young Uzbeks over the next few years, it is unlikely that it would decline by 100 per cent, to the level of the Russians. It is more likely that this decline would be offset by a proportional rise in the total number of Uzbeks in the younger age-groups at the expense of the Russians. In other words, a decline in fertility among the indigenous nationalities would still be slow in making itself felt in the republican birth rate as a whole.

Indeed, precisely because of these factors, some scholars have suggested the possibility that Uzbekistan's birth rate may even rise in the near future. One Uzbek demographer argues that present marriage patterns alone may be leading to a higher birth rate for Uzbekistan,[36] and trends in natural growth and migration also suggest that Uzbekistan's birth rate may go up before it goes down. The growing proportion of young Uzbeks in the republic's population resulting from natural growth, and the probability of greater out-migration of Slavs, will leave Uzbekistan in the coming decades with a more homogeneously Asian population which is younger and more inclined towards traditional family values than the republic's population of the past twenty years.

Taking many of these factors into account, projections for Uzbekistan suggest that population growth in Uzbekistan will remain high to the end of the century, and that nationality differences in population growth-rates will persist well into the next century. The greatest possible birth rate decline envisioned for all of Uzbekistan's nationalities combined is to a level of 20.3 per thousand in the year 2000. Since these projections do not assume a rise in the non-Asian birth rates in Uzbekistan, they suggest that even radical declines in fertility will still keep local birth rates in the year 2000 well above those which characterised Uzbekistan's Russian population in 1970 (Table 1.9).

Migration, moreover, cannot be expected to offset the high birth rate, nor to equalise the nationality distribution in the republic's population. On the contrary, many analysts have regarded the recent Slavic out-migration from Uzbekistan as the beginning of a fundamental shift of Europeans out of Uzbekistan, while implying little change in geographical mobility among the indigenous nationalities. Increased Soviet efforts to encourage migration to labour-short areas of the non-Asian USSR continue to meet with little response among Uzbekistan's Asian population. Almost all Soviet projections expect the

48

TABLE 1.9   *Estimated and projected total population and vital rates – Uzbek SS 1975 to 2000*

Year	Population	Birth rate	Death rate	Rate of natural increase
1975	13 689	34.5	7.2	27.3
1980				
High Series	15 818	37.2	6.9	30.3
Medium Series	15 759	35.6	6.9	28.7
Low Series	15 634	33.1	6.9	26.2
Constant Series	15 805	37.6	6.9	30.7
1985				
High Series	18 467	37.8	6.4	31.4
Medium Series	18 208	35.0	6.4	28.6
Low Series	17 805	31.6	6.5	25.1
Constant Series	18 520	39.1	6.4	32.6
1990				
High Series	21 557	35.9	5.9	30.0
Medium Series	20 919	32.2	5.9	26.3
Low Series	20 073	28.1	6.0	22.1
Constant Series	21 778	37.6	5.9	31.8
1995				
High Series	24 956	33.5	5.4	28.1
Medium Series	23 733	29.1	5.5	23.6
Low Series	22 258	24.2	5.7	18.5
Constant Series	25 451	35.6	5.3	30.3
2000				
High Series	28 643	32.1	5.2	26.9
Medium Series	26 572	26.6	5.4	21.1
Low Series	24 231	20.3	5.7	14.6
Constant Series	29 539	34.4	5.1	29.3

NOTE   These projections are based on an estimated gross reproduction rate of 2.8 for Uzbekistan, 1975. The high series assumes a 20 per cent decline in fertility between 1975 and 2000; the medium series, a 39 per cent decline; the low series, a 57 per cent decline; and the constant series, a 12 per cent decline to gross reproduction rates in the year 2000 of 2.2, 1.7, 1.2 and 2.4 respectively.

SOURCE   Baldwin, Godfrey S. *Population Projections by Age and Sex: For the Republics and Major Economic Regions of the USSR: 1970 to 2000* series p. 91, no. 26, monograph prepared for the Foreign Demographic Analysis Division, US Bureau of the Census, Washington, DC, September, 1979, p. 84.

mobility of the local nationalities to rise in the coming decades; but few Soviets expect increased mobility among the Asians to assume an inter-republican character for some time to come. Barring any mass deportations or major upheavals in Soviet population policies, therefore, it appears that external migration to and from Uzbekistan will remain largely a non-Asian phenomenon at least to the end of the century. The net effect of inter-republican migration, therefore, will probably be minimal as far as Uzbekistan's total population is concerned, but will contribute to the increasing ethnic homogeneity of Uzbekistan as European migrants leave behind a growing Asian population.

In short, taking both natural growth and migration into account, Uzbekistan's population can be expected to grow to at least somewhere around 26 million by the year 2000 – or to double its 1975 level. If the higher estimates are adopted, it can be expected to reach almost twice the number recorded in the 1979 census, that is, to reach about 30 million people in 2000, as against 15 million in 1979. In addition, it will continue to be a young population, evenly divided between the sexes and increasingly Asian in composition. Compared with the growth rates of the total population over the previous twenty-year periods (30 per cent over the period 1939–59; 90 per cent, 1959–79), and taking into account the disparity between the growth rates of the Europeans and the Asians, all these factors are raising new and critical challenges for Soviet leaders. Soviet planners now appear to face the growing uncertainty of whether economic expansion in Uzbekistan will be able to keep pace with this rapid population growth, in terms of both production and consumption. Can Uzbekistan's economy grow rapidly enough to provide consumers with at least the present level of goods and services? Will it be able to provide a rapidly-growing working-age population with full employment? And if not, as Asians comprise a growing proportion of both the producers and the consumers in Uzbekistan, will economic strains become invested with ethnic meaning and begin to threaten the Soviet system in more fundamental political ways?

ECONOMIC GROWTH

One has only to compare the present level of development of Soviet Central Asia with that of neighbouring Afghanistan to be reminded of the enormous strides which Uzbekistan has made in little over sixty years. By almost all measures of economic growth, as well as by gross measures of social services (student enrolments, infant mortality, number of doctors or hospital beds per thousand inhabitants, etc.), economic change has been rapid in Soviet Central Asia, and Uzbekistan today is undoubtedly on a level far above that of her southern neighbours.

Until recently, moreover, there seems to have been a deliberate effort on the part of central planners in Moscow to keep rates of economic growth in the Central Asian republics high. Since the 1960s, Uzbekistan apparently has benefited from the inter-republic redistribution of national income disproportionate to its contribution. At least since the mid-1960s, the total value of used national income has exceeded produced national income there, on a level well beyond the USSR average.[37] And in terms of other budget data, Uzbekistan, like the other southern-belt republics, has consistently been assigned shares of its total turnover tax-collections which are well above average, if not at or near 100 per cent. Between 1967 and 1979, for example, an average of 92 per cent of total turnover tax was retained within Uzbekistan, as against 45 per cent for the RSFSR and an average of 53 per cent for the USSR as a whole.[38]

None the less, despite the rapid economic growth and the apparently disproportionate amount of investment in Uzbekistan relative to other republics, Uzbekistan's economy over the past two decades apparently has begun to be constrained by rapid population growth. In recent years, despite the high percentage rises in most economic indicators, economic development in most per capita terms in Uzbekistan has actually slowed. For example, while the growth rate of Uzbekistan's national income over the past two decades has exceeded that of the USSR as a whole, its growth per capita has lagged behind. Between 1971 and 1975 the average annual rate of growth of national income for the USSR as a whole was 5.7 per cent; for Uzbekistan, it was 6.9 per cent. In per capita terms, however, the rates were reversed: in 1966, per capita national income in Uzbekistan was at a level about 63 per cent of the all-Union average; by 1970, according to some estimates, it may have been as low as 54 or 58 per cent and by 1975, as low as 51 per cent.[39]

Similarly, in terms of production, total produced national income for the USSR stood, in 1975, at a level 263 per cent higher than in 1965; per capita produced national income was 221 per cent its 1965 level. For Uzbekistan, these proportions were 276 per cent and 170 per cent respectively – suggesting a rate of growth above the national average for total national income produced, but far below the national average when computed on a per capita basis.[40] Thus, despite the disproportionate amount of investment in Uzbekistan relative to other republics, since 1960, by most per capita measures, the development gap among these republics has actually widened. While some of this must be attributed to structural differences in the economies of the different republics, (see Chapter 3), the lag has been due largely to Uzbekistan's high level of population reproduction.[41]

As Gillula notes, the need to divert a larger share of used national income to consumption in order to keep the standard of living from declining may have contributed to the cutback in relative levels of capital formation in Uzbekistan. None the less, rising consumption needs brought about by Uzbekistan's rapid population growth have also increased at rates which have outpaced the growth of national income in these republics. While average annual wages and payments and benefits from the social consumption fund rose in Uzbekistan, 1960–75, retail sales per capita declined from a level 74 per cent of the all-Union average to 63 per cent over the fifteen years, and savings deposits per capita, from 45 per cent of the national average to 36 per cent.[42] According to a Soviet analyst, the level of consumption of food products and consumer goods in Uzbekistan presently lags far behind the estimated norm of per capita consumption.[43]

In other words, rapid development in Uzbekistan and the benefits which Uzbekistan has derived from central economic policies have been more than offset by high population growth there. Trends through the 1970s, moreover, suggest that as central priorities shift to Siberia and the Far East, these disproportions between economic and population expansion in Uzbekistan may intensify. Today, several Western analysts have noted an apparent curtailment of the policy of redistributing national income between regions to provide for higher levels of capital formation in less-developed republics. Instead, the share in total investments in Siberia and the Far East has been rising, at the expense of the southern tier in general.[44] Thus, according to several indicators, the strains of rapid population growth are already making themselves felt in Uzbekistan's economy. And if central priorities shift more dramatically towards Siberia, projections, while not cataclysmic, are not promising. Most reports seem to reaffirm Schroeder's view that 'on a per capita basis the relative positions of the Central Asian republics will continue to deteriorate, even though moderate overall growth will be achieved if plans are met'.[45]

2 The Labour Force

Against this background, what about the Asians as producers? What do economic trends imply for Uzbekistan's labour force? If the rate of economic expansion is lagging behind the growth of the population as a whole; and if the growth rate of the younger population is exceeding that of the older age-groups, what does this mean in terms of jobs, and in terms of providing Uzbekistan's young and working-age population with full employment? And what will be the relative places of the different nationalities in a tightening labour market?

The demographic trends already described – a high rate of population growth and a growing indigenous component – are only more pronounced with regard to the young and working-age populations, and thus hold serious implications for future labour utilisation in Uzbekistan. If Uzbekistan's total population is projected to grow rapidly over the next two decades, its working-age population will grow even more rapidly. If the indigenous nationalities will comprise a large and growing proportion of Uzbekistan's total population, they will comprise an even greater proportion of its working-age population. The effects of both natural growth and migration consequently will be more exaggerated on the size and composition of Uzbekistan's labour force than they will be on the total population. Against a background of slowing economic growth, therefore, concern has been expressed that their apparent corollary, potential for political unrest, might prove to be more pronounced as well. In this context, then, several questions are assuming major importance: how great is Uzbekistan's labour surplus today? How can it be measured? What do projections suggest for potential surpluses among the different nationality groups?

DEMOGRAPHIC TRENDS: THE WORKING-AGE POPULATION

Projections regarding the growth of Uzbekistan's working-age population are indeed dramatic. From 1959 to 1979, Uzbekistan's working-age population grew at the same rate or slightly more slowly than the republic's population as a whole.[1] For the coming two decades, however, both numerically and in proportion to Uzbekistan's total population, the size of the working-age population is expected to swell. According to one of the more conservative sets of projections,[2] if the total population of Uzbekistan is expected to grow by 99 per cent, from 1975 to 2000, from natural growth alone, the working-age population is projected to grow by 125 per cent in that same interval; that is, in the year 2000 it will be 225 per cent its 1975 level, or will have doubled and then increased by yet another 25 per cent. As a proportion of the total population, moreover, the change will also be notable: the working-age population comprised about 45 per cent of Uzbekistan's population in 1975; according to some estimates, by the year 2000, it may reach as high as 56 per cent. And finally, because of the population's continued young age-structure,[3] the high growth rate of the working-age population will not abate even at the turn of the century. Unlike the European parts of the Soviet Union – where the size of the working-age population will decline in number between 1980 and 1995[4] – in Uzbekistan the proportions are projected to remain stable for still some years to come (Table 2.1).

Barring any possible forced migration in the near future by Soviet authorities, migration is not projected to significantly alter these population projections. As discussed in Chapter 1, several Soviet estimates project that migration to Uzbekistan from other republics, mainly of people in the able-bodied ages, may remain marginal in the future, but that there will still be little outward migration from Uzbekistan on the part of the local population. Including migration, therefore, their estimates suggest that the total number of people entering Uzbekistan's labour force may reach an unprecedented magnitude. The working-age population of Uzbekistan grew by an average of about 136 000 people per year from 1965 to 1970, and by about 233 000 people per year from 1970 to 1975. Several scholars now feel it could grow by an average of 306 000 people per year from 1975 to 1980; 276 000 per year from 1980 to 1985; and 278 000 per year from 1985 to 1990 – all higher than the increments of any previous five year period.[5] Few statistics are available on the composition of the working

TABLE 2.1 *Projections of the working age population, Uzbekistan, 1975–2000 (thousands)*

	1975	1980	1985	1990	1995				2000			
					H	M	L	C	H	M	L	C
Male	3 093	3 852	4 556	5 218	6 065	6 046	6 003	6 057	7 130	7 026	6 858	7 146
Female	3 062	3 719	4 311	4 965	5 749	5 731	5 690	5 742	6 895	6 796	6 634	6 910
Both Sexes	6 155	7 571	8 867	10 183	11 813	11 777	11 692	11 799	14 025	13 822	13 492	14 056

NOTE H, M, L, C designate High, Medium, Low and Constant Series.
Numbers are as of 1 January. Figures may not add to totals due to rounding.

SOURCE Baldwin, Godfrey, S. *Population Projections by Age and Sex: For the Republic and Major Economic Regions of the USSR: 1970 to 2000* series P.91, no. 26, monograph prepared for the Foreign Demographic Analysis Division, US Bureau of the Census, Washington, DC, September, 1979, pp. 128–9.

age population by nationality. Two important points of consensus among Soviet demographers interviewed in Tashkent, however, were that the proportion of the local nationalities in the working-age population is growing more rapidly than their share in the total population; and that because of high levels of natural growth their share will continue to rise towards the end of the century.

In other words, relatively high fertility in Uzbekistan, at least for the next several years, will keep the proportion of the working-age population high, at a level almost half of Uzbekistan's total population throughout the 1990s. A growing share of this able-bodied population will be Central Asian. Although migration is declining, Slavs continue to move to Uzbekistan, apparently suggesting that they may continue to pre-empt or vie for jobs which a growing number of indigenous Central Asians might be seeking as well. Several Soviet planners have already expressed concern over this situation:

> As a result of the rapid growth in the spheres attracting labor, and in nationality ranks of the working class and specialists, possibilities have grown for providing sectors of the national economy with a labor force drawn from local labor resources. All the same, the absolute magnitude of migration in the republic is significant . . . Moreover, migrants settle in regions with high population density and already provided with a labor force, which makes regional use of local resources more difficult.[6]

By the year 2000, the working-age population of Uzbekistan will comprise as many as 14 million people, as opposed to about 6 million in 1975 and around 7.5 million people in 1980. More than 10 million will be of the indigenous nationalities. Will there, as Soviet officials insist, be employment for everyone? And if not, which nationality groups will be affected to a greater degree?

EMPLOYMENT IN SOCIAL PRODUCTION

Particularly in recent years, Soviet and Western analysts alike have become increasingly apprehensive about these trends: about the ability of Uzbekistan's economy to absorb this growing manpower supply, and about the kinds of social and ethnic issues implicit in an apparently unavoidably tightening labour market. 'Widespread unemployment and welfare burdens in Central Asia as a result of a growing labour surplus' have been forecast by Lewis, Rowland and Clem.[7] A. McAuley and A. Hegelson note that:

> the industrial resource base of the Central Asian region is modest and we cannot expect in the near future nearly sufficient employment for the growing masses of Central Asians ... Recent experience does not suggest that it will be easy to expand non-agricultural employment in these regions ... and agricultural intensification is limited by the immense capital investments needed for further development of irrigation in the water-deficient Central Asian region[8]

And as Massell adds, because of the continued influx of 'European, especially Slavic, settlers, professionals and supervisory political personnel' and the sustained high birth rate among the local Asian populations, 'it is all but certain that Moslem pressure on available positions will increase'.[9]

On the Soviet side, the same concerns have been expressed, with perhaps slightly more caution. Local journals continually, if somewhat obliquely, stress the need to find better outlets for their rapidly-growing working-age populations. And Ubaidullaeva – who, in interviews, praised the rapid growth of Uzbekistan's labour force as 'an important factor providing for the expansion of socialist reproduction of the labour force and for the development of the republic's productive forces' – nonetheless makes the same points more directly:

> In perspective, growth in the population of the able-bodied ages, by our accounts, will surpass the growth rates of the total population. This will make questions of rational employment one of the most important social and economic concerns.[10]

In other words, even those Soviet analysts extolling the rapid growth of Uzbekistan's labour force have stressed the extreme sensitivity and great difficulties of fully accommodating that labour force in Uzbekistan's economy.

Indeed, beginning in the 1960s there were already broad indications that Uzbekistan might prove incapable of fully absorbing its labour supply. As early as 1962, one Uzbek scholar, N. S. Esipov noted that despite the rapid expansion of Uzbekistan's economy, there were still problems in employing the large and growing labour force there. The quantity of work places (*rabochie mesta*), excepting agriculture, he noted, was indeed growing faster than the working-age population: for

Central Asia as a whole, the former had grown by 29 per cent between 1959 and 1962, as opposed to 15 per cent for the latter. But, he added, 'the absolute growth in the working-age population still exceeds the need for it in the economy'.[11]

Today, there is no single indicator to express the exact magnitude of labour surpluses or deficits in Uzbekistan, but a combination of indicators can provide at least a broad idea of general problems and trends. Despite some success in creating job opportunities, a general 'labour surplus' might already be evident in Uzbekistan and continues to grow.

The total Soviet civilian labour force is divided into three main sectors. The state sector includes all industrial and service occupations and the state-owned and operated portion of agriculture – that is, state farms (*sovkhozy*) and work in parts of non-agricultural enterprises and organisations involved in subsidiary agricultural activities. The collective farm sector includes occupations on farms which, technically at least, are owned and run by the farm members. Together these two sectors comprise the socialised economy (or social production), where the vast majority of the Soviet labour force is occupied. A third, private sector, however, also exists in the USSR, consisting of people working on private plots (full or part time) and a very small group of uncollectivised peasants and independent artisans. Most of the people working in the private sector who are not also working in social production are classified as working in the 'household and private subsidiary economy'. The socialised economy, however, is meant to be the main employer of the Soviet labour force, with full-time work exclusively in the private sector generally limited.

Judging by the published data of the three most recent censuses (1959, 1970 and 1979), Soviet authorities have indeed made significant gains in creating large numbers of employment opportunities in the socialised sector in Uzbekistan during the past two decades. The reported labour force occupied in the socialised sector of Uzbekistan's economy (i.e. excluding household and private subsidiary work) grew by about 30 per cent in the eleven years, 1959–70, and by another 46 per cent between 1970 and 1979. That rate of growth exceeded during the 1960s, and during the 1970s was about equal to the growth rate of Uzbekistan's working-age population (which grew by 25 per cent and 46 per cent during the same periods, respectively). The reported labour force in the socialised sector grew from 82 per cent of the working-age population in 1959, to 85 per cent in 1970 and 1979 (Table 2.2).

TABLE 2.2　Growth of the employed population relative to the working-age population, Uzbekistan, 1959–79 (thousands)

	1959	1970	1979
Total working-age population	3983	4989	7292
Reported labour force[a]	3263	4238	6201[b]
Working-age population minus reported labour force	720	751	1091
Annual average employment	2533	3709	4973
Reported labour force as % of working-age population	81.9	84.9	85.0
Annual average employment as % of working-age population	63.5	74.3	68.2

[a] excluding private subsidiary activity
[b] computed from census data, assuming the proportion of private activity is the same as for 1970.

SOURCE　Line 1: 1959 data from TsSU, *Itogi vsesoiuznoi perepisi naseleniia 1959 goda*, p. 48; 1970 data, from *Itogi . . . 1970 goda*, vol. II, p. 12; 1979 data from Baldwin, G. 'Population Projections by Age and Sex for the Republics and Major Economic Regions of the USSR: 1970–2000', monograph prepared for the Foreign Demographic Analysis Division, US Bureau of the Census, 1979, p. 128. Line 2: From *Itogi vsesoiuznoi perepisi naseleniia* . . . for each respective year. Line 4: Feshbach, M. 'Prospects for Outmigration from Central Asia and Kazakhstan in the Next Decade', *The Soviet Economy in a Time of Change*, Joint Economic Committee, US Congress, Washington, DC, 1979, p. 694.

In terms of absolute numbers, however, as Esipov suggested, the size of the working age population still may have exceeded the need for it in the economy. And despite the large increases for the employed population, beginning with the 1970s, this excess in the working-age population may have begun to grow. As illustrated above, the growth rates of the working-age and employed populations were comparable during the past two decades. But the disparity in the numerical increments to each category was great and widened with the 1970s. Whereas the working-age population grew by an average of about 91 000 people per year from 1959 to 1970, the reported labour force employed in the socialised sector grew by about 88 000 per year; whereas the former grew by about 256 000 per year from 1970 to 1979, the latter grew by only 218 000 per year. In other words, while that part of the able-bodied population not working in the socialised sector grew by about 27 000 people between 1959 and 1970, it grew by about 340 000 people – or by 12.5 times as much! – between 1970 and 1979. This represented an average growth of about 38 000 people per year from 1970 to 1979, as opposed to 2500 per year in the preceding decade.[12] Thus, despite the fact that the growth rate of the reported labour force exceeded or was equal to that of the working-age population, by 1979 more than one million people of working age were not employed in the socialised sector of Uzbekistan's economy – a growth of more than 50 per cent from the 1959 level (Table 2.2).

Because of Soviet definitional peculiarities, perhaps a more revealing measurement of the change in employment over the past two decades is provided by average annual employment. The labour force, as defined by Soviet statisticians, includes all individuals who claimed an occupation at the time of the censuses, regardless of how long they had been working. Annual average employment, on the other hand, relates the number of days worked by an individual during a given month to the number of calendar days in the month. Derived as the ratio of days worked to calendar days (including weekends), it takes seasonality and absenteeism into account and is therefore a more accurate measurement of actual full-time employment in the Soviet context.

Like the total labour force, annual average employment grew substantially between 1959 and 1979, from 2.5 to almost 5 million people. But particularly in the last nine years of that period, its growth of 34 per cent was still outpaced by the 46 per cent growth of the working-age population. While the latter was growing by about 233 000 people per year between 1970 and 1975, annual average employment was growing by only slightly more than half as much (136 000 per year). In 1970, annual average employment represented about 74 per cent of the total working-age population; in nine years, by 1979, that proportion had declined to 68 per cent (Table 2.2). The significance of this decline is perhaps best conveyed when contrasted with other regions of the USSR and with the all-Union average. Unlike that in Uzbekistan, annual average employment in the RSFSR grew slightly more rapidly than did the working-age population in the years 1970 to 1975. While the ratio of the labour force to the working-age population, from 1959 to 1975, remained relatively stable in the RSFSR and in the USSR as a whole, it declined by almost four percentage points in Uzbekistan.[13]

Much of this 'surplus' in Uzbekistan, of course, has been absorbed by the rise in the number of students in the able-bodied ages, a number which has grown rapidly over the past two decades. The proportion of the working-age population which is composed of full-time students has grown rapidly in Uzbekistan, and today, Uzbeks comprise the majority of full-time students at all levels of educational training (see Chapter 4). Even despite that tremendous expansion, however, the rapid growth in the number of employment opportunities and in the number of full-time students have still left, over the years, a large component of Uzbekistan's working-age population not working in the socialised sector and not studying, that is, ostensibly 'not employed'. Official Soviet statistics staunchly insist that 'unemployment' does not exist in Uzbekistan. As one Uzbek writes, 'Such a remote idea, like the word "unemployment" is absolutely alien to the people of our country since we have completely dispensed with it as far back as in the early thirties.'[14] While a small proportion of these people may not have been working or studying for a variety of reasons, therefore – such as disabilities, studying for exams, receipt of 'privileged pensions' or for other reasons remaining as a dependent within the household – the vast majority of this 'surplus' has been classified as occupied outside social production in the private sector.

To a certain extent, private subsidiary activity is an integral part of the workings of the Soviet economy, in labour 'deficit' and labour 'surplus' regions alike. An apparent excess of such activity, however, may also indicate the existence of substantial manpower reserves for whom work may not be available in the socialised sector:

> The size of employment in the household economy largely depends on the needs of social production for labor resources and their rates of growth. The higher the national economy's need for a labor force, and the lower the growth rate of labor resources, the greater the significance of household and private subsidiary work as a source of labor for social production. The lower the need for labor, and the higher the growth rates of labor resources, the smaller the role of the household economy as a source of labor.[15]

In attempting to gauge levels of 'non-employment' in Uzbekistan, therefore – although activity in private work should by no means be equated with 'unemployment' *per se* – large changes in the level of activity in household and private subsidiary work can be regarded as at least partially indicative of changes in the general demand for labour there.

ACTIVITY IN HOUSEHOLD AND PRIVATE SUBSIDIARY
WORK

Despite official pronouncements to the contrary, activity in household
and private subsidiary work is high in Uzbekistan, and the level has
grown throughout the past decade. Soviet census data boast a substantial decline in the proportion of the working-age population occupied
solely in Uzbekistan's private sector – a decline of about 2.5 times
between 1959 and 1970, from 16.7 per cent of the able-bodied
population, to 6.9 per cent. According to data from Egamberdyev, the
decline in private subsidiary agriculture and employment in household
work among Uzbekistan's rural inhabitants was approximately 50 per
cent.[16]

This decline as reported by official Soviet sources, however, was due
largely to two definitional and administrative changes, rather than to a
real shift of the able-bodied population from the private sector to the
socialised economy. The first change regards the role of pensioners. As
Rapawy has pointed out, the introduction of pensions in the early
sixties for collective farmers greatly compounded the problems of
accurate information-gathering as far as work in private subsidiary
agriculture was concerned. Whereas prior to 1964, in response to the
census questionnaire, a collective farmer may well have replied that his
main source of income was his private plot (since no other source of
income was available to him), after 1964 – although his private
activities may not have diminished – he would have been more apt to
reply that his main source of income was his pension. His actual activity
in private agriculture, however, might well have remained
unchanged.[17]

The second change regards seasonality. As both Egamberdyev and
Mikheeva have pointed out, in 1959 on collective farms only that part
of the able-bodied population which was participating in collective
agricultural work in December was considered working in social
production. In the 1970 census, the definition of employment in social
production was expanded to include the entire working age population
which had 'generally worked in collectivised agriculture during the
course of the year'. According to Egamberdyev, 'It is particularly due
to this fact that a sharp reduction of people employed in private
subsidiary agriculture and household work took place.' While neither
Mikheeva nor Egamberdyev was prepared to suggest an alternative set
of statistics, both confirmed that throughout the 1970s, 'factual emp-

loyment in the household and private subsidiary economy was significantly higher' than that reported in official publications.[18]

A better indication of the actual level of household and private subsidiary employment, then, is provided by another set of Soviet data for the seventh and eighth five-year plans. According to these estimates, the proportion of Uzbekistan's able-bodied population which was occupied exclusively in the household and private subsidiary economy declined from 31.8 per cent of the working-age population in 1959 to 18.2 per cent in 1970. Numerically, that meant a drop from about 1 274 000 in 1959 to 936 900 in 1970 – or a decline by about 26 per cent rather than the 50 per cent suggested by Egamberdyev – and to a level still extremely high. The number of people of the able-bodied ages occupied in household and private subsidiary work was projected to remain relatively stable at about 900 000 throughout most of the 1970s.

Although only fragmentary data are available on activity in the private sector for the 1970s, several Soviet commentators writing during the 1970s have suggested that even these projections may have been too conservative. In 1974, Ubaidullaeva suggested that, instead of remaining stable, the number of people occupied in the private sectors was actually rising, and could be expected to continue to do so for the next decade. Despite the growing number of job opportunities, she noted, 'the rapid growth of those employed in social production is not being accompanied by a decline (absolute or relative) of those occupied in the household and private subsidiary economy'.[19] The number of people occupied solely in household and private subsidiary work, moreover, is not expected to decline in the near future. Attempting to take several variables into account, Ubaidullaeva has suggested three sets of projections of the growth of the able-bodied population which will be occupied in household and private subsidiary activity through 1990. Her estimates, based on 1970 data, suggest that the number of people employed in the private sector in 1990 will range anywhere from close to 900 000 people to about 1.3 million people, or anywhere from 9 per cent to about 15 per cent of the total working-age population.[20]

Thus, during the past decade, the level of activity in Uzbekistan's household and private subsidiary economy has remained high. Today, the percentage of Uzbekistan's able-bodied population not employed in social production is among the highest of any of the Soviet republics. According to one estimate, in 1970, somewhere close to one quarter of all labour resources in Uzbekistan's cities did not take part in social production.[21] According to another, during the mid-1970s, more than one fifth of the labour resources of Samarkand *oblast'* were occupied exclusively in household and private subsidiary work, and 'significant labour reserves' were 'also expected in perspective.'[22] If we regard these numbers – as Soviet scholars do – as at least partially indicative of an absence of employment opportunities in social production, then a 'labour surplus' appears to exist in Uzbekistan, and may be growing.

THE WORKING AND NON-WORKING POPULATIONS BY NATIONALITY

Data on the workforce along nationality lines are scarce. None the less, information that is available suggest a further complicating factor. Not only does Uzbekistan face a significant, and growing number of seemingly 'unemployed' able-bodied population, but a disproportionate number of those who are not employed in social production, or who are occupied exclusively in household and private subsidiary activity are of the local Asian nationalities.

This is not to understate, it must be stressed, the tremendous strides which Uzbekistan has made in drawing the indigenous nationalities into the socialised labour force over the past sixty years. From the beginning of the Soviet era, Soviet policies have been oriented towards two major goals in Uzbekistan: towards developing the area as rapidly as possible, and towards establishing 'native cadres' from among the local nationalities. Due to the presence of a highly illiterate and unskilled indigenous population and an extremely low level of development, the first of these goals initially necessitated directing most of the capital and labour inputs to Uzbekistan from other, mainly European parts of the USSR, rather than generating them from within Uzbekistan itself. As mentioned above, during the first few decades of Soviet rule, the vast majority of industrial workers, teachers, doctors and other professionals were obtained from outside the Central Asian region. Russians represented 'the core on which to build'.[23]

At the same time, however, a policy was also adopted to bring more of the indigenous nationalities into the labour force. Despite resistance from among the indigenous and non-indigenous nationalities alike, throughout the 1920s the Soviet leadership stressed the need for 'korenizatsiia', or the 'nativisation' or 'rooting' of the new workforce in native soil. This entailed increasing the number and proportion of Central Asians in all sectors of the economy. During the first two decades of Soviet power, substantial efforts were made to move the indigenous nationalities into new economic sectors, to train them for new roles, and to advance them to new positions. Despite the influx of Europeans into Uzbekistan, therefore, the growth of an indigenous workforce was rapid.

None the less, workers and employees drawn from the local nationalities are not created overnight, and despite these advances, by the 1970s, the indigenous nationalities living in Uzbekistan were still disproportionately under-represented in the workforce relative to their total population. In 1970, while Uzbeks comprised 65.5 per cent of Uzbekistan's total population, and perhaps as high as 68 per cent of its working-age population, they accounted for only 57.5 per cent of the republic's population employed in social production. Of that 57.5 per cent, moreover, the majority were agricultural workers in the countryside. While Uzbeks comprised about 41 per cent of Uzbekistan's total urban population, they accounted for only about 30 per cent of the urban labour force. By contrast, in the same year, Russians comprised 12.5 per cent of Uzbekistan's total population; yet they accounted for more than 18 per cent of the republic's employed population, and close to 40 per cent of its employed urban population (Table 2.3).

Excluding collective farmers, moreover, Uzbeks in 1970 comprised only 51 per cent of the total number of wage-workers employed in all branches of Uzbekistan's national economy. This marked a rise of only eight percentage points from the 1959 level of 43 per cent. Thus, although the number of these wage-workers employed in the State sector grew by about 50 per cent over the intercensal period, 1959–70, about one third of the increment in the number of wage-workers was drawn from the non-indigenous nationalities.[24] Even though Asians in Uzbekistan comprise the overwhelming majority of the working-age population, therefore, they are still under-represented in the population of their republic employed in public work. Instead, as several local planners stress, 'the main part of the non-working and non-studying members of a family are people of the local nationality'.[25]

Perhaps of most significance with regard to activity in this sector, however, is its age, sex and skill-structure. Not only are most people occupied in the private sector Asian, but they are also mainly women, largely unskilled, and are concentrated in the younger age-groups and the prime working-ages. In 1975, out of an estimated 12–15 per cent of the able-bodied population of Uzbekistan working in household and private subsidiary work, about 95 per cent were women, and the vast majority were Central Asian women. This does not nullify, of course, the tremendous growth in the number of women employed in

TABLE 2.3 Nationality composition of the labour force, urban and rural, Uzbekistan, 1970 (percentage)

Nationality	Total Population		Urban Population		Rural Population	
	Total	of which Employed	Total	of which Employed	Total	of which Employed
Uzbeks	65.5	57.5	41.1	29.8	79.5	77.3
Karakalpaks	2.0	1.8	1.6	1.2	2.2	2.2
Russians	12.5	18.3	30.4	39.2	2.2	3.4
Tatars	3.7	5.0	7.7	9.2	1.4	2.0
Kazakhs	4.0	3.6	3.0	2.4	4.6	4.4
Tadzhiks	3.8	3.3	2.6	1.9	4.5	4.3
Other	8.5	10.5	13.6	16.3	5.6	6.4

SOURCE Chamkin, A. S. 'Motivy k trudu v sfere obshchestvennogo proizvodstva', doctoral dissertation, Tashkent, 1976, p. 45.

social production. From the onset of the first five-year plan, as a Soviet scholar writes, the goal of attracting women to social production was 'at the centre of attention of Party organisations'. And whereas women comprised less than 8 per cent of the total number of personnel in Uzbekistan in the late 1920s, they comprised about 43 per cent of all personnel in the mid 1970s.[26]

None the less, even by the 1970s the proportion of women in the workforce was still well below their proportion in the total and working-age populations of Uzbekistan, and the vast majority of working women were European. Only about 83 per cent of all women in the working ages were numbered among the reported labour force in Uzbekistan in 1970, as against 90 per cent of the men. And if women comprised approximately 42 per cent of Uzbekistan's workers and employees in the early 1970s, only about one quarter were indigenous. Instead, indigenous women today overwhelmingly dominate the household and private subsidiary economy. Rather than diminishing, the absolute number of women working outside social production has grown over the past decade, rising as much as 20 per cent in Uzbekistan in the period 1971–75.[27]

An analysis of the age structure, moreover, indicates that the population occupied in household and private subsidiary activity is not composed mainly of older people, as one might expect, but is young and middle-age. In 1970, 33 per cent of the population occupied in Uzbekistan's private sector was under thirty years old (aged 16–29), while another 33 per cent was aged 30–39. Only about 7 per cent of the women, and less than 13 per cent of the men were aged 50–59. Interestingly, the preponderance of the young and middle-aged is particularly true among the men in household and private subsidiary work. As Table 2.4 illustrates, whereas less than 7 per cent of the total number of women employed in the private sector were aged 16–19 in 1970, more than 25 per cent of the men were in that age group. Close to 60 per cent of the total number of men in private work were under 30. With each successive age-group, the number of men employed exclusively in private work declined. The majority of the women employed in private work were aged 20–49 (Table 2.4).

The age, sex and nationality structures of the population in private work, then, suggest two apparent, and somewhat different problems. For the men, one may assume that employment in the private sector is due to a lack of attractive opportunities elsewhere, either for work or for retraining. Among the young, (those aged 16–29), low participation rates in the socialised workforce can probably be attributed in

TABLE 2.4   *Composition of the able-bodied population employed in the household and private subsidiary economy of Uzbekistan, by age and sex, 1970 (as percentages)*

Age group	Both Sexes	By Age		By Sex	
		Male	Female	Male	Female
16–19	7.6	25.4	6.6	19.1	80.9
20–29	25.8	33.1	25.5	9.7	90.3
30–39	32.7	14.8	33.6	3.3	96.7
40–49	26.5	14.4	27.2	4.4	95.6
50–59	7.4	12.3	7.1	15.6	84.4
Total:	100.0	100.0	100.0	7.4[a]	92.6[a]

[a] Calculated by multiplying percentages in columns 5 and 6 by those in column 2 to derive the percentage of the total. 92.6 per cent of the total number of people occupied exclusively in household and private subsidiary activity in Uzbekistan, 1970, was female, 7.4 per cent, male.

SOURCE Egamberdyev, A. E. *Regional'nye problemy vosproizyodstva rabochei sily v Uzbekistane* (Tashkent: Fan, 1976) p. 52.

large part to the long delays among school-leavers or returnees from military conscription in finding employment, by the number of 'refuseniks' from educational establishments who are spending an additional year as a 'dependant' studying for exams, or the like. Among those aged 30–39, however, reasons for non-participation in the socialised labour force are more difficult to ascertain. While some proportion of that group may not be working because of various disabilities, the majority of men in private work in this age-group may also indicate a fairly large number of able-bodied males for whom work, or attractive opportunities are not available in social production. In any case, it indicates that some component of males in the prime working ages is working exclusively outside the socialised economy.

For the women – and thus for the vast majority of people employed exclusively in household and private subsidiary work – the issues go beyond the availability of work in the socialised sector. The reasons for their predominance in the private sector are generally assumed to be more directly linked to a tremendous lack of goods and services in Uzbekistan and the predominance of large families. As several Uzbek writers have noted, most of the women working exclusively in Uzbekistan's household economy are mothers with many children. Yet despite the prevalence of large families there, the level of child care facilities in Uzbekistan is presently only about 40 per cent that of the average level for the USSR as a whole. In the early 1970s, only about 13 per cent of Uzbekistan's children aged 1–7 could be accommodated in kindergartens and nurseries, or only about 300 000 out of a total of more than 2.3 million children in that age-group. The level, moreover, was much lower in the countryside than in the cities, being 5.2 per cent in Uzbekistan's rural areas as opposed to 34.4 per cent in Uzbekistan's urban areas.[28]

Similarly, the low level of technology in the home – and particularly in Uzbek homes – is also a tremendous constraint in attracting women to the labour force. While Soviet power has brought vast technological advances even to rural families (many rural families have televisions, radios, and even cars), washing-machines, dishwashers, modern plumbing, vacuum cleaners, etc. are still rarities in urban and rural areas alike. Indeed, one study estimated that women with a family of four or five people in the USSR as a whole expend more than 2000 calories per day on housework 'or just about the same amount of energy demanded by one shift in production'.[29] The Asian way of life, with its emphasis on large families and on an eternal abundance of food and hospitality, makes home life particularly demanding and time-consuming for a native woman. Especially because of the prevalence of large families among Central Asians, expanded services are necessary to free local women from the demands of household work if they are indeed to participate in the socialised labour force. 'At the present time, however,' an Uzbek scholar writes, 'a huge mass of human labour is used irrationally in the household economy because of limited social forms and means of servicing the population.'[30]

The low level of part-time work in Uzbekistan, high female turnover-rates, and low levels of education and skill among women are also reasons for low female participation rates in Uzbekistan's social-ised labour force. Few occupations in Uzbekistan allow for part-time work; the employment choice for women in Uzbekistan is generally between full-time work and no work at all. Again, large families among indigenous women usually tip the balance in favour of the latter. Several employers, moreover, privately expressed to me their wariness of hiring too many young, indigenous women, since 'they are sure to be taking many maternity leaves not too long after being hired'. And even on the job, women are often considered to be incapable of meeting the demands of work to the same degree as men, as one Uzbek put it, 'for a variety of physiological, familial, traditional and other reasons'.

In short, large and growing numbers of indigenous Central Asians in Uzbekistan, especially women, are not working in social production. Instead, many young people are occupied exclusively in household and private subsidiary activity, and indigenous female labour force participation remains low. During the 1970s, the level and quality of consumer goods and labour-saving technology and the provision of part-time work for women barely changed to encourage greater participation in social production.

UNDEREMPLOYMENT AND DISGUISED UNEMPLOYMENT

In assessing the extent of labour surpluses in Uzbekistan, it is important to look briefly at one other aspect of possible surpluses there: the efficiency with which manpower is being used within the socialised sector. Not only may a 'labour surplus' be suggested by the large proportion of people not working and not studying in Uzbekistan, but an additional 'surplus' is suggested by the apparently large internal reserves among people already employed in social production. Again, it is impossible to determine the exact extent of underutilisation of manpower in Uzbekistan. Not only are data scarce; but even if they were readily available, it would be difficult to create a conceptual framework within which to evaluate the data. None the less, general trends in terms of manning levels, use of working-time, turnover-rates and changes in labour productivity do suggest a substantial degree of 'disguised unemployment' or 'underemployment' in Uzbekistan in addition to the large numbers of people not working in social production.

Overmanning in Uzbekistan's enterprises and collective farms, for example, is high and widespread. High levels of manning, of course, are endemic to the Soviet system as a whole. Plan constraints and uncertainties connected with plan targets; uncertainties in the supply situation; uncertainties over whether plant personnel may be borrowed for work elsewhere; the fact that managerial salaries and bonus funds are often dependent, in part, on the size of a plant's labour force; high turnover-rates; and similar factors all encourage managers to attempt to acquire and hold excess labour everywhere in the USSR. A high level of seasonality in agricultural work, moreover, also demands a certain amount of overmanning in agriculture, since it requires high levels of manpower at certain times of the year and low levels at others. Yet an apparent excess of overmanning in Uzbekistan may be an indication that this practice is also a function of substantial manpower surpluses there, and not only an outgrowth of the Soviet economic and administrative systems alone. One set of statistics offered by Ubaidullaeva, for example, suggests that overmanning in Uzbekistan may have been as high as 18 per cent of the total planned labour force in 1970, and 14 per cent in 1979.[31]

Similarly – and related to manning levels – loss of working-time, infractions of labour discipline and the frequency of labour turnover in Uzbekistan are also substantially higher than the average for the USSR as a whole, helping to perpetuate lower productivity. Throughout the 1970s, Uzbekistan's use of the yearly fund of working-time was well below the all-Union average. In 1971, the number of failures to report to work per worker was on average one and a half to twice as high as the average for the USSR as a whole.[32] Throughout the 1970s, moreover, the number grew: the number of absences caused by simple failures to report to work rose in all sectors of Uzbekistan's industry, 1965 – 71, from 4.8 to 6.4 per cent of all absences, as compared with no rise from a steady 2 per cent for the USSR as a whole. Levels of labour turnover apparently also are higher in Uzbekistan than in non-Asian republics of the Soviet Union, and are rising.[33] These high levels of turnover, in turn, are closely related to loss of working-time: for example, the average Soviet worker who voluntarily leaves a job in industry will spend an average of one month looking for a new job; in Uzbekistan, this 'search time' is also longer than in Slavic areas of the USSR.[34] And finally, all of these factors have had their impact on labour productivity. Not only is labour productivity in Uzbekistan lower than in the rest of the USSR, but it is also growing at a slower, and often declining rate (see Chapter 3). During the past few years, labour productivity in some enterprises in Uzbekistan has not even grown at all, and in some cases has even declined.

It must be stressed, of course, that none of these variables is indicative of a labour surplus in Uzbekistan *per se*. High manning levels, losses of working-time, labour turnover or low productivity in Uzbekistan may be more a function of structural differences and changes in Uzbekistan's economy than they are a reflection of manpower surpluses or deficits alone. None the.less, the disparities between these indicators and those of other areas of the USSR suggest that they may reflect possible present and prospective manpower surpluses in Uzbekistan as well. As Brezhnev stated quite categorically at the 26th Party Congress in February, 1981:

In Central Asia and some areas of the Transcaucasus there is a surplus in the workforce, particularly in the countryside. This means that it is necessary to draw the population of these areas more actively into the development of the country's new territories.[35]

In short, differences of opinion abound concerning the extent of labour surpluses in Uzbekistan. Whatever the arguments, however, the magnitude of activity in the household and private subsidiary sector, and the extent of underemployment within social production have remained high and by many accounts are expected to grow. Despite substantial job-creation over the past two decades, a growing number and proportion of Uzbekistan's working-age population has not been employed in social production. Particularly during the 1970s, the growth of the working-age population in Uzbekistan began to outpace the growth of employment opportunities in the socialised sector. These factors suggest that the question of growing manpower reserves has become, and will continue to be a growing concern for policy-makers in Uzbekistan. Because of population dynamics, moreover, it appears that any growing imbalance between population and employment opportunities will affect the local nationalities more directly than Uzbekistan's non-indigenous nationality groups.

3 The Use of Labour by Sector and Location

As illustrated, labour surpluses, especially among the indigenous Central Asians, may be a growing problem in Uzbekistan. Perhaps a greater problem, however, is the fact that the different nationalities working in social production differ sharply in the sector and location of their employment. Despite efforts to industrialise Uzbekistan and to bring the indigenous nationalities into the industrial labour force, the indigenous Central Asians still predominate in agriculture and the service sphere, while heavy industry and construction have been developed mainly by non-indigenous personnel. Despite efforts to urbanise the indigenous populations, Central Asians remain largely rural or in the older, smaller towns where industry is poorly developed; the inhabitants of new cities, where industrial development and capital investment have been highest, are largely European. While Uzbekistan's economy has been dramatically transformed during the twentieth century, therefore, the traditional sectoral and locational divisions by nationality have been slower to change, and in many respects remain in force today.

For a regime with priorities explicitly in industrial development and in creating a native industrial workforce, the perpetuation of the traditional labour distribution by nationality would be the focus of concern under any conditions. Today, however, growing population pressures are making this division a more serious issue in more than just an ideological sense. Because of higher rates of population growth among the indigenous nationalities, the sectors and occupations which normally enter are gradually becoming saturated with manpower, as are the cities and regions in which they live. At the same time, industries and cities where Russians form a majority often have

72

immense shortages in their labour force. Thus, while a general surplus of manpower seems to characterise Uzbekistan's economy as a whole, a surplus is particularly large only in certain sectors and locations, that is, in the sectors in which Uzbeks tend to predominate, and the regions in which they tend to live. Aside from discussing labour surpluses *per se*, therefore, it is important to raise several additional questions: what is the nationality distribution of the labour force by sector and location? To what extent are sectoral and locational imbalances growing? And to what extent do these imbalances affect the different nationality groups?

EMPLOYMENT BY NATIONALITY

Pre-revolutionary Uzbekistan

A sharp split in employment by sector and occupation among Uzbekistan's nationalities predates the onset of Soviet power. Locked by barriers of high mountains on one side, and by inhospitable desert or inland waters on the other, Uzbekistan's geography allowed for settled agriculture only in certain areas – the foothills of the mountains, or farther along the rivers flowing from them; the rest of the territory was used mainly for grazing. Thus, Central Asians of the nineteenth century were characterised by two kinds of subsistence: that of the pastoral nomad, and that of intensive cultivation of the oases. In the villages locals lived by cultivation, crafts and trade: there was little industry to speak of among indigenous Central Asians aside from household industries (spinning wool, weaving rugs and saddle bags, embroidery, etc.), designed mainly to satisfy family needs. Any surplus was sold whenever possible, so that life in the villages tended to centre on the bazaars. Elsewhere, Central Asians led the life of a stockbreeder with regular seasonal migrations, and a margin of semi-nomads lay between the two groups. The indigenous 'intelligentsia' was limited mainly to local religious leaders and people in artistic creative pursuits.

The Russians who settled in the area from the mid-nineteenth century, on the other hand, were mainly government administrators, military personnel, traders and entrepreneurs and, with the coming of the railroad, employees in railroad and industry. Few Russian peasants migrated to Turkestan; indeed, unlike in the Kazakh steppes, until

1910, a clause in the government statute barred Russian peasants from settling on lands in Turkestan other than those newly brought under irrigation.[1] Almost all Russians, therefore, were settled in the towns and cities, and in most urban centres, Russians had their own cantonments built apart from the old native towns. As a nineteenth century British traveller noted with regard to Tashkent, this situation differed markedly from other colonised areas at the time:

> The two sections were distinctly separate. . . , far more so than in the capitals of India – Bombay, Calcutta or Madras – where the resident princes and noblemen and the native merchants mingled habitually in Anglo-Indian society and took a prominent part in government or the management of public institutions. . . In Tashkent, on the other hand, several obstacles preclude a similar amalgamation – the purely military character of the administration, the dearth of any wealthy or capable men among the natives, and the recency of the Russian conquest[2]

In social organisation, choice of occupation, and in location of settlement, there was a clear-cut division between the Russian and Asian worlds.

Equally clear cut was the place of Central Asian women in pre-revolutionary Uzbekistan. While women comprised the bulk of agricultural workers, they did not participate in the trades or public life. Secluded at home, veiled in public, women worked only in the fields, or in places where they would be secluded from men and worked mainly in manual, unskilled occupations. Cotton ginning and spinning of cotton yarns were regarded as women's work, as was the raising of silkworms. But more skilled occupations – such as unwinding the silk from the cocoons, dying the yarns and fabrics, or weaving the cotton silk, taffetas, satins and velvet – were the work of master craftsmen.[3]

Tsarist rule and the influx of Slavs to Uzbekistan certainly affected the social and economic organisation of Uzbekistan. In the late nineteenth century, agriculture began a transformation (completed in the 1930s) towards cotton monoculture. On this basis, industries arose to clean the cotton, process the fibre and press the seeds into oil. Vodka distilleries and wineries were established to cater to the local Russian populations. Mineral deposits, especially copper and vanadium, began to be worked, and other processing plants attracted local enterprise. For the most part, however, the manufacturing or proces-

TABLE 3.1   Nationality composition of industrial workers in Turkestan, by type
of work, 1914, as percentages

Type of Work	Total	Russians	Uzbeks
Production workers	100	22.6	77.4
Mechanised workers	100	86.0	14.0
Repair workers	100	77.3	22.7
Lowest-skilled workers[a]	100	20.9	79.1
Hired workers[b]	100	28.0	72.0

[a] *'Chernorabochii'*
[b] *'Rabochii na storone'*

SOURCE   Ubaidullaeva, R. A. 'Regional'nye problemy razmeshcheniia i
effektivnost' ispol'zovaniia trudovykh resursov v Uzbekskoi SSR',
doctoral dissertation, Tashkent, 1974, p. 167.

attracted local enterprise. For the most part, however, the manufacturing or processing was done in the European parts of the USSR.
Industry on the territory of Uzbekistan remained on a low level, and
was staffed mainly by Russians. Russian influence on local life was
limited and superficial.

Thus, by the time of the revolution, Uzbekistan was mainly an
agrarian and nomadic region, in which the major local activities were
herding livestock, farming, and trade on local markets. Uzbekistan's
indigenous urban population consisted mainly of merchants, traders,
craftsmen and religious figures, basically following, as Caroe notes, the
medieval guild system found in the bazaar quarters of most eastern
towns. Such factories as existed – mostly for cotton ginning and carding
– were dominated by Russians and Slavs, as were the railways and
telegraphs. What few locals did participate in the limited number of
industrial organisations were relegated to positions of labourers subordinate to Russian foremen. In general, industry, communications and
the military were in Russian hands (Table 3.1).

Post-revolutionary Uzbekistan

In the initial years following the onset of Soviet power, this economic
and occupational pattern was not substantially altered. During the
years of the New Economic Policy in the 1920s, smallholders con-

tinued to work on lands which they counted as their own. Herdsmen roamed the steppe, tending herds of camels, cattle, horses, sheep, goats. Both brought their produce for sale in the local markets. 'Except that the chiefs and big men had been removed, the social and economic system of agricultural production and distribution remained much as it had been before the revolution.'[4] According to census data, in 1926, workers and employees comprised just under 20 per cent of Uzbekistan's total population, against about 80 per cent for individual peasants and merchants.[5] The overwhelming part of Uzbekistan's population was occupied in agriculture; and of those people in industry, most were in handicrafts rather than in heavy industrial factories and plants.

With the beginning of the first five-year plan (1928–32), however, as throughout the USSR, this pattern was dramatically, and violently changed. For both political and economic reasons, the aims of Soviet policies became twofold: rapid industrialisation of Uzbekistan, based on its agricultural raw materials (mainly cotton and silk) and mineral resources; and the creation of an indigenous industrial workforce as well as skilled native cadres in all sectors of the economy. Economically, Central Asia was to become a supplier of cotton and certain fuel, mineral, food and other agricultural resources for the needs of the USSR as a whole. And in the words of one Uzbek scholar, political considerations were no less important: indigenous cadres in Uzbekistan were to have significance 'not only as an extremely important element of the productive forces, but also as the carrrier of socialist productive relations'. They were designed to play 'an enormous role in securing the economic and political foundations of Soviet power in Uzbekistan, in the construction of a socialist base for the entire national economy'.[6] Thus, the late 1920s saw a drive to settle pastoral nomads; develop mining and industry; and in general, to transform local craftsmen into workers, and particularly into industrial workers, as quickly as possible.

Although the results of this drive ultimately have been two-sided, there is little doubt that efforts towards these aims were great. Despite enormous resistance on the part of indigenous inhabitants, schools were created, oriented particularly toward establishing a native industrial workforce (see Chapter 4). Although toned-down from the violent campaigns of the early and mid-1920s, efforts continued to bring women into the mainstream of social and economic life. And as Bacon notes, attempts were made to create a native proletariat even among Central Asians without training: craft guilds were converted into 'professional unions' and artels were formed. Craft members were gradually brought under one roof, forming co-operative workshops into which, beginning in the 1930s, modern equipment and machinery were slowly introduced. While crafts were never wholly industrialised, factory-manufactured goods rapidly began to supersede them.

In the absence of indigenous workers, employees and an indigenous technical intelligentsia, however, realisation of all these aims also initially implied an influx of Europeans into Uzbekistan to staff the new enterprises and schools being created. Most of these in-migrants remained in Uzbekistan, themselves and their offspring participating in tasks which often they had come to teach locals to perform. The results of Soviet efforts, therefore, were ambiguous, at least in part contrary to the expressed aims of Soviet planners. While Russians trained Central Asians for industrial and other jobs, they simultaneously dominated both the industrial spheres and the higher skilled jobs in all economic sectors. By consequence, a pattern emerged wherein policies encouraged the indigenous nationalities to enter new sectors, but also paradoxically inhibited their entry into those sectors, particularly into industry.

Thus, as mentioned above, Russian in-migrants filled 85 per cent of the industrial labour force between 1929 and 1940. As Table 3.2 illustrates, between 1929 and 1937, 90 000 new workers entered heavy industry in Uzbekistan; of these, only 12 000 (13 per cent) were indigenous.[7] Until 1935, workers from the RSFSR formed more than half of the personnel of new enterprises in Uzbekistan, with other European republics also providing workers' cadres. And in the latter part of the 1930s, Russians continued to dominate Uzbekistan's industrial workforce. During the 1930s, only one fifth to one third of

TABLE 3.2   *Distribution of workers entering large scale industry, Uzbekistan 1929–40*

Years	Total number new workers	of which indigenous	other nationalities	Percentage workers of indigenous nationality
1929–32	57 000	4 000	53 000	6.7
1933–37	33 000	7 200	25 800	21.8
1938–40	20 000	4 500	15 500	22.5
Total:	110 000	15 700	94 300	14.3

SOURCE   Ubaidullaeva, R. A. 'Regional'nye problemy razmeshcheniia i effektivnost' ispol'zovaniia trudovykh resursov v Uzbekskoi SSR', doctoral dissertation, Tashkent: 1974, p. 171.

all workers in Uzbekistan were indigenous, while 'a significant, and sometimes even the main part of the working class . . . was comprised of other (and most often Russian) nationality groups'.[8] Within industry, Central Asians still avoided production-line jobs, entering the more sideline occupations such as maintenance or storage, or else the light industries or industries founded on traditional crafts or agriculture.

The growth of indigenous representation in the non-industrial sectors, on the other hand, was more rapid. Central Asians rapidly entered almost all of the tertiary sectors in Uzbekistan. And while key-positions remained in Russian hands, the indigenous nationalities were also accorded high Party, administrative and managerial positions in all sectors of the economy. The early 1930s, for example, saw an enormous growth in the number of Central Asians in the fields of medicine and education, and in the service sectors in general.[9] Between 1926 and 1936, the numbers of Uzbeks employed in non-manual work grew by eight times, as against only one and a half times or twice in the non-agricultural manual occupations. Although policies vacillated, those years showed tremendous growth in the number of Central Asian government and party personnel as well. Despite some fluctuation in indigenous Communist Party membership, between 1929 and 1941, the size of Uzbekistan's Communist Party almost doubled, from 36 093 to 72 068 people, and representation of the indigenous nationalities grew slightly more rapidly, from 17 072 to 35 169 people.[10]

The occupations which these new Central Asian Party and service personnel entered, moreover were not low level. Every First Secretary of Uzbekistan was an Uzbek. Central Asians entered the Bureau of the Central Committee, slowly surpassing the Europeans in membership, and became directors of hospitals, factories and institutes. By 1939, on the eve of World War Two, except for a small number of strategic positions (discussed later), representatives of the indigenous nationalities had filled many of the main administrative positions in Uzbekistan, while Russians predominated among the technical personnel.

The evacuation of factories during World War Two gave a great boost to economic development in Uzbekistan. Some major plants engaged in wartime tank production were transferred to sites in Uzbekistan where small factories of the same type already existed. A chemical plant evacuated from the Ukraine, for example, supplemented the electrochemical works at Chirchik in 1941, while plants from Kiev and Kherson supplemented the textile machinery plant in Tashkent. The further exploration and exploitation of natural resources (such as the discovery of natural gas, gold and other mineral resource deposits) led to the growth of new cities and industrial centres. Official aims were ostensibly the rapid and full development of Uzbekistan's economy, and full integration of the indigenous nationalities into all sectors of that economy. None the less, questions of efficiency and reliability continued to entail an influx into Uzbekistan of Europeans who, at least for the time being, remained to dominate the technical and industrial jobs. Despite rapid development, therefore, Uzbekistan by the 1970s still remained a largely agrarian republic, with the indigenous nationalities concentrated in the traditional service and agricultural spheres.

Thus, the success of Soviet policies to create indigenous local cadres has been very mixed. Analysis of Soviet data suggests that Soviet planners have made tremendous strides in diversifying the economy and bringing indigenous Central Asians into all sectors of the labour force. By the 1970s, Uzbekistan's economy had diversified immensely by comparison with its structure at the time of the October Revolution. Whereas in 1926 there were fewer than 150 000 workers and employees in Uzbekistan (comprising about 3 per cent of Uzbekistan's total population), in 1976 there were close to 3.5 million workers and employees, or 25 per cent of Uzbekistan's total population. As Table 3.4 illustrates, in 1929, only about 200 000 people were employed in the State sector, of which more than 20 per cent were employed in agriculture and about another 20 per cent in government administration. By 1975, government administration accounted for only 3 per cent, and agriculture, 17 per cent of all personnel in the State sector, while industry accounted for 21 per cent; education and culture, 14 per cent; construction, 12 per cent; and trade, housing, health, science and art, about 23 per cent. Measured numerically, the growth of an industrial labour force was great: whereas in 1929 Uzbekistan's industrial labour force comprised only 2800 people, by 1975 it had grown to 25 times that number, to about 700 000 people.[11]

None the less, these data mask broader structural changes. Despite this success, diversification of Uzbekistan's economy has still occurred more slowly than these large increases would suggest, and slowly relative to other parts of the USSR. Despite huge percentage increases in employment in the non-agricultural sectors in Uzbekistan, the actual numerical growth in the construction sector from 1950 to 1975 was only about three quarters that of the growth in state

TABLE 3.3   Average annual employment by branch of the national economy, Uzbekistan, 1929 – 75 (thousands)

Branch	1929		1950		1960		1965		1970		1975	
	Number	%	Number	%	Number	%	Number	%	Number	%	Number	%
State Sector												
Industry	28	14	254	28.6	371	23.7	492	23.6	579	21.9	697	20.8
Agriculture	45	22.6	121	13.6	304	19.4	365	17.5	414	15.7	582	17.4
Forestry	—	—	6	0.7	3	0.2	3	.1	3	.1	5	0.1
Transport	22	11.0	74	8.3	121	7.7	164	7.9	218	8.3	271	8.1
Communications	2	1.0	10	1.1	17	4.6	26	1.2	34	1.3	40	1.2
Construction	19	9.5	48	5.4	172	11.0	230	11.0	327	12.3	386	11.5
Other branches of material production[a]	12	6.0	104	11.7	135	8.6	188	9.0	249	9.4	311	9.3
Housing, communal economy, and personal services	—	—	21	2.4	32	2.0	57	2.7	82	3.1	106	3.2
Health services	7	3.5	60	6.7	107	6.8	137	6.6	181	6.9	232	6.9
Education and cultural services	15	7.5	109	12.3	174	11.1	276	13.3	371	14.0	478	14.3

Art	n.a.	n.a.	6	0.7	10	0.6	11	.5	13	.5	15	0.4
Science and research	2.5	1.3	15	1.7	37	2.4	53	2.5	63	2.4	82	2.5
Credit and insurance	4	2.0	7	0.8	7	0.4	8	.4	11	.4	15	0.4
Government administration	37	18.6	47	5.3	38	2.4	49	2.4	65	2.5	84	2.5
Other non-productive	5.5	2.8	7	0.8	7	0.4	26	1.2	33	1.2	38	1.1
Total State Sector	199	100	889	100	1565	100	2083	100	2642	100	3343	100
Collective farms	—	—	1369	60.6	1015	39.3	985	32.1	1042	28.3	1088	24.6
Total State and Collectivised	199	100	2258	100	2580	100	3068	100	3684	100	4431	100

a Trade, Catering, Material–Technical Supply and Procurement

— signifies negligible

SOURCE 1929: *Sovetskii Uzbekistan za 40 let*, 1964, p. 265. 1950–75: Rapawy, S., 'Regional Employment Trends in the USSR 1950–75', *Soviet Economy in a Time of Change*, compendium of papers submitted to the Joint Economic Committee, US Congress, vol. I, Washington, DC: Government Printing Office, 1979.

agriculture.[12] In the non-agricultural sectors, aside from construction, the most rapid growth rates in the labour force occurred in the science sectors, in housing and communal services and in education and culture while industry rated among those sectors with the lowest growth rates.[13] Compared with other parts of the USSR during the same time-period, these changes appear particularly unfavourable. Between 1950 and 1975, for example, employment on collective farms declined more than three times more slowly in Uzbekistan than it did in the RSFSR. By 1975, only 8 per cent of employment in the RSFSR was in collective agriculture, compared with 25 per cent in Uzbekistan, and only 8 per cent of the total labour force was in education and culture, against 14 per cent in Uzbekistan. On the other hand, employment in industry in the RSFSR was about 35 per cent of the total state labour force, against 20.8 per cent in Uzbekistan (Table 3.3).[14]

Finally, despite the diversification of Uzbekistan's economy, and the growth in the numbers employed in non-traditional sectors, the tradi-

TABLE 3.4   *Industrial labour force by branch of industry, 1960–75*

	1960		1975		1975 as %
	number	percent	number	percent	of 1960
Electric power	9	2.4	20	2.9	222
Fuels	8	2.2	12	1.7	150
Ferrous and non-ferrous metallurgy	3	0.8	3	0.4	100
Chemical and petro-chemical	11	3.0	29	4.2	264
Machine Building and metalworking	93	25	209	30.0	225
Timber, etc.	16	4.3	24	3.4	150
Construction materials	37	10.0	76	10.9	205
Light industry	126	34.0	199	28.6	158
Food industry	45	12.1	69	10.0	153
Other	23	6.2	56	8.0	243
All Industry	371	100	697	100	187

SOURCES   Rapawy, S. 'Regional Employment Trends in the USSR', *Soviet Economy in a Time of Change*, compendium of papers submitted to the Joint Economic Committee, US Congress (Washington, DC: Government Printing Office, 1979); and Voronovskii, Iu. B., 'Trudovye resursy Uzbekistana i ikh raspredeleniie', *Kommunist Uzbekistana*, no. 9, 1975, pp. 39 – 44.

tional distribution of labour among the nationalities still persists to a significant degree. The indigenous nationalities continue to be concentrated in light and food industries, the service sectors and agriculture, while Russians dominate heavy industry and sectors considered strategically important to the central authorities (e.g. the military in Uzbekistan, or sectors under all-Union jurisdiction). Within individual sectors, Uzbeks tend to dominate the highest- or lowest-skilled jobs outside the production process, while Slavs and other non-Central Asians comprise the vast majority of Uzbekistan's workers and technical cadres, particularly in heavy industry.

PRESENT SECTORAL EMPLOYMENT BY NATIONALITY

That non-Central Asians continue to dominate certain sectors and occupations because of Moscow's economic, political or strategic interests is beyond dispute. Any sector connected with Soviet military or defence interests is staffed primarily, if not entirely by non-Central Asians. In 1978, for example, only 14 per cent of the air and ground personnel at Tashkent's airport were Asian (not including stewards and stewardesses and freight transport), and only 10 per cent of the pilots. The military in Uzbekistan, as well as defence-related scientific research organisations, are almost entirely, if not exclusively European in composition. Given the importance of cotton, roughly 60 per cent of the leading cadres in agriculture, and a greater proportion of the non-administrative positions, have been staffed by non-indigenes for at least the past fifteen years.[15] Of all control organisations in Uzbekistan, only the internal police department – under the Ministry of Internal Affairs, in charge of law and order – is predominantly Uzbek in all occupational categories.

Similarly, certain occupations in Uzbekistan are reserved for Europeans in order to maintain control over the activities of the indigenous nationalities, or to ensure effectiveness of industrial plants or organisations particularly important to the central authorities. The Chairman of the KGB in Uzbekistan, the Second Secretary of the Uzbek Communist Party, and the Commander of the Turkestan Military District have always been non-Central Asians: between 1952 and 1981, for example, all five Second Secretaries of the Uzbek Communist Party, all six commanders of the Military District and five out of six of Uzbekistan's KGB chairmen have been non-Central Asians centrally appointed from Moscow; the remaining KGB chairman was a locally-recruited non-native. In addition, the First Deputy Chairman of the Council of Ministers, the Second Secretary of Central Committee of the Uzbek Komsomol and the heads of the Party organisational and agricultural departments of the Central Committee of Uzbekistan's Communist Party have traditionally been non-indigenous, whether recruited from outside Uzbekistan or recruited locally, the holder of these positions has often been appointed in Moscow.[16]

Lower down in the Party and government apparatus in Uzbekistan, while most *raion* and *oblast'* first secretaries are indigenous Central Asians, the heads of Departments of Organisational and Party Work, the heads of the Special (security) Section (the link to the state security apparatus, to the KGB) and almost all *oblast'* second secretaries and first deputy chairmen of *Obispolkoms* in Uzbekistan are non-indigenous.[17] At both the republican and local levels, these non-indigenous positions yield a considerable amount of authority or control. The First Secretary, for example, is given a great deal of publicity in Uzbekistan, and has general powers of leadership, supervision and co-ordination in his *oblast'* or region. While the functions of the second secretary are less clear, the consensus seems to be that they possess more real power and less visibility than the first secretary. They are generally responsible for organisational and personnel matters, often with special responsibilities in other areas as well. The same kind of division holds for other areas of government and Party work. The Chairman of the Trade Union Council, for example, has traditionally been a Central Asian; but the Council's secretary responsible for organisational activities has almost always been a locally-recruited European. In general, those positions concerned with cadres, the means of coercion and checking and verifying economic development are often staffed with non-Central Asians at all levels.[18]

Finally, in certain strategic sectors of Uzbekistan's economy, enterprise directors are often Uzbek, but their deputies – and often their entire staffs – are almost always non-indigenous. The Director of Tashkent's airport (an international airport, and the largest in Central Asia) for example, is an Uzbek, but all five of his deputies are Russians, as are seventeen of the nineteen directors of all the departments of the airport, and twenty-nine of the thirty-four deputy directors.[19] In particularly strategic industries, (for example, in many of those with all-Union significance) both the director and his deputy are often European, and Uzbek representation in managerial positions is totally absent. In 1979, for example, the director of the Chirchik Agricultural Machinery Plant (*Chirchiksel'mash*) was a European, as was his chief engineer, his main power specialist, the director of the Department of Capital Construction (*Otdel' Kapital'nogo Stroitel'stva*, or OKS), all their deputies and all the heads of the eleven departments. Only one of the forty bookkeepers, and only one of the eleven power-specialists were Uzbek (Appendix I).

These strategic occupations which are reserved exclusively for Russian occupancy, however, are for the most part limited in number.

Indeed, given the large number of party, government and management positions at all levels of Uzbek society, the number of positions reserved for non-native occupancy is small, limited mainly to second secretaries, department heads for organisations and individual strategic positions mentioned above. None the less, aside from the sectors and occupations connected directly with security concerns, the traditional and fairly sharp delineation in employment between the indigenous and non-indigenous nationalities still persists. Despite the decline cited above in the proportion of Uzbekistan's labour force employed in agriculture, the number of Central Asians employed in agriculture is still high and growing, while the number in industrial sectors remains relatively small. While approximately 35 per cent of Uzbekistan's total labour force were collective farmers in 1970, for example, that proportion was between 44 and 50 per cent among Uzbekistan's indigenous nationalities.[20] Similarly, Central Asians who have been brought into the non-agricultural sectors still tend to be concentrated in the service spheres rather than in industry. For example, if the indigenous nationalities comprised 35 per cent of all workers in the late 1970s, they comprised approximately 85 per cent of all publishing workers in Uzbekistan, while only a far smaller percentage of industrial workers.[21] Today, the teaching professions, law and trade are overwhelmingly indigenous in composition.

On the other hand, even though the proportion of Central Asians in the industrial, construction and other technical sectors has grown tremendously by comparison with its 1917 level, it is still low compared with the present representation of the non-indigenous nationalities, and low compared with the indigenous proportions of the working-age population. For the past few decades, for example, scientific research organisations in all fields have been almost entirely non-Central Asian in composition, and local representation has remained especially low in industry. In 1967, for example, Uzbeks comprised only 39 per cent of the men and 21 per cent of all women employed in industry; 35 per cent of all men and 8 per cent of all women employed in construction in the Uzbek republic; and 42 per cent and 9 per cent of all men and women respectively in transport. In communications, local representation was somewhat higher, reaching about 60 per cent of all men employed in that sector in the same year. The proportion of Uzbek women in the total number of employed women, however, was still low, at 11 per cent.[22] In all these categories, Uzbek representation was well below the proportion of Uzbeks in the total population. Between 1967 and 1973, moreover, the proportion of Uzbeks who were working in industry rose only slightly, from 31.2 per cent to 35.5 per cent and it rose mainly among Uzbek women; the proportion of Uzbek men working in industry barely changed.[23] And throughout the 1970s, this pattern showed little sign of changing. As Ata Mirzaev writes:

> A low level of employment in industry is characteristic for the entire indigenous population of Uzbekistan, including the urban population. As a result, at the present time the proportion of national working cadres in the republic's industry is very insignificant. This is especially characteristic for the very large industrial enterprises of Uzbekistan.[24]

Low participation on the part of Uzbeks in industrial or technical work is not changing rapidly relative to their population growth and their growth in other sectors. Instead, rates of growth of indigenous representation have remained higher in the service sectors than in the industrial sector.[25] If the rate of growth of Uzbek workers and employees in industry was notably low in 1960 to 1970, for example, the number of Uzbek scientific workers more than trebled during the same time-period; the number of those with the degree of *Kandidat Nauk* more than quadrupled. Today, Central Asians still tend to shy away from the industrial or technical sectors: in 1979, for example, less than one third of the 2500 people working on construction of the Tashkent metro had been drawn from the indigenous nationalities.[26] And despite some growth in an industrial workforce, in the same year Ubaidullaeva noted that 'the proportion of workers of the indigenous nationality in industry still remains relatively insignificant'.[27]

Within Industry

Within industry, the division between nationality groups is also pronounced: Russians still predominate in heavy industry, while Central

Asians form the majority of workers and employees in light industries and food and local industries. Throughout the 1970s, for example, 40–50 per cent of all industrial production personnel in Uzbekistan were in the light and food industries,[28] the remainder, in the heavy industrial sectors. Yet in a 'representative sample' of seven mainly heavy industrial enterprises in 1971, Uzbeks comprised less than one fifth of the more than 32 000 workers and employees. In 1978, there were only four Uzbeks numbered among the 113 employees at the Chirchik Agricultural Machinery factory (*Chirchiksel'mash*) just outside the city of Tashkent, and less than 2 per cent of the 15 000 workers of that plant were indigenous Central Asians. Only one employee and about twenty workers were Uzbek at the same factory's machine construction/repair administration of factory equipment, and a similar situation was apparent in the Chirchik Chemical Combine. Examples are numerous (see Table 3.5).

TABLE 3.5   *Nationality composition of selected enterprises, Uzbekistan*

Enterprise	Year	Percent Uzbek
Chirchik Agricultural Machinery Plant		
Employees	1978	3.5
Workers	1978	<2
Tashkent Agricultural		
Machinery Plant	1975	10
Tashkent Textile Machinery Plant	1971	12.8
Tashkent Tractor Factory	1971	7.8
Uzbek Chemical Machinery Plant	1971	5.5
Navoi Chemical Combine	1971	14.5
Uzbek Combine of Refractory Metals	1975	13.7
Tashkent Textile Combine	1975	15
Fergana Textile Combine	1971	27
Kokand Furniture Factory	1979	59
Andizhan Sewing Factory	1979	85

SOURCE   Interviews by Soviet investigators or by the author.

Indeed, according to one source, despite the apparently continuing rise in the number of Uzbeks in Uzbekistan's industry as a whole, Uzbek representation in certain industrial sectors in recent years has actually declined. According to Shister, between 1963 and 1967 the number of Uzbeks employed in ferrous metallurgy declined by 2 per cent; in machine-building, metal-working and the chemical industry by 1.5 per cent; and in non-ferrous metallurgy by 0.5 per cent.[29] Local interviews did not support the possibility that the number may have now risen substantially. On the other hand, Uzbek representation in light industries, food and local industries is high: the Andizhan Sewing Factory, in 1979 boasted over 2500 indigenous workers and employees (about 85 per cent of the factory's total personnel) of whom about 2300 were indigenous women. Almost all the 560 workers and employees at the Andizhan Furniture Factory in 1979 were Uzbek, and about 70 of the 119 workers and employees at the Kokand Furniture Factory were also indigenous. Today, the Tashkent meat and wine factories are staffed almost entirely with indigenous personnel, as are most of the food enterprises throughout the republic. Local industry is almost entirely in indigenous hands.

OCCUPATIONAL DISTRIBUTION BY NATIONALITY

Finally, despite immense successes in developing indigenous workers and an indigenous skilled labour force in all sectors of the economy, Central Asians tend to dominate certain jobs and positions while other occupations have remained entrenched in Russian hands. There is no doubt, of course, that along with rapid economic development, the number of workers, intelligentsia, specialists and skilled workers in Uzbekistan has risen tremendously over the past sixty years among the indigenous and non-indigenous nationalities alike. From 1965–75 alone, the number of specialists employed in Uzbekistan's economy more than doubled; and from 1960 to 1974, the number of Uzbek specialists with higher education more than quadrupled, from 40 700 people in 1960 to 165 500 in 1974.[30]

None the less, today Uzbekistan's indigenous nationalities are under-represented among the total number of workers in Uzbekistan relative to their share of the total population. They are under-represented among the number of specialists and the intelligentsia. And with regard to both categories, they are particularly under-represented in the industrial sectors. Instead, the indigenous nationalities in Uzbekistan today tend to dominate the highly-visible specialist and public contact positions – government ministers, enterprise directors, party or brigade leaders, teachers, cultural workers, etc. – and otherwise, the lower-skilled professions and occupations throughout the economy – lemonade sellers, salespeople, merchants in the bazaar. Where they have entered heavy industry, they still tend to dominate the lower-skilled occupations outside the production process, such as guards, truck drivers, or general service or storage personnel. Russians, on the other hand, are not represented in the lower-skilled jobs proportionate to their numbers in the population as a whole; they comprise the bulk of workers in industry; and they almost always dominate jobs demanding a high degree of technological training.

Among highly-visible Party and government personnel in Uzbekistan, for example, indigenous domination is high, and in many cases, almost universal. As already mentioned, Central Asians comprise the vast majority of government ministers and directors, and of Party secretaries at all levels of government and Party work. Most of the departments under the Central Committee of the Communist Party in Uzbekistan are at present (1983) headed by indigenous Central Asians. And in 1981, the indigenous nationalities comprised between two-thirds and three-quarters of the highest posts in Uzbekistan's central government and Party apparatus: they comprised eleven out of sixteen members of the Bureau of the Central Committee; four out of six members of the secretariat; three out of four members of the Praesidium of the Supreme Soviet; and six out of eight members of the Praesidium of the Council of Ministers, UzSSR. Except for part of the 1960s, this marks a fairly steady rise of indigenous representation since at least 1952.[31] While these positions originally may have been staffed with indigenous nationalities primarily because of their symbolic value, the growing numbers of Central Asians in these positions, and the functions associated with the positions themselves, suggest that Central Asian personnel have not been bereft of power or influence on local decision-making.

Outside the government and Party organs, moreover, most of the directorships throughout Uzbekistan's economy are also staffed by indigenous personnel. These are mostly in the administrative and service sectors but, especially in non-strategic industries, also occur frequently in the industrial sector as well. A recent breakdown of occupations by nationality in one region of Tashkent illustrates what appears to be a generally standard distribution of directorships and department heads by nationality. In the *raion* Party and government apparatus, the first secretary was a Central Asian nationality, his deputy a Slav; the same goes for the Department of Propaganda and Agitation. Outside the government and Party organs, many of the directorships of all other organisations were staffed by indigenous

Central Asians, especially in the service and government sectors but in industry and construction as well. 82 per cent of all directors of trade organisations, and all their deputies were indigenous Central Asians. All the directors, and most of the deputy directors of educational establishments (higher and secondary specialised), were of the indigenous nationalities, as were all the directors and deputy directors of the region's administrative organisations. In the industrial sectors, Central Asian representation was lower, but significant mainly in the light industries: 50 per cent of the directors of industrial enterprises, and 59 per cent of their deputy directors were indigenous; in construction organisations, 61 per cent of the directors, and only 24 per cent of their deputies were indigenous (Table 3.6).

With regard to the workforce, on the other hand, despite the success in developing workers among the indigenous nationalities, the growth of indigenous workers – particularly in the industrial and technical sectors – is still occurring slowly, with the number still lagging behind both the needs of the economy and the growth of the labour force as a whole. By way of explanation, the Soviet socialised work-force is broadly divided into workers, employees and collective farmers. The closest approximation to 'workers' would be the category of blue-collar workers in the West, consisting of personnel engaged largely in physical work. These are wage-workers, in the words of Feshbach, 'directly concerned with production, materials handling and the servicing of the production process'. 'Employees' correspond most closely to white-collar workers, and are further divided into three categories: engineering-technical personnel (*inzhenirnye-tekhnicheskie rabotniki*, or ITRs), including managerial personnel as well as some technical personnel (scientists, medical personnel, engineers, technicians, etc.); salaried employees (*sluzhashchie*), including administrative, clerical and professional personnel; and minor service personnel, or personnel whose work is not directly related to the production process, such as custodial workers, messengers, doormen, chauffeurs and guard personnel. (Guard personnel sometimes, although infrequently, form a separate category.)[32]

Throughout the 1970s, only about 40 per cent of all Uzbeks were workers – a particularly low representation by comparison with other republics of the USSR. While Uzbeks comprised 52 per cent of the total number of workers and employees in all sectors of Uzbekistan's economy throughout the mid-1970s, by 1973, they comprised only about 36 per cent of the total number of workers in Uzbekistan.[33] Similarly, despite the growth of specialists from among the indigenous

TABLE 3.6 *Nationality distribution of directors and deputy directors of all organisations and enterprises, Sabir Rakhimovskii raion, Tashkent, 1977*

Enterprise/Organisation	Director/First Secretary		Deputy Director/Second Secretary	
	Total	*of which indigenous nationality*	*Total*	*of which indigenous nationality*
Raion CP* and government organs:				
Raikom	1	1	1	1
Raikom of Komsomol	1	1	1	0
Raion Executive Committee	1	1	3	2
Industrial enterprises	34	17	32	19
Construction organisations	18	11	17	4
Transport organisations	7	6	7	4
Project and scientific research organisations	10	7	10	5
Administrative organisations	5	5	4	4
Trade and public catering organisations	17	14	17	17
Higher and specialised secondary educational establishments	6	6	6	5
Medical organisations	23	21	23	16
School and related organisations	36	28	38	22

* Communist Party

SOURCE Telephone directory for Sabir Rakhimovskii Raion, Tashkent, 1977.

nationalities, Central Asians are still under-represented in the total number of employed specialists relative to their proportion of the total population,[34] and Central Asian specialists, workers and intelligentsia are concentrated in the non-industrial sectors. As Table 3.7 illustrates, the Uzbek intelligentsia in Uzbekistan in 1970 was overwhelmingly concentrated in the 'mass' professions (defined as 'teachers, cultural workers, etc.'), and otherwise comprised the majority in the administrative, scientific and artistic professions; Uzbeks comprised less than one third of the intelligentsia in the productive sphere. This contrasts strikingly with the Russian intelligentsia in the USSR, among whom by far the highest proportion was in the productive sphere. In Uzbekistan, in 1970, the level of the Uzbek intelligentsia in the 'mass' professions was twice that of the level in the productive spheres; among Russians in the USSR as a whole, precisely the opposite was the case.

In industry, indigenous Central Asians tend to dominate the highest, most visible positions – heads of industrial ministries, or directorships of individual plants – and otherwise, the lower-skilled jobs – guards, truck drivers, and other jobs outside the production process. As already mentioned, the director of the Tashkent airport in 1979 was an Uzbek. Of the remaining 661 Uzbeks employed in the airport in 1979, however, 450 people, or 68 per cent were in the freight department, with the majority of the remainder concentrated in the repair, housing, motor pool, bookkeeping, or landing departments. Virtually no Uzbeks were represented in the departments of capital construction or planning. Similarly, almost two thirds of the personnel of the production department of the Navoi chemical fertiliser factory (*Navoiazot*) were non-indigenous in-migrants from the RSFSR, the Ukraine, Belorussia, the Transcaucasus and other republics of Central Asia.[35] Of the fourteen Uzbeks employed at the Chirchik Agricultural Machinery Plant in the same year, ten (almost three quarters) were employed as guard personnel (see Appendix 1).

Finally, despite efforts to raise the skill levels of indigenous Central Asian inhabitants, European in-migrants from other parts of the USSR continue to migrate to Uzbekistan to fill available skilled jobs. In 1973, more than 700 workers and specialists were sent from the RSFSR to the Navoi Chemical Combine. In order to construct the Tashkent metro in the early 1970s, about 900 skilled workers and specialists came from other European republics (of which 130 were engineer technical personnel, and 770, highly skilled workers). In general, one could broadly characterise Uzbekistan's economy today as one in which the indigenous nationalities dominate positions at all levels of

TABLE 3.7 Structure of the intelligentsia among Uzbeks and Russians, USSR, 1939–70 (per 10 000 gainfully-occupied people of given nationality)

Nationality	Administrative		Productive		Scientific		Artistic		'Mass'		Total Intelligentsia	
	1939	1970	1939	1970	1939	1970	1939	1970	1939	1970	1939	1970
Uzbeks	173	181	63	354	2	45	20	20	189	641	447	1241
Russians	261	269	493	1160	10	71	23	35	304	640	1091	2175
Total USSR (average of all nationalities)	249	258	423	973	10	64	24	33	301	625	1007	1952
Uzbek level as percentage of Russian level	66	67	13	31	20	63	87	57	62	100	41	57
1970 as per cent of 1939												
Among Uzbeks		105		561		2250		100		339		278
Among Russians		103		235		710		152		199		199
Total USSR		104		230		640		138		208		194

SOURCE Kulichenko, M. I. (ed.) Natsional'nye otnoshenia v razvitom sotsialisticheskom obshchestve (Moscow: Mysl', 1977). p. 97.

expertise in the non-industrial sectors, while occupying many of the highest and ostensibly the lowest jobs in industry. This pattern seems to have characterised Uzbekistan's labour force for the past several decades, and shows little sign of changing.

EMPLOYMENT OF WOMEN

This pattern in the sectoral and occupational distribution of labour by nationality is particularly true of women, and particularly of indigenous women. Women have made remarkable strides under Soviet power, and indeed have been brought into almost all sectors of the economy.[36] Despite this progress, however, women are still concentrated in agriculture and the service sectors; they predominate in the lower-skilled and manual jobs; and both disparities are particularly pronounced with regard to women of the indigenous nationalities. In 1975, for example, women comprised 42 per cent of all workers and employees in Uzbekistan's economy. But of those, more than two thirds were employed in state agriculture or the service sectors. Within the service sectors, the vast majority were concentrated in health and social security (comprising 73 per cent of all workers and employees in that sector in 1975) and education and culture (comprising 55 per cent of the total in 1975) (Table 3.8).

This sectoral distribution of the labour force by sex, moreover, contrasts greatly with other parts of the USSR. Unlike the European parts of the USSR, where men tend to dominate industry and women, the service sectors, women in Uzbekistan are under-represented in both industry and almost all sectors of the service sphere. For example, in most of the European parts of the USSR, 80 per cent of all workers and employees in public catering, more than 85 per cent of those in the health professions, and more than 70 per cent of those in education are women. In Uzbekistan, women comprise less than 50 per cent of this workforce; as noted in Table 3.8, only in the health-care services is their representation high (about 75 per cent).[37] Within industrial and technical spheres, a division is especially clearcut. Soviet leaders tend to laud the rise in female participation in the industrial sectors. Yet despite this rise, women comprise only a small proportion of the population employed in construction and transportation work and in heavy industry.[38] While women comprised 47 per cent of Uzbekistan's industrial workforce in 1975, the vast majority were concentrated in light industry and food production, and mainly in the textile and sewing industries. With regard to the occupational distribution of

TABLE 3.8 *Percentage women in the total number of workers and employees by branch of the economy. Uzbekistan, 1975*

	Percentage women in the total number of workers and employees of given branch of the economy					Women in given branch as percentage of total number of women workers and employees				
	1965	1970	1973	1974	1975	1965	1970	1973	1974	1975
Total women workers and employees in the national economy	40.0	41.3	41.9	42.2	42.4	100.0	100.0	100.0	100.0	100.0
In industry (industrial-production personnel)	43.5	45.3	46.7	46.5	47.0	25.6	24.0	23.7	23.2	23.1
Agriculture	38.5	40.3	40.0	40.5	40.6	16.9	15.3	15.3	16.5	16.7
In State farms, subsidiary and other State agricultural enterprises	40.8	42.6	42.0	42.4	42.4	16.3	14.7	14.7	15.9	16.1
Transport	16.3	16.2	15.4	15.3	15.3	3.2	3.2	3.0	2.9	2.9
Communications	47.5	48.2	48.0	49.3	48.3	1.5	1.5	1.4	1.4	1.4
Construction	20.2	20.2	20.5	20.2	20.0	5.6	6.3	6.0	5.7	5.4
In construction-installation work	18.0	18.3	17.2	16.9	16.5	4.0	4.5	4.0	3.8	3.6
Trade, public catering, material-technical supply and sales, and procurement	39.8	42.7	44.4	46.0	46.7	9.0	9.7	10.2	10.2	10.3
Housing-communal economy and services	36.9	38.7	38.6	37.9	36.6	2.5	2.9	2.9	2.9	2.7
Health service, physical culture and social security	73.1	73.7	73.3	72.1	72.5	12.0	12.2	12.3	11.7	11.9
Education and culture	51.8	52.7	53.4	54.5	54.6	17.1	17.9	18.2	18.4	18.4
Art	29.6	31.7	32.0	31.0	33.4	0.4	0.4	0.3	0.3	0.4
Science and scientific services	37.5	41.5	43.1	44.5	43.6	2.4	2.4	2.4	2.5	2.5
Credit and State insurance	55.5	59.0	61.0	61.6	62.2	0.6	0.6	0.7	0.7	0.7
Government administration and administration of co-operative and social organisations	41.8	46.4	47.6	48.2	48.4	2.5	2.8	2.9	2.9	2.9

SOURCE 'Tsentral'noe Statisticheskoe Upravlenie' *Narodnoe Khoziaistvo Uzbekskoi SSR v 1975 g.* (Tashkent: Uzbekistan, 1976).

TABLE 3.9 *Specialists with higher and specialised secondary education employed in Uzbekistan's economy, by sex and specialisation (Data for 15 November 1977)*

Specialisation	(1) Total Number of Specialists (in 1000s)	(2) Total Number of Women Specialists (in 1000s)	(3) Women as % of Total Number of Specialists, by Specialisation	(4) % of Total Number of Women Specialists
I. All specialists with higher education employed in the economy, of which, by specialisation received in educational establishment:	450.4	189.8	42.1	100
engineers	100.8	28.4	28.1	15.0
agronomists, livestock specialists, and veterinarians	22.1	3.9	17.6	2.1
economists	33.1	14.3	43.2	7.5
goods managers[1]	3.9	n.a.	n.a.	n.a.
doctors[2]	37.1	21.1	56.9	11.1

teachers and university graduates,[3] librarians and educational-cultural workers	235.7	113.0	47.9	59.5
II. All specialists with secondary specialised education employed in the economy, of which:	466.8	248.9	53	100
technicians	169.5	50.8	30.0	20.4
agronomists, livestock specialists, veterinary workers	23.1	3.8	16.5	1.5
planners and statisticians	50.0	24.4	48.8	9.8
goods managers	26.0	n.a.	n.a.	n.a.
medical workers (including dentists)	110.1	93.4	84.8	37.5
teachers, librarians, and educational-cultural workers	71.6	54.1	76.0	21.7

NOTES 1) 'tovarovedy'; 2) Does not include dentists with secondary medical education; 3) Does not include geologists (included under engineers') and lawyers, doctors and economists, who are included in the corresponding group of specialisations.

SOURCES Columns 1 and 2: Ts.S.U. *Narodnoe Khoziaistvo Uzbekistana v 1977 godu* (Tashkent: Uzbekistan, 1978) pp. 218 and 219. Columns 3 and 4 calculated from columns 1 and 2.

women in Uzbekistan, the same pattern prevails: in all spheres, including the service sectors, women tend to be concentrated in the lower-skilled or unskilled jobs proportionate to their numbers (Table 3.9).[39]

Thus today, while more than half the able-bodied population of collective farms in Uzbekistan is female, women comprise less than 3 per cent of the approximately 22 000 skilled staff working on agricultural machinery – and close to 99 per cent of the manual labourers on state farms.[40] In industry, about half of the manual workers are women, or slightly higher than their proportion in the total industrial labour force.[41] Even in the service sectors – where the majority of female specialists are concentrated – women are still concentrated in the lower positions: in 1977, while slightly more than one third of the 32 000 scientific workers in Uzbekistan were female, women comprised only one eighth of the *Doktor Nauk* (PhDs) and only about one tenth of the professors, members and correspondent members of the Academy of Sciences – against more than one third of the junior scientific workers and assistants, the lowest rung on the academic ladder. In the medical field, women comprise more than 75 per cent of the medical personnel. But in 1970, they accounted for only 39 per cent of the head doctors and heads of medical establishments, as opposed to 96 per cent and 98 per cent of the nurses and heads of pre-school institutions respectively.

All these distinctions – prevalence in the agricultural and service sectors and in the lowest skilled jobs – are particularly true of indigenous Central Asian women. While indigenous women comprise the vast majority of female labour in agriculture, throughout the 1970s they comprised only 24 per cent of all female workers and employees in Uzbekistan's state sector.[42] Of those, moreover, most were concentrated in the service sectors and the light and food industries, while few indigenous Central Asian women were employed in heavy industry. Not atypical of Uzbekistan's heavy industrial enterprises, for example is the Andizhan machine construction factory which I visited in April 1979. Of a staff of 2900 people, 46 per cent were Uzbek and 54 per cent European. Of the 561 women employed there, however, none were of the indigenous nationalities.

Lastly, in the industrial sectors and certain other sectors where both European and Asian women are employed, non-indigenous women tend to dominate the higher-skilled positions. In one sewing factory which I visited in the Fergana Valley, of almost 3000 workers and employees, 2743 were female, of whom about 85 per cent (2337) were Uzbek women. The occupational data, however, suggest that the Uzbek women were concentrated in the lower-skilled jobs: while about 60 per cent of the female engineer-technical personnel and 70 per cent of the white-collar workers were Slavic, close to 90 per cent of the female industrial workers were Uzbek. Thus today, there still exists a fairly clear division between Russians and Uzbeks in sectoral employment, and between indigenous and non-indigenous women.

LOCATIONAL CONSIDERATIONS

The sectoral and occupational distribution of the nationalities in Uzbekistan is partly attributable to, and certainly compounded by the location of Uzbekistan's people and natural resources. In addition to a still somewhat traditional distribution of occupations among the different nationalities, longstanding territorial divisions by nationality also persist, with each perpetuating the other. As mentioned in Chapter 1, for example, urbanisation in Uzbekistan has been rapid during the years of Soviet power, as has been the expansion of arable land. As many Soviet scholars are quick to point out, before the Bolshevik Revolution few modern urban settlements existed in Uzbekistan. Since the early 1920s, over 149 cities and urban settlements have been created there, through both the construction of new cities and the conversion or reclassification of rural settlements into urban ones. By 1976, there were 76 cities and 86 urban settlements in Uzbekistan, with about 5.5 million inhabitants in them. Similarly, the amount of sown land in Uzbekistan grew by more than 700 000 hectares (almost 25 per cent) from 1940 to 1976.

Despite the rapid urbanisation – although Russians no longer reside in explicitly military outposts – non-Central Asians, mainly European, are disproportionately over-represented in Uzbekistan's urban areas and most developed regions and *oblasts*, while the indigenous Central Asian population is still overwhelmingly rural. Within the urban areas, moreover, Europeans have generally tended to settle in the new, industrial cities which have been created during the years of Soviet power; urban Uzbeks are concentrated in old small and medium-size towns.

In large part, the distribution of nationalities by region in Uzbekistan has been shaped by the location of Uzbekistan's natural resources as opposed to her population resources. Industry in Uzbekistan, based largely on the extraction and processing of mineral raw materials, has tended to develop close to the resources in question, and is therefore often remote from the traditional Uzbek villages and towns. Thus, given the low mobility and lack of industrial skills among the indigenous populations, new cities created during the years of Soviet power have been comprised mainly of Russians. Cities created for the exploitation or processing of certain raw materials – cities such as Navoi or Chirchik, for the development of the chemical industry; Gazli or Mubarek, for the extraction of natural gas; Angren for coal extraction; Almalyk, Inchichki, Burchmulla, Mardzhandulak, for the extraction of non-ferrous metals; Gasgan or Gazalkent, for marble; or settlements in the Kyzylkum desert, for the extraction of gold – are still primarily, if not exclusively, non-native in composition. In general, cities which were founded for the development of large-scale heavy industry – including Bekabad, Akhangaran, Angren, and others – are also populated principally by non-indigenes. On the other hand, few Europeans migrated to the older small and medium cities where Uzbeks have been concentrated for over a century, or to rural areas. These areas, therefore, are almost exclusively indigenous in composition, and their populations have proved reluctant to move elsewhere.

The net effect in terms of population has been that today, more than half the populations of all industrially developed centres in Uzbekistan are European by nationality, while the population of Uzbekistan's old, smaller cities and rural areas is almost entirely Central Asian.[43] In 1970, in the new small industrial towns of Uzbekistan (where more than 70 per cent of the employed population was employed in industry) the indigenous nationalities comprised only 20 per cent of the total population. In the small towns where industry was less developed (where employment in industry comprised an average of about 47 per cent of total employment) the indigenous nationalities comprised about 60 per cent of the total population (Table 3.10). As Ubaidullaeva notes, in the mid-1970s, the productive fixed capital stock in Tashkent's industry alone was more than twice that of all other *oblasts*. But at the same time, she noted, 'almost 80 per cent of the indigenous population lives precisely in these other *oblasts*, and mainly in rural locations'.[44]

Thus, the distribution of the different nationalities by sector and location have tended to perpetuate each other: the continued imbalance in location between industrial development and the traditional Uzbek urban centres is one main reason why Uzbeks are so under-represented in the industrial sectors cited above:

TABLE 3.10 Selected economic and nationality indicators by type of city, Uzbekistan, 1970

Indicator	New small and medium cities with developed heavy industry	Old large cities with multisectoral industry	Old small cities with main industry the primary processing of agricultural raw materials
Percent of total number of cities	22	15	63
Percent of total urban population	21	62	17
Indigenous nationalities as per cent of population	20	50	60
Percent of labour resources employed in social production	72.1	70.5	73.8
Per cent of employed population in industry, construction, and transport	70.4	53.7	46.6

SOURCE Mikheeva, V. 'Trudovye resursy malykh i srednykh gorodov Uzbekistana i perspektivy ikh ispol'zovaniia', doctoral dissertation, Tashkent 1975.

Very often when choosing the location for construction of a new object only the economics of construction are taken into account. Insufficient attention to the presence of labour resources leads in a series of instances to difficulties in staffing the labour force in the industrial enterprises brought under construction ... Enterprises, although built with the intention of utilising the local nationalities, in fact are staffed by in-migrants from other regions of the country [45]

The fact that Uzbeks continue to live in areas remote from Uzbekistan's raw materials and industry has inhibited their entry into the industrial sectors connected with them. The location of Europeans, on the other hand, has been directly connected with the exploitation of raw materials and the development of Uzbekistan's industrial base.

SECTORAL AND LOCATIONAL IMBALANCES

To a government intent upon raising the level of industrial development in Uzbekistan and creating workers' cadres from among the indigenous nationalities, the persistence of traditional patterns of employment and settlement by nationality would cause concern under any circumstances. Today, however, as with the questions of 'unemployment' and 'underemployment' discussed above, population pressures and traditional governmental priorities in heavy industry are intensifying the divisions between Uzbeks and Russians rather than diminishing them. Differences in growth rates of employment by sector have led to increasing labour 'surpluses' in agriculture and shortages in industry. Differences in population growth have led to growing labour surpluses in rural areas and old, small towns, and to potential shortages in new industrial cities and large urban centres. In other words, because of high rates of natural growth among the indigenous nationalities, the sectors and locations in which Central Asians predominate may gradually become saturated with manpower, at the same time that there are labour shortages in many European-dominated sectors and cities within Uzbekistan.

AGRICULTURE

Because of high rates of population growth in Uzbekistan's rural areas, and because of the tendency of rural inhabitants to enter agricultural occupations, several indicators in the 1970s–80s have suggested an increasingly rapid saturation of agricultural manpower in Uzbekistan. The amount of land per agricultural worker on Uzbekistan's farms, the use of working-time on collective farms, and the proportion of able-bodied collective farm members working full-time have all declined during the past decade, particularly in predominantly Uzbek regions. With mechanisation the order of the day, these trends are expected to intensify.

In terms of availability of land, for example, because of rapid population growth in rural areas, (discussed in Chapter 1), the amount of arable land per collective farmer in the past two decades has begun to decline. According to one estimate, the number of rural inhabitants per sown hectare in Central Asia rose by 25 per cent between 1959 and 1970, after having remained stable for at least a half century;[46] and Soviet scholars concur that the situation is not changing. In a recent study of labour use in Uzbekistan, Ubaidullaeva considered the optimal amount of land per able-bodied collective farmer to be an average of 3.0 hectares. In many of Uzbekistan's collective farms today, however, the level is far below that. In the collective farms of Andizhan *oblast'* in 1972, the average was 1.32 hectares per collective farmer; in the collective farms of Fergana *oblast'*, 1.24 hectares; and in the collective farms of Namangan *oblast'*, 1.33 hectares.[47] According to Ubaidullaeva's estimates, based on the amount of land per worker, in the mid-1970s more than 57 500 able-bodied collective farmers were redundant in the collective farms of Namangan *oblast'* alone.[48] As another Soviet scholar remarked only a few years later 'The growth of the able-bodied population in agriculture is overtaking the growth of arable land.'[49]

The use of working-time in Uzbekistan's agriculture has mirrored this decline. Since the 1960s, the number of man-days worked per able-bodied farmer has dropped significantly in most of Uzbekistan's collective farms. According to one report, in 1965, one able-bodied collective farmer in Samarkand *oblast'* worked 172 man-days; in 1973, he worked 153.[50] And throughout the 1970s, the number of man-days worked per collective farmer continued to decline. In 1970, Ubaidullaeva posited the optimal number of mandays worked per able-bodied collective farmer at 270 man-days per year, and Egamberdyev, at 280 per year. By 1975, however, the actual number of man-days worked on Uzbekistan's collective farms was an average of 213, and in several *oblasts* it was as low as 180–190.[51] Average annual output per working and per able-bodied collective farmer also remained steady or declined during the early and mid-1970s, while in many cases, the growth rate of labour productivity in agriculture slowed, or even declined, as well. During the ninth five-year plan, labour productivity declined in the collective farms of Bukhara, Kashkadar'ya and Khorezm *oblasts*, and showed only modest, if any growth in the remaining *oblasts*.[52]

Seasonality of agricultural work has often been cited as one of the main reasons for the labour surpluses in Uzbekistan's agriculture. In October of 1970, for example, about 1 350 000 people were working in the collective farms of Uzbekistan; during the winter months of December, January and February, an average of only 600 000 people worked.[53] Several analysts have questioned whether the 750 000 collective farmers not working during the winter months should be considered 'surplus' labour, since ostensibly they are needed during the fall, summer and spring. None the less, while seasonality may compound the problem of the use of agricultural labour, it is apparently not the only, nor even the main reason for the present manpower reserves in Uzbekistan's agriculture. Instead, studies have shown that many of these excess farmers are not utilised even at the busiest periods of the year:

It is clear from the data that because of the seasonality of agricultural production, it is essential to have labour reserves at about 8–12 per cent of the potential labour force in collective farms. None the less, a study conducted in the planning sector for the use of labour resources indicated that a significant part of collective farmers did not participate in social production even in the period of maximum stress of agricultural work.[54]

Agricultural labour surpluses are apparently growing due to high rates of population growth among rural inhabitants of Uzbekistan, and the inability of agricultural expansion to keep pace with that growth.

With mechanisation the order of the day, moreover, this situation is not expected to change. The stock of cotton-picking machines in Uzbekistan's collective and state farms, for example, has grown rapidly over the past two decades. For the last few years of the 1970s, in the light of the planned amount of mechanisation, one Soviet scholar expected about 26 000 people to be freed from cotton cultivation in Kashkadar'ya *oblast'* alone. In the absence of a mass movement of agricultural personnel to other sectors, calculations presented at an agricultural conference in Fergana (September 1976) suggested that with the planned amount of mechanisation, labour expenditures per hectare in all the cotton-growing areas of Uzbekistan would decline on average to 24–28 man-days per year in the near future.[55]

Uzbekistan's agricultural labour surplus, moreover, is particularly pronounced among women, and especially among indigenous female collective farmers. Indigenous women comprise a large proportion of Uzbekistan's agricultural workers, and especially of its unskilled workers. Thus, in the light of increased mechanisation in the countryside, Soviet writers cite increasingly large unused or poorly-used reserves of female labour there. 'Because of their weak participation in social production', women work fewer man-days per year than men, have a smaller amount of land per worker, and exhibit a higher degree of seasonality.[56] As the least mobile part of Uzbekistan's population, moreover, indigenous women comprise the smallest proportion of workers moving to newly-opened agricultural lands. Thus, Soviet analysts have placed increasing significance on the fact that the declining employment and economic activity of collective farmers in Uzbekistan 'in greatest degree is affecting women', who rarely find work in other sectors.

In sum, several indicators have pointed to large and growing reserves of agricultural manpower in Uzbekistan's economy. In 1958, 87 per cent of all able-bodied members of collective farms in Uzbekistan participated in collective-farm work; in 1970, this proportion was 80 per cent in the collective farms of Khorezm *oblast'*; less than 75 per cent in the collective farms of Andizhan, and Surkhandar'ya *oblasts*; and less than 70 per cent in the collective farms of Samarkand and Tashkent *oblasts.*[57] According to one Uzbek author, in 1973, 'labour reserves were more than 50 000, and possibly more than 100 000 people in collective farms of the Fergana Valley alone'. As he writes, 'The decline in the proportion of those working to the total number of labour resources of Uzbekistan's collective farms . . . is explained basically by the fact that the labour force freed on account of introducing complex mechanisation is not finding a use within the collective farm.'[58] And today, the situation has not changed: 'In the absolute majority of collective farms (in Uzbekistan), the existence of labour resources significantly exceeds the need for labour in (agricultural) production.'[59] Throughout the 1970s, while the average annual number of collective farmers continued to rise, availability of land per collective farmer, use of working time, average annual output per collective farmer, output per able-bodied collective farmer and the growth rate of labour productivity declined.

NON-AGRICULTURAL SECTORS

By contrast with agriculture, manpower shortages characterise Uzbekistan's industrial and construction sectors. According to one account, Uzbekistan, in 1976, had just about the lowest proportion of its labour resources employed in industry relative to the USSR as a whole. Only 22 per cent of all workers and employees were employed in industry, against an all-Union average of 35 per cent; only Turkmenistan, with 20 per cent of its workers and employees in industry, had a lower level.[60] And despite a high level of 'unemployment' and of underemployment in the non-industrial sector, Uzbekistan's industry has been characterised by significant manpower shortages. As Maksakova writes:

> Along with the existence of potential labour surpluses distributed in the household and private subsidiary economy, there is a shortage of labour in almost all the republic's leading industrial enterprises and in construction organisations. The shortage of industrial – production personnel or of personnel employed in construction – assembly work constitutes 5–10 per cent, and in some leading enterprises it is significantly higher.[61]

According to another Soviet scholar, the Ministry of Light Industry in Uzbekistan was able to fill its plan for hiring new workers by 95 per cent in 1969, and by only 86.3 per cent in 1971. In the Ministry of Construction, the corresponding proportions were 94 per cent and 85 per cent.[62] In 1975, Ubaidullaeva notes, the shortage of labour in Uzbekistan's industrial sectors was about 528 600 people; and since the mid-1970s, industrial labour productivity in Uzbekistan – already low in the early 1970s – has grown relatively slowly compared to other parts of the USSR.[63]

In the service sectors, the picture is more mixed. Although not as glaring as in agriculture, there are also suggestions that Uzbekistan's service sector consumes a high degree of manpower relative to the needs of industry. As mentioned above, if the proportion of labour resources in Uzbekistan's industrial sectors rose by 64 per cent between 1959 and 1973, it grew by 81 per cent in the service sector, and from a higher starting point.[64] The proportion of personnel in the non-productive sphere rose from 26 per cent of all personnel employed in the state sector in 1960, to about 31 per cent in 1975. Several

Soviet writers have cited large reserves in the use of working-time in the service sectors, and high rates of turnover in Uzbekistan's service enterprises. Continued expansion of the service sector is anticipated for the future, to absorb part of the labour released from agriculture. But in over thirty-five interviews, Soviet officials and scholars expressed the hope that the growth rate of employment in the service sphere would slow relative to that in industry, and labour resources from service sectors could be siphoned off for work in the economy's more productive sectors where labour is greatly needed.

LOCATIONAL IMBALANCES:

Again, problems of sectoral dislocations in Uzbekistan are compounded by the territorial distribution of labour resources by nationality. Despite the high level of employment and growing labour surpluses in agriculture, for example, the need for agricultural manpower in certain regions of Uzbekistan is still high. As discussed above, surpluses in the traditional agricultural regions, such as the Fergana Valley, are large and growing. Yet between 1966 and 1970, the need for agricultural labour in land newly opened for arable farming, especially in the Hungry Steppe, was estimated as somewhere between 100 000 and 110 000 people.

Similarly, while many new small and medium-size industrial cities in Uzbekistan are suffering severe shortages of industrial manpower, in Uzbekistan's old smaller towns and cities, a Soviet scholar writes 'there is a considerable lag in the use of labour resources, not only by comparison with all-Union indicators as a whole, but also by comparison with other Union republics... Since most of the inhabitants of (old) small and medium cities are indigenous,' she adds, and because of differing rates of natural growth among the different types of cities and rural areas, this situation is threatening to become 'a tremendous socio-economic problem'.[65]

A study conducted by Mikheeva in 1974 illustrates this more graphically, and particularly her data on four types of cities: large cities with 'complex economic development' (type I); small, medium and large industrial cities with high rates of employment (type II); local small and medium economic centres with weakly-developed industry but with levels of employment equal to that of the republican average (type III); and similar small and medium local centers, but with levels of employment below the republican average (type IV). The results of

Mikheeva's study are summarised in Appendix 2. In essence, Mikheeva notes that the first two types of cities have largely European populations; the latter two types are comprised largely of indigenous Central Asians. She then documents three essential points: that employment, levels of production, number of industrial production personnel, labour productivity and capital assets installed in enterprises have all been much lower in the small local centres (types III and IV) than in the new industrial cities; that growth rates in employment in social production have also lagged by comparison with industrial cities; and that, because of higher rates of natural increase in the smaller cities, the disparities among these types of cities will probably only widen.

In 1970, for example, Mikheeva noted that levels of gross production in old, small towns were less than half those of the industrial centres; the average number of industrial production personnel, less than one third that of industrial cities; and capital assets installed in enterprises, more than four times lower than in Uzbekistan's industrial cities. As much as 15 per cent of the labour resources in small, mainly Uzbek urban centres were working exclusively in the household and private subsidiary economy; in the new industrial, mainly Slavic cities, this proportion was about 5–6 per cent. With regard to growth rates, if employment in social production in the new cities grew by an average of 93 per cent from 1959–1970, it grew by as little as 61 per cent in the smaller, largely indigenous cities. The birth rate in the smaller, mainly Uzbek cities, hovering around 34 births per thousand population in 1973, was much higher than the birth rate of 21.5 per thousand for Uzbekistan's more industrialised cities. This suggests that problems of excess labour in the former group of cities may not significantly abate in the near future. (See Appendix 2.)

Thus, taking into account present levels of development and employment, demographic factors and prospects for demographic change, Western and Soviet observers alike have projected increasing labour surpluses in Uzbekistan's small towns where the indigenous nationalities are concentrated. Barring any dramatic change in investment patterns or demographic policies (see Chapter 4) large labour shortages have been projected for new, mainly European industrial cities in Uzbekistan (see Appendix 2.) Because of the growth of the able-bodied population and differing rates of migration among the cities, there is 'a growing need for labour in the industrially-developed cities, and in local economic centres with a level of employment at the republican average'. However, 'the other groups of cities ' Mikheeva notes 'have a sharply expressed opposite tendency, where the growth of the able-bodied population considerably exceeds the growth of the need for them in the labour force'.[66]

IMBALANCES BY OCCUPATION

If there are manpower surpluses in agriculture and shortages in industry, surpluses in small towns and shortages in industrial ones, all sectors and regions in Uzbekistan are experiencing shortages of *skilled* labour. Despite the growth in specialists and skilled workers described, and despite general labour surpluses in agriculture, in 1974, little more than half the demand for specialists in agriculture was met in Uzbekistan.[67] In the early and mid-1970s, more than half the personnel in trade did not have a specialised education, and more than 20 per cent did not have even a secondary education.[68] For the service sphere, Egamberdyev notes that 'rates of preparation of cadres for the service sphere in Uzbekistan are low'.[69] Shortages of skilled personnel, however, are especially acute in the industrial and technical sectors. In the mid-1970s, the 'acute' need for skilled workers, and the 'poor knowledge of technology and of technological production' was cited by one Soviet scholar as 'one of the basic reasons for ... the still-significant unused capabilities in many sectors of production'. According to this writer, a large part of wastage, poor use of equipment, and breakdowns are caused by 'the impermissible lag in the professional training of cadres by comparison with the rate of introduction of new technology'.[70] In 1976, Mikheeva referred to a 'chronic shortage of skilled cadres' in Uzbekistan's enterprises, where the supply of skilled cadres was meeting less than 87 per cent of the republic's needs. The supply of specialists with higher and secondary education in Uzbekistan, she concluded in 1976, 'noticeably lags behind both the optimal and all-Union levels'.[71]

In view of the importance placed on the industrial and technical sectors, the shortages of specialists in these sectors have been especially disturbing to Soviet planners. Skills in Uzbekistan, these planners note, have risen among Uzbekistan's population, but they have not risen rapidly enough to meet the demands of an expanding industrial base. Jobs in Soviet industry, for example, are classified on a seven-group scale from one (unskilled) to seven (highly skilled). Uzbekistan's industry has seen significant growth in the past decade in the number of personnel in the higher-skilled jobs. Between 1965 and

1972, the average skill level in Uzbekistan's industry rose from 3.1 to 3.3. In the coal industry, it rose from 4.0 to 4.5; in oil-processing, from 3.25 to 3.6; in electric power, from 3.15 to 3.6; in construction of industrial materials, from 3.4 to 3.5; in the food industry, from 3.0 to 3.1.[72] By 1972, about two thirds of all industrial workers in Uzbekistan had been rated in the third or higher skill bracket, and more than half were in the fourth or higher skill rankings.

Despite their skill-ratings, however, skill-levels of industrial personnel in Uzbekistan are still low and 'lag behind the needs of contemporary production'.[73] In 1973, almost two thirds of the total number of industrial workers had received only an elementary level of education. Less than 7 per cent of all industrial workers in Uzbekistan had received secondary specialised education or higher, and at least one third of all directors of industrial enterprises, department heads and their deputies had received a maximum of an elementary level education. In 1976, with particular regard to industry, Egamberdyev wrote that 'the level of skilled workers lags behind the needs of contemporary production. . . . The lag attests to the high proportion of manual labour in the republic's industry and the inadequate use of labour resources of the economy'.[74]

The situation may also be characterised by a comparison of the average workers' skill-rating in Uzbekistan with that in the USSR as a whole. As well as lagging behind the production needs of Uzbekistan, 'In almost all sectors of industry' Egamberdyev writes 'there is a lag in the average skill-ratings from the Union average'.[75] Using data for 1972, Ubaidullaeva noted that the differential of average workers' skill-ratings in Uzbekistan with those of the USSR as a whole was 'especially serious' in the labour-intensive sectors in Uzbekistan. In machine building, the average skill-rating for Uzbekistan was 2.9, as against 3.1 for the USSR as a whole. In woodworking, the ratings were 2.9 (Uzbekistan) and 3.2 (USSR); in light industry, 2.8 and 3.4; in the textile industry, 3.4 and 3.6; and in the food industry, the average rating in Uzbekistan was 3.1, against an average of 3.3 for the USSR as a whole.[76]

Finally, with regard to the different nationalities, one finds a particularly acute lack of specialists among the indigenous nationalities in all sectors. The proportion of indigenous specialists in agriculture rose from 1 per cent of the total number of Uzbeks employed in agriculture in 1939 to only about 9 per cent in 1970.[77] As Table 3.11 illustrates, this proportion was much lower than that among the Russians in the USSR (who were more than three times higher in each category) and

TABLE 3.11   *Proportion skilled personnel in total number of agricultural personnel, Uzbekistan, 1959–70 (as percentages)*

Nationality	Total Skilled		Directors and Specialists		Technicians	
	1959	*1970*	*1959*	*1970*	*1959*	*1970*
Uzbeks	6.5	9.2	2.2	2.5	4.3	6.7
Russians (in the RSFSR)	15.7	27.9	4.5	6.8	11.2	21.1

SOURCE   Bromlei, Iu. *Sovremennye etnicheskie protsessy v SSSR* (Moscow: Nauka, 1977) p. 127.

was growing more slowly. Few statistics are available on the number of industrial specialists by nationality. But as Ata Mirzaev noted in 1978, in view of an 'increasingly complex' labour situation, 'the training and formation of workers' cadres from among the indigenous nationalities, especially in industry, is now one of the most important social-economic problems'.[78]

Similarly, almost all regions of Uzbekistan are experiencing shortages in skilled manpower, but these shortages are particularly acute in rural areas and in small and medium cities. Again using Mikheeva's division of urban areas, Uzbekistan's industrially-developed new cities (group II) have a higher ratio of specialists with higher and secondary education than the cities of group IV. The ratios are 1:1.7 and 1:0.32 respectively; the average for Uzbekistan as a whole is 1:1.3. The industrially-developed cities also have the highest levels of educational training and attainment among the population occupied outside social production (see Appendix 2). As another study observed, the labour shortage in a number of enterprises is apparent

not because all labour reserves are actually used up, but because the supply does not correspond to the demand: enterprises are experiencing a need for skilled labour; but reserves, distributed mainly in the household and private subsidiary economy, for the most part do not satisfy this need by their level of education and skill.[79]

According to Soviet analysts, the degree and type of specialisation among Uzbekistan's population is one of the major factors inhibiting movement of the indigenous population to work in new sectors and locations, and one of the most important constraints on their effectiveness even when these transfers have been made.

4 Labour Policies

Soviet authorities have placed considerable hopes on a number of policies to modify the traditional differentiation described in Chapter 3, and to mitigate the growing labour surpluses described in Chapter 2. They have expanded educational opportunities to accommodate greater numbers of people, particularly of the indigenous nationalities. They have designed educational training to shape attitudes as well as teach new skills, in order that indigenous Central Asians will enter those sectors and regions where manpower is most needed. And in economic-policy making, they have stressed the need to create the jobs and incentives necessary for educational policies to be effective. As a preliminary to consideration of the political implications, therefore, it is necessary to analyse these two sets of policies, to determine what the effects of Soviet policies on manpower use may have been to date, and what the likely effects of education and economic planning may be in the future.

EDUCATION

As at the national level, Soviet policy-makers regard education as a major instrument of social transformation in Uzbekistan. The large numbers of people working exclusively in household and private subsidiary activities; the labour shortages in certain sectors and geographical areas, and surpluses in others; the survivals of traditional values and ideas among the indigenous nationalities which may be inhibiting population movement between sectors and geographical locales are all attributed in large part to low educational attainment and skill among the indigenous nationalities. Soviet planners, therefore, consider education as fundamental to solving all these manpower

112

issues, despite the problems' complexities.[1] To the extent that education affects manpower use, therefore, how successful have Soviet policies been to date? To what degree has educational expansion in Uzbekistan kept pace with population growth? To what extent has it addressed the growing sectoral and locational imbalances in Uzbekistan's economy? And with regard to both issues, how differently has it affected Uzbekistan's varied nationality groups?

GENERAL EDUCATIONAL EXPANSION: EARLY YEARS

As Table 4.1 illustrates, the indigenous populations of Central Asia were among the least educated peoples in the Russian Empire before the onset of Soviet power. Efforts to create a skilled labour force within Uzbekistan, however, were begun almost immediately after the Bolshevik Revolution. In 1918, the Turkestan Peoples University – the first institute of its kind in Central Asia – was opened in Tashkent, and two years later became Tashkent State University. With the decree on education in Turkestan signed in 1920, the first groups of professors and equipment began to arrive at the university early the following year, marking, as one Uzbek scholar put it, 'the beginning of mass education of skilled specialists – of engineers, agronomists, doctors, economists and others' in Uzbekistan.[2] Schools and part-time courses were also developed in the towns, and three-year schools were

TABLE 4.1   *Educational attainment by nationality in Imperial Russia, according to the 1897 Census*

Nationality	Persons with more than elementary education per 10 000 population
Russians	120
Lithuanians and Latvians	40
Armenians and other Indo-European peoples of the Caucasus	108
Georgians	107
Jews	90
Turkic peoples	3
Mongolian peoples	3
Russian Empire, Total	110

SOURCE   Bromlei, Iu., *Sovremennye etnicheskie protsessy* (Moscow: Nauka, 1977) p. 124.

opened for rural children and youth. A network of short-term courses was created for adults, in order to eradicate technical illiteracy. Thus, despite the enormous problems associated with educational training – especially in the way of language – a system of general, specialised secondary, higher, and professional institutions were gradually created, as well as on-site training programmes. Within twenty years of the consolidation of Soviet power in Uzbekistan, there were over 5400 general educational schools and close to 130 higher and secondary specialist educational establishments in Uzbekistan, with a total of about 1.3 million and 44 000 students studying in them respectively.

Efforts to train workers for industrial and technical work were particularly emphasised. Because of the pace and magnitude of economic development in Uzbekistan during the early years of Soviet power, most workers were trained directly in production. Throughout the first two decades of Soviet rule, most of Uzbekistan's new workers were drawn from youth who, upon finishing seven years of schooling, entered gainful employment immediately and received training either individually or within a brigade. Among adults, training on the job was also prevalent, either for basic training, or for retraining of those who had transferred from agriculture to industry. By 1940, close to 500 000 people had learned new skills on-the-job.

Because of the shortcomings of on-the-job training, special vocational schools were also set up on the eve of World War Two for people of all ages before they entered the labour force. The first of these were factory schools (FZU, or schools for factory/plant apprenticeships), and 'schools for the apprenticeship of mass professions' (ShUMPy). While an improvement over on-the-job training, however, these schools were organised under the jurisdiction of individual enterprises, and thus prepared cadres primarily for work in the enterprise to which they were attached. It was difficult to secure a skilled workforce for new enterprises, or for enterprises in which these schools did not exist. In the 1940s, therefore – although throughout the late 1920s and 1930s factory and plant education systems existed – a general government system for the overall vocational training and distribution of Uzbekistan's labour force was created. On the basis of the FZU, a network of professional technical schools and colleges, the PTU, was established. While workers continued to be trained on the job, these PTUs were designed to become the dominant form of cadre preparation for the future.

Soviet planners also stressed the expansion of education among women in Uzbekistan. From almost total illiteracy before the Revolution, women were gradually brought into all levels and types of educational training. By the 1949–50 school year, 500 000 women were enrolled as students in Uzbekistan, of whom 371 000 were indigenous women. Women thus comprised approximately 41 per cent of the total student enrolment, and indigenous women, close to 31 per cent.[3]

Since the 1960s, then, four main types of education have existed for training workers and specialists in Uzbekistan's economy: higher

TABLE 4.2   *Student enrolment by type of educational establishment, Uzbekistan, 1978 (beginning of school year)*

Type of educational establishment	Total students (in 1 000s)	Per cent of total	Per 1000 population
Total number of students in all forms of education	5 647.7	100	367
In general education schools:	3 875.8	68.6	252
of which, day	3 659.1		
evening/correspondence	216.7		
Specialised secondary education	218.7	3.9	142
of which, day	148.7		
evening	19.0		
correspondence	51.0		
Higher education establishments	266.6	4.7	173
of which, day	142.7		
evening	37.3		
correspondence	86.6		
Vocational schools[1]	194.8	3.4	127
of which, PTUs[2]	184.2	3.3	120
of which, day	176.1		
evening	8.1		
Studying on-the-job and other types of study[3]	1 091.8	19.3	709
Total population:	15 389.0		

[1] Includes professional technical educational establishments, sectoral professional schools and schools of the FZU
[2] As at 1 January 1979. Includes schools in the system of educational establishments under the State Committee of the UzSSR for Professional Technical Education
[3] Does not include the network of educational establishments for political education

SOURCE   TsSU, *Narodnoe Khoziaistvo Uzbekskoi SSR v 1978 godu* (Tashkent: Uzbekistan, 1979) pp. 265, 266, 273, 207.

educational establishments, secondary specialised educational establishments, vocational schools (PTUs) and on-the-job training. Table 4.2 shows a breakdown in enrolment in these different types of educational establishments at the beginning of the 1978 school year. While all four types of education are important in different ways and designed to achieve different purposes, Soviet planners have continued to emphasise PTUs as the most 'progressive' type and deserving of priority treatment for development. The general consensus among Soviet policy-makers at least throughout the past decade seems to have been that PTUs, or a single centralised system of vocational training should be 'the main form of training skilled workers among graduates of the eighth to tenth classes of secondary schools for professions with a complex profile demanding longer terms of instruction'.[4] The preparation of skilled workers on the job, while it has its merits, is now regarded as primarily for the training or retraining of Uzbekistan's adult population and for raising the skills of already qualified workers.

EDUCATION AND MANPOWER SURPLUSES

The growth in the number of all four types of institutions and students in Uzbekistan has been impressive, but serious problems still remain in the ability of education to combat Uzbekistan's general labour surplus. From hardly any in 1917, 7261 general educational institutions had been constructed in Uzbekistan by 1976, as had more than 40 institutes of higher learning, 177 secondary specialist educational establishments, and 273 PTUs. Between 1940 and 1978, the number of students studying in institutes of higher learning grew by more than fourteen times, from 19 000 to 267 000 people; the number of students in secondary specialised educational establishments, by almost nine times, from 25 000 to 219 000 people; and the number of students in PTUs – non-existent in 1940 – had reached almost 195 000 by 1978. In 1960, about 10 000 new workers had been prepared in schools and PTUs; by 1970, that number had more than quadrupled, to 41 800.[5]

Among the indigenous nationalities, moreover, the growth in the number of students in all types of education has been even more pronounced. Between 1928 and 1958, the proportion of Uzbeks among higher-education students increased from one-seventh to one-third of the republic's total.[6] According to another source, the indigenous nationalities comprised more than 57 per cent of all full-time and evening students in higher educational establishments in the 1960–1 school year. As Table 4.3 illustrates, according to this source, in 1960–70 the proportion of the indigenous nationalities in the total student body grew to 63.5 per cent in 1970. A similar pattern of growth was true for specialised secondary educational establishments. And while no data on nationality enrolment in PTUs are available for 1960, according to a Soviet dissertation, the indigenous representation in PTU daytime study had grown to about 69 per cent by 1970 (Table 4.3).

Throughout the 1970s and 1980s, Uzbeks have comprised roughly two thirds of all full-time students in Uzbekistan's higher and secondary specialised educational establishments and in PTUs. Relative to their numbers fifty years earlier, the number of Uzbeks enrolled in universities and colleges in Uzbekistan in the 1966–7 school year had risen 225-fold, and the number of Uzbeks in vocational schools, 19-fold. And recent acceptance data suggest that indigenous representation is not diminishing. For example, of approximately 32 000 students accepted for daytime study in Uzbekistan's higher educational establishments for the 1978–9 school year, 71 per cent (about 24 000 people) were Uzbek.[7] In 1978, the indigenous nationalities constituted 81 per cent of all entrants to Uzbekistan's PTUs; indigenous women comprised 15 per cent of all entrants, a growth of over ten percentage points since 1971.[8]

Despite this progress, however, educational expansion in Uzbekistan still lags behind both the needs of Uzbekistan's economy and the growth of its able bodied population. The rapid growth of educational establishments continues to be outpaced by high population growth, even while the needs of a rapidly growing economy for skilled manpower continue to mount. Although educational expansion has been substantial, its inability to meet these needs is reflected in the number of entrants to educational establishments relative to the student age of population, and the declining overall student-share of the working-age population. Between 1970 and 1978, for example, the number of students accepted to the three primary types of higher and secondary education almost doubled, growing from 107 200 to 205 700 over the eight-year period. Despite this growth, however, less than one quarter of all people reaching working age each year in Uzbekistan continue their studies to learn a particular skill; the rest go directly to learn a skill on the job in different sectors of the economy.[9] As a Soviet scholar wrote in 1979 'A large gap has appeared between the number of young people who are entering working age and their opportunities for

118

TABLE 4.3 Indigenous representation among students by type of educational establishment (thousands)[a]

	1960/61			1970/71		
	Total	of which indigenous	% indigenous	Total	of which indigenous	% indigenous
Higher education	101.3	58.0	57.4	232.9	157.7	63.5
Specialised secondary education	53.3	29.0	54.7	165.0[b]	101.6	61.7
PTUs	18.2	n.a.	n.a.	58.2		
PTUs (daytime study only)	n.a.	n.a.	n.a.	45.5	31.5	69.0

[a]Includes all age groups, including personnel undergoing retraining, people on leave from production, etc.; unless otherwise designated, includes full-time and evening students.

[b]Official estimates place the 1970–1 figure at 163 000 students. See TsSU, *Narodnoe khoziaistvo Uzbekskoi SSR 1978 goda* (Tashkent: Uzbekistan, 1979).

SOURCE Lines 1, 2 and 3 from A. E. Egamberdyev, (ed.), *Regional'nye problemy vosproizvodstva rabochei sily v Uzbekistane* (Tashkent: Fan, 1976) p. 158, and R. A. Ubaidullaeva 'Regional'nye problemy razmeshcheniia i effectivnost' ispol'zovaniia trudovykh resursov v Uzbekskoi SSR', doctoral dissertation, Tashkent, 1974, p. 177. Line 4 from A. B. Fedorova, 'Analiz podgotovki rabochikh kadrov v Uzbekistane' unpublished doctoral dissertation (Tashkent).

specialised and vocational training.' The number of young people annually reaching working age in Uzbekistan, this scholar asserted, 'presently exceeds the possibility of being accepted by an educational institution by a factor of approximately three'.[10] Despite significant educational expansion in the 1970s, the share of the total working-age population which entered these educational establishments grew only negligibly, from 2 per cent of the working-age population in 1970, to 2.8 per cent in 1978.

The picture is not brighter regarding the total student-share of the working-age population. Indeed, the proportion of the total working-age population enrolled in all levels of higher and secondary specialised education has declined since 1970. In 1970, 213 400 students were enrolled in higher and secondary specialised educational establishments (4.3 per cent of the working-age population). While the number of students grew between 1970 and 1979, this growth did not keep pace with that of the working-age population, and the proportion of students declined to between 3.9 and 4.0 per cent of the working-age population.[11] The share in PTUs remained relatively unchanged. The bulk of the growth in the working-age population, therefore, was absorbed primarily by on-the-job training, whose level rose from 10 per cent of the working-age population in 1970, to 15 per cent in 1979.[12] As another Soviet scholar wrote in 1975, the number of educational establishments and student places in Uzbekistan is 'of course insufficient, considering the existence of a large number of people wishing to study in the given schools'.[13]

Finally, despite the growth in the size of their student body, PTUs still account for only a small contingent of students in Uzbekistan. And despite the high priority accorded them, the expansion of PTUs in particular 'still lags behind the development of the sectors of production' – 'as a result of which' Ubaidullaeva writes 'a significant proportion of young people begin work without professional training, and enterprises continue to experience a shortage of skilled workers'.[14] During the 1970s, enrolments in Uzbekistan's PTUs relative to the total student body were only about one third the all-Union average.[15]

It should be stressed, of course, that this is not to diminish the successes Soviet planners have achieved in increasing the number of students, and particularly indigenous students, accepted to educational establishments in Uzbekistan beyond the eighth class. The data are only intended to illustrate that this high rate of growth has none the less been outpaced by economic and demographic demands; and that the high number of 24 000 or 79 000 Uzbeks accepted to Uzbekistan's

higher educational establishments and PTUs respectively is still significantly below the number of people entering working age, the vast
majority of whom are indigenous.

EDUCATION BY SECTOR AND LOCATION

Like the problems of the labour force discussed above, shortcomings in
educational training in Uzbekistan have only been compounded by
problems of sector and location. For the past two decades, Soviet
writings have increasingly referred to 'disproportions between the
types of educational training and the needs of the economy' in Uzbekistan, and have stressed the need to correct a situation where
'training of the population is occurring in an unplanned, haphazard
manner'.[16] A large part of Uzbekistan's student population, and
particularly of the indigenous nationalities, have been entering those
fields where labour surpluses already exist, and not the industrial or
technical sectors where specialists are needed.

There is little doubt, of course, that education in Uzbekistan has not
only expanded numerically, but has diversified immensely during the
past four or so decades, and that it continues to diversify in order to
rectify these deficiencies. In 1940, more than 70 per cent of all students
in higher and secondary specialised education were studying in departments of health or education, while only about 9 per cent were in
studies concerning industry and construction. In the 1978–9 school
year, the number of students in health and education had declined to
41 per cent of the total, while the proportion of students in industry
and construction had grown to almost 27 per cent.[17] Similarly, in 1940,
six *oblasts* in Uzbekistan were lacking even one institute of higher
learning, and two *oblasts* were lacking a single secondary specialised
educational establishment as well. By 1978, every *oblast* in Uzbekistan
had at least one institute of higher learning and at least seven secondary specialised educational establishments.[18] In 1978, PTUs prepared students for over 259 professions – 'for everything from hair-
dressing to electronics' – and about two-thirds of all PTUs and half of
all PTU students were located in rural areas.[19] By the late 1970s, the
trend toward geographical diversification with an emphasis on industry appeared to be continuing.

Yet despite the successes in developing educational training for all
geographical areas and economic sectors in Uzbekistan, the same
problems persist: educational establishments still tend to be concen-

trated in Uzbekistan's largest cities or towns, and the indigenous nationalities still tend to be concentrated in studies leading to work in the service or agricultural spheres while Europeans dominate industrial studies. In the 1978–9 school year, for example, Central Asians comprised 74 per cent of the entering class in Uzbekistan's higher educational establishments. Yet of that number, they comprised about 82 per cent of approximately 11 000 students then in pedagogical institutes,[20] and at least 92 per cent of all students in the Tashkent Agricultural Institute. They comprised only 42 per cent of the 3534 students at the Tashkent Institute for Engineers of Railway Transport (TIERRT), and about 45 per cent of the total enrolment at the Tashkent Electrotechnical Institute of Communications (Table 4.4). Data on graduates of general secondary educational establishments between 1968 and 1974 showed an actual decline in the proportion going into industry, transport and communications, with the largest proportion going into agriculture, and the largest percentage rises in trade, public catering, housing and services (Table 4.5).

Similarly, while today about 80 per cent of all students in Uzbekistan's PTUs are of the indigenous nationalities, they are concentrated primarily in the rural PTUs and in agricultural studies. For several years, local planners have been stressing the need to locate PTUs which will train cadres for non-agricultural sectors, or for sectors 'of an urban profile', in the countryside.[21] Despite the necessity to re-locate industrial training, however, 'this most important matter in the republic is only beginning to be activated'.[22] In 1967–8, Egamberdyev notes, rural PTUs prepared no one for industrial professions, and in 1969, only 127 people. Lest one assume that more progress occurred during the 1970s, 'at the present time' Maksakova wrote in 1975 'the preparation of skilled workers' cadres for industrial sectors from among rural youth is not being carried out'.[23] As Shister notes, in 1977, only about 19 per cent of all graduates of PTUs were directed to work in industry, and only 19 per cent to construction. This latter proportion of PTU graduates directed to construction was the same as in 1970.[24]

Soviet planners have also met with limited success in attracting rural youth to studies in the cities or to industrial courses of study. As one Uzbek scholar noted 'cadres prepared in rural PTUs consist almost exclusively of representatives of the indigenous nationalities, but in urban PTUs, the native share does not correspond to their proportion in the total population'.[25] In the 1968–9 school year, rural youth comprised only about 40 per cent of the entering class of urban PTUs in Fergana *oblast'*, even though throughout the late 1960s and 1970s

TABLE 4.4 *Enrolment in higher educational establishments by nationality, Uzbekistan, 1 October, 1978.* * (Daytime only)

Educational establishment	Total enrolment	Indigenous	Non-indigenous	% Indigenous	% Non-indigenous	% Unknown
Tashkent Polytechnic Institute Im. A. R. Beruni	15 691	10 772	2 967	69	19	12
Fergana Polytechnic	3 518	2 610	379	74	11	15
Tashkent Motor Vehicle Institute	3 601	2 729	380	76	11	13
Samarkand Architectural–Construction Institute	2 690	2 064	253	77	9	14
Tashkent Institute of Textile and Light Industry	3 492	2 718	490	78	14	8
Bukhara Technical Institute of Food and Light Industry	973	872	65	90	7	3
Tashkent Institute of the National Economy	4 897	3 927	512	80	10	10
Tashkent State University	8 856	6 241	1 753	70	20	10
Samarkand State University	5 386	4 316	536	80	10	10
Nukus University	3 195	3 072	54	96	2	2
Tashkent State Pedagogical Institute of Foreign Languages, Im. F. Engels	1 346	1 118	85	83	6	11
Tashkent Institute of Engineers of Railway Transport	3 534	1 475	1 491	42	42	16
Tashkent Electro Technical Institute of Communication	2 844	1 267	1 169	45	41	14
Institute of Engineers for the Irrigation and Mechanisation of Agriculture	7 249	6 043	679	83	9	8

Institution						
Tashkent Agricultural Institute	4 339	3 995	148	92	3	5
Samarkand Agricultural Institute	2 664	2 554	22	96	1	3
Andizhan Institute of Cotton Growing	1 722	1 578	73	92	4	4
Samarkand Medical Institute	4 527	3 774	363	83	8	9
Andizhan Medical Institute	4 326	3 296	500	76	12	12
Central Asian Medical–Pediatrics Institute	4 730	3 888	522	82	11	7
Tashkent Medical Institute	8 253	6 376	1 107	77	13	10
Tashkent Pharmaceutical Institute	1 759	1 444	167	82	9	9
Termez State Pedagogical Institute	1 426	1 325	37	93	3	4
Kokand State Pedagogical Institute	1 537	1 423	65	93	4	3
Samarkand Co-operative Institute	2 427	2 051	177	85	7	8
Institute of Culture	1 954	1 351	427	69	22	8
Andizhan Pedagogical Institute of Languages	1 346	1 118	85	83	6	11
Tashkent Polytechnic Institute, subsidiary no. 1 in Dzhizak	220	189	8	86	4	10

*For the purpose of this table, indigenous nationalities are comprised of Uzbeks, Kazakhs, Kirgiz, Tadzhiks, Turkmen, Karakalpaks; 'non-indigenous' nationalities consist of Russians, Ukrainians, Belorussians and Jews. Since there was no breakdown between Bukharan and European Jews, the non-indigenous figures could possibly be slightly overstated.

NOTE   The data obtained from the Ministry of Higher and Specialised Secondary Education (MINVUZ) provided a total enrolment figure for each educational establishment, and a numerical breakdown by nationality. The latter figures did not add up to the former, by a margin ranging between 2 and 15%. I have therefore included both the numerical and percentage figures for both the indigenous and non-indigenous nationalities, as they appeared on Minvuz's forms.

SOURCE   The Ministry of Higher and Specialised Secondary Education, UzSSR, Tashkent, Uzbekistan, 1979.

TABLE 4.5   *Distribution of graduates of daytime general secondary schools who were fitted with work, by place of work, UzSSR, 1968–74 (as percentage)*

Type of work	1968 Total	Urban	Rural	1974 Total	Urban	Rural
In industrial enterprises	16.1	44.7	6.1	12.4	35.5	5.9
In construction organisations	5.4	10.1	3.8	6.3	10.6	5.2
Transport and communications enterprises	2.6	6.0	1.4	2.4	5.5	1.6
Agriculture	64.1	14.4	81.5	65.1	14.3	79.7
Trade and public catering	2.7	6.6	1.3	3.6	9.4	1.3
Housing and services	1.5	3.7	0.7	2.4	5.3	1.6
Education, culture and health	4.5	8.1	3.3	2.9	7.6	1.7
Other	3.1	6.4	1.9	4.9	11.8	3.0
Total	100.0	100.0	100.0	100.0	100.0	100.0

SOURCE   Abdullaev, Sh. 'Nekotorye voprosy professional'noi orientatsii molodezhi', *Regional'nye demograficheskie issledovaniia*, monograph prepared by the Ministry of Higher and Specialised Secondary Education, UzSSR and Tashkent State University (compilation of works no. 548), Tashkent, 1978, p. 99.

the population of that *oblast'* was more than two thirds rural. In 1977, a special study on Uzbekistan's higher educational establishments showed that 'an insignificant proportion' of the republic's intelligentsia had been drawn from rural Uzbeks. And in Tashkent State University – the largest higher educational establishment in Uzbekistan – only 10 per cent of the teachers today are originally from rural areas of the republic. As Egamberdyev writes:

> In the light of the existence of a potential labour surplus in the countryside and insufficient provision of workers' cadres in the republic's industrial sectors, the designated scales and proportions of training a skilled labour force from among the rural population in urban vocational-technical schools is manifestly insufficient.[26]

In 1979, this statement was confirmed by senior Uzbek officials in the administration of PTU affairs. In an interview with Messrs Dzhuraev and Goldenberg, Deputy Chairman and Administrative Director respectively of the Uzbek State Committee on Professional Technical Education, I was told that agricultural PTUs in Uzbekistan are still almost exclusively Uzbek in composition, while the number of Uzbeks in construction or industrial PTUs – although growing – is still minimal.

It was Dzhuraev's opinion that the difficulties in training rural youth for non-agricultural professions and in attracting them to the cities for educational training has been one of the greatest constraints in diminishing sectoral imbalances in employment in Uzbekistan's economy.

Within industrial educational spheres, moreover, Central Asians who are studying industrial subjects still tend to concentrate in studies leading to work in light industry and food industries, while Europeans dominate training programmes leading to work in heavy industry.[27] Uzbeks who are enrolled at industrial or highly technical institutes in Uzbekistan tend to drop out at a slightly more rapid rate than Europeans. In the first-year class of the Construction Department of the Institute of Transportation in Tashkent, 1978–9, of 181 students, 75, or about 41 per cent were Central Asians – a ratio the Institute has tried to maintain for the past several years. In the fourth- and fifth-year courses, however, there were only 37 and 38 Central Asians represented, out of total class sizes of 135 and 138 students respectively. In other words, the number of Central Asians had declined by half, and their proportion in the student body had been reduced to about 27 per cent.

Again, the concentration in studies leading to work in the service sector or light and food industries is particularly true of women in Uzbekistan. While more than 37 per cent of the 1978 entering-class in all higher educational establishments were women (and while 70 per cent of those were indigenous women) most were concentrated in the cultural and service spheres. Women constituted about half the students accepted to institutes under the jurisdiction of *Minpros* (pedagogical institutes and institutes of language and literature). And half the approximately 2500 indigenous women accepted in the sixteen institutes of higher education under central ministerial control were concentrated in the three medical institutes of Tashkent, Samarkand and Andizhan. At the same time, only one-tenth of the students enrolled in the Tashkent Motor Vehicle Institute in 1978 were female; and of the 900 students comprising the 1978 entering-class of the Samarkand Agricultural Institute and the Andizhan Institute of Cotton Production, only 7 per cent were women (Table 4.6). It should be noted, moreover, that although the proportion of indigenous women in the total female entering-class is high in most sectors, their drop-out rate is also higher than that of non-indigenous women and of male students.[28]

TABLE 4.6 *Number of students enrolled in selected institutes of higher education in Uzbekistan, by sex, 1978*

Institute	Total Enrolment	of which, women	% women
Tashkent Polytechnic Institute, Im. A. R. Beruni	15 691	4 102	26.1
Fergana Polytechnic	3 518	1 080	30.7
Tashkent Motor Vehicle Institute	3 601	386	10.7
Samarkand Architectural-Construction Institute	2 690	505	18.8
Tashkent Institute of Textile and Light Industry	3 492	1 585	45.4
Bukhara Technical Institute of Food and Light Industry	973	231	23.7
Tashkent Institute of the National Economy	4 897	—	—
Tashkent State University	8 856	4 125	46.6
Samarkand State University	5 386	2 455	45.6
Nukus University	3 195	1 641	51.4
Tashkent State Pedogogical Institute of Foreign Languages, Im. F. Engels	1 346	923	68.6
Tashkent Institute of Engineers of Railway Transport	3 534	1 358	38.4
Tashkent Electro Technical Institute of Communications	2 844	1 071	37.7
Institute of Engineers for the Irrigation and Mechanisation of Agriculture	7 249	—	—
Tashkent Agricultural Institute	4 339	677	15.6

NOTE There are at present 42 higher educational establishments in Uzbekistan, of which 12 are under the jurisdiction of *Minvuz*, 14 under *Minpros* and 16 under other ministries and agencies. The first 11 institutes in the above table are under *Minvus*, the remaining 4 under other ministries and agencies.

SOURCE Ministry of Higher and Specialised Secondary Education, Tashkent, interviews May, 1979.

In terms of geographical distribution, as mentioned above, educational establishments in Uzbekistan have become more evenly dispersed throughout the republic. But despite the increased construction and wider geographical distribution of institutes and colleges, by 1979 about half of the republic's forty-three higher educational establishments, and more than half of the roughly 270 000 students enrolled in them, were still concentrated in the city of Tashkent; about one-third of all students enrolled in secondary specialised educational establishments were concentrated in Tashkent *oblast,* where the proportion of Russians in the total population is greatest. In 1975, Ubaidullaeva noted that almost three quarters of all students entering PTUs came from rural areas. As illustrated above, however, most of these students remained in rural PTUs pursuing agricultural studies. Today, about 30 per cent of the total number of graduates from urban secondary schools go on to full-time study; in rural areas, only 15 per cent continue their studies.[29]

A final problem, discussed below, is the apparently growing number of young people in Uzbekistan who are trained in one field and then choose or are sent to work in another. This problem was highlighted, for example, by B. A. Allamuradov, First Secretary of the Uzbek SSR Komsomol in March, 1982 when he noted the 'particularly disturbing trend' that only half of all graduates of Uzbekistan's higher educational establishments and *tekhnikums* were working on Uzbekistan's collective and state farms. 'At the same time' he noted 'one out of every ten agronomists and more than one third of the engineers, technicians and machine operators in the rural community do not have a specialised education.'[30] This was echoed by Sh. Rashidov, First Secretary of the Communist Party of Uzbekistan until his death in November 1983, when he noted that 'only one out of every five graduates in Uzbekistan today chooses a job corresponding to the vocational training he acquired in school'.[31] The implications of all of these imbalances, especially when viewed in nationality terms, are locally considered quite serious. A scholar from Turkmenistan summed it up briefly:

In spite of the success which has been achieved, the degree of qualitative development in manpower resources and the workforce's level of general and specialised training – especially for cadres of the indigenous nationalities – do not meet the modern demands of a quickly-growing national economy in the Central Asian republics. Therefore, on the one hand, the national economy's requirements for manpower are not being completely met in these republics and, on the other hand, the population's requirements are not being met at work.[32]

RECENT POLICIES

Recent educational policies in Uzbekistan have emphasised the continued expansion of vocational, higher and specialised secondary educational training, particularly in industry; better distribution of educational establishments throughout the republic; quotas in existing educational establishments, both by region of the republic and by nationality; and more intensive vocational orientation and propaganda to better orientate students towards meeting the needs of the economy. The *Main Directives of Development of the Economy of the USSR 1976–1980* (XXV Congress, CPSU) called for linking the further development of the Soviet educational system 'with the needs of scientific-technical progress'. This theme was repeated at the XXVI Party Congress in February, 1981, and the nationality aspects especially were again highlighted in Andropov's speech of 21 December 1982, marking the sixtieth anniversary of the USSR.[33]

Within Uzbekistan, several administrative and other measures have been formulated to expand and improve education and training, especially in industry. A branch of the All-Union Scientific Research Institute of Vocational-Technical Education was created in Tashkent in 1979 to study 'the social economic development of vocational technical education in Central Asia'.[34] As discussed in Chapter 5, educational quotas have been established by region and nationality, generally in favour of the lesser-developed regions and indigenous nationalities. And greater attention has been turned towards professional orientation among secondary school students and recent graduates, and towards more rational distribution and better placement of specialists throughout the economy. A decree of December 1971, for example, called for the better organisation and direction of youth to enterprises and state farms. Throughout the past decade, vocational 'orientation' centres have been set up in Uzbekistan's major cities.

Lectures and excursions during the eighth to tenth classes and work on the part of Uzbekistan's Komsomol complement these policies. Today, secondary educational establishments in Uzbekistan organise compulsory excursions, discussions, lectures, etc. as part of their curriculum, and frequently make special arrangements with neighbouring enterprises. Evening lectures and discussions have included such topics as: 'All Types of Work are Good – Take Your Pick', 'Any Work Here is Held in High Esteem', 'My Favourite Profession'. Vocational counselling has grown in Uzbekistan, both within and outside existing enterprises: within enterprises such as the Tashkent Textile Combine, for example, offices for vocational advice and orientation have recently been opened; and in 1979, a new vocational counselling organisation was opened in Tashkent for residents of the entire city. At the 22nd Komsomol Congress in Tashkent (30 March, 1982), B. A. Allamuradov, First Secretary of the Uzbek SSR Komsomol, stressed the role of the Komsomol in these efforts as well:

> More people must be encouraged to work in industry and construction. Can we accept the fact that production capacities are being underutilised in many republic branches just because of a shortage of manpower? It is here that all links of the Komsomol have much to do.[35]

Yet if the record of the past is any indication, forecasts that education and training will catch up with economic and demographic needs are not promising. A decree of November 1971, of Uzbekistan's Central Committee and Council of Ministers foresaw the construction of 266 new PTUs by 1975. By 1975, however, only half the planned number had been constructed. Despite the growth of vocational counselling centres, enrolment in industrial and technical institutes among the indigenous nationalities remains low. And despite the work of vocational centres, there is still a tremendous reluctance among Central Asian graduates to enter work in the industrial sectors. As one Uzbek economist wrote in 1978, 'despite the wide development in the republic during the past ten-year period of work in the professional orientation of youth, its positive sides still have not been fully developed. Among boys and girls entering working life, a one-sided orientation still strongly governs the choice of profession and spheres of attraction to work. The overwhelming majority of Uzbekistan's youth begin their career-path from agricultural production'. As he adds 'a one-sided, agricultural orientation among youth going on to work complicates satisfying labour needs in other sectors'.[36]

Today, education and professional orientation are still stressed as means for shaping the labour force. But success appears no more promising, and administrative constraints further impede their effectiveness. 'In working out plans for expanding the training of skilled cadres' Egamberdyev writes:

in some sectors the need for individual specialities is not studied; there is no connection between plans for training cadres in vocational schools and the direct need for them in collective and state farms. ... Young people do not approach the selection for study seriously, and there is no close connection with the directors of general educational schools[37]

In other words, educational expansion and diversification in Uzbekistan is occurring, but slowly. Despite the immense growth and diversification of Uzbekistan's educational system, educational expansion has not kept pace with the growth of the working-age population, nor with the needs of the economy. The indigenous nationalities still predominate in studies leading towards work in agriculture and the service sectors, while Europeans comprise the majority of students in more industrial or technical departments and institutes. While Soviet planners may regard education and propaganda as one of the most important policy tools at their disposal, therefore, it has still had severe drawbacks. In some cases it may even be perpetuating some of the very trends it was designed to alter.

ECONOMIC POLICIES

Particularly during the past fifteen years, Soviet policy-makers have come to appreciate that more than education is needed to modify manpower distribution in Uzbekistan. The concern to formulate labour policies to address these problems has been reflected in administrative changes and in the growing numbers of conferences and seminars on the subject. In 1956, the State Committee on Labour and Wage Problems was founded in Uzbekistan; in 1967, the republic level State Committee on Labour Resources Utilisation was created. In 1976 – along with the transformation of the All-Union Committee on Labour and Wages to that on Labour and Social Problems and the shifts associated with that change – these two committees were combined into the Committee on Labour and Social Problems with all-Union rather than republican significance and, according to its present first deputy chairman, Y. T. Zakirov, with widely expanded powers and responsibilities.[38] Today, this committee is under the jurisdiction of both Uzbekistan's Council of Ministers and the State Committee on Labour and Social Problems in Moscow.

Similarly, many other institutes and committees in Uzbekistan have expanded their research into the realm of manpower. The Population

Laboratory at Tashkent University was officially created in the early 1970s to study both demographic and manpower problems in Uzbekistan and Central Asia. New departments on the use of labour resources have recently been created as part of certain *oblast'* executive committees. And according to one Uzbek academic, interdisciplinary committees are now being set up 'within university and government organisations and linked with every factory and establishment' to study all aspects of labour utilisation in Uzbekistan.[39] Prior to 1960, few conferences were held on labour problems in Central Asia. Between 1965 and 1978, over twenty-four all-Union and republican conferences, symposia and seminars have been held concerning the overall use of the growing labour force in Uzbekistan and Central Asia as a whole, the growing sectoral and locational imbalances and nationality issues as they relate to manpower problems in both respects.[40]

As reflected in these seminars, conferences, studies and administrative changes, a fairly clear set of policy imperatives has developed. Almost all recommendations and policy proposals concerning labour use in Uzbekistan have emphasised the need for expanding job opportunities in all sectors of the economy, and for shifting the employment structure in favour of the non-agricultural sectors. Water diversion schemes, the opening of new agricultural lands and the expansion of labour-intensive industries in Uzbekistan are all viewed as means for providing Uzbekistan's growing labour force with full employment. Likewise, greater expansion of the consumer economy – in terms of increased construction of homes and apartments, day-care centres, etc. – is intended to diminish the need for employment in household work and to reduce labour turnover. The location of new industries and service organisations in labour surplus areas and encouragement of commuting are intended to address the sectoral and locational factors compounding the employment situation. And better organisation of labour in all sectors and geographical areas is designed to address all employment problems in a 'complex' manner. Each of these policies has been regarded as essential for solving the economic and social issues associated with labour use in Uzbekistan, but each policy has also had its drawbacks.

WATER DIVERSION

Central Asian policy-makers regard plans to divert water from Siberian rivers to Central Asia as a significant way of creating job opportunities for Uzbekistan's local populations. While plans to divert water from the Ob' and Irtysh rivers in Siberia to Central Asia have been in the making since 1951, a directive issued in December 1978 called for the technical-engineering specifications of the construction work to begin in 1980. The proposal calls for diverting part of the Ob' River into the basin of the Aral Sea, mainly for irrigation in parts of Central Asia and Kazakhstan, but also for industry and population use. According to the 1978 decree, a 'technical and economic rationale' for the first stage of the scheme was to be completed in 1980, along with a full study of the volume of work involved and a plan for its implementation. Today, completion of the plan is regarded as a potentially major source of new employment opportunities for Uzbekistan's population. One writer on this topic in Uzbekistan, Anatolii Ershev, has stated this directly, echoing the feelings of many of his colleagues:

> it must be recognised that, without additional sources of water or, to be more specific, without the diversion of some of the flow of the Siberian rivers to our region, it will be difficult for us to provide employment in the public sector for all the children being born today when they come of age. An analysis by economists has shown that industry alone is quite incapable of coping with this task.[41]

According to Ershev's estimates 'every cubic kilometre of water will provide 50 000 jobs in Uzbekistan'.

None the less, the water scheme is already behind schedule, there is some doubt that plans will be implemented, and there has been a continuing debate as to just how extensive the job opportunities created by the venture ultimately would be, particularly for the indigenous nationalities, even if the scheme were to get underway very soon. The draft guidelines for the XXVI Party Congress made only a brief reference to the water diversion scheme, mentioning little with regard to a timetable for implementing it. The guidelines mentioned only that

> preparatory work is to commence on transferring part of the outflow of northern rivers to the Volga River basin, as well as continuing the scientific and design studies for the transfer of the Siberian river waters to Central Asia and Kazakhstan.

Enormous controversy continues to surround the plan, with some observers certain of its implementation, but with stray opposition still coming from Siberia and other quarters of the USSR and abroad.[42] In short, because of the innumerable uncertainties involved in such a vast project, few people have attempted to project a timetable within which plans may possibly be implemented and completed. Thus, whatever the number of jobs that ultimately could be created, the effects of a water diversion scheme on local manpower use, even if implemented, would be a long time in making themselves felt.

NEW LANDS

The further augmentation of arable land in Uzbekistan is also designed to create new jobs, to absorb the excess manpower in Uzbekistan's agricultural sector. From the early 1920s until the mid 1960s, the amount of irrigated land in Soviet Central Asia more than doubled, requiring an investment, from the end of World War Two to the mid-1960s alone, of more than 1500 million roubles.[43] Since irrigation of the Hungry Steppe was begun in 1941, irrigation work in the Hungry Steppe, parts of the Fergana Valley, the Karshi Steppe, and the lower reaches of the Amudar'ya and Zeravshan rivers have all opened tremendous opportunities for expanding agricultural work. And today, plans for further augmentation of arable land continue. Significant expansion of irrigated land in Uzbekistan was planned for the current five-year plan period, (1981–5) intended to redistribute agricultural labour resources from labour surplus areas to newly-opened, labour-short lands. The plan calls for continuing the development of the Karshi and Dzhizak steppes, and for bringing between 450 000 and 465 000 hectares of irrigated land in Uzbekistan into use.[44] According to Ubaidullaeva, every 462 hectares opened for irrigation in Uzbekistan may require upwards of 100 new workers. According to another Uzbek scholar, the collective farms and state farms of Chirakchin, Kamashin, Kitab, Shakhrisabs and Yakkobad regions – each with twice as many people per 100 hectares of irrigated land as the republican average – could and should be the source of labour for the newly-opened lands of the neighbouring Kasan, Karshi, Ul'ianov and Guzar regions.[45] Present plans stress this as well.

Policies to encourage migration to these new lands have tended to include elements of both compulsion and incentives. A large colony of Crimean Tatars, for example, was compulsorily resettled on the Hungry Steppe in 1944 and has not yet been allowed to return home. For the most part, however, recruitment policies to create permanent cadres in these regions have included methods such as 'social summons' for youth through Komsomol organisations, organised recruitment (*orgnabor*), directing youth after graduation from educational institutions, the planned transfer of workers and employees from existing enterprises and establishments, and economic incentives. According to the 1979 interview with Zakirov, financial incentives include bonuses and such tax holidays as the receipt of a rent-free apartment (which remains rent-free for two years), the provision of all moving expenses, family allowances (with the amount varying by place and distance), and receipt of credit, should the individual or family wish to buy the house or move livestock there. No less important, he added, through campaigns, the media, posters, lectures, etc. large amounts of propaganda also encourage the population to migrate.[46]

Despite these policies, however, the need for labour in newly-opened regions remains high, and the numbers leaving labour-surplus collective farms, very low. As mentioned above, in 1970, labour shortages in Uzbekistan's newly-opened agricultural state farms were estimated to range between 100 000 and 150 000 people, and there was little indication that migration would increase. A common theme throughout the 1970s is summed up by one scholar in the earlier part of that decade: 'Practice indicates that the forms and methods of redistributing the labour force have turned out to be insufficiently effective'. Despite some movement to newly opened lands, migration has been limited, and 'state farms of the Hungry Steppe are still insufficiently supplied with permanent cadres'.[47]

Even should mobility among Uzbekistan's rural population rise, moreover, prospects would still appear no more encouraging. According to an article in *Pravda Vostoka*, the expansion of arable lands in Uzbekistan will not be sufficient in itself to absorb the additional people that must be drawn into production in order to maintain labour-force participation rates at present levels.[48] As a 1975 republican Gosplan report for Uzbekistan noted 'the growth of the working-age population is already surpassing the growth of arable land. The possibilities for extensive development of production in agriculture are very limited. . . . The rural population must be attracted to non-agricultural spheres.'[49]

EXPANSION OF INDUSTRIAL AND SERVICE SECTORS

With this as background, Soviet planners – in Moscow as well as Central Asia – have also begun to emphasise expanding labour-intensive industries and organisations in Uzbekistan. Planners in Moscow have long called for the establishment in Central Asia of labour-intensive industries to absorb the high level of manpower in the southern republics, while keeping in mind the pending labour shortages for the USSR as a whole. To an even greater extent, Uzbekistan's local planners have emphasised the need to expand labour-intensive industries and establishments in Uzbekistan, especially in order to utilise the indigenous rural populations now occupied in agriculture. Particularly in the light of the increasing mechanisation of agriculture, local planners have intensified calls for the rapid transfer of manpower from agriculture to non-agricultural work. As one such planner wrote:

New industrial construction must solve an important socio-economic task – to create favourable conditions for drawing the native rural population into industrial work. This cannot always be achieved by the construction of enterprises in need of highly-skilled workers who have great professional knowledge and productive experience accumulated through more than one generation. Construction of only such enterprises means creating great difficulties in providing cadres and attracting the workforce from labour-short regions. In the light of this, the problem of the adaptation of national cadres to industrial work, in essence, is not solved. Therefore, it is very important in these regions to build enterprises in such sectors which could be staffed by the indigenous population. Experience shows that light industries and food industries, as well as some sectors of the extractive industry, can be regarded as such enterprises.[50]

Similarly, local planners have consistently stressed the importance of locating these labour-intensive enterprises in rural areas and in old, small towns. As early as 1965, the Uzbek academician E. Tashbekov referred to the need to 'more rationally distribute the productive forces in Uzbekistan – to reduce the growing disparity between Uzbekistan's working and non-working populations'.[51] Since then, local planners have reiterated his views, stressing the nationality implications and social dimensions more explicitly as well. As one such planner noted in the mid-1970s:

The correct choice of location for the construction of enterprises has great significance for these [Central Asian] republics. It is well-known that the indigenous inhabitants, and they comprise the basic reserve of labour, live mainly in rural localities or in small and medium-sized cities. In the republican capitals and large cities a high proportion of the population is of the non-indigenous nationalities. It therefore follows that one should distribute enterprises in those regions where there is a high proportion of people of the indigenous nationalities.[52]

In the 1979 interview with Zakirov I was told that 'the disproportions in the choice of profession by nationality in Uzbekistan is due mainly to the location of the different industries; industries must be located where the rural population can be brought into them'.

One of the major policies designed to address this problem, therefore, has been the construction of agro-industrial complexes. These complexes, while demanding high efficiency and productivity, are mainly intended (a) to diminish the effects of seasonality on the rural labour force, by using labour more evenly throughout the year; (b) gradually to encourage rural inhabitants to enter the industrial sphere; (c) to increase levels of skill and educational training; (d) and, generally, to absorb surplus manpower which is growing rapidly on Uzbekistan's farms. Reports from Gosplan, UzSSR have called for locating enterprises or departments for processing agricultural raw materials in the Fergana Valley, Dzhizak *oblast'*, and in other densely-populated rural areas of the republic. And the importance of developing agro-industrial complexes continues to be expressed on all-Union levels.[53]

Similarly, planners continue to emphasise policies for locating more labour-intensive industries in small and medium cities. The XXIV Party Congress of the CPSU focused particular attention on the problem of rationally employing the labour resources of small and medium-sized cities. The congress proposed 'to locate small specialised enterprises and subsidiaries of already existing large urban plants and factories in small cities and workers' settlements'.[54] This was repeated at the XXV Party Congress, and again at the XXVI:

> The policy of restricting the growth of major cities is to be consistently carried out. Small and medium-size towns are to be developed. Specialised and highly productive manufacturing capacities and subsidiaries of enterprises and associations are to be located in these towns.[55]

Despite these calls for expanding labour-intensive industries in Uzbekistan, however, and for locating them in lesser-developed areas where Central Asians predominate, these policies have proved to be only marginally effective, and the broader goals of increased participation of the indigenous nationalities in the non-agricultural sectors of the economy have not been met. Investment priorities in Uzbekistan, in practice, have still remained with large scale and heavy, capital intensive industries and with the cities and regions in which these industries are located. Moreover, even those enterprises which have been constructed in rural areas or in old, small towns are not necessarily drawing the majority of their new personnel from the agricultural sectors or from among the indigenous nationalities.

As Pokshishevskii, for example, noted a decade ago, despite calls for greater investment in light industry and food industries, the sectors enjoying highest priority for rapid development were not labour intensive. More recent interviews with economic planners in both Moscow and Tashkent suggest that priorities have not altogether changed. In practice, despite an acknowledged need to absorb a growing working-age population, planners tend to feel that 'first place in importance is still heavy [that is, capital-intensive] industry'.[56] In 1976, a Soviet economist in Uzbekistan noted that more than 70 per cent of the total amount of capital investment directed towards the development of Uzbekistan's industry is channelled to the heavy or highly technical industrial sectors (that is, the fuel, electric power, chemical and machine construction industries). Only about 10.5 per cent of total capital investment goes to light industry.[57]

In terms of geographical investment, small cities in Uzbekistan have been receiving only a small share of total investment in Uzbekistan. Throughout the 1960s, most of the capital investment in Uzbekistan was channelled to industrial settlements and the largest cities, generally the *oblast'* centres. In some *oblasts*, the proportion of capital investment even declined from year to year, as the proportion directed to large cities increased. And recently, despite the rapid population growth in small local centres and calls for increased investment there, the pattern has not changed. For example, one report for the eighth five-year plan gives some indication of the differences in investment in Uzbekistan's cities. According to this report, from 1966–70, 537 million roubles, or 46.6 per cent of total capital investment in industrial construction in Uzbekistan, was being directed to cities of the second group cited above, that is to new industrial cities; 483.3 million roubles, or 42 per cent was being directed to large old cities; only 131.5 million roubles, or only 11.4 per cent of the total volume of investment was being channelled to old small cities. At the end of the 1960s, an average of 67 million roubles per year were being invested in new small and medium cities in Uzbekistan, and an average of eight enterprises were being constructed in them. In old small cities, only 6.6 million roubles per year were being invested, or less than one tenth that amount for the construction of an average of three enterprises per city. In many of the old small cities, the author noted, during the five-year-plan period not one enterprise, or only one enterprise was being constructed.[58]

Interviews conducted during 1978–9, while providing few overall statistics, suggest that priorities have not changed. More than fifteen interviews with economists in Moscow and Uzbekistan suggest that despite the acknowledged need to absorb a growing working-age population, investment priorities are still in heavy industry. Indeed, several local observers suggested that despite the fact that local officials appear aware of the need to build more labour-intensive industries in small and medium-size towns, the high proportion of investment determined in Moscow precludes their making any substantial change in existing priorities, and constrains their own ability to construct enterprises in areas where raw materials or heavy industry do not already exist. In other words, capital investment during the past two decades has continued to be channelled to the large urban centres, or to those cities and regions where industry and an industrial infrastructure already exist.

Furthermore, even those enterprises which have been constructed in rural areas or small and medium cities have not necessarily drawn most of their new personnel from the intended sources – that is, either from the agricultural or private subsidiary economic sectors or from among the indigenous Central Asian population. On the contrary, studies undertaken throughout the 1970s indicate that as new enterprises are opened in Uzbekistan's rural or mainly indigenous areas, they are often staffed largely by Europeans, and/or by individuals from non-agricultural sectors. This is often true whether the aim is to open new industrial enterprises in small cities, to open industrial enterprises in new lands; or to open or staff new non-industrial or trade or service organisations in the countryside.

For example, one study undertaken in Uzbekistan in the early 1970s dealt directly with the question of staffing new enterprises with indigenous personnel. Despite the predominance of Uzbeks in the Fergana Valley, this study noted, a large share of the personnel in the new enterprises located there was being drawn from non-Central Asian populations – whether from among local Europeans or in-migrants from other republics. The study was comprised of thirteen new enter-

prises in five cities in the Fergana Valley, ranging from heavy industries, such as construction material and mechanical engineering plants,
to light industries such as textile and silk factories.[59] Although Uzbeks
comprised more than 66 per cent of the total population of the cities
where the enterprises were located, they comprised only about 45% of
the new cadres – as against 37 per cent for the Russians. In addition,
the traditional division of employment among nationalities was also
glaringly maintained, and particularly with regard to Uzbek women.
The indigenous nationalities were primarily attracted to light industry
and food industries: while Uzbeks comprised over 70 per cent of the
new cadres brought into the textile factories, they comprised only 10
per cent of the 819 new workers and employees in the fertiliser factory.
Sexual divisions by nationality were maintained: most of the Uzbeks
attracted to the new industries were male (54 per cent), while most of
the Russians, or almost 70 per cent, were female; and in the heavy
industrial sectors, few, if any indigenous women were represented.
While Uzbeks comprised 27 per cent and 11 per cent of the new
entrants to the two industrial construction materials enterprises, not
one of the Uzbeks was female.

Other studies, moreover, suggest that only a small share of personnel in new industrial enterprises continues to be drawn from the
agricultural or private subsidiary sectors, whether the enterprises have
been constructed in small urban areas or in the countryside. As one
Soviet scholar in Uzbekistan noted in 1976, between 1966 and 1976
only 2.5–3 per cent of all new personnel in a 'representative sample' of
new enterprises came from the household and private sector.[60] As
Ubaidullaeva noted in 1974:

> Studies on the processes of formation of the labour force in Uzbekis-
> tan's new industrial enterprises indicate that even in *oblasts* where a
> surplus of agricultural labour resources essential for employment in
> other sectors of the economy exists, this rich source is insufficiently
> used in providing workers.[61]

As but one example, Ubaidullaeva notes that of 2500 workers who
came to the Namangan Silk and Men's Fabric Combine in 1969, only
520, or 16 per cent were former collective farmers; and of 5867 people
who entered new industrial enterprises in the Fergana Valley, only
5–7 per cent were former collective-farm women.[62] At 1 November
1970, Uzbeks who came directly from collective and state farms
comprised only 0.8 per cent of the industrial production personnel of

such large plants in Uzbekistan as a major tractor assembly plant and the Chirchik Agricultural Machinery Plant (*Cherihiksel'mash*), and migrants from rural areas comprised only 2 per cent of the workers of the Tashkent Agricultural Machinery Plant (*Tashsel'mash*).[63] As Ata Mirzaev noted in the late 1970s, in general 'the indigenous rural population participates to a very low extent in building the republic's working class'.[64]

Another study conducted in Uzbekistan in the mid-1970s found the situation unchanged in the case of enterprises constructed in the Hungry Steppe. Of all new personnel in construction organisations in the Hungry Steppe, this study found, more than 70 per cent changed jobs to work in a different sector after migrating. None the less, more than half the new personnel (about 56 per cent) had formerly worked in another sector of industry or construction. Only 14 per cent of the personnel had been drawn from agriculture, and only about 12.5 per cent, from the service sector (Table 4.7).[65]

TABLE 4.7   *Sectors of the economy in which migrants formerly worked before moving to construction organisations or enterprises in the Hungry and Karshi Steppes (percentages)*

Industry	22.7
Construction organisations	17.6
Agriculture	14.0
Enterprises of construction industry	12.7
Service sphere	12.5
School graduates	21.5

SOURCE   A. S. Chamkin, *'Motivy k trudu v sfere obshchestvennogo proizvodst-va'*, doctoral dissertation, Tashkent, 1976, p. 75.

Finally, a local study conducted on the composition of personnel in trade and the services in rural areas of Tashkent *oblast'* (1971) indicates that the picture is not necessarily much brighter with regard to non-industrial sectors in the countryside. Of a total of 1097 new workers and employees in the consumer co-operative in Tashkent *oblast'*, for example, only 300 (27 per cent) had been drawn from agriculture, and only 29 per cent from the non-productive sphere. Of 347 new service personnel, only 81 (23 per cent) had been drawn from agriculture, while an almost equal number (77) had been drawn from industry. A disproportionately low number of new personnel, moreover, were indigenous: of the 347 new people drawn into the

TABLE 4.8 Selected survey data on trade and service personnel in rural areas of Tashkent Oblast'. 1971

	Personnel of Trade Co-operative						Personnel in Service Sphere					
	Total Number	of whom men	of whom women	Total as %	of whom men	of whom women	Total Number	of whom men	of whom women	Total as %	of whom men	of whom women
A. Sources of Formation of Labour Force: Total	1097	538	559	100	49.0	51.0	347	168	179	100	48.4	51.6
of which:												
First job	89	44	45	100	49.4	50.6	30	5	25	100	16.6	83.4
From agriculture	300	178	122	100	59.3	40.7	81	39	42	100	48.1	51.9
From industrial sectors	145	58	77	100	40.0	60.0	77	48	29	100	62.3	37.7
From non-productive sphere	315	166	149	100	52.7	47.3	137	68	69	100	49.6	50.4
By assignment	235	89	146	100	37.8	62.2	22	8	14	100	36.4	63.6
B. Nationality Composition												
Total	1097	538	559	100	49.0	51.0	347	168	179	100	48.4	51.6
of which:												
Uzbeks	574	386	188	100	67.2	32.8	137	58	78	100	42.3	57.7
Russians	141	26	115	100	18.4	81.6	70	28	42	100	40.0	60.0
Tatars	145	31	114	100	21.4	78.6	52	27	25	100	51.9	48.1
Koreans	84	11	74	100	13.1	86.9	39	4	35	100	10.3	89.7
Other	221	93	123	100	42.1	57.9	110	54	56	100	49.1	50.9

SOURCE R. A. Ubaidullaeva, ('Regional'nye problemy razmeshcheniia i effektivnost' ispol'zovaniia trudovykh resursov v Uzbekskoi SSR'), doctoral dissertation, Tashkent, 1974; Survey Data Appendix.

service sector, less than 40 per cent were Uzbek, while just over 20 per cent were Russians, and mainly Russian women. Of the 1097 new personnel in the co-operative trade organisation, about 50 per cent were Uzbek, while about 12.5 per cent were Russian – and again mainly Russian women. Of the combined total for both groups, then less than 26 per cent had been drawn from agriculture; only 49 per cent of all new personnel were Uzbeks and only 18 per cent of the total number of new personnel were Uzbek women. (Table 4.8).[66]

The fact that new entrants to these enterprises do not come from the labour surplus sectors or areas of Uzbekistan leads to yet another problem in labour use there. It means that very often the labour force in these new enterprises is created at the expense of existing local enterprises, often leaving the latter with their own labour shortages. As the same author writes, 'cadres are completed mostly by attracting personnel from local enterprises and organisations; these in turn therefore lose a sufficiently large number of their skilled cadres. This naturally, must reflect negatively on their work'.[67]

Thus, some progress has been made towards drawing more members of the indigenous nationalities into industry and towards relocating the rural population into non-agricultural sectors. On the whole however, efforts to staff new non-agricultural enterprises with indigenous Central Asians, and especially with workers released from agricultural production, have not been entirely successful; the process is proceeding at a very slow rate.

ORGANISATION OF LABOUR

In addition to these policies, and in response to the difficulties in altering the sectoral and locational distribution of Uzbekistan's labour force, Soviet planners have begun to emphasise the necessity for better organising labour in existing enterprises and in rural areas. Even though immense imbalances exist in the sectoral and locational distribution of labour, misuse of existing resources only compounds the problem in both agricultural and industrial work. Despite existing labour surpluses in agriculture, for example, and the increasing number of non-working collective farm members, hundreds of thousands of urban students and professionals are sent to the countryside each year to help handpick the cotton crop. This phenomenon, moreover, is more than simply the result of seasonality and the higher demand for labour at harvest time. Many collective farmers choose not

o work at this time; the use of students and professionals for agricul-
ural work is also a direct reflection of the use, or misuse of agricultural
abour.[68]

According to Ubaidullaeva, for example:

A general characteristic of collective farms is that all work is done by
collective farmers; workers and specialists are only called in from
the side when those specialists are not available on the collective
farm, or when work in the collective farm cannot be finished on time
by the collective farm's labour alone. Paradoxically, however, in the
republic's collective farms, including in the most densely-populated
oblasts, labour of people called in from the side is used not in light of
a shortage, but with a surplus of the collective farm's own labour
resources and with a high level of mechanisation of the production
processes.[69]

n 1971, she noted, about 60 000 city dwellers were called to work in
Jzbekistan's collective farms, while more than 20 000 collective far-
ners of the able-bodied ages, 'at the very height of the harvest work'
lid not participate in collective farm work. At the same time, the
ggregate amount of working time spent on the farm declined: it was 4
er cent lower than it had been in July, and 5 per cent lower than the
verage aggregate time worked in industry. On the whole, in the
nonth of November 1971, the number of man-days worked per
ollective farmer was 20 per cent lower than in July, even though the
umber of man-days worked by outsiders in Uzbekistan's collective
arms remained high during that same period.[70] As Table 4.9 illus-
rates, between 1960 and 1970 the number of outsiders grew by 15 500
eople (24 per cent). Throughout the 1970s, the number of outsiders
vorking in Uzbekistan's collective farms did not diminish.

TABLE 4.9   *Use of outsiders in collective farms of Uzbekistan*

	1960	1965	1970	1971
Average annual number of outsiders in agricultural work	67 300	81 500	82 800	82 000
Number of collective farmers not working a single man-day	58 800	29 300	20 700	18 000

SOURCE   R. A. Ubaidullaeva, 'Regional'nye problemy razmeshcheniia i
effektivnost' ispol'zovaniia trudovykh resursov v Uzbekskoi SSR',
doctoral dissertation, Tashkent, 1974, pp. 256–7.

In other words, non-agricultural populations are used for work on collective farms during the harvest even when labour surpluses exist on Uzbekistan's farms. Throughout the 1970s the number of outsiders participating in the harvest remained high even in the labour-surplus collective farms of the Fergana Valley, where the level of outside personnel was about 6–7000 people each year. As Ubaidullaeva described six collective farms in Namangan oblast:

> as a result of insufficiently using their own labour resources, these collective farms, calculated per 100 hectares of arable land, each lose 133 man-days of collective farmers' valuable time. By thus sensing a labour shortage, these collective farms run to the services of people attracted to agricultural work from the side, in order to fulfill their production plan.

In the collective farms of this group, the average yearly amount of actual time worked in social production was only about 165 man-days per able-bodied collective farmer; the 'irrational expenditures' associated with the process of using outside labour on these farms were estimated to be about 76 000 roubles.[71] As another Uzbek scholar estimated, if all the collective farms of just one of Uzbekistan's *oblasts* in 1973 had used their existing reserves of labour correctly, then agricultural output, with an unchanged level of labour expenditure, would have exceeded actual output by 42 per cent.[72]

Similarly, despite the labour shortages in industry, this sector, as elsewhere in the USSR, is also guilty of immense misuse of labour; and in both sectors of the economy, specialist labour, so desperately needed, is wasted. The wastage caused by overmanning, poor time use, absenteeism, turnover, etc. is discussed in Chapter 2. In addition, despite shortages of skilled workers in many sectors of industry and construction, many of the existing trained workers and employees do not work according to the level of their education and skills; rather, they are in lower-level jobs and occupations. In 1970 for example, about 3000 specialists with higher education in Uzbekistan's economy were employed in jobs which did not demand a higher education.[73] In the same year, only about 50 per cent of the agronomists and veterinarians with a higher education and only about 70 per cent of those with specialised secondary education were working in agriculture 'while the remainder were employed in sectors not at all connected with agriculture'.[74] Research in industrial enterprises in Uzbekistan showed that only 58 per cent of the engineers and 48 per cent of the echnicians were working in their specialty.[75] Among engineering-echnical personnel (*inzhenerno-tekhnicheskie rabotniki*, or ITR) in he Tashkent Tractor Factory, only 26–50 per cent of working-time vas spent on fulfilling basic functions of engineering-technical work; he remainder was devoted to functions 'not at all connected with the esponsibilities of ITR work' and primarily demanding few, if any kills.[76] By the early 1980s, moreover, the situation had barely changed, and was generating significant official concern, perhaps best llustrated by Brezhnev's speech in Tashkent in March 1982. Speaking n Uzbekistan, he commented that 'unfortunately specialists among ou are quite often used as they should not be'. He criticised the general misuse of specialists throughout the economy, especially in Jzbekistan's collective and state farms.[77] Again, examples of poor utilisation of labour are many.

Finally, Soviet planners have increasingly begun to emphasise other organisational changes – such as two-shift work, part-time work and imilar measures – as yet another means of countering under-employment and structural dislocations in manpower use, given Uzbekistan's low level of capital investment and high level of labour availability. Existing levels of two-shift work, for example, are exceedingly low in Uzbekistan, leaving ample opportunity for expansion provided that inputs can be increased to sustain an extra shift. In a tudy of 465 enterprises in Uzbekistan conducted in the early 1970s, 45 enterprises (75 per cent of the total) had less then two shifts, or a oefficient of two-shift work less than 2. The level of two-shift work, moreover, was especially low in small cities where labour surpluses are particularly severe, and in local industries and construction industries each with a coefficient of 1.1), and in mechanical engineering (1.4). Especially since mechanical engineering is one of the main sectors of ndustry in Uzbekistan (with 40 per cent of all workers in heavy ndustry employed there) possibilities for expanding job opportunities hrough two-shift work are deemed extremely promising. Of the light ndustrial enterprises surveyed, many had only one shift, and most of hose were located in small cities.[78] In the study of 465 enterprises, herefore, the author concluded that an additional 111 200 people ould be employed in those enterprises alone if two-shift work were to e organised 'which would increase by more than 30 per cent the umber of personnel now employed'.[79] These conclusions were considered particularly important in addressing the need to raise the participation of the indigenous nationalities in social production.

None the less, aside from acknowledging the importance of better organising agricultural work, better using skilled workers in industry, and expanding two-shift work in all sectors, the effects of policies designed to reorganise labour use have also been minimal. Despite official appeals for a more rational use of the agricultural manpower surplus, thousands of students are still sent to the fields every autumn, leaving Uzbekistan's urban areas for up to three months at a time. Skilled personnel are still found in manual and low-level occupations in all sectors of the economy. And if the past decade provides any record to go on, one should be wary of undue optimism in terms of the ability of two-shift work to provide significantly greater job opportunities as well. Despite calls for the expansion of two-shift work in Uzbekistan, the level actually declined during the early part of the 1970s. According to Ubaidullaeva, the proportion of all industrial workers working two-shift work in Uzbekistan diminished significantly, especially in mechanical engineering, in construction, and in local industries where opportunities for employment of indigenous Central Asians was considered most promising.[80]

Even if successful, moreover, many of these same organisational policies would also have the serious opposite effect of releasing more manpower into the unused labour pool than is presently projected from natural growth, migration, and from household and private subsidiary work alone. Between 1966 and 1970, for example, enterprises under the system of the Ministry of Cotton Ginning Industry in Uzbekistan spent approximately 67 million roubles carrying out measures for the 'technological perfection of production'. While the economic effect was estimated to be a savings of several million roubles, hundreds of individuals were also released from work there and needed to be provided with work elsewhere. With regard to the 1970s, according to Tashkulova, 'the constant modernisation of existing equipment, the introduction of new technology, and mechanisation and automatisation of labour-intensive production processes', while permitting an economic saving perhaps as high as 300 million roubles during the ninth Five-Year Plan, also freed over 20 000 people during the same time-span who needed to find work elsewhere.[81]

With particular regard to women in Uzbekistan, policy discussion in Uzbekistan has begun to focus on two main means of encouraging women to enter the labour force in greater numbers: greater provision of goods and services, and provision for part-time work. The XXVI Party Congress placed increased emphasis on greater provision of consumer goods and labour-saving services for the coming five- and ten-year plans. Among the points envisaged for the eleventh five-year lan (1981–5) were 'raising the level and perfecting the structure of consumption of material goods and services'; 'improving their quality and widening their range'; 'facilitating work in the home'; 'raising the standard of all kinds of services' and 'expanding the advantages and benefits for families having children and for working mothers'.[82] At the same time, the idea of providing women with shorter working-days is apparently becoming a serious consideration in the formulation of present employment policies.[83]

None the less, the extremely low level of goods and services in Uzbekistan still suggests that Soviet planners are unlikely to create enough labour-saving devices to free a significant number of women from the household sector in the near future. As mentioned in Chapter 2, only about 13 per cent of all children aged 1–7 in Uzbekistan can be accommodated in kindergartens and nurseries. The most optimistic projections advanced by Soviet scholars suggest that the proportion may reach as high as 33 per cent of all children in the 1–7 age group by 1990, but most projections suggest that even this level is unrealistic, and that a high degree of female employment in household work will by necessity be retained for some time to come.[84] Furthermore, offering part-time work for women appears to be presenting the same problems as in other parts of the USSR, such as combining flexible work-shifts with standardised production schedules, adjusting payment norms, etc. Thus, little has been implemented along these lines so far in Uzbekistan, and most women still face the option of either full-time work or none at all. 'Far into the future' an Uzbek writes:

> with the development of the productive forces of society, the necessity for household work – connected with the preparation of food, laundry, repairing an apartment, etc. – will disappear. Economic conditions will be created such that carrying out the household economy will become counterproductive for the family itself, not just for society as a whole. 'The household economy,', M. V. Solodkov and R. N. Samar feel, 'will outlive itself economically only at the stage of communism, when the needs of the family for food, clothes, shoes, living space, etc. will be satisfied free of charge, in accordance to need, from the social consumption funds.[85]

However realistic the prediction, however, it appears that the low availability of employment opportunities, low levels of goods and services and low levels of education and training among indigenous women will continue to keep a large component of Uzbekistan's

female Central Asian population occupied outside production, i
household and private subsidiary work, for some time to come.

In his speech of March 1982, Brezhnev referred to the sectora
imbalances and generally poor use of labour in Uzbekistan, and calle
for more effective policy measures to combat them – sentiment
echoed in Andropov's speech nine months later:

> The full use of labour resources is very important. It is no secret tha
> in this republic there is still a labour surplus, especially in th
> countryside. At the same time, in a series of sectors of industry an
> construction, there are not enough working hands. For this reason
> for example, one quarter of the capabilities of the Tashkent Textil
> Combine and one half of the Bukharan Textile Combine are no
> being fully used. It is essential to take serious measures – to organis
> study, create incentives for personnel, raise the consciousness o
> people. Here lies a great amount of work for the Party and Sovie
> organs, and for the Komsomol.[86]

There is no reason to doubt the sincerity of Brezhnev's or Andropov'
words. Nor is there any reason to doubt that change is occurring i
Uzbekistan, and that efforts to utilise workers and specialists mor
efficiently, particularly from among the indigenous nationalities, hav
not been altogether without success. The problem is the rate at whicl
these changes are occurring, because simultaneously, population pres
sures continue to grow in rural areas, in small cities and towns, and i
sectors where indigenous Central Asians form the vast majority of th
labour force.

Part II

The Problem: Politics and Economics

To summarise Part I, Uzbekistan's economy has grown and diversified immensely since the Revolution, as has the number of indigenous Central Asians working in all sectors of the labour force. None the less, a fairly sharp division in the employment of the indigenous and non-indigenous nationalities – and particularly of indigenous and non-indigenous women – still persists. The indigenous nationalities in Uzbekistan comprise the vast majority of the population not working in social production, while Europeans are overrepresented in the socialised labour force. Europeans dominate the highly technical or heavy industrial sectors of Uzbekistan's economy, while the indigenous nationalities are concentrated in agriculture, the service sectors or in the light and food industries. The indigenous nationalities live mainly in the least-developed small and medium-size cities in Uzbekistan with fewest prospects for development, while Europeans are disproportionately represented in the large cities or industrial centres. Because of different population growth rates and only partly effective policies, these disparities are widening.

A logical conclusion to be drawn from this situation is that questions of labour and nationality will inevitably lead to a growth of political tension in Uzbekistan. By examining the data, it seems appropriate to conclude that the indigenous nationalities must be dissatisfied with the economic and social position they hold in their own republic today, and that, as disparities widen, they will undoubtedly demand entrance into European-dominated regions and jobs tomorrow. Many Western observers have therefore drawn three conclusions from this situation: that the indigenous nationalities are discriminated against; that they are consequently disadvantaged, both economically and socially, compared with the Slavs in their midst; and that as population pressures

149

intensify, political pressures will grow as well. If these conclusions are correct, the labour situation would only exacerbate broader economic and social tensions which are growing in Uzbek society at large, and trigger perhaps dramatic expressions of political unrest. Indeed, one Western observer has cited questions of labour and employment in Soviet Central Asia as among 'the most major problems' threatening the cohesion of the USSR today.[1]

While there is no doubt some truth to these conclusions, however, other variables have tended to mitigate or change the situation as well. The purpose of Part II, therefore, is to analyse some of these other variables, to suggest what the political implications of Uzbekistan's labour situation in fact may be. Each of the following chapters discusses one of these commonly-drawn conclusions. After a brief elaboration of the conclusions themselves, Chapter 5 discusses the question of discrimination and to whose advantage labour and nationality politics in Uzbekistan in fact work. It discusses hiring practices and job preferences in Uzbekistan to determine which nationality groups have access to desired opportunities and where nationality preferences in fact lie. Chapters 6 and 7 discuss the questions of material and social subordination: they examine real incomes (Chapter 6) and tradition and culture (Chapter 7) to determine which occupations in Uzbekistan in fact provide the highest incomes and the greatest prestige. Finally, Chapter 8 discusses somewhat revised political implications which take these other factors into account. The ways in which these additional factors may affect and be manifested among the various nationalities in Uzbekistan's labour force constitute among the most crucial components of any discussion of labour use in Uzbekistan designed to extend beyond employment *per se* into the realm of politics.

5 Who Gets Hired for What?

COMMON ASSUMPTIONS

The political implications of the labour situation described above constitute an extremely important issue in Soviet Central Asia, but there is some debate as to just how. As suggested, several Western observers have drawn three main conclusions from Uzbekistan's labour situation. The first is that in order for this situation to be the case, the indigenous nationalities in Soviet Uzbekistan must undoubtedly be discriminated against in their own republic. These writers feel that the relative failures of Soviet policies to date indicate that these efforts are only verbiage to conceal an overall discriminatory policy against the Central Asians. Because of their implicit strategic nature, it is assumed, most industrial and technical enterprises in Uzbekistan are staffed primarily with Russians and Slavs, to ensure greater political reliability and efficiency. Similarly, most of the new industrial cities and regions springing up in Soviet Asia are built along Russian and European lines, dramatically different and alien from the traditions and culture of the local nationalities. Thus, despite the fact that the non-working population may be rising among the indigenous nationalities, these writers feel that entry of the local nationalities into the more modern and labour-deficient sectors is impeded by both blatant and subtle discrimination. The indigenous nationalities are assumed to be directly denied entrance into some sectors; and their poor knowledge of Russian, the presence of hostile environments and other subtle forms of discrimination impede them from entering others. As Asian-dominated sectors become increasingly saturated with manpower, the argument goes, Russians continue to migrate for available industrial and technical jobs, apparently pre-empting the occupations which there is an increasing need for indigenous people to fill.[1]

Following this assumption, the second common conclusion is that because of the higher wages and higher prestige accorded personnel in the industrial and technical sectors in the USSR, the indigenous nationalities are disadvantaged, both materially and socially, *vis-à-vis* the European nationalities living within their own homeland. By concentrating in the service sectors and agriculture and in the least developed locations, it is assumed, the indigenous nationalities apparently earn lower wages and are accorded lower prestige than the Europeans in their midst. Since entry into industrial work, moreover, apparently requires not only training, but migration to European-dominated cities and regions, life in an alien environment, and competition with more highly skilled Europeans for jobs in enterprises where Russians already form the vast majority of personnel, the indigenous nationalities are also deemed to have few prospects for advancement. As one Western scholar writes:

> Muslims predominate in agriculture and stockbreeding, while Russians predominate in such technical fields as mechanical engineering, communications and building and finance as well as in industry ... The status of Muslims in the economy is therefore still subordinate to that of the Russians.[2]

The third conclusion is that as population pressures intensify, as sectoral and locational imbalances grow, as the sectors in which the Asians now predominate become saturated with manpower, as educational attainment and mobility among the indigenous nationalities increase and as the locals become increasingly cognisant that higher earnings and greater prestige can be attained elsewhere, the indigenous nationalities will begin demanding entrance into cities, sectors and enterprises which traditionally have been dominated by Europeans. The result is expected to be increased competition between the indigenous and non-indigenous nationalities for scarce desirable jobs to which the former, in the view of these writers, have long been denied access.

If these assumptions are correct, their implications in political terms would be enormous. As Massell correctly notes, a sense of deprivation on the part of any ethnic or national group in itself creates a taut situation. 'It is precisely at such a time of perceived deprivation and discrimination that inchoate and disparate perceptions of a separate cultural and ethnic identity may most readily be fused into a powerful sense of solidarity.'[3] As Massell notes, growing demographic and economic pressures in Uzbekistan would only compound these tensions and accentuate other areas of discontent. In other words, as pressures build, the argument goes, ethnic- and class-consciousness might well fuse into a powerful political force, as indigenous Central Asians become more aware of their status both as a distinct ethnic group and as a deprived social and economic class. The end-result would be the prospect of growing tension in Uzbekistan which would threaten not only stability within the area, but some of the very levers of control upon which Moscow has relied for decades.

The requirement of modernisation and the inter-ethnic co-operation have led masses of men and women to shed traditional ties, to acquire needed skills, and to move to fill the newly available roles and positions, in the expectation that these positions are without exception theirs to fill. However, the imperatives of security and control have dictated the continued entrenchment of Slavs in authoritative, supervisory, and management positions in minority republics, especially in Central Asia. These conflicting imperatives may well lead to role-saturation in the region and deepening native frustration.[4]

While there is undoubtedly some truth in all of these conclusions, however, one is also led to question why it has been so difficult to attract the indigenous nationalities into social production, particularly in the industrial and priority sectors, even when they have been accorded preference in hiring practices. Even when enterprises have been built close to Central Asians' homes and demanded little change in their life-styles, Soviet planners have failed to attract large numbers of indigenous Central Asians to the higher-paying, more-prestigious industrial and technical sectors. Even when urban living conditions (aside from containing smaller private plots) are not so qualitatively different from ways of life in the countryside, the vast majority of the indigenous rural populations have uniformly refused the wage and other incentives to move to the cities and towns, or to new agricultural lands. In short, even when opportunities have been offered precisely to the indigenous populations, there still has been no sign that Central Asians in fact desire those jobs which Europeans hold. Indeed, most indications have implied the opposite, that indigenous Central Asians actively resist efforts encouraging them to take these jobs. Ultimately one is led to question, therefore, whether the ethnic employment structure in Uzbekistan is solely the result of discrimination against the indigenous nationalities – that is, whether it is merely the result of acquiescence on the part of the indigenous nationalities to hidden unfair hiring practices, regardless of the expressed aims of Soviet policies – or whether other factors are playing a role, making the situation more mixed and changing the political implications inherent in it.

NATIONALITY HIRING PRACTICES: 'AFFIRMATIVE ACTION' AND NEPOTISM

The commitment on the part of Soviet planners to attract more of the local nationalities into the socialised labour force, and particularly into the industrial sectors, is described above. So, too, is the ambivalence which this commitment has reflected over more than sixty-five years of Soviet rule. From the first five year plan on, members of the indigenous nationalities were to be brought into all sectors and occupations of the economy, but certain key positions and sectors were to be staffed by Europeans. Indigenous Central Asians were to be trained to staff highly-skilled positions; but in the meantime, it was certainly easier for enterprise managers or individuals, under pressure to fulfil their plans, to transfer workers and specialists from outside the republic and to give preference to Russians and other non-indigenous groups within Uzbekistan who already had the necessary training. Today, the same ambivalence persists: despite the continued stress on creating workers and specialists from among the local nationalities, certain jobs in Uzbekistan are reserved exclusively for Europeans. In addition, there is often a great temptation for local managers to give preference to non-indigenous personnel in jobs demanding particular skills or a high degree of efficiency or reliability.

As already mentioned, however, the jobs reserved for Europeans are limited in number. And otherwise, in the vast majority of sectors and occupations in Uzbekistan's economy, a type of 'affirmative action' has been implemented, to meet quotas generally in favour of the indigenous nationalities. As will be illustrated, while *de jure* jobs and opportunities are to be allocated in Uzbekistan irrespective of race or nationality, the local nationalities, *de facto*, generally have greater access to employment and training opportunities than do the Europeans residing in Uzbekistan. The indigenous nationalities receive priority treatment in entrance to many training programmes; once enrolled, grading policy is often easier for them; and upon graduation, more jobs are available to them than to their European counterparts. Should an enterprise manager hire too many Russians, in fact, he will risk accountability for actions contrary to the spirit of Soviet cadre policy and may suffer unpleasant consequences.

Indeed, over the past several years, this type of 'implicit' affirmative-action policy has slowly become a well-entrenched and often explicitly stated part of official Soviet policy. In separate interviews, over forty directors of institutes, enterprises and government establishments stressed to me the importance of giving local nationalities 'more opportunities' in hiring procedures, even if their qualifications are not as high as those of the Slavs. A Russian professor at Leningrad University explained that it is 'natural' and 'taken for granted' in almost all republics of the USSR that 'privileges will be accorded the local people within the boundaries of their own republics'. As a member of the faculty of the Tashkent Pharmacology Institute explained 'The Russians have their republic where they can study. If they are not accepted to this institute, they can always study at an institute in the RSFSR. But if an Uzbek is not accepted here, where else can he go? For this reason, preference for locals is necessary, and is becoming well institutionalised.' Indeed, two émigré scholars, V. Zaslavskii and Yuri Luryi, noted as late as 1979 that 'the role of nationality as a factor of preference or discrimination has increased more and more'.[5]

Thus, during the past decade – except for a very limited number of occupations – the education and employment situation in Uzbekistan has assumed a character where nationality preferences are expressed overtly at every step of an individual's career, from education to employment opportunities to job security. Places in higher and specialised secondary educational establishments, for example, are supposedly free and allocated strictly on the basis of merit. In practice, however, entrance to higher education in Uzbekistan is extremely costly and nationality often plays a greater role than does merit in acceptance procedures. Implicit, if not explicit, quotas have been established in all educational establishments above the tenth class, generally biased in favour of the indigenous nationalities.

In 1978, for example, out of a total of about 3000 applicants (of whom 2243 were indigenous) to the Bukhara State Pedagogical Institute, 825 people (of whom 718 were indigenous) were accepted.[6]

TABLE 5.1 *Competition for admission to selected higher and specialised secondary educational establishments, Uzbekistan, by sex and nationality, 1978*

Educational Establishment	Applicants				Acceptances				% of given category accepted			
	Total	Indige-nous	Women	Indig. Women	Total	Indige-nous	Women	Indig. Women	Total	Indige-nous	Women	Indig. Women
Total Minvuz	38 507	29 527	12 007	8 359	13 255	9 456	4 488	3 051	34	32	37	36
% of total	100	77	31	22	100	71	34	23				
Selected Institutes												
Tashkent Polytechnic	9 133	7 015	1 772	852	3 815	2 531	842	422	42	36	48	50
% of total	100	77	19	9	100	66	33	11				
Tashkent University	5 937	4 640	2 569	1 768	1 925	1 298	832	507	32	28	32	29
% of total	100	78	43	30	100	67	43	26				
Samarkand University	2 849	2 442	1 293	1 013	1 170	771	488	363	41	32	38	36
% of total	100	86	45	36	100	66	42	31				
Nukus University	2 023	1 867	959	936	855	700	371	347	42	37	39	37
% of total	100	92	47	46	100	82	43	41				
Bukhara Institute of Light & Food Industry	1 705	1 021	434	338	385	335	101	79	23	33	23	23
% of total	100	60	25	20	100	87	26	21				
Tashkent Auto and Road Institute	3 433	2 804	308	148	825	572	73	37	24	20	24	25
% of total	100	82	9	4	100	69	9	4				
Fergana Polytechnic	2 615	1 962	556	378	765	600	220	155	29	31	40	41
% of total	100	75	21	14	100	78	29	20				
Total Minpros	26 456	21 956	13 850	12 025	7 450	6 146	3 825	2 908	28	28	28	24
% of total	100	83	52	45	100	83	51	39				
Selected Institutes												
Tashkent Pedagogical Institute	5 700	4 893	3 613	2 976	1 200	912	698	488	21	19	19	16
% of total	100	86	63	52	100	76	58	41				
Fergana Pedagogical Institute	3 228	2 285	1 403	1 060	775	635	430	340	24	28	31	32
% of total	100	71	43	33	100	82	55	44				

Bukhara Pedagogical Institute	2987	2243	1381	1272	825	718	381	302	28	32	24
% of total	100	75	46	43	100	87	46	37			
Andizhan Pedagogical Institute	1285	1127	671	607	375	331	187	168	29	29	28
% of total	100	88	52	47	100	88	50	45			
Samarkand Pedagogical Institute	1128	933	415	374	500	452	348	120	44	48	32
% of total	100	83	37	33	100	90	70	24			
Tashkent Oblast' Pedagogical Institute	1086	850	574	490	375	328	178	157	35	39	32
% of total	100	78	53	45	100	87	47	42			
Other Ministries and Organisations	39051	31798	13467	9708	10968	7784	3812	2531	28	24	26
% of total	100	81	34	25	100	71	35	26			
Selected Institutes											
Tashkent Institute of Engineers of Railway Transport	2058	1137	706	189	733	295	293	62	36	26	33
% of total	100	55	34	9	100	40	40	9			
Tashkent Institute of Communications	1523	863	471	171	675	344	224	83	44	40	49
% of total	100	57	31	11	100	51	33	12			
Institute of Irrigation and Mechanisation of Agriculture	5624	4980	638	420	1625	1414	203	133	29	28	32
% of total	100	89	11	7	100	87	12	8			
Tashkent Conservatory	317	105	197	43	190	92	122	50	60	88	116
% of total	100	33	62	14	100	48	64	26			
Tashkent Agricultural Institute	3786	3682	436	397	935	930	118	85	25	25	21
% of total	100	97	12	10	100	99	13	9			

SOURCE Ministry of Higher and Specialised Secondary Education, May, 1979.

Thus, competition for entrance to the institute was one out of every three applicants for the indigenous nationalities, and one out of seven for the non-indigenous applicants. Similar levels of competition were reflected in admissions data for the Fergana, Dzhizak, Samarkand and Tashkent *oblast'* Pedagogical Institutes.[7] The same bias in educational acceptance procedures was evident in several non-pedagogical institutes as well: in the Tashkent State Conservatory, indigenous Central Asians comprised 33 per cent of the applicants and 48 per cent of the entering class. In some industrial sectors, such as the Bukhara Technological Institute of Light and Food Industry, the disparity was even larger (Table 5.1).[8]

This is not to suggest, of course, that competition is uniformly lower among the indigenous nationalities than it is among the Europeans in Uzbekistan. As Table 5.1 also illustrates, occasionally admissions are biased in favour of the non-indigenous nationalities; rarely, however, is that bias very large. For the most part, Soviet acceptance procedures seem to be oriented towards awarding the indigenous nationalities between 66 and 80 per cent of the acceptances for each educational establishment. In only six of Uzbekistan's forty-two higher and specialised secondary educational establishments did Central Asians comprise less than 66 per cent of the entering-class in 1978, while they comprised over 80 per cent of the entering-class in eighteen of the establishments. Because of the number and quality of the indigenous applicants, it seems safe to assume that where competition is dramatically different among the nationalities it is generally weighted in favour of the indigenous nationalities, and often especially in favour of indigenous women.

Similar regional quotas have been established for most institutes weighted in favour of the lesser-developed *oblasts* and locations. As Table 5.2 illustrates, for example, 85–90 per cent of all qualified applicants from the Karakalpak ASSR and from Dzhizak, Namangan and Surkhandar'ya *oblasts* were accepted to educational establishments under the Ministry of Higher and Specialised Secondary Education (Minvuz) and the Ministry of Education (Minpros) in 1978. All these regions are among the lesser-developed in Uzbekistan and are mainly indigenous in composition.[9] On the other hand, less than 75 per cent of the qualified applicants – and less than 26 per cent of the total number of applicants – from Tashkent and Bukhara *oblasts* were accepted for admission. These *oblasts* are among the more highly-developed *oblasts* in Uzbekistan, with the largest percentage of Slavs. Given the fact that the quality of applicants on the whole was often

TABLE 5.2 *Acceptances for educational establishments under Minvuz and Minpros by* oblast', *Uzbekistan, 1978*

Oblast'	Number applicants	Number Passing exam	Number accepted	% applicants who passed exam	% qualified applicants accepted
Karakalpak ASSR	4541	1227	1117	27	91
Andizhan *oblast'*	4467	1506	1257	33	83
Bukhara *oblast'*	5922	1984	1465	34	74
Dzhizak *oblast'*	3083	1278	1123	41	88
Kashkadar'ya *oblast'*	6685	2173	1675	33	77
Namangan *oblast'*	3323	1185	1011	36	85
Samarkand *oblast'*	9295	3458	2871	37	83
Surkhandar'ya *oblast'*	4585	1311	1117	29	85
Syrdar'ya *oblast'*	2599	989	784	38	79
Tashkent *oblast'*	9482	3422	2480	36	72
Fergana *oblast'*	5236	1683	1362	32	81
Khorezm *oblast'*	3833	1453	1087	38	75
Tashkent city	11620	6149	4901	53	79
From other republics	6045	2187	2026	36	93
Total	80716	30005	24276	37	81

SOURCE Data from the Ministry of Higher and Specialised Secondary Education (Tashkent, UzSSR, May, 1979).

lower in the former group than in the latter, the data suggest at least some degree of 'affirmative action' on the part of Soviet planners.

The same situation is perhaps more sharply illustrated within individual institutes. Planned intake for the Tashkent Pedagogical Institute (TashPI) in 1978 was approximately 100–50 people from each of the *oblasts* of Andizhan, Samarkand, and Kashkadar'ya, even though the number of applicants differed markedly. Planned competition for entrance, therefore, ranged from one acceptance out of every two applicants in Andizhan *oblast,* to one out of every six in Kashkadar'ya *oblast.* In the final selection, virtually all the qualified applicants from the Karakalpak ASSR and from the Andizhan, Dzhizak, Namangan, Syrdar'ya, and Fergana *oblasts* were accepted for admission, as against 89 per cent of those who passed the exam in Tashkent *oblast.*[10]

Similarly, the Tashkent Institute of Communications, with a ratio of applications to acceptances of 3:1, is considered to have a moderate level of competition for Uzbekistan's major institutes. In 1978, the institute accepted 650 people from approximately 1550 applicants. Of

400 applicants from Tashkent, 150 people were accepted in that year; the lowest grade on the entrance examinations, out of a possible 25, was 20. From Dzhizak, Syrdar'ya, and Namangan *oblasts*, however, all 35 applicants were accepted without any competition; the average scores of these applicants, while not specified, were, according to one source at the institute, 'well below 20'. Similarly, all applicants from among the indigenous nationalities passed the examination from other Central Asian republics were also accepted.[11]

As Tables 5.1 and 5.3 illustrate, these biases in acceptance procedures at educational establishments are sometimes applied to a greater degree among women, and particularly among indigenous women. As Table 5.1 illustrates, in 1978 42 per cent of all applicants were accepted to the Tashkent Polytechnic; at the same time, 48 per cent of all female applicants were accepted, and 50 per cent of all applications from indigenous women were accepted for admission. Women accounted for 19 per cent of the applicants to the Tashkent Polytechnic, and 33 per cent of the entering class. A similar situation was apparent in the Fergana Polytechnic and in the Tashkent Institute of Communications. In terms of a regional bias, from every *oblast* except Tashkent and the Karakalpak ASSR, the proportion of indigenous women applicants who were accepted to educational establishments was equal to or exceeded the proportion of total applicants accepted. Given the fact that indigenous women may often fall among the less-qualified applicants,[12] the difference suggests a fairly pronounced bias in their favour.

On the whole, competition for entrance to all educational establishments under Minvuz in 1978 appeared to be relatively easier in many of the less-developed *oblasts* than it was in Tashkent *oblast'*, provided one could pass the basic entrance exam. Ninety-one per cent of all qualified applicants were accepted in 1978; only 72 per cent of all qualified applicants from Tashkent *oblast'* were accepted, and 79 per cent from the city of Tashkent. The quality of applicants from Tashkent may be generally higher than those from other *oblasts*: only 27 per cent of the total number of applicants in the Karakalpak ASSR passed the entrance exam in 1978, as against 36 per cent of the applicants from Tashkent *oblast'*, while 53 per cent of all applicants from the city of Tashkent did. In other words, empirical evidence could suggest a type of affirmative-action policy in Uzbekistan by both region and nationality which has been implemented in practice as well as in theory. Acceptance procedures often tend to favour the indigenous nationalities even when they may be the lesser-qualified applicants, to

TABLE 5.3 *Competition among indigenous female applicants to educational establishments under Minvuz and Minpros by oblast', Uzbekistan, 1978*

Oblast'[1]	Indigenous Women Applicants	Indigenous Women Acceptances	% Total accepted (both sexes)	% Indigenous Women Accepted
Karakalpak ASSR	1740	418	25	24
Andizhan oblast'	993	304	28	31
Bukhara oblast'	1701	485	25	29
Dzhizak oblast'	578	235	36	41
Kashkadar'ya oblast'	1159	308	25	27
Namangan oblast'	700	241	30	34
Samarkand oblast'	2292	702	31	31
Surkhandar'ya oblast'	678	193	24	28
Syrdar'ya oblast'	500	177	30	35
Tashkent oblast'	2994	637	26	21
Fergana oblast'	1072	388	26	36
Khorezm oblast'	996	287	28	29
Tashkent City	na	1008	42	na
From other republics	na	413	34	na

SOURCE Data from the Ministry of Higher and Specialised Secondary Education, May, 1979.

maintain certain ethnic and regional quotas which favour them in almost all educational establishments.

A further indication that the indigenous nationalities are often given preference in entrance to educational establishments is illustrated by the system of bribes. Substantial bribes are often paid in order to be accepted to any college or institute in Uzbekistan; for the most part, the amount of each bribe depends on the popularity of the educational establishment in question. The bribe for a native however, is almost always substantially lower than that for a Russian student, and very often, an Asian may pay nothing at all while a Slav may be obliged to pay several thousand roubles. Although evidence is mainly anecdotal, according to several informants, in 1978, Jews paid an average bribe of about 5000 roubles and needed a minimum score of 22 on the entrance examination (out of a top score of 25) for admission to the Tashkent Polytechnic Institute. Russians paid an average bribe of 3000 roubles and Uzbeks paid anything from 2000 roubles to nothing at all, depending on their sex, place of origin or connections. Uzbeks from collective farms paid anything from 0–1000 roubles in bribes for entrance to the institute. Uzbek women rarely paid any bribe and were frequently accepted with a minimum score of 18 on the entrance examination. If indigenous women received a lower grade, they alone, apparently, had the option to retake the examination.

Upon acceptance to an institute, moreover, representatives of the indigenous nationalities often continue to receive priority treatment. Special courses have been organised to supplement the normal course-load for those Asians who have not had adequate training before entering the institution: at the Tashkent Communications Institute, these take the form of additional classes each week and private tutorials. Finally, according to many sources, even the grading system in Uzbekistan's institutes often is weighted heavily in favour of the local nationalities. Professors and instructors at several Tashkent institutes told me they had been explicitly instructed to grant only passing grades or higher to the majority of the Central Asian students, and were often severely restricted in the number of the highest grades – 'fours' and 'fives' (equivalent to As and Bs in US universities, and a first and upper second in British universities) – they could award to Russians or Jews.

Upon graduation, the indigenous nationalities often receive better access to jobs; and 'affirmative action' continues on the enterprise and professional level as well. In the staffing of managerial and skilled positions, in industry as well as the service sectors, positions in most sectors are filled quite deliberately with Uzbeks. In instances where Uzbeks still do not possess the same skill-levels as their Russian counterparts, a Russian or European may be asked to direct the operation of a school or enterprise; but once the organisation in question is functioning at moderate capacity, the European is almost always replaced by an Asian. The story of one Russian professional is typical: three times he had been appointed director of an enterprise just being established, and three times he had been replaced by an Uzbek once the enterprise in question had begun to function at moderate capacity. An interview with an administrator at the Uzbek ballet revealed that leading roles are often transferred from dancers of non-Asian nationalities to Uzbek dancers 'even though the latter may not be as talented'. Several Russians in 'middle-level' positions commented that 'job security is non-existent, so long as local officials are intent upon implementing "nationality policies" in the working world'.[13]

This preference for the indigenous nationalities in State policy, moreover, has been reinforced by a kind of 'old boy' network in Uzbekistan, which functions along nationality lines. Anthropologists have often cited 'nepotism' as perhaps a traditional ingredient of Soviet Central Asian tradition and culture, or indeed, as a fundamental component of the entire kinship system and tribal and clan structure which has characterised Central Asian society for centuries:

> We condemn nepotism; the Central Asiatics found themselves upon it. Nepotism is used here in the broadest meaning of surrounding oneself with one's kin in the normal course of things, in any undertaking, civil or military . . . Nepotism is not a crime in Central Asia. It is not favoritism for one's kinsmen; it is the natural order of things in a kinship-based society. All social groups are composed of kinsmen.[14]

Rooted in the tribal and clan traditional structure, the type of nepotism often associated with the influence of family and tribe continued to be felt in the post-Revolutionary period. Rather than abolishing this phenomenon, affirmative action has simply allowed it to flourish within the Soviet context. Today, cadre selection for certain positions according to clan or tribal structure has created, in Bennigsen's words 'a curious and unexpected "familial" or genuinely mafia-type character to local Communist Party organs'.[15] More specifically, another study on Soviet Central Asia notes:

Asiatic man normally goes to his kinsmen if he wishes to start any kind of enterprise. And if he is secretary of a Party cell, he will see to it that his various sons, coursins, nephews, uncles work side by side with him in other key posts. If they get better pay for this, it is only natural because their kinsman is the local chief.[16]

In other words, with economic development, the importance of kin in Asian society, and the fundamental role of blood ties or ancestry in almost all undertakings and institutions, has simply been transferred to modern day-hiring practices in Uzbekistan. The Soviet government's affirmative-action policy has only tended to reaffirm, if not intensify this process over the past few decades. It is still true that 'every Muslim official [always gives] jobs first to his relatives and people from his area'.[17] Until recently, however, few indigenous Central Asians were in skilled or high enough positions to affect greatly the composition of the workforce as a whole. Today, the large inroads the indigenous nationalities have made in the labour force have meant that more Asians are in positions to allocate jobs and opportunities to 'their own'. Thus, granting more positions of authority to the indigenous nationalities has tended to open up more opportunities for the indigenous populations as a whole, and the snowball effect continues.

Indeed, perhaps one of the most revealing indicators of opportunity by nationality in Uzbekistan is the choice of nationality on one's passport. Parents wishing to ensure the best possible future for their children in Uzbekistan, and to provide them with the widest possible choice of opportunities as they grow older, whenever possible choose an Asian nationality for the child's passport. Almost all the children of mixed marriages whom I met throughout Uzbekistan were designated as 'Uzbek' on their passports, regardless of whether one or other parent was a Russian, Slav, Armenian, Tadzhik or any of the other nationalities in the USSR. 'When you are in Uzbekistan' many of them explicitly stated 'it is easier to be Uzbek. When you are in Russia, it is better to be Russian.' A Russian passport, it is widely believed, will prove to be a handicap for the duration of one's entire student and professional career if one plans to remain in the Uzbek republic.

PREFERENCES

If the indigenous nationalities on the whole may have greater opportunities for work and training in most sectors of social production, why do they predominate among the ostensibly non-working or 'underemployed' populations of their republic, and in the least prestigious and lowest-paying jobs and sectors? Certainly dislocations between skills, location and available opportunities play a large role in inhibiting the entrance of Central Asians into social production as a whole and into the industrial and technical sectors in particular, as do questions of female employment. But as illustrated by affirmative action and by the number of opportunities open especially to the indigenous nationalities, clearly an element of preference is also involved. Uzbekistan's indigenous populations often deliberately resist seemingly attractive offers for work or training opportunities, preferring to remain in household and private subsidiary work or in work which clearly has an overabundance of labour. Once employed, they deliberately resist efforts to enter the industrial sectors, preferring instead to remain in agriculture or the service sphere.

Of 944 people who were in need of work in Samarkand during 1976, for example, only 52.3 per cent, or 419 people expressed a desire to take part in social production. In another study (1977), of 760 women employed exclusively in the private and household sector, 66 per cent (500 women) did not work and expressly did not want to work in social production. Of the remaining 260, almost all expressed a desire to work only if certain conditions were met (for example, pertaining to salary, number of working hours, proximity to home, etc.). Few were actively and unconditionally seeking employment in the socialised sector. At the same time, as illustrated in Chapter 4, plants constructed specifically to attract local inhabitants to social production are often able to draw only a small proportion of their labour force from the local nationalities.

Taking underemployment into account, moreover, the number of indigenous Central Asians employed in the socialised economy but desiring to work at least part-time outside social production is also high, despite incentives encouraging full-time participation in social production. As illustrated in Chapter 7, a study of the values of different nationality groups carried out in Uzbekistan in 1974 suggested that Uzbeks, once employed in the socialised sector, have more of a tendency to work part-time in the household and private sectors than do Russians. In a sample of 1995 workers and employees of 'multi-nationality' enterprises in the Hungry Steppe, over 57 per cent of the Uzbeks interviewed wished to work in the household economy in addition to their present employment, against 33 per cent of the Russians.[18] The directors of various enterprises suggested to me (sometimes in jest, sometimes not) that any manager had to have an extra supply of workers on hand, as Asians tended to disappear during the work day 'to tend to their other affairs'.

A similar situation is apparent in the sectoral and occupational preferences among the different nationalities. Informal surveys undertaken by myself and other Western and Soviet scholars suggest that despite low wages and growing surpluses in agriculture and higher wages and deficits in industry, the most popular occupations among the indigenous nationalities in Uzbekistan are in the managerial service and agricultural occupations, while the least popular are in heavy industry. While this trend has been noted for the USSR as a whole, it has been particularly pronounced among the Central Asians. In an interview with the First Deputy Minister of Higher and Specialised Secondary Education, UzSSR, I was told that such preferences among Uzbeks are becoming stronger and more generally accepted. 'The service and household professions' he noted '(professions such as salespeople, etc.) today seem to be valued quite a lot more'.[19] This sentiment was underscored by the late Uzbek Sh. R. Rashidov, First Secretary, at a speech, March 1982, when he stressed that parents often 'feel that their children should work in science, culture or the arts and not in production'.[20]

That these statements reflect active preferences for particular jobs and sectors rather than a passive acceptance of existing delineations is reflected in applications for admission to educational establishments in Uzbekistan, and in the acceptance procedure for employment opportunities upon graduation. In 1978, close to 32 000 indigenous Central Asians applied for entrance to institutes of higher learning under the jurisdiction of ministries and organisations other than the Uzbek Ministry of Higher and Specialised Education (*Minvuz*) and the Uzbek Ministry of Education (*Minpros*). Of those, 37 per cent (about 12 000) applied to one of the four agricultural institutes (i.e. the Institute of Irrigation and Mechanisation of Agriculture, the Tashkent and Samarkand Agricultural Institutes and the Andizhan Institute of Cotton Growing), and about 8000, or 26 per cent of the indigenous applicants applied to one of the two medical institutes (Tashkent and Samarkand). Only 863 of the applications from the indigenous nationalities, (2.7 per cent), were to the Tashkent Institute of Communications, and only 1137, (3.6 per cent) to the Tashkent Institute for Engineers of Railway Transport (TIERRT). Similarly, in 1978, 33 per cent of all indigenous applicants to educational institutions under

Minvuz applied to one of Uzbekistan's three universities, while only 5 per cent and 3 per cent applied to the Tashkent and Bukhara Technological Institutes of Light Industry and Food Industry respectively, and only about 6–7 per cent applied to the Fergana Polytechnic. These proportions seem to reveal a decided preference for the non-industrial sectors among the indigenous nationalities.

On the other hand, of the 7253 *non*-indigenous applicants who submitted applications for entrance to educational establishments under these ministries and organisations, 1581, (22 per cent) applied for entrance to one of these two institutes, the TIERRT or the Institute of Communications. The remaining non-indigenous applicants were fairly evenly dispersed among the remaining fourteen institutes. Put another way, more than 80 per cent of all those who submitted applications to pedagogical institutes under Minpros were indigenous Central Asians, as opposed to little more than 50 per cent of the applicants to the TIERRT, the Institute of Communications and the Uzbek Institute of Physical Education, and only about 33 per cent at the Tashkent State Conservatory (Table 5.4).

These preferences, moreover, are again more clearly pronounced with regard to women. As Table 5.4 illustrates, of the 9700 indigenous women who applied to the sixteen institutes under other ministries and organisations, 54 per cent applied to one of the two major medical institutes (Tashkent and Samarkand) or to the Central Asian Pediatric Institute. Less than 2 per cent applied to the TIERRT and to the Tashkent Institute of Communications. In general, of the approximately 30 000 indigenous women who applied to the 42 higher and specialised secondary educational establishments in Uzbekistan, 40 per cent applied to the fourteen pedagogical institutes under Minpros to become teachers.

Similar preferences by nationality are apparent in Uzbekistan's Professional Technical Institutes (PTUs). In an interview in 1979, R. Kh. Dzhuraev, Deputy Chairman of the State Committee, UzSSR on Professional Technical Education, told me that the most popular courses of study among the indigenous nationalities applying for entrance to PTUs are in auto transport, domestic services and agriculture, with about eight to ten applications for each place. Competition is also fierce in PTUs of folkcraft, most of which are located in Andizhan and other regions outside Tashkent.

Finally, nationality preferences are again reflected in the system of bribes in the Uzbek SSR. The bribes noted above which must be paid

TABLE 5.4 *Structure of applications for admission to higher and specialised secondary educational establishments under ministries and organisations other than Minvuz and Minpros, by sex and nationality, Uzbekistan, 1978*

Name of Educational Establishment	Indigenous Applicants	%	European Applicants	%	Women Applicants	%	Indigenous Women Applicants	%
TIERRT	1 137	4	921	13	706	5	189	2
Tashkent Institute of Communications	863	3	660	9	471	3	171	2
Institute of Irrigation & Mechanisation of Agriculture	4 980	16	644	9	638	5	420	4
Tashkent Agricultural Institute	3 682	12	104	1	436	3	397	4
Samarkand Agricultural Institute	1 867	6	40	1	120	1	115	1
Andizhan Institute of Cottongrowing	1 286	4	196	3	132	1	107	1
Tashkent Medical Institute	5 684	18	934	13	3 479	26	2 813	29
Samarkand Medical Institute	2 679	8	632	9	1 594	12	1 397	14
Central Asian Paediatric Institute	1 725	5	607	8	1 579	12	1 068	11
Tashkent Pharmacological Institute	937	3	254	4	683	5	461	5
Samarkand Co-operative Institute	2 511	8	286	4	792	6	630	6
Uzbek Institute of Physical Culture	549	2	494	7	122	1	25	.3
Tashkent Theatrical Art Institute	743	2	251	3	225	2	145	1
Tashkent State Conservatory	105	.3	212	3	197	1	43	.4
Tashkent Institute of Culture	1 044	3	438	6	840	6	472	5
Total	31 798	100	7 253	100	13 467	100	9 708	100

SOURCE Ministry of Higher and Specialised Secondary Education, UzSSR, May, 1979.

to gain entrance to certain educational establishments and jobs in Uzbekistan also reflect a decided preference among the indigenous nationalities for work in agriculture and the service spheres rather than for industrial and technological pursuits. In 1978, the average bribe for entrance to the Tashkent Medical Institute was approximately 10 000 roubles. For the Tashkent Polytechnic, it was about 3000 roubles. For many of the local polytechnics, bribes were only about 50 roubles. And in many instances, particularly with regard to the latter two, indigenous applicants often paid nothing at all. Similarly, as discussed in Chapter 6, bribes are often paid for access to jobs in Uzbekistan: these range from almost zero for positions in certain heavy industrial enterprises, to upwards of thousands of roubles for certain positions in the service and agricultural sectors, from sales or stocktaking positions to the directorships of service or agricultural organisations (see Chapter 6). Preference for these non-industrial jobs and sectors are naturally linked to locational choices among the local populations. The deliberate preference among the indigenous nationalities for employment in the service and agricultural sectors often explains their reluctance to migrate from rural to urban areas, or from the smaller, lesser-developed cities to the industrial ones.

Paradoxically, then, there is an undisputable element of choice involved in the predominance of the indigenous nationalities in the lowest-paid and least-prestigious sectors and jobs in their own economy, and often for residence in the least-developed regions. This, in turn, can only lead one to question whether these sectors and occupations are in fact the lowest-paying and least-prestigious, or whether other factors might be playing a role in determining the desirability of different jobs among the nationalities. The ethnic distribution of occupations in Uzbekistan cannot be only the result of discrimination, lack of skills or poor knowledge of Russian on the part of the indigenous nationalities. These reasons would not be sufficient in themselves to explain why an Uzbek would deliberately resist efforts to draw him/her into the industrial labour force, choosing instead to pay several hundreds, or even thousands of roubles in bribes to become a watchman at a meat factory, a low-level policeman, or a lemonade seller on a Tashkent street corner. And they certainly would not explain why an Uzbek already qualified to be an industrial worker would choose instead to return to his collective farm.[21]

From the evidence available, it must be concluded that activity outside the socialised sector or in the non-industrial sectors often meets the needs and wants of the local population more than activity within social production or, more specifically, within heavy industry. To the degree that my residence in Uzbekistan allowed some understanding of local daily life and the workings of the Soviet system, it may be suggested that, in addition to the factors mentioned above, this situation is due to two additional, and perhaps more fundamental reasons. These reasons concern (a) income and (b) differing attitudes towards work, professional aspirations, life-styles, traditions and values. Within the context of Uzbekistan, preferences among the indigenous nationalities appear to be founded in solid economic and social reasons which are more powerful determinants of behaviour than questions of language, location, or training alone. What appear to be the lowest-paying sectors and occupations in Uzbekistan's economy may in fact be among the most remunerative; what appears to the Western analyst to be the 'subordinate status' of the local populations may, in local terms, represent one of the highest rungs on a different social ladder.

6 The Structure of Incomes

'Income' Alistair McAuley has written 'is far from a straightforward concept in the USSR, and there have been years of controversy about how it should be measured.'[1] Attempts to determine relative living standards of different populations within the USSR have long preoccupied Western scholars. This is true not only because of the same constraints which confront analysts of similar problems in other countries, but also because, particularly in the USSR, there is no clear way to determine individual income levels in the first place. A wage in the Soviet Union is only one of several components of an individual's income and not always the most important, depending on the regions and people involved; yet data on other sources of income are extremely scarce. Whatever the handicaps, however, even the most cursory analysis of incomes in Uzbekistan is essential, since, as everywhere, incomes largely determine the distribution of its labour force. In the context of Uzbekistan, they help clarify the reasons for the distribution between Uzbekistan's employed and non-working populations, and largely explain the sectoral preferences and nationality distribution of the employed population.

This study divides the different sources of income into three main groups, of which wages, and earnings from work in the socialised economy comprise the first group. This category includes money earnings from employment in the state sector, and both money earnings and receipts in kind from work on collective farms. In the state sector, it includes direct payments to employees, including various bonuses paid out of special profit and other funds, annual leave pay and other emoluments such as subsidised housing and cafeteria meals.

The second group of incomes covers benefits from the social consumption fund. This includes a number of services provided by the Soviet state, either free of charge or at subsidised prices, such as

171

pre-school child-care, education, and medical and social security services. The social consumption fund supports schools, children, cultural-educational and medical establishments, sanitoria and houses of rest, as well as providing stipends and pensions. This category also includes transfer payments.

The final group, private earnings, includes both money incomes and income-in-kind from work in the private sector. Variously known as the 'second economy', the 'parallel economy', the 'counter' or 'unofficial' economy and 'private enterprise', its monetary component includes income from the sale of homemade items or of produce grown on private plots by collective farm, state farm and some urban households, as well as from other private activities, both legal and illegal. For the purposes of this book, private income-in-kind is also used to include both the value of output – of agricultural produce from private farming activities or otherwise – consumed within the household, and also additional income-in-kind obtained by 'barter' of privately-produced goods unobtainable in government stores. Income-in-kind received from work on collective farmlands, however, is considered part of wages, since it is accrued on the basis of work in social production.[2]

For the purposes of this study, the distinction between legal and illegal private activity in Soviet Uzbekistan, and in the USSR as a whole, should be slightly expanded. While most economic activity in the USSR rests on the principle of state ownership, three types of private activity are permitted in the Soviet system: (i) activity on one's private plot, (ii) in housing and construction, and (iii) in certain professions. Private plots, for example, can be cultivated both by collective or state-farm peasant households or by individuals living in an urban or rural area whose primary employment is outside agriculture. As Grossman points out, it is estimated that in 1974 private agriculture accounted for about one third of all man-hours expended in Soviet agriculture and almost one tenth of all man-hours expended in the USSR's economy as a whole; its contribution to production and distribution was at least as high.[3]

Similarly, by law, private ownership of housing is allowed, mainly for the owner's own occupancy (although some exceptions exist). Today, about half the Soviet population, and about one quarter of the total urban population resides in privately-owned housing. Finally, the law also permits private activity in certain professions (such as physicians, dentists, teachers and tutors); in certain household, repair and personal services in rural areas; in some crafts and trades in the prospecting and extraction of some valuable metals (for example, in gold prospecting), and in some other circumstances. The sale of used personal objects to other persons is also permitted.

On the other side is illegal private activity, some of which is also illegal in Western systems and some of which is generally legal behaviour in the West, but all of which is widespread in the USSR. Unlike in the West, Soviet law explicitly prohibits an individual from privately employing another individual (except in the case of household help); 'speculation', that is, purchasing and re-selling objects with the intent to profit; privately possessing foreign currency or monetary metals; conducting business with foreigners (except for authorised persons), or plying crafts and trades for private gain. Also prohibited by Soviet law is the use of socialist property for private gain, stealing from the state and co-operatives, as well as from private persons, giving or taking bribes (in money or in kind) and generally violating any laws, regulations, norms, directives or plans governing daily activities among all strata of the employed population, in all sectors of the economy. Private production and distribution of goods and services is also explicitly forbidden.[4]

Although in Soviet law the line between the two types of private activity is fairly well-drawn, in practice the legal quite frequently overlaps illegal private activity and both types of activity abound. In agriculture, limitations which are placed on the areas of plots or on livestock holdings are often exceeded; inputs for agricultural production – such as fodder, fertiliser, water, tools, means of transport, etc. – are often acquired illegally from the socialised sector and produce is frequently sold through middlemen or at collective farm markets at prices above the ceilings set by Soviet law. While in principle private construction is often legal, much of it involves acquiring materials on the black market, illegally hiring construction help, using state-owned vehicles without authorisation, bribing officials, and violating the law in other ways which lead to private gain. And while the law also provides for some private activity in the professions, 'all of these provide loopholes for illegal trading and activity'[5] as well. In Grossman's words, the end-result is a 'two-tiered' (or many-tiered) structure, wherein two levels of prices and incomes exist simultaneously. On one tier are controlled wholesale and retail prices and official wages; on the other tier are the corresponding 'free' prices – reflected in the collective farm markets and in the 'black' and 'grey' markets – and additional 'unofficial' incomes earned from participation in such activity. Incomes from private activity, legal or illegal, rarely, if ever, show up in Soviet statistical handbooks.

It is often assumed that the bulk of an individual's income in the

USSR is derived from the wage paid for work in social production, and that income from private activity – that is, from the 'second tier' – comprises but a minor supplement to these official earnings. Although more attention has been paid in recent years to the role of private incomes in the USSR (in the work of Grossman, Speckler, Ofer, Wiles, and others), many Western observers assume that a family's or individual's welfare depends primarily on the wage-scale of the sector in which he/she/they are employed; and, conversely, that those households where a majority of the members are working outside social production or in the lower-paying sectors within social production are subsisting on meagre means indeed. Given the sectoral distribution of occupations by nationality – where the indigenous nationalities predominate in the non-working population and the population in agriculture and the service sector – they conclude that the indigenous nationalities in Uzbekistan receive smaller earnings than the Europeans there. This, in turn, leads to the general conclusion that the indigenous nationalities are financially-deprived relative to the Europeans in their republic.

In certain republics, however, the private economy is large and private incomes often equal or exceed official incomes. In Uzbekistan, legal private activity is extremely widespread; and even illegal activity has acquired its own generally-accepted system of operation which, in many cases, is not widely regarded as 'criminal' at all. In other words, both types of private activity in the USSR can be extremely remunerative, and have become an integral part of local Uzbek society. When the private economy is taken into account, therefore, income distribution among the different nationalities in Uzbekistan acquires a very different face from that suggested by official statistics alone. Because of higher participation rates in the private economy, Uzbekistan's indigenous nationalities may in fact often receive higher incomes than their European counterparts in the same republic. In analysing the effects of labour distribution by nationality, therefore, it is essential to analyse both these income components in Uzbekistan, to suggest what the actual income disparity among the nationalities residing there may be.

OFFICIAL INCOMES: TIER ONE

Official wage data suggest what appear to be two very simple, if not universal conclusions: that, officially at least, incomes are significantly lower among the population not working in social production than they are among the employed population; and that wages are lower among personnel in the agricultural and especially the service sectors than they are among industrial and construction personnel. Almost by definition, official incomes among adults not working in social production are minimal in Uzbekistan, if any payment is received at all. Stipends for working-age persons enrolled in studies, or payments to mothers with many children rarely equal a wage or salary. One would expect, therefore, that earnings among Uzbekistan's populations employed in social production would be higher than those among the ostensibly unemployed.

The same principle applies to incomes by sector. Soviet wage-policy establishes basic wage rates, bonus arrangements and job-classification systems for each branch of the state sector which are designed to be free of discrimination of any kind. But since the principle of Soviet communism – to each according to his need – has not been translated into practice, substantial differences still prevail in pay by sector and by occupation. As a Soviet economist noted:

> The fairest distribution of wages would not be an equal fixing of wages, but wages according to needs, irrespective of labour contribution to the social economy. But the Soviet Union is not yet rich enough to put this system into effect, and there are still people who do not consider work to be their main social duty. Therefore distribution according to labour prevails and will prevail for a long time yet in socialist society. Without it, the level of social wealth required for the transition to the Communist principle of distribution according to needs cannot be attained ... Work which is more complex, skilled, qualified and important for the development of the economy is paid higher than simple and easy work.[6]

Thus, as throughout the USSR, wage rates in Uzbekistan are still higher in the most-needed sectors of the economy, such as heavy industry and construction, and lower in the light and food industries or in the non-industrial sectors of the economy. As Tables 6.1 and 6.2 illustrate, they are highest in the heavy industrial sectors (mainly fuels and metallurgy), transport and construction, and lowest in agriculture, light industry, food industries and the service sectors.

As Table 6.1 illustrates, for example, in 1981 the highest monthly wages for workers and employees in Uzbekistan were in industry (industrial/production personnel) at 168.4 roubles per month; in construction (at 210.9 roubles per month, and 220.0 roubles per

TABLE 6.1　　*Average monthly wage of workers and employees by sector of the economy, Uzbekistan (in roubles)*[a]

	1940	1965	1970	1975	1980	1981
Total for the Economy	29.7	89.2	114.8	136.6	155.5	158.8
Industry (Industrial-production personnel)	27.6	93.7	123.5	151.9	166.7	168.4
Agriculture	22.9	69.0	97.5	121.0	150.9	154.2
of which, State farms, subsidiary and other State agriculture	19.7	67.2	97.8	120.1	151.3	154.6
Transport	31.9	102.9	131.0	171.7	185.9	191.2
of which, railway	33.8	93.7	116.2	148.3	165.5	175.4
automobile, etc.[b]	30.5	106.0	134.8	176.9	190.0	194.4
Communications	30.8	69.8	91.7	122.3	130.9	132.7
Construction	31.4	114.1	154.1	178.9	205.4	210.9
of which, construction-assembly work	28.1	115.2	159.0	185.6	214.7	220.0
Trade, public dining, material technical supply, sales and procurement	25.2	71.5	92.3	106.2	129.1	131.6
Housing-communal economy and personal services	25.6	67.7	85.6	100.5	117.0	118.8
Health services	26.8	80.9	92.6	98.7	120.5	122.9
Education	31.7	93.5	108.9	125.2	132.0	132.7
Culture	20.7	73.4	87.0	94.0	105.6	106.0
Art	37.9	73.9	90.2	96.2	116.1	114.8
Science and scientific services	42.7	111.5	127.5	147.1	161.8	164.7
Credit and insurance	33.9	80.5	97.6	113.9	144.8	148.4
Government administration	42.1	100.2	113.9	123.6	144.0	145.1

[a] Does not include additional payments and taxes from the social consumption fund.
[b] Automobile, urban electric, water and other transport, and trucking organisations.

SOURCE　TsSU *Narodnoe Khoziaistvo Uzbekistana v 1981 godu* (Tashkent: Uzbekistan, 1982) p. 188.

month in construction-assembly work); and automobile, urban electric, water and other transport, and loading and unloading organisations (191.2 roubles per month). Average monthly payments in agriculture were only 154.2 roubles per month; and wages in art and culture were 106 and 114.8 roubles respectively, or less than half the monthly wage paid for construction assembly work. Put another way,

TABLE 6.2 *Average monthly wage of workers and employees, by sector of industry (in roubles)*

Sector of Industry	1965		1970		1975	
	Industrial Production Personnel	of which workers	Industrial Production Personnel	of which workers	Industrial Production Personnel	of which workers
Electric power	107	96	132	117	162	149
Fuels	131	123	154	144	196	187
Ferrous and non-ferrous metallurgy	128	124	165	155	187	183
Chemical and petrochemical	106	101	135	129	163	155
Machine-building and metalworking	103	102	134	134	164	166
of which, machine building	103	101	137	137	168	170
Timber, wood-working and pulp and paper	93	95	126	128	152	155
Construction materials	103	102	144	143	173	174
Glass and china	92	92	136	131	146	141
Light industry	78	78	104	105	130	132
of which textile	81	83	110	113	140	143
cotton cleaning	93	97	128	130	181	192
Food industry	77	76	102	101	132	132
All industry	94	92	123	122	152	152

SOURCE TsSU *Narodnoe Khoziaistvo Uzbekskoi SSR 1975 goda*, (Tashkent: Uzbekistan, 1976) p. 69.

wages in agriculture and all sectors of the service sphere (except for science) – sectors where the indigenous nationalities predominate – were all below the republican average; wages in heavy industry transport and construction – staffed more heavily with Europeans – were all well above the republican average, by as much as 61 roubles per month, or over 730 roubles per year.

Within industry, as of 1975, the highest wages were in the fuel, ferrous and non-ferrous metal, construction material and cotton cleaning industries (187, 183, 174 and 192 roubles per month respectively) – again where Europeans often predominate. The lowest wages were in the light and food industries (132 roubles per month); within industry, these are the indigenous enclave. Wages in the fuel, ferrous and non-ferrous, cotton cleaning and construction material industries were each above the average industrial wage in 1975, by 29, 23, 19 and 14 per cent respectively; the average wage in light industry and food industries, on the other hand, was only 86–87 per cent that of the average industrial wage (Table 6.2).

Trends over the past two decades, moreover, suggest that the sectoral wage gap in Uzbekistan may not necessarily be narrowing. From the early 1960s to mid 1970s, wages in industry, transportation and construction grew more than twice as fast as those in most spheres of the service sector. Whereas wages in industry grew by about 62 per cent from 1965 to 1975, and in transport, by 67 per cent, they grew by only 22 per cent in health and in government administration and by only 34 per cent in education and culture over the same time-span. As McAuley notes, 'the growth of *kolkhoznik* well-being [in the early 1970s] was considerably slower than it had been in the preceding decade', and was slower, in 1970 to 1974, than the growth among state employees.[7] As Table 6.1 illustrates, data for 1981 suggest that the situation may be changing, as wages in the agricultural and some of the service sectors grew more rapidly in the latter part of the 1970s. But by 1981, the wage gap among sectors was still wide, with wages in construction and transportation, for example, still at least 50 per cent higher – or as much as 1360 roubles greater per year – than in housing, health, culture and art.

Similarly, bonus arrangements – incentive schemes, premia systems and regulations with regard to other wage supplements – are also more remunerative in the heavy industrial sectors. Supplements play a greater role, for example, in the actual earnings of workers in non-ferrous metallurgy (17.4 per cent) while having hardly any effect in the clothing and textile industries. Rewards from incentive schemes are particularly significant in the machine-building and woodworking industries (in the form of payments for overfulfilment of norms) and in non-ferrous metallurgy and in the coal industry (in the form of premia).[8]

All this would suggest significantly higher incomes in certain sectors of Uzbekistan's economy than in others. However rational the wage scale may be on economic grounds, therefore, because of the distribution of labour described above, such differences cannot help but assume strong ethnic overtones. The sectoral and occupational distribution of labour among the different nationalities in Uzbekistan would imply, at least according to official wage data, that Russians in fact are more highly paid than are the native populations in Uzbekistan. As Nove and Newth note 'this does not mean Kamal Aliyev is paid less than Ivan Petrov on principle; if they work in the same factory and do the same work, they will be paid the same amount'.[9] But in the light of the priorities given to Russian-dominated sectors and occupations, official data on wages would suggest the conclusion which several Western analysts draw that 'the indigenous nationalities are deprived relative to outsiders.'[10] By dominating the most highly paid sectors, it is assumed, earnings among Russians in Uzbekistan could vary from anything between 50 and 100 per cent greater than the average wage among Uzbeks in the service sector. Similarly, since higher-skilled positions in any sector undoubtedly carry with them higher wage rates than do subordinate positions in the same sector – and since, as illustrated above, the former are also dominated largely by Europeans – occupational differences by nationality would also imply large disparities in income between the indigenous and non-indigenous nationalities employed in the same sector. In many cases, the differences would appear to be substantial.

As discussed in the first part of this chapter, however, wages do not necessarily comprise an individual's entire income in the USSR, and in some cases comprise only a small proportion of total personal income. Perhaps particularly in Soviet Central Asia, 'non-wage' income and income from the private sector – legal and illegal – play an important role in household budgets. Paradoxically, when the role of private activity in Uzbekistan's economy is taken into account, the relation of real incomes among sectors and among the working and non-working populations in social production may often be precisely the converse of that suggested by official data. Before discussing income differentials among the different nationalities, therefore, it is essential to consider the nature and extent of private subsidiary activity as a whole, and the magnitude of earnings which may be accrued from such activity.

PRIVATE ACTIVITY: TIER TWO

Differences of opinion on the magnitude of private activity in Uzbekistan in particular, and in the USSR as a whole abound. There is little doubt, however, that in most parts of the USSR, a shortage of retail goods at official prices is largely compensated by activity in the private sector. Indeed, although ideologically antithetical to their aims, even Soviet sources have described this fact:

> The structure of production in private subsidiary agriculture in large part is determined by the structure of production in the socialised economy: as a rule, the private sector supplies those products which are not produced in the socialised sector.[11]

This is equally, if not especially true in Uzbekistan. As Nove notes, whether between regions or different groups 'when we compare living standards by using data on prices and incomes, we implicitly assume that goods can be bought'.[12] If a worker earns an average wage of 160 roubles per month, and if official reports indicate that meat costs two roubles per kilo, the implicit assumption is that he and his family are well-fed. Since Tashkent is the *'gorod khlebnyi'**, we take for granted that food supplies are amply and readily available to Uzbekistan's inhabitants.

Yet Uzbek food stores are more devoid of meat, cheese, fresh fruits and vegetables than are other government stores in many parts of the USSR, and consumer goods there are in even shorter supply. As already noted, the level of goods and services in Uzbekistan is below the all-Union average. According to official statistics, there is one third less meat sold at retail prices in Uzbekistan; one third less milk, and far fewer consumer goods, both in quantity and variety.[13] Although this is in part due to the largely rural nature of Uzbekistan, and in part to the different consumption patterns of inhabitants of the southern tier of the USSR,[14] it also suggests that shortages of many basic food and

---

* Literally, 'bread city', implying that Tashkent is a city where food is in more plentiful supply than in other parts of the USSR.

:onsumer goods are particularly great in Uzbekistan as well. As ≥lsewhere in the USSR, shortages of food and consumer goods tend to ead to a rise in private activity, both legal and on the black market. One would assume, therefore, that as the availability of goods and services diminishes, the private activity – both legal and illegal – surrounding those goods will grow. In Uzbekistan, constant shortages of almost all basic goods and services at retail prices have allowed private activity to flourish.

Although data on private activity are scarce, this is borne out by Soviet data with regard to legal private activity in agriculture. Because of the inability of the socialised sector to meet the population's needs in basic foodstuffs, the role of private agriculture in Uzbekistan is particularly large, and growing:

> Every year our republic achieves great success in agriculture. How-
> ever, the level of production of grain, meat, milk, and of some other
> agricultural products and of animal husbandry still is not satisfying
> the growing needs of the population. That is why in Uzbekistan the
> private subsidiary economy plays a significant role.[15]

By 1977, according to one account, 821 000 collective farm households, more than 500 000 families of *sovkhoz* personnel, the main mass' of the rural intelligentsia and part of the urban population were involved in private subsidiary agriculture.[16] In 1978, the amount of land 'under cultivation for individual use' in Uzbekistan had grown from 80.4 thousand hectares in 1960 to 116.6 thousand, or by close to 50 per cent.[17] And by the late 1970s, production in private agriculture had grown to a level at least 20 per cent of total production. According to official Soviet sources, in 1965, output from private plots accounted for 15.2 per cent of the total production of agricultural products in Uzbekistan; in 1970, 18.8 per cent; and in 1977, 19.5 per cent.[18] More realistic and also conservative estimates suggest that it now accounts for about 26-29 per cent of total output – and none of these statistics includes illegal production or output from unreported private sub-sidiary agriculture.

Thus, whatever the exact figure, the resulting level of private agricultural production in the late 1970s was high by comparison with the USSR as a whole, particularly with regard to certain foodstuffs. Again according to official sources, in 1978 private subsidiary agriculture in the USSR as a whole accounted for 29 per cent of total vegetable, meat and milk production in the USSR, 34 per cent of total

TABLE 6.3   *Production of private subsidiary agriculture as percentage of total output, selected products, Uzbekistan, 1978*

	USSR	Uzbekistan
Potatoes	61	35
Vegetables	29	49
Meat	29	49
Milk	29	62
Eggs	34	41
Wool	19	45

SOURCE   V. Zhivaev, and I. Gritsenko, 'Lichnoe podsobnoe khoziaistvo v sisteme sotsialisticheskikh proizvodstvennykh otnoshenii.' *Kommunist Uzbekistana*, no. 9, 1980, p. 42.

egg production, and 19 per cent of the total amount of wool (Table 6.3). In Uzbekistan, these proportions were in some instances more than twice as high. Private subsidiary agriculture in the Uzbek republic accounted for about 50 per cent of the republic's total meat, vegetable and wool production; 62 per cent of its milk production, and 41 per cent of total egg production. Only in the production of potatoes did Uzbekistan's private sector play a lesser role than it did on average for the USSR as a whole.[19]

The importance of the private subsidiary economy in the production of agricultural products naturally finds its corollary in consumption. A large part of consumer demand in Uzbekistan is met by the private economy. In 1980, there were over 500 markets and bazaars in Uzbekistan, thirty of which were in Tashkent; in Tashkent alone, according to a Soviet source, more than 270 000 tons of various fruit and vegetable products were sold each season – allegedly accounting for more than half Tashkent's annual consumption.[20] With regard to particular products, Soviet writers admit that 'the main needs of the rural population in animal products is satisfied basically by the private subsidiary economy', or that the private sector also 'satisfies more than half the needs of the population in most livestock products'.[21] The amount of meat sold in urban collective farm markets grew by 225 per cent, or more than doubled between 1965 and 1974, while total meat production rose by only 54 per cent and government purchases, by 27 per cent.[22] Trade on collective farm markets in general has shown a constant increase in large Uzbek cities over the past fifteen years. And although the foregoing estimates on the sale of private produce through Uzbekistan's collective farm markets are conservative, they further underestimate the role and magnitude of the private economy in Uzbekistan, since they exclude those parts of private production sold to the government in other parts of the country and through illegal channels.

Data on the legal private production and consumption of non-agricultural goods and services – such as construction, household goods or private activity in the professions – are more scarce in Soviet statistical handbooks and scholarly writings. Their level is only suggested by such indicators as the degree of private housing in Uzbekistan, or broad statements regarding the level of trade in second-hand goods. For example, private housing is notably more prevalent in Uzbekistan than in all other republics in the USSR, with the exception of Georgia and the Ukraine. In 1977, 35 per cent of all housing in Uzbekistan was privately owned, as opposed to 18 per cent in the RSFSR. (In Georgia, the level was 41 per cent, in the Ukraine, 37 per cent). Uzbekistan today also has more privately owned housing per capita than does the RSFSR.[23] Although not quantifiable, 'less measurable' forms of legal private activity in Uzbekistan, including trade in second-hand goods, are also, as one local scholar put it, 'proverbial'.

On the illegal side, the magnitude of private activity in Uzbekistan also appears to be particularly high. As elsewhere in the USSR, as Feifer notes, 'reliance on the ordinary supply system is fading'; instead, because of continuing shortages of almost all goods and services at retail prices, illicit stealing from the state 'is practised by almost everyone' in different ways and to different extents:

> The peasant steals fodder from the *kolkhoz* to maintain his animals, the worker steals materials and tools with which to ply his trade 'on the side', the physician steals medicines, the driver steals gasoline and the use of the official car to operate an unofficial taxi.[24]

Indeed Grossman suggests 'one might perhaps assert that the right to steal on the job, within certain conventional limits, is an implicit but integral part of the conditions of employment in the Soviet Union'.[25] Individuals 'moonlight' on the side, providing household repair and construction services, automotive repairs, home-made clothing and utensils or transport services. On a higher level, fiddling with statistics and socialist 'norms', or theft of socialist property for resale or for 'black' manufacture or production of highly sought-after goods are allegedly commonplace in Uzbekistan. From operations of private groups of building contractors to full-fledged underground entrep-

reneurs, large-scale private production is also widespread, and greas-
ing the wheels at every level of 'parallel' private activity is the system of
bribes, personal favours, gifts of time and connections which has
evolved to protect the individuals involved from discovery and/or
punishment. Indeed, in the words of some Western scholars, the
situation seems to have led not only to a growth in a 'second economy',
but to the creation and growth of a type of 'second polity' – a system of
informal power relationships directed toward private gain as well –
wherein large sums are paid to law-enforcement officials, inspectors,
and government, party and other personnel with power and
influence.[26]

While high throughout the USSR, illegal private activity and corruption appear to be especially highly developed in Transcaucasia and
Central Asia. In the case of Uzbekistan, this is suggested by recent
legislation, the emergence of more books specifically related to
economic crimes in Uzbekistan and recently-increased propaganda
campaigns to combat private 'entrepreneurship'. Official rules and
regulations have singled out Uzbekistan and Georgia for comment and
admonishment on weakly administering legislation against economic
crime and corruption.[27] Films and books have emerged recently,
strongly attacking illegal economic activity.[28] In the words of a local
Uzbek jurist, discussing 'models' of economic crimes of embezzlement
is a 'voluminous' task by comparison with other types of crime.[29]

In other words, by almost all accounts, the private sector continues
to play a major role in Uzbekistan in providing goods unobtainable
from the socialised sector. And since the 'goods famine'[30] in the USSR
as a whole is not projected to decline, Uzbekistan's private subsidiary
economy can be expected to remain strong. In the words of a Soviet
economist:

> The necessity for the products of the private subsidiary economy still
> remains, since social production as a whole still does not satisfy fully
> the growing needs of the population. Tendencies towards its diminu-
> tion are not to be observed.[31]

INCOMES FROM PRIVATE ACTIVITY

For the purpose of this book, two main points are important. First,
private activity, legal and illegal, is widespread in Uzbekistan, and

earnings from private activity can be extremely high. In addition to payments from the state, a collective farmer in Uzbekistan may earn hundreds more roubles monthly by selling produce from his private plot on the private or collective farm market. A teacher in an institute may earn thousands of roubles each term by accepting bribes and tips to give higher grades on entrance and other exams. The director of a shoe factory may augment his income by thousands of roubles every few months, by falsifying records and/or distributing or producing 'black' finished goods or raw materials; and a local Party secretary can augment his income by literally tens of thousands of roubles each year, by accepting bribes to exert (or not to exert) his power and influence in any number of ways.

The second important point, however, is that while private activity may be high in Uzbekistan, opportunities for participation in the private economy are not uniform by sector, occupation or location. Instead, they depend upon the access one has to particular goods and services for which there is excess demand, or the power or control one has over individuals who have such access. If a factory worker steals materials from his production line, whether for his own consumption or for resale on the black market, those materials must have some value for himself or someone else: his family can eat meat; they cannot eat ball-bearings. If an enterprise director falsifies statistics to provide himself with a surplus of goods to be sold through private channels, there must be a market for those goods. For a teacher to accept bribes in order to help someone enter an institute, there must be competition to enter that institute which goes beyond the quotas set by official planners.

In other words, if incomes from the first 'tier' of economic activity in Uzbekistan are relatively insensitive to demand – providing each working individual with a basic income regardless of the demand for his services – the second tier is based upon demand. Participation in the private economy is therefore inextricably linked to the particular good or service over which an individual has some kind of direct or indirect control and upon the nature of that control. Employment in different sectors, locations and jobs therefore provides not only different wages, but also different opportunities to engage in other types of private activity.[37] In considering income differentials among the various nationality groups in Uzbekistan, it is essential to analyse the extent to which lower incomes among Uzbekistan's population in household and private subsidiary activity or in the agricultural and service spheres may be offset by earnings from private activity.

INCOMES FROM THE HOUSEHOLD AND PRIVATE SUBSIDIARY ECONOMY

Activity in the household and private economy can augment a household's income in three ways. First, providing produce for consumption within the household, participation in the private subsidiary economy substantially diminishes expenditures on the cost of living (and often allows the family to consume food products simply unavailable elsewhere). Second, because of general shortages, it allows for significant monetary income from selling the excess. Finally, for the same reason, it allows for greater access to other scarce goods and services by an informal system of barter.

Many observers regard the first of these income components, consumption of private produce within the household, as the main attraction of work in private subsidiary agriculture, since it allows for substantial savings on food and other products. In this sense, because of the large number of consumers within each household, incomes from the private subsidiary economy are viewed as particularly significant for the indigenous populations, where large families prevail.[33] As others have noted, the level of consumption within a household that can be supported by a given wage depends upon the size of the household and labour force participation rates; that is, it depends on the proportions of household members who are employed and who are dependants. While large families in Uzbekistan may consist of a large number of wage-earners, they also generally contain a greater number of dependants. For the same reason, consumption of private produce is also significant with regard to non-food goods. The production of household items, sewing one's own clothing, etc. are activities which occupy a significant share of women's time in Uzbekistan and diminish clothing and other household expenditures greatly.

In terms of monetary income and exchange for goods in kind, however, rewards from participation in the private subsidiary economy are also large. In 1980, in the markets of Tashkent alone, there were more than 13 000 stalls selling fruit and vegetable products at prices often two to five times official retail prices.[34] During the year I spent in Tashkent, the official price of meat was between two and three roubles per kilo; on the market, it often sold for between eight and twelve roubles per kilo. Eggs, when available in government stores (an extremely rare occurence), cost 15 kopeks each; on the market, they sold for twice as much. I never discovered the official prices of oranges or cottage cheese (*tvorog*), since they were never available in government stores during that entire year; on the market during the winter months, however, oranges cost from two and a half to three roubles each, while cottage cheese was about four to four and a half roubles a kilo. As a result, individuals selling their produce at those 13 000 stalls in Tashkent's markets received high earnings for the sale of even a small amount of fresh produce. Because of the demand for these goods, moreover, they were also able to exchange their food and animal products for other goods in short supply (for example, clothing, jewellery, or an endless supply of other consumer goods).

Estimation of the actual level of income from the private subsidiary economy presents a number of problems, including the absence of more than anecdotal data on production and pricing in the private subsidiary economy and the fact that whatever data is published in official Soviet texts are fragmentary and misleading. Even where accurate production figures may be provided, moreover, several problems impede utilising them to determine the income levels which work in the household and private subsidiary provides.

Perhaps the most important problem, for example, is determining the value of privately produced output. A large share of the marketed output from the private subsidiary economy is sold on collective farm markets, at prices which, as illustrated, are substantially higher than those received for similar products sold to the State. A large share is sold through private channels beyond the control of the State. Estimating the exact extent of private production, therefore, and evaluating its value in the light of inconsistent pricing in the USSR greatly complicate efforts to estimate the monetary incomes accrued from activity in the private subsidiary economy.

In addition to gauging the value of monetary income from private production, a second problem arises in ascribing a value to private produce consumed at home. Whether it should be evaluated in terms of state prices or collective farm market prices would have to depend on the good and its availability in government stores. Indeed, private output consumed at home often includes food products and other homemade goods and clothing which are unavailable even on collective farm markets in the first place.

A final problem lies in ascribing monetary value to barter, and to non-monetary transactions involving the trade of privately produced goods for various, otherwise unattainable goods and services. If an individual offers a lamb in lieu of a 1000 rouble bribe to be placed on the waiting list for a car, do we ascribe a value of 1000 roubles to the animal? If he should decide instead to trade the lamb for two winter coats which, on the black market, would otherwise cost him 300 roubles, does the value of that lamb now depreciate to one third of what it was before? If the individual should choose to consume the lamb as part of a festival or picnic, is the same lamb now worth only the cost of a meal? The massive problems implicit in determining the value of output from household and private subsidiary work become increasingly complex as more variations are envisioned.

Because of these handicaps, estimates on monetary income alone from private activity in Uzbekistan range from an average of about forty roubles per month, to thousands. Official Soviet data suggest that private subsidiary agriculture alone accounts for about 25 per cent of a collective farmer's income. Conservative Western calculations suggest that incomes from the private sector account for at least about 35 per cent of total personal incomes among collective farmers, and income from 'other sources', about 27 per cent.[35]

The important point illustrated by these varied estimates, however, is that high incomes can be earned from private agriculture alone, at the same time that such activity significantly diminishes the cost of living. Taking the private sector into account, by 1977, the incomes of collective farmers who were also occupied in private subsidiary agriculture had grown to a level at least equal to that of Uzbekistan's average worker and employee. According to one Uzbek scholar, in 1977 income from the private subsidiary economy comprised less than 1 per cent of total income for the latter, and 25 per cent of total income in collective farm families. Using one of the lowest Western estimates, this would mean that the average income for collective farmers in Uzbekistan in 1977 was an approximate 195 roubles per month, as opposed to an average wage of 140 roubles per month among Uzbekistan's workers and employees.[36] Combined with the income accrued from private produce sold outside the *kolkhoz* markets, from the sale of household items other than agricultural produce, from barter and the exchange of privately-produced goods for other services, and from the value of private production consumed within the household, total incomes from household and private subsidiary activity can be assumed to be higher.

An attempt to compute the magnitude of these additional sources of private income in Uzbekistan – from the sale of non-agricultural, privately-produced items, from barter, from private produce sold through channels other than collective farm markets – would of course, be a lesson in futility. Virtually no data are published, and even if they were, the problems described above in interpreting that data would only be compounded immensely. A few examples, however, should provide some illustration of the form and magnitude this extra activity may take.

An Uzbek mother of nine children living on the outskirts of a major Uzbek city during the late 1970s preferred to remain occupied outside social production in 'household work', despite the fact that her children were at an age where 'they could take care of themselves', and despite efforts on the part of local authorities to draw her into social production. Ironically, the reason for her preference was primarily financial. At home, while her children were at school or work, she sewed Uzbek dresses and other festive clothing generally unavailable in Uzbekistan's stores for private sale among her city's local inhabitants. With an output of at least two dresses per week, and with each dress sold at 80–100 roubles, her monthly income thus became some 640–800 roubles each month (minus a minimal cost of materials, since the fabric was often supplied by the buyer). Work in the household economy thus provided her with a total monthly income four to six times the average wage in Uzbekistan in 1976. 'To help support nine children,' she said 'this kind of work is essential.'

A similar case concerns the urban schoolteacher who, rather than teach a full day, spent his afternoons selling home-grown vegetables in the local market. The high cost of food-products in Tashkent's markets has already been discussed. By consequence, the additional income earned by this schoolteacher apparently greatly exceeded what he would have earned by working an additional shift, or 'stavka' at his institute. Casual observation indicated that both types of activity are frequent, particularly among the indigenous populations.

In terms of access to other scarce goods, moreover, the private economy is also extremely lucrative by means of a form of barter rather than by monetary transaction. Thousands of roubles are paid in bribes to be placed near the top of a waiting-list for a car or other consumer goods in Uzbekistan. Because of the shortage of meat, however, a bribe of one or two lambs can often place an aspirant at the top of a waiting-list even more rapidly than a large sum of roubles. Today, several informants have suggested that the number of collective farmers possessing a car may well exceed the number of urban residents who acquired a car through monetary transactions alone. Access to the limited meat supply in Uzbekistan is often beyond what money can buy.

None of these stories is exceptional. Yet they all elude the statistician's eye.[37]

THE ROLE OF PRIVATE INCOMES BY SECTOR OF SOCIAL PRODUCTION

Like the private subsidiary economy, numerous problems are involved in estimating real incomes from illegal or semi-legal second economic activity. Data are extremely scarce; and even when data are available, ascribing monetary value to barter and consumption at home again makes their analysis extremely tenuous. Similarly, types of second economic activity are so varied that they, too, could not lend themselves to a uniform analysis. A Soviet source cites over eighty distinct methods of embezzling finances from industrial enterprises alone.[38] The many different types of economic crime in non-industrial sectors suggest that the actual number of variations is enormous.

Of most importance for this study, however, are the opportunities for private activity by sector and location. There is little doubt that, by nature, certain sectors provide greater opportunity for private activity than do others. As a Soviet author of a book on corruption, A. D. Davletov remarks:

> Plundering in various sectors of the economy is characterised by various modes and methods of extracting material and financial valuables ... The plunderer's actions, including the masking of the theft, to a great extent are determined by external circumstances, including the particularities of the technology of production, the economic operations, the bookkeeping accounts, etc.[39]

Davletov posits several factors upon which participation in the private economy depends, the most important of which are the following:[40]

1. The *type and character* of activity of the enterprise, organisation or individual (i.e. what is produced or constructed, in what volume, etc.).
2. The '*conditions of activity*' (i.e., the procedure of receiving and storing raw materials; the technological process; procedures for distributing/issuing the product and of registering the object and accounts; document circulation; procedure of stocktaking, guarding, control, etc.).
3. The '*production connections*' essential for receiving, transporting and distributing material values;
4. The *rules and regulations* governing different sectors and opera-

tions (i.e. norms and rules for stocktaking, the existence of normative acts, etc.).

5. The *opportunities* which are available to 'criminal groups' for
embezzlement.

5. The *surrounding circumstances*, i.e. the location of the enterprise or
operation, the needs of the immediate population, etc.

He concludes that because of the different opportunities provided by
different sectors, 'embezzlement' and 'plundering' in Uzbekistan are
most prevalent in the cotton-cleaning industry, construction, government, trade and agriculture. In other parts of the book, he suggests that
embezzlement is at least as high in light industry and food industries
and among government and Party personnel. As illustrated in Chapter
3 of this book, most of these are mainly indigenous sectors.

Activity in agriculture, for example, not only provides access to
private earnings from one's private plot, or opportunities for the theft
of tools, fodder or working time; it also provides easy access to
larger-scale illegal activities. Since farms are often subject to less
stringent controls than are other state-owned enterprises and organisations, they can frequently provide illegal undertakings with their
premises, transport, labour or with regard to, say, currency
conversions.[41] As several émigrés have pointed out, an entire system of
under-reporting harvests and over-reporting losses has also evolved,
with the remainder of agricultural produce sold through private channels. Close connections with local industries also provide the collective
farm leadership with goods and services in exchange for part of that
agricultural produce.

Like agriculture, activity in the service sectors provides direct access
to goods or services in short supply and thus also provides access to
augmented incomes. During the 1978–9 academic year, a physician's
official average wage in Uzbekistan was well below the average wage
for Uzbekistan as a whole, at about 110 roubles per month. But
because of the 'tips' that physicians are paid – for particular services, or
for access to drugs, hospital admissions, places in queues, sick leave,
abortions or simply more attentive care – the average income among
doctors often appeared to be at least six times greater. Although in
principle medical care in the USSR is free, bribes are habitually paid to
receive adequate care. During 1978–9, abortions in Tashkent allegedly 'cost' the equivalent of a thirty rouble bribe; child deliveries, an
average of fifty roubles; medical excuses, ten roubles and more major

operations upwards of several hundreds of roubles to several thousands paid to the physician or surgeon alone. Thus, one doctor with five years of experience who worked in a delivery ward earned upwards of 4000 roubles each month – although his official monthly salary was only 110 roubles. Another surgeon with an excellent reputation in Tashkent – with an official basic salary of 170 roubles per month – allegedly earned a staggering 10 000.

In teaching, trade or other sectors of the service sphere, a similar situation is apparent. Entrance to selected institutes or higher educational establishments is often characterised by fierce competition. This competition, in turn, has led to a situation wherein candidates for admission, or their parents, must often pay large sums to gain entrance to choice educational institutions and then again to remain in them once they have been enrolled. Thus, again during the 1978–9 academic year, an average of 10 000 roubles was paid in bribes for admission to the Tashkent Medical Institute – of which approximately half, according to one source, was divided among the admissions committee consisting of five of the institutes's teachers. During the same year, at another institute, a teacher received a fifty to one hundred rouble bribe from approximately fifty students in return for the assurance that they would pass their mid-term and final exams. Her ninety rouble salary was therefore augmented by between 2500 and 5000 roubles in one term.

'In trade,' Davletov writes 'especially typical is the payment of bribes to an inspector, and to responsible persons of the bases to distribute a variety of goods which are "convenient" for a crime; the sale of deficit goods at higher prices or via "*speculanty*"; etc.'[42] In trade, the same access to a particular good or service also influences actual incomes. Salespeople augment their incomes by selling items under the counter, by selling information on where to queue, by directly stealing goods or, as in the case of meat or food products, by directly manipulating the quality of the cut or the precision of the scale and increasing his or her own income accordingly. The manager of a trade co-operative may augment his own income by directing the inflow/outflow of goods, fudging statistics, by-passing normal channels for the sale of goods by selling them on the side at highly inflated prices, etc. Thus, in 1979, a shoe salesman in Tashkent received a monthly salary of eighty roubles; but by selling 'left' (or 'black') shoes, by fudging records or by selling shoes 'under the counter', his net actual earnings were approximately 200 roubles per day – approxinately 4000 roubles per month. Directors of the local markets receive bribes from almost all collective farm vendors so that they will not notice if prices exceed the ceiling set by Soviet law, or if the vendors are in violation of any one of a number of other regulations.

The same may be true in certain sectors of transport, construction, light industry and food industries. Individuals with means of transportation at their disposal – truck drivers, taxi drivers, owners of private automobiles – often earn high fees by using them to transport black goods, or by running personal taxi businesses.[43] The theft of construction materials or the sale of repair services on a private basis are only two of the myriad ways of augmenting incomes in construction. In the light industry and food industries, opportunities for private activity apparently exist at every level. Fudging statistics, theft of finished goods and various other methods provide workers and employees in these enterprises with ample opportunities to augment their wage. By stealing meat for his/her own consumption or resale, a worker on the production line of a meat factory may earn approximately 2000 roubles per month – minus the bribe paid to the security guard so that the latter 'will look the other way'.[44] Indeed, the director of one light industrial factory is a noted 'millionaire' in Uzbekistan, often referred to as 'Uzbekistan's Rockefeller'.

Perhaps of most importance in such a scheme – given the ever-present possibility of detection or arrest – are the individuals occupying Party and government posts. These posts are not necessarily connected with a particular good or service, but carry an immense amount of control over individuals who are. Thus, law enforcement officials – such as the regular police; the special economic police (the OBKhSS);* personnel in prosecution; functionaries in the bureaucracy who handle the allocation of certain goods (such as automobiles, housing or other goods or services); inspectors; control and monitoring organisations; Party officials; or personnel in control of awarding degrees, prizes and titles – frequently and regularly receive sizeable bribes to exert (or not to exert) their influence in an individual's or enterprise's favour. Indeed, this system of bribe-taking among officials is strengthened by the element of 'family circles' within it.[45] In addition to the earnings accrued from such activity, moreover, individuals in Party and government posts in Uzbekistan also receive access to

---

The Otdel' Bor'by Khishcheniiami Sotsialisticheskoi Sobstvennosti, or OBKhSS.

special stores, bonuses, perquisites, etc.

On the other hand, opportunities for additional private earnings from heavy industry or technical research institutes – where, as illustrated, Europeans predominate – are limited. A worker in Tashsel'mash (the Tashkent Agricultural Machinery Plant) earns an average of about 200 roubles per month – a wage well above the average wage for Uzbekistan as a whole. With additional piecework or especially high qualifications he can possibly raise his wage to 250 roubles. But because of the nature of his product, opportunities to earn additional income 'on the side' are almost non-existent. I was often told that an additional sixty or seventy roubles from private activity on the part of these workers is considered extremely high. Thus, the maximum monthly wage which a heavy industrial worker on the production line of this factory could earn in 1979 was allegedly about 300 roubles.

Similarly, an air-traffic controller at the Tashkent airport earns 150 roubles per month, based upon a forty hour shift each week. If he is rated among personnel of the first class, he earns an additional ten roubles and if he knows, say, English, he earns an additional seven and a half roubles per month. With few opportunities to work on the side however, these sums comprise the bulk of his income. The total monthly income of these employees, two highly-skilled controllers told me, rarely exceeds 200 roubles. Indeed, because of this situation several heavy industrial enterprises in Uzbekistan (and elsewhere in the USSR) have earned the nickname '*nevynosimye*' enterprises – a play on the Russian word for 'insufferable'. Literally, this word means 'unbearable' or 'un-carry-able' – implying that work in these enterprises is insufferable simply because nothing can be carried out for resale or for additional profit elsewhere.

Isolated examples, of course, cannot be compiled, averaged or standardised to be indicative of a population as a whole. While one shoe salesman in Uzbekistan may earn 4000 roubles per month another may earn 100; while one heavy industrial worker may find few opportunities to earn additional income in the private economy another may find several. In countless conversations in Uzbekistan however – and in a series of interviews conducted subsequently among Soviet émigrés in the United States – it emerged that broad generalisations can be drawn, and *opportunities* for the greatest financial and other gain in Uzbekistan may indeed be found in the services and agriculture, rather than in heavy industry.

REAL INCOMES BY OCCUPATION

The same principle applies in the distribution of earnings by occupation within particular enterprises and organisations. As discussed in Chapter 3, indigenous Central Asians who have been brought into the heavy industrial and technical sectors over the past several decades, albeit on a relatively small scale, tend to dominate the most highly visible specialist and public contact positions – enterprise directors, or heads of certain departments – and otherwise tend to dominate the lower-skilled occupations outside the production process. If Russians dominate the specialist jobs or work directly in the production process, Uzbeks in heavy industrial enterprises are preponderant as guards, warehouse chiefs or low-level white-collar personnel, or on the business side in supply and marketing. Given the distribution of wages, this would imply correspondingly lower earnings among the Uzbeks employed in these enterprises than among the Russians. Again, however, these lower-skilled positions are often the positions which offer the greatest possibilities for private gain. Actual earnings among the lower-skilled, non-production personnel, therefore, may often be significantly higher than those of workers on the production line.

In the words of Davletov, for example, private economic activity in the industrial spheres occurs most frequently in the acquisition, storage, stocktaking, accounting, control, transport and marketing of a good – but rarely in its development or production. The exception, of course, is if the good in question is a highly-sought-after item which workers may find advantageous to 'plunder' on the assembly line (such as some items produced in the food or light industries). This rarely occurs, however, in heavy industrial enterprises, simply because items on the assembly line will rarely bring profit elsewhere. The plunderer must, in the words of Davletov, be able to 'take control of one or more of these] steps, or else discover a loophole'.[46]

Thus, opportunities for private earnings lie in occupations which have control over a finished good (distributors, truck drivers, guards) or control over the registration and documentation of raw materials or goods – the jobs, in other words, which indigenous Central Asians often occupy. In the Tashkent airport, bribes are frequent among the service personnel, to ensure timely delivery and collection of goods, to send off wares, to receive tickets for passenger flights, etc. Thus, while a highly-skilled air-traffic controller may receive average monthly earnings of roughly 200–300 roubles, several ticket-sellers receive

more than twice as much. In heavy industrial enterprises, watchmen
are bribed not to notice what is transported through their factory's
gates. In general, 'connections and friendly relations of trade personnel with supply and marketing personnel of production enterprises
Davletov writes 'do not remain a secret'.[47] Rarely, however, would
production workers participate in or benefit from such private activities.

The real value placed on each job, then, is perhaps better reflected
where data are available, in the bribes paid to obtain certain jobs than
in the official wages paid to the job holders. As mentioned in Chapter
5, each job in the USSR can be ascribed a monetary value, based upon
the opportunities for additional income or perquisites embodied in it
In Uzbekistan during the 1970s, the highest 'prices' were paid for jobs
in the service and agricultural spheres: often upwards of tens of
thousands of roubles to become director of a collective farm or director
of an institute, and upwards of tens or hundreds of thousands of
roubles to become a government minister.[48] Workers in an Uzbek
meat factory in 1977 paid approximately 2000 roubles each to receive
their jobs, and close to 1000 roubles are allegedly paid to receive work
as a lemonade-seller on a Tashkent street corner. An air-traffic
controller, on the other hand, paid a maximum of 500 roubles to
receive his job and several of his colleagues paid nothing at all.
'Want-ads' dot factory bulletin boards throughout the republic for
work in heavy industrial enterprises which also do not require a bribe
to be hired.

In short, one is left with a paradoxical situation whereby 'work which
is more complex, skilled, qualified and important for the development
of the economy', (to use the words of Grigoriev quoted earlier), in fact
often provides lower incomes than work often described as 'simple and
easy'. While magnitudes vary widely, jobs characterised by low wages
can often provide additional incomes many times the net earnings of
work in high priority sectors. In the light of Uzbekistan's ethnic
employment structure, this is *not* intended to suggest that Central
Asians uniformly earn more than Europeans: Slavs in urban service or
construction occupations may earn equally high second incomes as
their Central Asian counterparts, and many Central Asians may in fact
earn little or nothing on the side. What it is intended to suggest,
however, is that precisely by dominating the agricultural or service
spheres, light industry or food industries – or by remaining in the
population not working in social production – the indigenous
nationalities tend to concentrate in those jobs with greater *possibilities*
for private gain. The end-result is that – regardless of whether they

make use of these opportunities – indigenous Central Asians often have *access* to far higher income streams than do the Slavs in their midst.

CONSUMPTION PATTERNS

If private activity is in fact so widespread, particularly among the indigenous nationalities, why do the indigenous nationalities appear to be economically more disadvantaged than their Russian counterparts within the same republic? Their adobe homes without heating or plumbing, their lack of refrigerators or other modern appliances, their notable absence on planes destined for the Black Sea in the heart of the unbearably hot Uzbek summer – everything would suggest that the Uzbeks must be economically disadvantaged within their republic, whatever the level of allegedly lucrative private activity among them. If Uzbeks earn so much from the private sector, then why the apparent poverty?

Although there are richer and poorer groups among Uzbeks just as there are among most nationality groups in the USSR, an apparent disparity in living standards between the Asians and Europeans so often noted by travellers to Central Asia, it appears, is not due mainly to real differences in earnings between the two groups. Rather, it may be explained to a significant degree by different consumption patterns among the nationalities. As already mentioned, Uzbek values and ideas have changed significantly over the past sixty years and these changes are reflected in the consumer preferences of the local population. Uzbeks, for the most part, are proud of the new industries which have developed in their republic and luxuriate in many of the benefits that have accrued from Moscow. Many Uzbek families – and particularly rural collective farmers – have cars, and almost all Uzbeks have television sets, radios and electricity. They often value machine-made goods more than they do traditional handmade items. And gifts at Uzbek weddings often include Soviet shoes, black-market makeup or Western-style clothing.

At the same time, however, Uzbekistan's local residents in most other ways still exhibit traditional consumption patterns. To a great extent, they deliberately avoid expenditures on many modern items, preferring to spend roubles on their own traditional goods or festivals. I spent hours, for example, discussing the merits of modern kitchen appliances with several Uzbek women – the merits of modern refrigeration as opposed to their deep holes in the ground, or the benefits of modern ovens compared with their traditional clay ovens, or *tandoor*. These women staunchly insisted that modern home conveniences are generally useless, and refused to buy them. On the other hand, they reserve vast sums of roubles for festivals, or for celebrations of births, marriages, circumcisions and deaths.[49] Priding themselves on their hospitality, they prefer never to be without the means to provide sumptuous feasts at a moment's notice.

This persistence of traditional values is reflected in terms of savings. Amounts in savings deposits have risen in Uzbekistan over the past sixty years, to a level at the end of 1978 of about 182 roubles per person – a level only about one third of the USSR average.[50] Yet as Birman estimates, these deposits constitute only a small fraction of the actual savings of Uzbekistan's indigenous population. Instead, the 'age-old mentality of hoarding currency (and other valuables)' which Louis Duprée ascribes to the Afghan population across the border appears strong among the Asian populations in the USSR as well,[51] and vast amounts of roubles are saved within the home. Indeed, while Birman estimates that savings 'under mattresses' in the Soviet Union as a whole comprise 50 to 60 billion roubles, between 25 and 33 per cent of these unofficial savings, he estimates, (about 15 billion roubles) are now concentrated in the Central Asian republics alone.[52]

Thus, after a trip through the mountain ranges of Uzbekistan, one would hardly imagine the mountain shepherd to be exceptionally privileged. Housing conditions appear to be worse than the most poverty-stricken rural areas of the Western world; communities are often without running water; many of the modern goods which have accrued to urban Uzbekistan have not appeared in his mountain village. Yet these same mountain shepherds are often envied as among Uzbekistan's wealthiest inhabitants. Because they, in practice, have a partial monopoly on Uzbekistan's meat production – a glaringly 'scarce' good – they are seen as earning tremendous sums from private sales of meat alone. Their larders are rarely without an ample supply of beef and lamb – meat which urban residents scarcely dream of attaining; their wedding ceremonies and gifts are often among the most elaborate; and several times I was reminded of not only legendary Uzbek mountain residents who had invaluable sums of gold and silver coins stashed away under their earthen floors.

In a more general sense, it is the rare Uzbek who dreams of trips to Paris, or even to Eastern Europe or to the Black Sea. Rarely would he or she wish to buy washing machines, or Soviet household amenities generally available in Uzbekistan's government stores. Russians, on the other hand, regard with contempt what they consider to be the backward custom of hoarding durables underground, or lavishly spending all one's 'earnings' on ceremonies and gifts. They tend to prefer to spend roubles on household goods, or summers in the Baltic away from Uzbekistan's desert heat. To the visiting Westerner's eyes, therefore, the Russian appears to be 'better off', but only when Western standards are applied. Within the framework of indigenous lifestyles, quite the opposite could well be the case.

In other words, different consumption patterns make it particularly difficult to determine which nationality groups 'live better' in Uzbekistan. The measuring rod would have to be adjusted to account for discrepancies in consumption patterns – an impossible task, since living standards, judged in local terms, are not always as they appear to the Western eye. What is important here, however, is that the potentially high earnings from the private sectors cited above are not contradicted by low living standards among the local populations. On the contrary, under certain circumstances activity in the private sector may prove to be more lucrative and more advantageous in terms of raising one's living standard than full-time work exclusively in social production.

In short, one is forced to revise the preliminary conclusion suggested above, that the indigenous nationalities comprise a financially-disadvantaged social class and continue to be denied access to the most remunerative occupations within their own republic. Russians indeed tend to dominate the highest-paid jobs and sectors, but actual earnings from the native-dominated sectors (agricultural and the services) can often greatly exceed those of the European-dominated sectors and jobs. This is not to suggest, of course, that individuals employed in the traditional jobs are uniformly better off than those in other sectors, nor that this disparity is simply masked by different consumption patterns; from the evidence available, such an assertion would be impossible either to defend or refute. What it does suggest, however, is that there are often viable economic incentives for an individual to remain full-time in household or private subsidiary activity, or to participate in the private economy at the expense of full-time work in social production. The result is that – regardless of whether or not advantage is taken of these opportunities – the access to higher-income streams tends to encourage the indigenous nationalities to remain in the traditional sectors, rather than moving to the heavy industrial or more modern spheres.

7 The Role of Culture

If income differentials are perhaps the overriding factor colouring labour force distribution by nationality, they are not the only factor. Cultural attitudes and traditions also partly determine the preference for particular occupations among the different nationality groups. In the preceding sections, the employment distribution by nationality was approached mainly as the result of external circumstances, that is, as the result of different demographic behaviour among the nationalities, different educational levels, place of residence and proximity to industrial centres, incomes, and some element of discrimination against one or another of the nationalities. Yet differences in behaviour are determined by internal, or cultural, as well as by external sets of factors. Even where external circumstances may be identical, groups of people often behave differently because of attitudinal differences or differences in tastes, values and aspirations.

Thus, aside from economic factors, prestige, the quality and interest of the work and other social and cultural reasons also play a role in occupational choices in Uzbekistan, and often in markedly different ways among Uzbekistan's nationality groups. As Glazer and Moynihan so aptly point out

> Every society establishes norms – socially established values – selected from a universe of such values ... It can be thought a good thing to be wealthy, alternatively to be poor; to be dark or to be light; generous or mean; religious or atheistic; fun-loving or dour; promiscuous or chaste ...

> As between different ethnic groups, which have made quite different selections from the universe of possibilities, the norms of one are likely to be quite different from those of another, such that individu-

200

als who are successful by the standards of their own groups will be failures by those of the other . . .

Ethnic groups bring different norms to bear on common circumstances with consequent different levels of success – hence group differences in status.[1]

The indigenous nationalities in Uzbekistan comprise a society which for centuries has been quite distinct from that of the Russians. These various historical experiences have shaped different values, aspirations and outlooks which have proved markedly resistant to change. In Uzbekistan today, therefore, the norms and values of the local population often contrast sharply with those of the Slavs, and evaluations of 'desirable' or 'prestigious' work among the two groups often do not coincide. As suggested above, Western observers often assume that the indigenous nationalities not only receive lower incomes in Uzbekistan, but also occupy less prestigious occupations than the Europeans in their midst. But at the risk of oversimplifying societal or cultural generalisations, one must pose several questions in a social as well as economic vein: what is the role of 'culture' in Uzbekistan's labour force distribution? How does it differ among Asians and Slavs? And how might these differences, too, affect the evaluation and distribution of occupations among Uzbekistan's nationality groups?

THE IDEA OF CULTURE AND ITS PERSISTENCE

Determining the effect of culture and tradition on behaviour is complex anywhere in the world. The first problem, of course, is defining the elements of a 'culture' itself. 'Culture' has been defined only in its broadest terms, as the sum of basic values and beliefs, perceptions of history and politics, the foci of identification and loyalties, and the knowledge, perceptions and expectations which have been shaped among a nation or group by a specific historical experience.[2] When one attempts to narrow this definition, however, to apply to a specific nation or group, the task is laden with difficulties. Because of the 'informal logic of life', in Geertz's words, attempting to identify individual elements of a culture is

like trying to read (in the sense of 'construct a reading of') a manuscript – foreign, faded, full of ellipses, incoherencies, suspi-

cious emendations and tendentious commentaries, but written no
in conventionalised graphs of sound but in transient examples o
shaped behaviour.[3]

The observer's own cultural biases undoubtedly distort the 'reading' o
other cultures, making it easy to slip into generalisations and
stereotypes. Indeed, all too frequently the observations suggest more
about the observer than about what has been observed.

Even tentatively isolating specific features of a particular culture
moreover, leads to other problems in measuring their effects or
behaviour. Clearly people behave differently in various parts of the
world. The African is different from the Frenchman; the Asian often
appears to have different attitudes, values and aspirations from the
European. The extent to which this is the result of varying cultures
however, as opposed to external circumstances has become the focus
of considerable controversy. The controversy ranges between those
who regard culture as a major, distinct and measurable determinant o
behaviour in all societies and those who underplay its significance and
regard it as a fundamentally minor determinant.

Without examining the merits of each argument here, the consensus
appears to be somewhere in the middle: that while structures shape the
norms and aspirations of a people, so too, to a considerable extent, do
cultural factors. As Berliner notes, culture does not uniquely determine behaviour, but acts as a schedule, prescribing the different forms
of behaviour that are appropriate under specific conditions.[4] Aspirations, accepted norms and perceptions of one's place in the world
depend on the legacy of centuries of experience, as well as on the
circumstances of an immediate time and place.

That cultural differences are reflected specifically in economic
behaviour is a theme which has gained attention in recent years. Here
in particular one sees the interplay between culture and externalities.
The general argument seems to be that people with the same values
may behave differently depending on their position in the social or
economic structure of a particular society; but that position cannot be
divorced from an individual's values. In other words, an individual's
place in economic life in part determines behaviour; cultural values
however are involved in the decision on how, or even whether, to
participate in economic life.

Indeed, this interaction between culture and social structure as it
pertains to economic activity has led to the defining of a relatively new
discipline, which the American economist Kenneth Boulding has aptly

labelled 'cultural economics'. In an article published as part of a symposium on culture in the social sciences, Boulding asserts the need to analyse the interplay of culture with consumer preferences, acquisition of skills and economic trends in general. 'The whole structure of terms of trade' he writes '... is an integral part of any set of cultural relations ...'[5] Boulding calls for further analysis of the processes by which certain ideas and interests become fashionable or unfashionable, and how they affect economics.[6] 'Cultural economics' he concludes at one point 'must look upon both preferences, skills and techniques as essentially learned in the great processes of cultural transmission . . . Social learning, indeed, is the central concept of culture.'[7] As was echoed by a colleague, in general, 'Humane communities tend to have distinctive characteristics which last over time ... and collectives have dynamic laws with respect to development and change.'[8] Although the exact mechanisms for studying these differences are unclear, many social scientists agree that cultural patterns affect economic behaviour, both in production and consumption, and that this effect is enduring despite external changes.

For the most part, Soviet leaders and scholars have also acknowledged the enduring effects of culture on behaviour, even though the Soviet system is based on the opposite premise, that is, that economic structure is a far greater determinant of behaviour than culture, and thus that the development of socialism and communism in the USSR will gradually eradicate cultural and behavioural differences among the peoples living there. 'When the new has just been born,' Lenin noted over sixty years ago, 'the old always remains stronger for some time.'[9] Today, the durability of culture and tradition, and the fact that differences in behaviour persist in Soviet society continues to be acknowledged on the most official levels.[10]

Regarding economic activity, Soviet scholars agree that the effect of culture on work behaviour is also strong and enduring. Lenin emphasised at the onset of Soviet power that 'the assertion of a new consciousness, of a Communist relation to work, is a complex and long process, which will occupy "an entire historical epoch"'.[11] Today, the inevitable eradication of cultural differences which was to come with the construction of communism – while still regarded as inevitable – is admitted to have been only partial. Still today, in the words of one Soviet scholar, 'National differences condition specifics in the way of life; they appear in labour activity, daily life, and in the spiritual culture, language, and psychology of nations and peoples ...'[12] And still today, this is considered to be particularly true among the Soviet

Central Asians. Speaking of the 'lack of correspondence' between rates of technical progress and attitudinal change in the USSR, another Soviet scholar in the 1970s singled out Central Asia as illustrative of a particularly large attitudinal lag:

> If this [lack of correspondence] is characteristic for our society in general, then it is all the more noticeable in the republics of Central Asia, which in an economic sense in a relatively short historical period completed a leap unparalleled in scope ... In the consciousness and behaviour of some parts of the population, traditions and survivals continue to be preserved which, by their character and content, are not compatible with the socio-economic level of the development of society.[13]

In the light of the acknowledgement, then, that culture affects economic behaviour; that cultural differences among peoples and nationalities can be wide and enduring; and that these facts are at least as true in Soviet Central Asia as elsewhere, one must broach two questions in any analysis of labour issues in Uzbekistan: to what degree and in what ways do different cultures among the indigenous and non-indigenous nationalities imply attitudinal differences towards labour force participation? And in what ways do they affect work behaviour? 'Work' a Soviet scholar writes 'supposes the process of the continuity of generations. The existence of any labour act is senseless without consideration of the earlier sum of human experience . . .'[14] Given the vastly different historical experiences of the indigenous and non-indigenous nationalities in Uzbekistan, one would expect to find substantial differences in attitudes, norms and behaviour among them still today.

CULTURE AND THE LABOUR FORCE IN UZBEKISTAN

Characteristics of the pattern of work in pre-Revolutionary Turkestan are discussed in Chapter 3: the predominance of agriculture and trade and the disdain for low-level industrial work among the indigenous nationalities, the subordinate position of women, and the predominance of a rural way of life. Indigenous men in Turkestan were mainly agricultural workers, nomads, and traders, in a tightly-knit society where farming, nomadism, trade and war were regarded as the proper pursuits of man. As in subsistence economies elsewhere, the indigenous nationalities were tied to the land or livestock in an interdependent system, residing in homes and rural villages which answered particular economic and social needs. Women were regarded as unfit for participation in social intercourse; their proper place in the workforce was quite clearly in the fields or in the home. To the degree that these attitudes were due to the influence of religion, the general character of 'orientalism', or to the general character of pre-modern societies is difficult to measure. As a sum total, they formed a comprehensive and explicit set of norms which had remained relatively unchanged for centuries.

These values and attitudes towards work, female employment and way of life contrasted greatly with those of the Slavs who migrated to Turkestan during the latter part of the nineteenth century, and with the ideals and goals of the new Soviet regime in the early 1920s.

> Marxism was the result of the impact of systematised Western social philosophies, in the hands of very able and embittered men on a double-storeyed, ill-cemented Russian society ... The formulas of Marxism, deriving from the West and not from the East, were at all points at variance with an age-old tradition, a tradition resting in part on the faith of Islam, and in part and equally significantly on that sort of positive insouciance, the hallmark of the free-born horsemen of the steppe.[15]

As discussed in Chapter 3, the majority of Slavs who migrated to Uzbekistan both before and after the Revolution were military personnel, administrators or professionals – teachers, industrial or Party workers, or the like – whose life-style and professional aspirations were fundamentally different from those of the Asian nomads, peasants and merchants whom they encountered. Trained in the manner of the West and, in the post-Revolutionary period, perhaps imbued with the fervour of socialist construction, the European immigrants were mainly urban and oriented towards the values and training of the Western world. Women in the Slavic worlds were neither veiled nor secluded from working in the public domain. Officially, industrialisation was regarded as a positive drive to construct a new social order and powerful state.

Notwithstanding the sharp differences between the two worlds, the Slavs who overran Uzbekistan strove deliberately to transform the Uzbeks' environment, traditions and attitudes regarding work and social interaction. This meant, then, imbuing the indigenous peoples with a new perception of the value of industrial and 'progressive' forms of work, encouraging urbanisation, and changing attitudes – among male and female alike – towards the participation of women in the labour force. Drawing the local nationalities into a modern workforce was intended not only to contribute to economic growth, but gradually to dilute and transform traditional values and beliefs, to weaken the hold of the past, and hence to eradicate any real or potential political opposition.

More than sixty years after the Revolution, the results of these efforts have been mixed. As illustrated above, the transformations effected in Uzbekistan since the Revolution have indeed been great. With rapid economic change in Uzbekistan, moreover, there is no doubt that attitudes among the local populations have changed as well, in many ways conforming to Soviet standards. Uzbeks in large part regard many of the transformations which have occurred in their republic with a sense of pride and accomplishment, and see themselves as having played, and as playing, a central role in that modernisation process. At the same time, however, deeply ingrained values and ideas die hard, and the attitudinal changes normally associated with modernisation have been only partial. 'In passing to review some of the events of a tangled past,' Caroe writes 'it will be well to bear in mind how enduring is the influence of the two environments, one of the desert and the other of the sown.'[16] The imprint of the past is reflected in deeply psychological ways, which greatly affect behaviour in the economic realm and modernisation as a whole.

With regard to occupational choices, for example, the strong aversion to industrial labour, so colourfully depicted by travelogues of nineteenth-century travellers to Turkestan, still persists. In a dissertation completed in Tashkent in 1967, an Uzbek scholar suggested that industrial work among indigenous inhabitants of pre-revolutionary Turkestan was avoided by all but the lowest strata of society – even if other types of work in which they engaged may have been equally arduous. 'Before the Revolution' he writes 'it was characteristic that the main contingent of indigenous personnel working [in the oil industry of the Fergana Valley] was from the poorest levels of the peasantry, who for many years had worked in large landholdings of the *bei*.'[17] The Hungarian traveller, Vambery, also refers to the disdain for manual work and the preference among indigenous men for trade. After the Revolution, Muzaparov writes, only the most deprived classes entered the fuel or heavy industrial sectors.

Today, the decided preference among Uzbeks for work in the non-industrial spheres is notable. As Bacon suggests, the Uzbeks share with the peoples of Southern Asia the notion that educated people should not soil their hands with manual labour.'[18] Instead, white-collar jobs are sought, and trade and agriculture remain high on the list of preferences. Indeed, addressing the problems of labour distribution in March 1982, the late First Secretary of Uzbekistan, Sharif Rashidov, noted the local emphasis placed upon work 'in science, culture or the arts and not in production'.[19] 'More people' he stressed 'must be encouraged to work in industry and construction.' Yet as if in response to the speech itself, I was surprised to hear frequent comments from local Central Asians along the lines of: 'we are traders'; 'we are farmers', and 'we are poets'. 'Want ads' for industrial jobs appear unattractive to indigenous Central Asians, and remain largely unanswered.

A continued preference for the traditional sectors, of course, and a native reluctance to embrace new technological sectors in a modernising society are not unique to Soviet Asia. They stem largely from local or peasant psychology in general, and from the way in which modernisation and economic development occur. With regard to the former, for example, the American anthropologist James C. Scott's analysis of peasant psychology in South-east Asia is perhaps instructive. The subsistence ethic' he notes, has a strong moral as well as an economic dimension: the preoccupation with subsistence mentally ties the peasant to the land or the source of subsistence, reducing any inclination to move away from that source even if higher incomes may be offered elsewhere.[20] Changes in forms of land-ownership or the introduction of new forms of wage employment, therefore, threaten this security and are resisted. As Scott writes:

> there is a correspondence between the logic of the subsistence ethic and the concrete choices and values of much of the peasantry in South-east Asia. At the level of village reciprocity, occupational preferences, and the evaluation of tenancy and taxation, there appears to be a clear inclination to favor those institutions and relationships which minimize the risks to subsistence, though they may claim much of the surplus. These preferences grow out of the precarious human condition of subsistence farmers but they also take on a moral dimension as a claim on the society in which they live.[21]

The 'violation of this claim by the economic and social transformations of the colonial period' is the subject of Scott's analysis of South-east

Asian development. He suggests that inhabitants of traditional societies often regard the introduction of industry and other wage-paying sectors divorced from the means of subsistence not with favour, but with suspicion.

These considerations are only compounded by the process of modernisation itself. Modernisation tends to build on the old, and cannot immediately and totally uproot traditional norms and values. In essence, the 'normal transition' generally entails what another anthropologist, Clifford Geertz describes as readjusting a bazaar and agrarian economy to a more modern society, of shifting or defining trading patterns, of adapting collective and settled forms of traditional peasant society to the more varied needs of a modern economy.[22] Geertz cites, for example, the broad continuum in Indonesia from bazaar-trader to store proprietor, and from bazaar-craftsman to factory manager in carpentry, the garment-making trades, or household industry and manufacturing. Individuals tend to gravitate towards occupations which are familiar to them, or which demand little change in routine or pace of life.

Indeed, similar transitions to those in Uzbekistan can be seen in several countries of the contemporary Islamic Middle East. The rapid influx of capital and technology has led to two separate labour markets in much of the Arab world, where the indigenous populations often remain outside the modern sector.[23] Several analysts of Middle Eastern affairs have referred to the same preference for academic and literacy courses over vocational or technical education in, for example, Saudi Arabia and the Gulf States,[24] and to the lack of sufficient push- or pull-factors to attract the local population to urban areas or the non-traditional sectors.[25] Despite numerous government programmes to encourage the opposite, many indigenous Middle Easterners throughout the Arab world prefer to remain in the services or trade. As two Western specialists on manpower in the Middle East have noted, technology in many parts of the Arab world has been employed 'only to preserve a traditional life-style'.[26]

Despite the rapid rate of industrialisation and the influx of technology in Uzbekistan, similar transitions have occurred there as well. Maintaining attitudes typical of many third-world farming and nomadic communities, the indigenous nationalities in Uzbekistan continue to avoid the industrial sectors or manual work. The context for agriculture or trade – the mechanisms or channels for conducting work – may have changed somewhat in response to new circumstances or Soviet control; but the indigenous nationalities in Uzbekistan have still continued to practise their traditional merchant and agricultural occupations. Today, Uzbekistan's bazaars may no longer be the centre of city activity that they were a century ago, as goods are also sold through co-operatives and state-owned stores. None the less, they still thrive as centres for the sale of agricultural produce, household goods, crafts and art. Elizabeth Bacon, another American anthropologist who studied Central Asia, notes:

> replacing the leisurely commerce of the old bazaar, there seems to have been on the one hand a partial reversion to a direct trade between producer and consumer; and on the other, a modern type of free enterprise in which alert entrepreneurs ship fruit and vegetables by bus or train to cities outside the oases sometimes as far as Moscow, or buy up scarce factory-made goods for resale in the local market ... The oasis peoples' cultural interest in trade has retained its vitality, but the forms have been greatly modified.[27]

As long as circumstances allow – and certainly as long as economic incentives to enter industry remain minimal – indigenous Central Asians seem intent upon remaining in work associated with commerce, agriculture or the arts. Even in the capital cities, one has only to roam through the market place – amidst the aroma of Asian spices, the colourful interplay of Asian dress and the clamour of Central Asians bartering produce or crafts – to sense how little the imprint of the past has faded.

This attitude towards occupational choice has remained intertwined with native attachment to a rural life-style and particular forms of housing, community and kin organisation. The extended family in pre-Revolutionary Turkestan was both a unit of consumption and production, an independent world unto itself. Because of the importance of the extended family, the indigenous inhabitants constructed homes in order that several generations live in one household. In addition to the dwelling proper, homes included a courtyard and garden, and rarely exceeded one storey. In Central Asian terms, Russian urban life provided few advantages over rural settlement. It therefore provided few incentives to move to the towns, and no model to change indigenous patterns of life which had developed over centuries to meet local needs.

Today, the preference for a rural way of life – a preference which goes beyond the question of preferring agriculture or industrial work – remains a major determinant among Uzbekistan's indigenous nationalities in their choice of occupation. The type of housing, smaller agricultural plots and more structured and rigorous way of life associated with Uzbekistan's new industrial urban areas are tremendous constraints on encouraging rural Central Asians to move to new cities built recently to meet industrial needs.[28] Several correspondents have cited accounts of Central Asians who, after several years' residence in the cities, have moved back to the villages. According to one reporter, the head of a Tadzhik family was content to cut his salary by over 75 per cent to move back to the countryside after several years' residence in Dushanbe. 'For reasons of economic expediency and social psychology,' the reporter concluded 'the Tadzhik attached greater value to a one-storey private home and garden than to a city apartment.'[29] This attitude seems typical of many, if not most Central Asians in Uzbekistan, who are reluctant or unwilling to trade the intimacy, leisure and/or practicality of their adobe homes or rural life-style for the alien features of modern Soviet housing or conventional urban environments. Indeed, other observers have referred to local fears that because so many Uzbeks – even talented university graduates – prefer a rural life-style and are maintaining or seeking employment in the less-intensely urbanised areas, Tashkent might become even more Russianised than it is.[30]

Reinforcing the effect of rural life-styles on occupational preferences among the indigenous nationalities is its negative corollary: Russian dominance of the new industrial cities and enterprises in Uzbekistan. Because Slavs have tended to dominate the industrial sectors and new urban areas, Russian has become the main language of industry, and new industrial cities, Russian domaines. This factor perpetuates the notion among Uzbekistan's indigenous populations that industry and newly-constructed urban areas are in fact alien to their culture and heritage. It thus further impedes their entrance into the industrial sectors and migration to new cities and towns.

Lastly, rigid attitudes determining the place of women in the Central Asian workforce have been slow to change as well. Considered, at least in a public sense, among the lowest elements of society, women in pre-Revolutionary Uzbekistan were confined to the physical work which men shunned. Veiled in public, generally segregated from men, women did not aspire to participate in the trades or public life, nor was it regarded as fitting that they do so. Rather, women were confined to agricultural work in the fields, or domestic work within the home. Although perhaps exaggerated, the observations of nineteenth-century travellers to Turkestan are none the less revealing in this regard: 'While the poor women are fatiguing themselves with their laborious occupation,' Vambery writes 'their lord and master is accustomed to snore through his noonday siesta.'[31] Or as another nineteenth-century traveller put it:

> They spin, embroider – very well too – cook, and do most of the work, as the men are too lazy to do more than look after the horses ... The men devote themselves almost entirely to the care of their horses, leaving all the work to be done by the women, and leading in general a lazy, shiftless life, although when it comes to riding they are indefatigable, and will go hundreds of miles without seeming to be in the slightest degree tired.[32]

Although the context has greatly altered today, the traditional attitude towards participation of women in the labour force persists in large measure. Official Soviet claims stress the enormous strides women have made in entering the industrial sectors or particular professions, and the fact that equal opportunities in employment and wages are open to them as they are to men. Regardless of the opportunities open to them, however, indigenous women are still often discouraged, by husbands, family and local public opinion, from participating in social production, or work in the public domain. Today, when women do work outside the home, their choice of occupation is more often circumscribed by tradition and culture than by actual opportunities, prospects for economic gain, or government policy. Casual observation in Uzbekistan, particularly outside the main cities, affirms the widespread conviction that a woman's place is in the home, or in particular sectors which are rather rigidly regarded as 'women's work'. As already shown, working women are generally concentrated in low-skilled agricultural work or in factories producing domestic goods. Indigenous men and women alike often desire that their wives or daughters work in isolation from men – hence the predominance of indigenous female industrial employees in, for example, sewing factories.

Within particular professions, moreover, the place of women in Uzbekistan today is also more often determined by social attitudes than by salary or opportunity. For example, I was often told that in the legal profession, litigation is 'mainly men's work', since 'in a courtroom, women are not taken as seriously'. The public nature of litigation is regarded as contrary to the proper place of women; many topics (such as rape) are regarded as subjects not fit for public discussion by women; and allegedly, many Uzbek men on trial have simply refused to talk to female prosecutors.

Today, these attitudes with regard to participation in the workforce are pervasive. Perhaps of most significance, however, is the fact that all these attitudes are felt among indigenous women and men alike. The predominance of indigenous men in the non-industrial jobs, and the low female labour force participation rates in certain sectors, do not appear to be solely, or even mainly, the result of discrimination on the basis of sex or nationality. Rather, they seem to result in part from strong cultural attitudes which are still upheld by the society as a whole. Often, therefore, official efforts to encourage industrial employment, greater geographical mobility or higher female participation rates among the indigenous nationalities are regarded as an assault on deeply-held convictions and cultural attitudes, rather than as a liberation from them. The fact that Russians dominate certain 'undesirable' sectors or jobs is often regarded with favour by the indigenous Central Asians, rather than with disdain.

STUDIES ON CULTURAL CHANGE AND CONTINUITY IN UZBEKISTAN'S LABOUR FORCE

Until recently, few studies, Soviet or Western, directly addressed any of these attitudinal questions connecting labour and nationality issues. Nationality studies were confined to ethnographies, or studies in the art, history or languages of the various nationalities. Manpower studies focused on economics and planning without reference to culture or nationality.

Beginning in the late 1960s, however, the need for linking the two began to emerge. Cultural and attitudinal questions regarding the different nationalities began to be viewed in the USSR as a crucial component of studies on the workforce and manpower planning, and the turn of the decade saw increasing calls to focus attention on their interconnection. 'Until most recent times' one Uzbek social scientist wrote in 1974 'motivation towards work, with some exceptions, was not looked at in direct connection with the development of national relations in our country . . . although practice shows that an analysis of nationality relations is essential on all levels in which they occur.'[33] 'The personal aspect of nationality relations' he added 'is now only beginning to become an object of close study.' Slightly earlier, a Soviet ethnographer in Moscow, V. Pokshishevskii suggested that a generally neglected and 'important field for further research' should be:

the problem of the preference expressed by different nationalities and even ethnic groups for particular occupations; on the greater or lesser ease with which they acquire work habits and vocational skills; and, correspondingly, about the potential for attracting them to various branches of the economy, to the cities, etc. . . . Ethnic diversity is not only a problem in national-cultural terms, in forming one socialist nation, but also in different production habits.[34]

By the 1970s, several Soviet scholars were beginning to address the persistence of sharp differences in work preferences and habits among the different nationalities.[35] The renewed attention focused on these concerns seemed to confirm the hypothesis that various 'cultures' are reflected in different ways among members of the workforce, and that these cultural attitudes and qualities have been more enduring than was anticipated by Soviet leaders decades ago. Unfortunately, however, few of these scholars pursued the problem much beyond addressing the need for further studies. Few attempted to analyse the precise realms in which differences were to be found or the precise ways in which these differences could be studied.

A few studies which did address some of these issues in more detail, however, were conducted by Soviet scholars within Uzbekistan. In 1974, the Soviet social scientist A. S. Chamkin completed a study to provide some deeper analysis of different cultural values among personnel of the same enterprises, that is, among personnel working in the same external circumstances in Uzbekistan, but of different nationalities. More specifically, he attempted to analyse 'the dynamics of inter-nationality relations on an individual level and the intensity and direction of their development in the sphere of social production'. His hypothesis was the same as that described above: that the process of development involves both continuity and change, and that traditional attitudes, therefore, still play a central role in labour force participation in Uzbekistan.

From the point of view of Marxist sociology, the national strongly retains its specific features in culture, domestic life, traditions and habits. In the early stage of development, each nation has, due to objective reasons, clearly expressed specifics of an established economic profile. The character of production, therefore, forms a definite pattern of work habits, professional knowledge and value orientations.[36]

Chamkin's aim was twofold: to measure how persistently the habits and value orientations associated with that early stage of development in Uzbekistan were still evident in the mid-1970s; and to measure how much they had drawn closer to those of the Russians in the light of the broader social changes which had occurred over the past half century.

Between 1971 and 1974, Chamkin conducted social research in seven industrial enterprises and construction trusts in the newly-opened areas of the Hungry and Karshi Steppes. In the original study, 1995 people were surveyed; in 1974, a control study consisting of 525 people was conducted in the knitwear firm 'Malika' in Tashkent and its subsidiary in Dzhizak. All the enterprises and organisations researched by Chamkin had been established at the beginning of the 1960s. Generally, all the organisations and enterprises were characterised by 'a high level of specialisation', a fairly high level of capital intensiveness, and an 'acute deficit' in the labour force.

Because the regions in which all the enterprises had been established were generally devoid of their own labour resources, the main source

TABLE 7.1   *Place of origin and dates of settlement of the labour force,*
Chamkin's study, 1971 – 4

Region	Percentage of Labour Force
Given city or region	25.8
Other city/region, same *oblast'*	9.4
Other *oblast'*, Uzbekistan	12.8
Other republic	52.0
Total:	100.0
Time of Settlement	
Born in given city/region	25.8
Migrated 1930 – 40	3.4
1940 – 50	6.7
1950 – 56	5.3
1956 – 60	4.6
1960 – 65	13.7
1965 – 70	26.0
1970 and later	14.5
Total	100.0

SOURCE   A. S. Chamkin 'Motivy k trudu v sfere obshchestvennogo proizvodstva', unpublished doctoral dissertation, Tashkent, 1976, pp. 68–9.

TABLE 7.2   *Skill-level of labour force, Chamkin's study,*
by age, sex and nationality (as percentage)

Age	Unskilled *	Semi-skilled *	Skilled *	Total
Under 18 years old	–	–	2.8	–
From 18–25	20.8	20.5	35.2	–
25–30	16.5	25.4	21.1	–
30–40	26.4	36.1	27.5	–
Over 40	36.3	18.0	13.4	–
Total	100.0	100.0	100.0	–
Sex:				
Both sexes	23.0	36.6	40.4	100.0
Women	36.9	42.1	21.0	100.0
Men	20.4	31.8	47.8	100.0
Nationality:				
Uzbeks	27.6	41.3	31.1	100.0
Russians	14.3	38.9	46.8	100.0
Other	15.8	39.4	44.8	100.0

[a] Literally, *nesoderzhatel'naia, malosoderzhatel'naia* and *soderzhatel'naia*
work. Chamkin regarded the contents of work as 'the sum of functions fulfilled
in the work process, the basis of which is technological progress.' In compiling
his classification, he took into account the level of mechanisation of work and
the level of necessary skills. *Nesoderzhatel'naia* work was defined as work
wherein workers are employed in simple production operations without using
machines or in those occupations which do not demand professional training.
This category includes such occupations as construction engineers, scaffolders
and various types of workers in occupations which can be learned in one week
or less. The average level of education in this group was 7.8 classes. Workers in
the category of *malosoderzhatel'naia* work were employed to work on simple
machinery. Their work averaged between one and two months to learn, and
included such categories as operators and their assistants, motorists and crane
drivers. The average level of education was 7.6 classes. Workers in
soderzhatel'naia work were employed in manual work using instruments
rather than machines. These professions—such as metal craftsmen, electri-
cians, welders and carpenters – generally take between one and two years to
learn in a vocational school (PTU) or up to six months to learn on the job. The
average level of education in this category was 8.3 classes. 'Although their
work is manual', Chamkin writes, 'the use of an instrument demands a certain
amount of knowledge and production experience' (p. 56).

SOURCE   A. S. Chamkin, 'Motivy k trudu v sfere obshchestvennogo proizvodstva', Unpublished doctoral dissertation, Tashkent, 1976:
pp. 126–9 for lines 1–5; p. 59 for line 7; pp. 123–4 for lines 8–9;
p. 56 for lines 10–12.

of cadres in each case was in-migrants from other *oblasts* and regions of Uzbekistan, and from other republics.[37] The age, sex and skill structure was overwhelmingly young, male and with low levels of educational training,[38] and the nationality composition of the selected enterprises was largely non-indigenous. 48 per cent of all personnel were Russian, 21 per cent Uzbek, and 31 per cent other (consisting of 18 per cent Tatar, 6 per cent Ukrainian, 3 per cent Korean, and 4 per cent other). The proportion of Uzbeks varied with each enterprise and organisation: The Yangier combine was 8 per cent Uzbek; the Bekabad combine, 13 per cent Uzbek; and the Dzhizak enterprise, 26 per cent Uzbek, all drawn mainly from the city itself or from neighbouring surrounding areas. As Table 7.2 illustrates, however, in almost all the enterprises, Uzbeks were more highly represented in the lower skilled jobs, and Russians, in the higher skilled occupations. Almost 70 per cent of the Uzbeks surveyed were employed in unskilled or semi-skilled occupations, while 47 per cent of the Russians were in skilled occupations. Tables 7.1 and 7.2 summarises Chamkin's sample.

The technical or industrial nature of the enterprises; the age and place of origin of the personnel surveyed; and the sex, educational and nationality compositions of the enterprises all suggest that the Uzbeks in his survey were among the most 'modernised' and the most culturally advanced segments, in Soviet terms, of the Uzbek population. The majority of Uzbeks surveyed were mainly young, single, and male; they had entered an industrial or technical occupation; and in a republic whose indigenous population is characterised by extremely low geographical mobility, they had changed their place of residence to do so. None the less, Chamkin's results suggest that despite their high level of 'modernisation', certain traditional and cultural traits still persist, colouring aspirations, values and general attitudes towards one's place in the labour force.

Some of Chamkin's findings are summarised in Table 7.3. In broad terms, the main distinctions he drew between the attitudes of the Uzbeks and Russians in Uzbekistan's industrial labour force concerned general social and cultural values:

> Uzbeks are involved in social self-administration and with the collective acceptance of decisions on questions of social life; they exhibit great interest towards active social vocations. Russians, on the other hand, are attracted more towards enhancing cultural values (studies, reading artistic literature, going to movies, theatre and concerts).[39]

TABLE 7.3   *Social and cultural values, by nationality (shown as percentage, 'multi-nationality', Chamkin's study, Uzbekistan, 1974)*

Values	Uzbeks	Russians
Active participation in social life	15.5	9.5
Desire to study	16.6	22.6
More time to devote to studies	10.5	11.2
Reading artistic literature	28.8	40.4
Going to movies, the theatre, concerts	16.6	22.4
Rationalisation and innovation for work	–	7.2
Participation in artistic do-it-yourself circles	–	5.2
Amateur occupations	13.1	13.8
Participation in sports	15.6	18.8
Watching television	31.8	23.9
Work in the household economy	57.6	32.6
More time to spend with the family	47.0	52.8
To find additional work of some kind	15.1	8.9
Simply to rest	4.5	10.6

SOURCE   A. S. Chamkin, 'Motivy k trudu v sfere obshchestvennogo proizvodstva', Unpublished doctoral dissertation, Tashkent, 1976, p. 100.

With particular regard to the labour force, however, his findings are especially revealing. Despite some overlap in the level of job satisfaction and reasons for dissatisfaction, Chamkin's study confirms some preference among Uzbeks for private and household work and their preference for non-technical activities by comparison with their Russian counterparts. Close to 58 per cent of the Uzbeks surveyed placed significant value on work in the household economy in their daily lives outside the workplace, as opposed to fewer than 33 per cent of the Russians. At the same time, Chamkin notes the aversion to more technical pursuits: 'The total absence among Uzbeks of those wishing to occupy themselves with rationalisation and innovation for work speaks to the fact that they still have not acquired all the heights of productive mastery.'[40] Especially in light of the fact that Chamkin's sample was comprised of among the most 'modernised' segments of Uzbekistan's indigenous population – specifically, among young, Uzbek males who had already entered the industrial and technical sectors and had largely moved their place of residence to do so – the disparities that it portrays are all the more significant.

Chamkin's ultimate conclusions regarding differences in attitudes and values among Uzbeks and Russians in the industrial workforce are ambivalent. On the one hand, he suggests that cultural differences in attitudes towards work may not be as enduring as other aspects of culture and tradition.[41] On the other hand, however, his study suggests that cultural aspects of nationality still significantly affect attitudes towards work and professional aspirations:

> Nationality relations appearing in the production sphere are determined not only by socio-economic and political laws, but also by psychological laws conditioned by life circumstances and world views... Nationality relations permeate the sphere of general and specific factors forming motivations to labour.[42]

These cultural attitudes, he concludes, affect not only attitudes towards work once on the job, but also the choice of type of work. 'In the choice of profession' he writes 'particularities of family upbringing, concrete social surroundings, nationality, local traditions, and personal qualities of the individual play a great role'.[43]

Thus, Chamkin concludes that broadening the nationality distribution of personnel in enterprises and improving the contents of work should ultimately lead to a unity of interests and values among the different nationalities. What his study underlines, however, is that this unity is still far from being attained. Instead, in light of the nature of his sample, the cultural and attitudinal differences which still persist among the indigenous nationalities would undoubtedly be exhibited only more strongly if they could be studied among the Uzbek population at large. Ultimately, then, his study demonstrates that despite tremendous change, 'cultural predilections' in Uzbekistan for certain types of activities still persist and will be a long time in disappearing.

An earlier study which produced findings consonant with Chamkin's is a dissertation completed by an Uzbek social scientist, Sh. Muzaparov, on cultural changes among Uzbek workers in the oil industry of the Fergana Valley. Although conducted five years before Chamkin's, and oriented more towards shifts in life-style than towards attitudinal changes *per se*, his study suggests the same duality. While certain practices have changed among indigenous oil workers, Muzaparov notes, a change in attitudes has not necessarily followed, despite the participation of these workers in Uzbekistan's industrial vanguard.[44] Having had the opportunity to live among and visit indigenous workers in the Fergana Valley, I feel these conclusions still appear to be justified and pertinent.

Finally, similar conclusions were presented by the Soviet social scientist M. F. Soldatov, in Tashkent in 1972. In a book designed to 'shed light on the existence and interplay of objective and subjective factors in the formation of Communist relations towards work',[45] Soldatov concludes that moral, subjective factors in an individual's relation to work are as important in determining one's behaviour as material factors of incomes or type and level of production. Of most interest in Soldatov's discussion, however, is the echo of Bacon's analysis that past traditions and habits have not merely been retained, but have perhaps even been strengthened in simply an altered form:

> The law of the negation of the negation suggests not a simple retention, not the mechanical repetition of elements of the old in the new, but their appearance in a form new in principle . . . This situation can be illustrated by traditions of work which are transferred from one generation of workers to another.[46]

Traditional attitudes, he suggests – towards work, associated life-styles and towards female participation in the labour force – have not merely persisted. Rather, they may also have acquired a somewhat new, perhaps strengthened form within the context of contemporary Soviet society.

CULTURAL POLICIES AND THE LABOUR FORCE

Soviet policies regarding native behaviour and attitudes in the labour force have generally proceeded on the assumption that change in the economic and social structure will by itself affect cultural change in Uzbekistan. Planners have therefore largely focused their efforts on urbanisation, industrialisation and raising educational levels of the indigenous nationalities as means to eradicate the 'cultural hangovers' enumerated above.

Particularly in recent years, however, Soviet planners have also increasingly attempted to eradicate or alter work habits and attitudes of the indigenous nationalities directly. The importance of lectures in schools and vocational counselling is discussed in Chapter 4. In addition, other strategies have increasingly been emphasised to shape attitudes among the older or already-working population. By creating new holidays and traditions, for example, or intensifying propaganda campaigns, Soviet planners have been trying to shape a new native psychology directly. The 'psychological preparation towards work' is now considered to be 'one of the most important tasks of labour upbringing'.

In terms of the media, for example, books, newspapers, lectures in factories, television and radio programmes, and factory publications have all become, in the words of one Soviet writer 'a most powerful force on the ideological front'[47] when it comes to manpower questions. 'The Communist Party of Uzbekistan' he writes 'regards radio and television as a most powerful weapon for the ideological upbringing of the masses, and directs constant attention to raising their role in the international upbringing of the workers.' Thus, while the number of newspapers, television broadcasts and radio programmes have greatly increased over the past two decades, their content has also been carefully monitored in a way that goes beyond purely political considerations. Indeed, one newspaper in Uzbekistan several years ago was ordered to 'systematically publish material on positive examples which will educate the working people in the spirit of collectivism, of brotherly friendship of peoples, of socialist internationalism, of Soviet patriotism, and which will broadly show the economic and cultural connections of Uzbekistan with other union republics ... 'Another was told 'to discuss more widely the question of ideological work, educating the working people in the spirit of internationalism and Soviet patriotism'.[48] Other smaller party and factory newspapers over the years have been required to do the same.

Today, therefore, all these modes of mass communication stress the value of work, particularly in labour shortage sectors, and the importance of increased female labour force participation. Numerous articles and stories have appeared where the plot describes the migration of an Uzbek (often female) from the countryside to one of Uzbekistan's cities; his or her acquisition of a new skill; and the person's rapid rise to a well-paid position in a modern Uzbek factory. All factories must periodically conduct lectures and seminars on 'ideological questions of patriotism and proper work habits'.[49] And during the year that I lived in Uzbekistan, countless television and radio programmes – with such titles as *We will be Workers, We are Building BAM*, or *Industrial Uzbekistan* – addressed the same themes.

Similarly, Soviet planners have attempted to shape work behaviour and attitudes by creating new 'traditions' and holidays. The introduction of new rituals as a tool of cultural management is discussed in some detail in a recent book by Christel Lane. Ritual, she notes, performs a crucial ideological or regulatory function in society, and has long been emphasised as a policy tool by Soviet leaders.[50] Rituals, or 'traditions' which express the values and norms of Soviet socialism are today intended to channel feeling in a new direction, or develop or inculcate new Soviet value-orientations. A Soviet scholar in Uzbekistan confirmed this idea: 'The most effective means in the struggle against reactionary traditions and customs is the introduction of new traditions and customs into the life of the Soviet people.'[51]

The exceptionally large number of labour holidays and rituals – especially as they relate to industry – illustrates the importance placed upon shaping attitudes towards work in particular. New holidays have been designed with hopes that they will implant enthusiasm among personnel, raise productivity and obliterate other values and beliefs perceived as a brake or hindrance on future economic and social change. In Central Asia, as Lane points out, Soviet work holidays have been created and superimposed over religious festivals, to downgrade the religious component of annual festivities and upgrade the importance of labour. They have been created in conjunction with certain tasks, to increase labour discipline or the quantity and quality of production. Finally, they have particularly surrounded certain individuals, trades or occupational groups, either to raise the status of certain professions in public opinion (especially industrial or manual labour), or to raise the 'ideological consciousness' among personnel in occupations particularly lax in productivity, political enthusiasm, or support for the present Soviet regime.

Thus, during the past two decades, holidays such as the Day of Construction Workers, Day of the Metallurgist, and Hammer and Sickle Day have been created 'to be conducted under the banner of mobilising the working people of the city and countryside to raise the social content in creating the material-technical base of communism'.[52] The holiday of Hammer and Sickle Day, for example, is designed to reinforce the unity between workers and collective farmers, between town and country, between industry and agriculture. As Lane suggests, it clearly emphasises the importance of the urban and industrial working-class. In Central Asia, I was told, this kind of orientation is designed to both glorify industrial work, and enhance enthusiasm and unity among all sectors. During the year I was in Uzbekistan, holidays such as the Day of the Miner were marked by large parades and fanfare. According to L. K. Shek, a scholar of these issues in Uzbekistan, the Central Committee of the Communist Party continues to emphasise that these holidays should play 'an important role in the communist upbringing of the working people'.[53]

Finally, similar policies (goals) have been approached by means of awarding medals, presenting banners, establishing honour boards, sending letters to families or enlisting the help of local Party or youth organisations, with the same hopes of changing values and orientations of recipient and spectator alike. Hundreds of medals, banners or other awards are presented each year in acknowledgement of good work behaviour. Periodic letters are sent to families, to discuss an individual's work performance. And in March 1982, the late First Secretary of Uzbekistan, Sharif Rashidov, once again emphasised, as countless officials had done before, the role of the Komsomol in Uzbekistan as being to 'popularise the Soviet way of life more extensively, clearly and thoroughly; instil young people with high spiritual interests and needs; raise the standards of daily life; and promote new socialist traditions, customs and standards of behaviour on a broad scale'.[54]

Examples of these types of policies are countless. Despite their extensiveness, however, evidence suggests that their success has been limited. Lacking historical or emotional depth, newly-created Soviet holidays often tend to deaden rather than enhance emotional responses, especially in Central Asia where local traditions remain strong. As Shek notes:

New habits and rituals are increasingly entering the life of the working people. However, they still have not found wide acceptance among the population... The tie to the old traditions is still alive. People uphold the old way not because it is more attractive then the new, but by force of centuries-old habits which, as is widely known, do not disappear in a short time.[55]

According to several local writers and interviewees, there seems to have been little evidence of a shift in values in Uzbekistan, even in areas where propaganda output is extremely high. Indeed, it has sometimes been argued that while many indigenous Central Asians go through the motions of Soviet rituals and celebrations, their own religious holidays may have assumed renewed attractiveness, as these appear so much richer and more meaningful by comparison. These same writers continue to note, moreover, that success in changing values towards work has been limited among the younger population as well. 'It is very important that young workers be taught how to adapt themselves to the new social life and to respect the opinion of the collective, its traditions and its work' one observer writes. 'Unfortunately such attitudes are not to be found in a large number of enterprises.'[56]

In short, the results of efforts to change indigenous attitudes described above have been modest. This does not mean, of course, that indigenous attitudes have necessarily become more self-assertive or solidified than in the past, echoing the resurgence of traditional values in other parts of the world. Nor does it mean that attitudes will not necessarily change in the future. What it does suggest is that cultural attitudes are markedly resistant to change; that they still affect labour and nationality questions in Uzbekistan; and that they persist despite efforts to eradicate them. In the words of Brezhnev, changing attitudes among the indigenous nationalities will be 'the work of many years and decades'.[57]

In summary, in so far as the cultures of the indigenous and non-indigenous nationalities differed greatly, a situation was created early on in Uzbekistan where Central Asians gravitated toward certain occupations, and Slavic in-migrants, towards others. This was due in part to two distinctly different sets of standards, values and hierarchies among the indigenous and non-indigenous nationalities in Uzbekistan, as well as to other external factors. Early Soviet leaders assumed that as Uzbekistan's economic and social structures became transformed, the two hierarchies would merge, and thus the occupational distribution of labour by nationality would change as well.

'Cultural change', however, has occurred slowly among the indigenous nationalities in Uzbekistan. At present, therefore, one could argue that the labour distribution by nationality in Uzbekistan is as much an outgrowth of different traditions and values among the different nationalities as it is of individual external circumstances. The predominance of the indigenous nationalities in the able-bodied population not working in social production; their predominance in the service sectors and agriculture; or their low female participation rates are not only the result of different educational levels, places of residence, language, family size or discrimination. They are also the result of cultural proclivities which have persisted among the indigenous nationalities despite the transformations which occurred in their republic. The indigenous nationalities have long accorded more prestige and status to the traditional occupational categories than those where Europeans predominate and in many respects continue to do so today.

Today, Soviet policy-makers appear to be attempting to study and address these cultural concerns more directly than in the past. None the less, as illustrated in Chapters 6 and 7, Soviet policies have offered few incentives, economic or otherwise, to encourage rapid cultural change in any meaningful way. On the contrary, traditional social values in Uzbekistan have rather been sustained by the income and wage structure and economic policies there. For the time being, therefore, both the persistence of tradition and culture, and the unofficial or semi-official economies among Uzbekistan's indigenous nationalities tend to reinforce each other in perpetuating the same distribution of labour which was set in motion a century ago. For these reasons, then, labour distribution by nationality in Uzbekistan cannot be attributed to Slavic discrimination or prejudicial government policies alone; it is an outgrowth of native preference and overall development processes as well. In analysing labour distribution by nationality, questions of income distribution and prestige suggest a variety of factors affecting occupational choices and employment decisions. In so doing, they suggest their own series of implications extending beyond questions of labour use to broader political, social and explicitly nationality issues in Uzbek society as a whole.

8 Looking Ahead

The data discussed in Part I suggest the potential for immense political unrest in Uzbekistan. As illustrated, economic strains are growing among a rapidly expanding and relatively immobile population. Labour surpluses are growing and affecting the Central Asians to a greater degree than the Europeans. Sectoral and locational manpower imbalances continue to grow, with the indigenous nationalities concentrated in the traditional sectors and not entering other occupations essential for future economic expansion. On the whole, the data suggest that while urbanisation, industrialisation and modernisation have been occurring rapidly in Uzbekistan, the local nationalities have been only partly included in those processes and on a level well below their representation in the public's population as a whole. The combination of growing economic strains and relatively low native participation in the economy's most modern spheres would suggest that political unrest might follow, and be articulated in ethnic terms.

As suggested in Part II, however, economic and cultural factors in Uzbekistan diminish the apparent instability inherent in this situation. Undoubtedly part of the reason the indigenous nationalities are reluctant to migrate to cities and towns and to enter industrial sectors stems from negative factors: their lower levels of education; language barriers; the association of industry with alien environments; and, however limited, some degree of discrimination. But an equally, if not more important reason for the perpetuation of these trends derives from positive factors as well: the preference among the indigenous nationalities for a rural way of life; their aversion to manual and industrial labour; and the fact that an individual occupied in the agricultural or service sectors can often earn a higher income and sustain a higher standard of living in Uzbekistan than his industrial or urban counterpart. While tensions within the labour force are undoub-

225

tedly growing, therefore, a number of mitigating factors have emerged simultaneously, both as a result of Soviet policies and in defiance of them. Hiring policies, the private and second economies in Uzbekistan, controls within the workforce imposed from above, and cultural factors all tend to alleviate the economic and political pressures implicit in the employment situation.

By providing preferential hiring for the indigenous nationalities, for example, 'affirmative action' has lessened the sense of discrimination which is so often a cause of political or social unrest among other ethnic groups throughout the world. It has thus contradicted the contention mentioned above that 'perceived deprivation and discrimination' in Uzbekistan 'might readily be fused into a powerful sense of solidarity'. Instead, hiring practices in Uzbekistan seem to be raising the self-confidence of the indigenous Central Asians and fostering the sense that in many ways they are legitimate contributors to the development of their own republic and not merely Russian subjects or bystanders.

The second and private economies lessen ethnic tension and disaffection in the economic realm. As discussed above, a sense of economic deprivation among the indigenous nationalities was suggested as another likely cause of potential unrest in Uzbekistan. While official incomes might be higher among Uzbekistan's European populations, however, the second and private economies tend to redistribute incomes in the Central Asians' favour. The role of the private economy thus diminishes the argument that economic deprivation among the indigenous nationalities might give rise to increasing dissatisfaction and ethnic tension. Instead, there is a pervasive sense among Russians and Uzbeks alike that Asians often have access to far greater income streams than Europeans.

Of no less importance, the second economy also works to stifle the articulation of dissatisfaction in a direct political sense. Because by its very nature participation in the second economy is illegal, everyone who participates is, according to Soviet law, a criminal. As illustrated above, this fact does not seem to be a strong deterrent to participation in the second economy. But it does foster a pervasive, and very deep sense of 'implication' which diminishes the inclination to take political risks as well. There is a sense that 'rocking the boat' in Uzbekistan – sticking one's neck out to pursue political or nationality demands – could easily lead to arrest, conviction, or the end of one's career on other unrelated, but technically justifiable economic grounds. The risks of even the most minor political offences or demands, therefore – risks of livelihood and profession – apparently far outweigh the potential gains. In the words of a local inhabitant, 'everyone in Uzbekistan is under an economic pistol', which has become one of the most de-politicising forces in Uzbek society during the past ten to fifteen years. The pervasive fear of detection, particularly as it is reflected in economic transactions, very often leads to political complaisance.

Closely tied to both these factors – affirmative action and the second economy – is the possible vested interest among the élite in Uzbekistan in perpetuating the status quo. The extent of this, of course, is impossible to gauge, and among particular elite groups undoubtedly varies widely. It is important to stress, however, that native elites are by no means a homogeneous group in Uzbekistan promoting native interests across the board, and they may often be more conservative than their non-elite counterparts. There is little doubt that Fainsod's analysis of the attitudes of new governing élites is in part true of Uzbekistan today:

> Revolutions begin with the defeat and elimination of an established ruling group. But they also create fresh opportunities for social categories that had previously been suppressed and inert. They make it possible for the abler and more ambitious members of the newly-activated groups to rise in the social scale and to attain influence. In a fundamental sense a revolution only begins to consolidate itself when it calls forth new energy from below to defend its conquests.
>
> In many respects the Bolshevik Revolution followed this classic pattern. It dethroned an established ruling caste and set a profound social revolution in motion. It tapped fresh talent from the lower depths of society and harnessed it to the revolutionary chariot. It gradually welded together a new governing apparatus ... It built its own network of revolutionary beneficiaries with vested interests in the perpetuation of the new order.[1]

Today, many Uzbek élites owe their status to this political climate, and are 'at a minimum uneasy about change'. As an Uzbek commented to one foreign visitor 'In America they say that the Russians have russified our culture; that's not true. It was done by certain Uzbeks.'[2]

Cursory observation suggests that this vested interest may often be economic as well as political. Positions in the Party and government élite in Uzbekistan provide not only the greatest degree of perquisites and political power, but also the greatest access to second economic activities. Thus, it is possible that many of Uzbekistan's elite groups would feel the sense of 'implication' more than other citizens, and have more at stake from participation in overt political or nationalist activity. In short, as in many societies, any change in the established order – political and economic – could be inimical to the élites' own financial interests as well as to their political future. Ironically, activities in the second economy may often make Uzbekistan's Party and government élites more reluctant to press for any large-scale change, politically or economically related, even though they might be in the most opportune position to do so.

Reinforcing these considerations are other economic controls built into the employment situation and economic system itself. The ministerial arrangements dividing control between Moscow and Tashkent; the policy of keeping the bulk of heavy industry in Uzbekistan under all-Union jurisdiction; and the cadre policy itself, of keeping Slavs in certain key occupations throughout Uzbekistan also exert a modicum of control in a generally subtle way over the possibility for overt political action.

From the cultural side, several other factors decrease potential for political or nationality unrest in the labour force. In contrast to the assumptions of those who argue that the indigenous nationalities appear to carry lower status and prestige than do the non-indigenes in Uzbekistan, standards and criteria for evaluating jobs in the labour force are not uniform among the Asians and Slavs. Instead, the persistence of traditional attitudes towards work often implies that the Central Asians enjoy *more* prestigious occupations, in local terms, than do the Russians in their midst.[3] In both a political and economic sense, therefore, this diminishes social and professional competition between the two main groups, since each group's goals are often quite different. Each nationality in Uzbekistan seems to have different opportunities and choices; each possesses different criteria for making those choices; and each seems cognisant of its opportunities, and limitations.

In a social sense as well, the lives of the Asians and Europeans in Uzbekistan are visibly separate. In large part, the indigenous and non-indigenous nationalities live and work in different regions and sectors of the republic, so the lives of the two groups rarely overlap during and after working hours. Most cities in Uzbekistan have separate sections – a Russian quarter and a native quarter – and separate clubs, cinemas, tea-houses, and the like. Intermarriage between Asians and Slavs occurs infrequently. A type of voluntary, self-imposed segregation, therefore, continues in both work and leisure hours. Ironically, the division of nationalities by occupation more often implies increased competition among the indigenous nationalities for scarce jobs, rather than direct competition between them and Europeans. All these factors – cultural and economic – tend to lessen the nationality conflicts generally associated with growing labour problems in Uzbekistan.

In ethnic and political terms, therefore, the labour situation in Soviet Central Asia presents a mixed picture, and the political effects are equally mixed. There is undoubtedly some truth in the assumptions that present sectoral and locational imbalances and somewhat greater mobility among the indigenous nationalities have increased nationality problems today as well. But in political terms, a policy of preferential hiring for the indigenous Central Asians, the private economy, and differences in attitudes and aspirations among the nationalities all tend to mitigate the ethnic tensions implicit in these conclusions. Two worlds exist side by side in Soviet Central Asia: each evaluates jobs and opportunities within different economic and social frameworks, and thus each regards itself as 'superior' to the other. This juxtaposition tends to stabilise what might otherwise appear to be a highly unstable environment.

None the less, even though there would thus appear to be a standoff, the labour situation is not static. Demographic, social and economic pressures are growing, and their impact on the situation may now be giving birth to different kinds of ethnic and political tension. By upgrading nationality as a major criterion in job competition, Soviet style 'affirmative action' might now be developing this sense of 'superiority' into greater self-assertiveness among the indigenous nationalities, while fanning resentment among the Slavs. While affirmative action has provided the indigenous Central Asians with new and wider opportunities, by its very nature, it has simultaneously made ethnic affiliation an essential ingredient, if not one of the main determinants of upward mobility in Uzbek society. By consequence, nationality has come to pervade every aspect of professional and student life: an Uzbek, in Uzbekistan, can go farther the more he asserts himself *as an Uzbek*, while a Russian often has limited choices simply because he is a Russian. The pride or sense of accomplishment, therefore, with which an Uzbek may regard his professional attainments is consciously and inextricably linked to his ethnic heritage, sharpening ethnic differences and animosities in the process. Ironically, then, by mitigating ethnic disaffection in one way, affirmative action may be promoting ethnic awareness in another way. 'Affirmative action' may now be giving the Uzbeks a new confidence *as Uzbeks*, that whatever roles they desire are, by right and merit, theirs to fill, and the republic, theirs to govern.

Equally important, 'affirmative action' is also reinforcing ethnic identity and animosity among Uzbekistan's European populations. Analogous to affirmative action in the United States, Europeans in Uzbekistan are beginning to sense that, strictly on the basis of race, they are being denied access to jobs for which they have equal, if not better qualifications than their Asian counterparts. A number of Slavs bitterly resent the notion that they are treated as foreigners. Instead, Europeans in Uzbekistan tend to feel they should be treated at least as equal co-habitants of Uzbekistan, if not as more knowledgeable and experienced 'elder brothers'. 'I've lived here all my life,' one Russian in Tashkent put it 'My parents lived here, and my grandparents lived here. It's my home too!' 'We taught them everything they know' another Russian worker declared 'and now all you hear is "Hire more Uzbeks! Hire more Uzbeks!" Even if a place is already one hundred per cent Uzbek, you still hear them yelling it!' Thus, 'affirmative action' works as a constant reminder of one's separate ethnic identity among the indigenous and non-indigenous nationalities alike – a fact which neither could escape at any career stage. While alleviating tensions in one way, therefore, hiring practices in Uzbekistan are simultaneously promoting nationality differences and feeding ethnic awareness and animosity in other ways.

A similar situation applies to incomes. While the private and second economies may redistribute incomes among Uzbekistan's population, they have not necessarily reduced income differentials among the nationalities. Instead, as noted above, they may have simply reversed the balance, often making income among the indigenous nationalities highest. While this diminishes any sense of economic deprivation on the part of the indigenous nationalities, it also has another side. The often higher incomes among indigenous Central Asians, and the entire mechanism of protection and favouritism based on familial or nationality ties, may be bringing a whole series of other animosities to the fore on the part of Asians and Slavs alike. 'Envy and animosity among the nationalities' one local Slavic inhabitant of Tashkent remarked 'is generated and intensified by the second economy.' Thus, while the goal of Soviet policies in the socialised economy is to keep income differentials and competition low – in part to reduce class and nationality conflict – these policies increase competition in the second economy, cause greater discrepancies in wealth, and thus may be exacerbating ethnic tensions as well.

Lastly, the same ambiguity inherent in Uzbekistan's labour issues may be evident with regard to cultural factors. As discussed in Chapter 7, the indigenous and non-indigenous nationalities often apply different standards to the evaluation of various kinds of work and thus avoid direct competition for existing opportunities. But growing population pressure, coupled with fairly uniform aspirations, has been increasing competition *among* indigenous Central Asians for a more limited number of jobs in the traditional sectors. Regardless of whether this competition is limited to the indigenous nationalities, the resulting frustration is still often articulated in ethnic terms. As competition intensifies, these grievances tend to intensify as well. As mentioned, Soviet policies are attempting to alter this situation by somehow bringing local values and aspirations into line with 'Soviet' norms. But there is another danger inherent here as well: success in these efforts does not necessarily imply a relaxation of nationality tension either. Even the present slow transformation of values and ideas among the indigenous populations is proving to have political repercussions, as the innumerable dislocations and frustrations associated with change become articulated in ethnic terms. Should the aspirations of the indigenous nationalities become identical to those of the Europeans, Massell's fears can certainly be expected to materialise.

One is left, then, with a paradoxical situation in Uzbekistan, where the same sets of factors work for both political stability and restiveness. There is little doubt that animosity among the different nationality groups in Uzbekistan's workforce is increasing. It now stems, however, from a sense of 'superiority' on the part of each nationality group rather than from deprivation, and from the fact that the different nationalities remain separated in the workforce rather than totally integrated. The indigenous nationalities do not regard themselves as a deprived social class in Central Asia, but rather as economically and culturally superior to the Slavs in their midst. They have not been excluded from the more modern 'Russian world' as much as they have resisted Soviet efforts to integrate them fully into that world.

In a political sense, then, Uzbekistan's indigenous nationalities have become both better able to advance in society and more generally self-assertive. But because so much of their new status depends upon informal mechanisms, they may also have become more reluctant to press for any large-scale changes which could upset that informal system. Local grievances have perhaps become sharper, but so, too, have the benefits which come with being of the local nationalities in Uzbekistan and not rocking the boat. Assured of their own moral and cultural superiority, the Russians, for their part, seem hardly ready to press for Russian nationality interests in a republic which, nominally at least, is not their own. Thus, the present maintenance of political stability seems to rest on the tenuous balance between these two outlooks.

PROSPECTS

Soviet policies – aimed at social homogeneity and economic 'rationality' – are threatening to upset this balance by directly encouraging the indigenous nationalities to enter the socialised work force, particularly industry, and by trying to make it economically and socially more attractive for them to do so. While affirmative action continues, Soviet policies are aimed at diminishing the role of the illegal private economies, and accelerating social change and transformation of attitudes among the local nationalities to bring them more in line with Soviet standards.

Prospects for political unrest stemming from Uzbekistan's labour situation, therefore, depend upon two main economic and cultural considerations. The first is the degree to which Soviet policies will be successful in expanding Uzbekistan's socialised economy to keep pace with rapid population growth there – and, related to that, the future role of the private and second economies. The second concerns the rate of change in cultural attitudes and aspirations among the indigenous populations, the degree of ethnic interaction, and the level of frustration which normally accompanies cultural dislocations anywhere in the world.

On the economic side, probably the greatest concern will be whether the growth of Uzbekistan's economy can keep pace with the growing needs and wants of a rapidly expanding population and whether it will be perceived as in fact doing so. Because of rapid population growth, the traditional sources of stability in the USSR – such as full employment, a type of welfare system, rising living standards, educational opportunities, subsidies on necessary goods and services and a low rate of inflation – are already threatened in Uzbekistan. Should economic growth slow at an even greater rate relative to population growth, competition for jobs will increase, availability of goods per capita will decline, and regardless of which nationality groups are affected most, conflict and tension among the nationalities will undoubtedly grow. In terms of jobs, the experience of other republics has not been encouraging. 'When opportunities for social and occupational advancement became poor,' two Soviet émigrés write, 'general dissatisfaction grew and came to be projected into inter-ethnic attitudes.'[4] One can assume that native disaffection in Uzbekistan would rise as well if fewer jobs became available for the indigenous nationalities to fill. In terms of consumption, the implications are equally important. Despite the greater provision of certain consumer goods in Uzbekistan, sentiment is widespread that the availability of most foodstuffs in government stores has already begun to decline, as has the general quality of Uzbek life. Prices of many important consumer goods have risen in recent years. Crime in Uzbekistan – from petty crimes to felonies – has grown tremendously. And there are already signs that discontent arising from these perceived changes is becoming imbued with ethnic overtones. 'Ten years ago there was meat,' one hears many Uzbeks assert 'then the Russians started to come. Now try to find some!'

It is the rare Uzbek, of course, who has analysed actual meat availability in Uzbekistan and has then attempted to determine the relative positions of the different nationalities in the republic's economy. Even if he or she had, there would have been no statistical basis to assume that a Russian in Uzbekistan is any more privileged than the indigenous populations. Indeed, quite the contrary may more often be the case.

None the less, a population's emotional reactions to economic or political issues usually are not based on thorough analyses and rational appraisals of an entire situation. Instead, they emerge from a particular situation or issue and develop as they encompass other emotions and perceptions perhaps totally unrelated. Members of the indigenous nationalities will rarely deny the successes of Soviet development policies in Central Asia. But that acknowledgement does not necessarily imply greater political loyalty to the central authorities. Instead, one is reminded of the 'Law of Colonial Ingratitude', as Hugh Seton-Watson calls it, which often leads to greater rifts between the centre and individual nationality groups:
.

'Certainly,' an imaginary Uzbek intellectual will think 'there has been vast progress in our country. But this has been the result of all the hard work and the talents of us Uzbeks. If we had not had those Russians sitting on our necks, we should have made still more progress.' Unfair, perhaps, but a *zakonomernost'* – a regularity – of history so far.[5]

Thus, however unjustified their feeling may be, indigenous Central Asians have begun to hold 'the Russians' responsible for everything, from long lines at stores, to shortages in consumer goods, to the rise in crime and 'hippy cultures' infecting their republic. It makes little difference that the Russians who came to Uzbekistan during the past fifteen years had little impact on meat availability in most government stores – or that the decline in most per capita indicators in Uzbekistan has been due to rapid indigenous, rather than Slavic, population growth. For the indigenous nationalities, a perceived worsening quality of life has already become linked with the presence of 'outsiders' in their republic. The possibility of a more extreme economic slowdown in Uzbekistan, therefore – or the disappearance of many basic goods, services and job opportunities altogether – would hold immense ethnic implications which go beyond purely economic considerations alone. It could spark deep-seated nationalist hostilities and resentments which would be difficult to contain.

Closely linked to future economic performance, prospects for tension in Uzbekistan's labour force will also depend on the role of the private and second economies. Should the private economy prove unable to fill the gaps of the socialised economy, these same reactions would be triggered more decisively. Equally important, a dramatic change in the availability of consumer or producer goods would also trigger considerable disruption and disaffection in other ways as well. According to several local inhabitants in Uzbekistan, either a glut of desired goods on the official market, or their disappearance even on the black market would lead to discord among those involved in the unofficial markets over a division of profits, a struggle for leadership, a lowering of buying power, a rise in the magnitude of bribes and a total disruption of the economic system on which daily life in Uzbekistan depends. Should Soviet policies significantly disrupt the private economy, therefore, this would be tantamount to disrupting a well-entrenched pattern of social and economic behaviour for producer and consumer alike. This, too, could well lead to political instability, unless offset by far greater provision of other goods and services which the socialised economy seems unable to deliver.

On the non-economic side, prospects for nationality tension within the workforce will also depend on the degree to which Soviet policies are successful in truly changing the cultural values and orientations of the local populations; the rate of that change; the amount of true increased inter-ethnic contact; and the degree to which cultural assertiveness and renewed sense of pride will be translated into political assertiveness. Rapid cultural changes associated with modernisation are by nature destabilising anywhere in the world. As Cyril Black suggests, a cultural or traditional heritage, rapidly undermined by the process of modernisation, leads to 'fundamental uncertainty as to norms and values'[6] in any environment. Local communities dissolve; urbanisation alters family structure; broad societal changes profoundly alter male/female relations and general patterns of identity. The result is that when accepted status demarcations are thrown rapidly into disarray, one is rapidly forced 'to anchor social positions to new moorings'.[7] The task is not always an easy or smooth one.

These dislocations are only exacerbated by increased ethnic contact and levels of social change. Little is known about the extent to which these in fact may fuel political instability. The past experiences of other countries, however, and the vast number of countries in the world now troubled by ethnic restiveness within their borders, could suggest that regardless of who is economically advantaged or disadvantaged, inter-group contacts might be more likely to lead to discord than understanding in Soviet Central Asia as well.[8] Similarly, as societies grow more socially and economically sophisticated, ethnic tensions and 'chauvinist excesses' have also tended to increase.[9] Thus, potential for discord in Uzbekistan's labour force will depend largely upon the extent to which Soviet authorities press for economic and social changes there, and the ways in which they do so.

Finally, the potential political effects of labour issues cannot be analysed in isolation from other aspects of life. The ultimate political content of all of the above factors is directly related to phenomena which go beyond the labour force *per se* – such as religion, language, culture, foreign policy, Soviet military force, or other practical and emotional considerations. As already discussed, severe discontent or upheaval in any one of these areas could set off a chain reaction leading to unrest and new demands in others. As also discussed, however, none of these issues is clear cut. They are all issues with which Moscow must contend, but which would be unlikely on their own to trigger any widespread discontent to challenge seriously the maintenance of political order.

In terms of religion, for example, Islam undoubtedly commands the allegiance of a large and rapidly growing segment of the Soviet population, and could be a rallying point for the expression of discontent. As elsewhere in the Muslim world, however, Muslims can often be deeply, even violently divided among themselves – on issues of faith as well as on secular issues – and have a variety of other aspects to their identities and personalities. The Muslim peoples of the Soviet Union are no exception: they are geographically, economically and socially diverse and contact among them is often limited.

It therefore appears too one-sided to suggest that a 'Muslim society' in the USSR, 'united by the bonds of history, culture and tradition' comprises one of the most 'urgent' threats to the 'cohesiveness of the USSR' – or that 'an inevitable confrontation is unfolding' between Islam and the Soviet State.[10] While certain aspects of Islamic awareness and religious practice may have grown in the USSR, their particular paths of growth have diverged markedly among different Islamic groups; there is little evidence to suggest that 'behind "Homo Sovieticus" now looms "Homo Islamicus"'. At the same time, however, religion, in its myriad forms, does remain an important consideration in formulating policy and mitigating nationality unrest, in Uzbekistan as elsewhere. So far, Soviet policy seems to have been successful in keeping the Soviet Muslim community fragmented, in part appeased, and without a clear cut issue which could possibly divide all Muslims from non-Muslims, or on which Soviet Muslims might unite against Moscow.

Similarly, questions of language and culture by themselves would be unlikely to trigger widespread unrest which could significantly undermine political stability. None the less, as the outcry over curtailing local language use in the Caucasus and Central Asia suggests, they, too, are issues where emotions run high.[11] As in the area of religion, Soviet policy-makers appear to be cognisant of the dangers of directly attacking local language use or the persistence of 'cultural hangovers'. Instead, they tend to accept the persistence of certain aspects of local language use and culture while simultaneously attempting to loosen linguistic and cultural ties in the long run.

In other words, the first three issues of religion, language and culture are characterised by the same duality as labour issues: policies and practices connected with them are presently both feeding and containing national awareness. Any sign of nationalist tension in one arena could set off a string of reactions in the others. But at present, none by itself implies an often-assumed inevitable, head-on confrontation with the central Soviet leadership.

The ever-continuing build-up of the Soviet military or Soviet intervention in other countries of the Middle East is also exerting a dual effect on nationality relations. However limited the amount of information among Soviet Asians, recent events in Iran and Afghanistan apparently have strengthened the self-confidence of Soviet Asians and given Islam renewed legitimacy in their eyes. The Soviet invasion of Afghanistan may have heightened their animosity towards the central authorities, as Soviet Asians witnessed a full-scale military attack on their 'ethnic kinsmen' across the border. But these same events, with the assistance of Soviet reportage and propaganda, have also highlighted the darker side of Soviet domestic politics and international intrigue and confrontation. 'However much we may dislike the Russians,' an Uzbek commented 'separation would inevitably mean becoming embroiled in international politics and being eaten up by foreign imperialists'. Similarly, the invasion of Afghanistan highlighted the fact that the central authorities have not only the levers of institutional controls at their disposal, but a powerful military apparatus which they are prepared to use when they perceive their interests as threatened. The ever-present possibility that the Soviet military might intervene in local Central Asian affairs further diminishes the inclination among Soviet Asians to promote political unrest at home, and reduces their interest in using international affairs as an instrument of confrontation against the central authorities. In other words, policies with regard to all these areas tend to heighten nationality awareness and tension in Uzbekistan, but they also tend to diminish the potential for nationalist expressions in any overt or explosive way.

Other factors containing political unrest in Central Asia are more practical or emotional in character, such as the lack of means among Central Asians for decisively promoting nationalist demands, their economic dependence on Moscow and basic emotional features of the local Asians in general. Even if nationalist sentiment were strong in Uzbekistan, and aims clearly defined, factors such as lack of leadership and arms, lack of control of communications, disorganisation, little co-ordination of efforts and other practical constraints imposed by the Soviet political and social system would make effective advancement of these aims almost impossible. Although some circumvention of controls is possible, most of the means of communication in Uzbekistan are rigidly controlled, making a free interchange of ideas impossible. Few Asians ever serve in the military in their own republics or have access to arms in their own homelands; thus the people who do bear arms in Central Asia are largely Slavs, who feel little affinity with the local population in the first place. 'If we tried to do anything more than grumble' two self-proclaimed Uzbek nationalists commented in 1979 'we'd be squashed in the twinkling of an eye. We're a little republic, you know.' As far as has been determined, there is little *samizdat*, or underground literature, in Uzbekistan, and no organisational work explicitly directed towards advancing nationalist demands.

In addition, there is no consensus on what local demands are, even should the Central Asians be in a position to advance them. Demands and desires of the indigenous nationalities range from simply having more meat on the market to forming a separate country. And opposition to the central Slavic authorities is often further diffused by discord and fragmentation among the Asian nationalities. The indigenous nationalities in Uzbekistan can often be as divided among themselves as they are with the Russians. In the autumn of 1977, for example, a large 'race riot' broke out in the dormitories of Tashkent University. About 180 people were involved in the fighting that ensued, and policemen were called in to make arrests. The interesting part, however, is that few, if any Slavs were involved. The Uzbeks from the Fergana Valley, calling themselves the '*Fanovtsy*'[12] fought against the Uzbeks from the Syrdar'ya region, mainly from the city of Dzhizak. Each regarded the other as 'uncultured', and bitterly fought each other with rocks, stones and fists.

Similarly, social, economic and attitudinal rifts have appeared between urban and rural Uzbeks and among the different indigenous nationalities residing in Uzbekistan. Montgomery has referred to the existence of urban upper- and middle-class Uzbeks in Uzbekistan who to a great extent are bilingual and bicultural, and often have loyalties and allegiances quite genuinely oriented in Moscow's direction. They form a layer quite distinct from Uzbeks from other areas or economic levels. Montgomery describes this situation in Tashkent:

> This urban élite group, which is the main interface with the European-dominated central Soviet government, may develop interests which are divergent from those of the Uzbek intelligentsia and administrators in the smaller cities and rural areas where the majority of the Uzbeks live, producing a pronounced Uzbek cultural and social dichotomy.[13]

In many parts of the countryside, large Korean populations live on hostile terms with local Uzbeks. A sometimes-heated debate continues on the precise nationality status of the Khorezm Turks,[14] and longstanding animosities between the Uzbeks and Tadzhiks still often come to the fore in different parts of Central Asia.

Another practical constraint on the expression of nationality discontent is the fact that Central Asia is dependent on Moscow for many benefits and necessities and knows it. While the Asian chauvinist might consider Central Asia extremely rich in natural resources, the area also imports many necessary natural resources and manufactured goods from other parts of the USSR. How well Uzbekistan, or Soviet Central Asia as a whole, could survive without Moscow's aid is a major question which at least sobers the would-be Central Asian separatist. For the most part, the indigenous nationalities in Uzbekistan seem reluctant to 'rock the boat' since, as one Uzbek put it, 'all things told, things could be worse. Perhaps things are better the way they are'.

Indeed, the fact that many Soviet Asians sincerely believe that, despite animosities, 'perhaps things are better the way they are' is probably the single most important factor containing expressions of nationalist sentiment in Uzbekistan. The importance of habit, inertia and a general political passivity among Uzbekistan's population plays a tremendous role in determining future political behaviour there. However great their antipathy towards the Russians may be, Uzbekistan's indigenous nationalities appear to have a rather passive view towards politics. As one observer described other neighbouring groups, there is a sense in Central Asia that 'politics goes beyond the people. It is something that happens to you', and not something you shape. Members of an intensely inward-looking society, the Soviet Asians tend to concentrate on day-to-day concerns, ever conscious that 'things are not so bad' and that 'things could be worse'. Indeed, in many cases, indoctrination, propaganda and the habits of conformity have transformed this into tacit support for the political regime.

Soviet policy options, then, appear to be based on maintaining a balance between the dual effects of all these factors – economic, social, attitudinal and military. The central authorities do not appear to be considering any dramatic policies regarding Central Asia, such as forced mass deportation of the indigenous nationalities to other parts of the USSR, deletion of nationality from Soviet passports or its diminution as a criterion for social or economic advancement, massive augmentation or sharp cutbacks in economic investment in Uzbekistan, or the extension or curtailment of wide-ranging political powers to the indigenous nationalities, locally or on an all-Union scale. Rather, the central authorities seem inclined towards steering a delicate course, as they have done for the past sixty-five years, between visibly encouraging some aspects of tradition and culture and subtly discouraging or eradicating others; between encouraging modernisation and economic development in Central Asia and keeping the area clearly dependent on Moscow; and ultimately, between fostering national pride among the indigenous nationalities while reminding them that they are part of a larger whole which Russians firmly control. With regard specifically to the labour force, the authorities appear intent upon maintaining a balancing act as well. Their strategy seems to be to invest only limited resources in Central Asia, while still providing basic employment opportunities – even if these reflect inefficient labour use; to provide a minimum level of consumer goods and services without triggering widespread social and economic discontent; and to continue to allow, if not encourage, at least the legal private economy to function with few impediments. In other words, while Soviet leaders are promoting social and economic change in Uzbekistan, they seem to be as conscious of 'not rocking the boat' as their Central Asian counterparts. They appear intent upon providing at least the economic minimum – in terms of jobs and consumption – to dilute grounds for strong, legitimate discontent and to stifle opposition; and they appear intent upon keeping other Soviet policies intentionally ambiguous.

In conclusion, it should be noted that even if the tensions implicit in all these issues could be precisely measured and defined, their implications for Soviet Asia would still be unclear. While there are vast differences between the Uzbek experience and the experience of West European national and ethnic groups, the Basques, Bretons, Catalans, Cornish, Irish, Scottish, Welsh and other groups all illustrate that linguistic assimilation need not lead to a growing feeling of unity and solidarity in the first place; and experience elsewhere suggests that lack of linguistic assimilation is not always indicative of impending doom. Despite the pre-1920 slogans that declared Gaelic and Irish identity to be inseparable, Gaelic is spoken by only a small minority in Ireland today;[15] and yet the fact that English has become the common language there does not indicate that the English and Irish have moved closer together. Demands for bilingual education among Hispanics in the United States, on the other hand, do not imply that the same violent political self-assertiveness will follow, turning Washington into another Ulster. Regarding religion and political structure, Brown points out that national pressures have become, if anything, a *more* serious problem for the federal authorities in Yugoslavia since the extension of federal rights to the republics there,[16] even though nationalist pressures have been contained by similar measures in Canada. And Islam has proved to be a dividing as well as unifying force throughout the Middle East.

With regard to the labour force itself, the impacts of ethnic tensions resulting from the economic realm are also unclear. A large part of this study has focused on the relative affluence or deprivation of the different nationality groups in Uzbekistan as a source of ethnic and political unrest. Yet even these disparities would not necessarily spell restiveness or stability. Ethnic consciousness grew substantially among the Flemish of Belgium during the 1960s, even though Flanders received a disproportionately large share of Belgian investments at least during the first eight years of that decade. Nationalist feelings are strong among the Croatians and Slovenes of Yugoslavia and the Basques and Catalans of Spain, even though the two groups are financially better off than the Serbs and Castilians respectively. And on the other side, a 1975 Gallup poll in the United States showed that, even when the recession was well under way and blacks had been most affected, young blacks comprised the group which was most optimistic about their chances of success for the immediate future.[17]

Individuals and groups, then, react in unpredictable ways to different conflicts, loyalties and circumstances. As several writers have pointed out, any incendiary event or speech, even unrelated, could radically transform nationalist sentiment from a passive to active energy and could make any one of the above issues a rallying point for the assertion of nationalist demands. But then again, it might not.

In Soviet Central Asia, economic and social change is occurring, accompanied by the same frustration, questioning and dissatisfaction which has accompanied similar changes and upheavals in other areas of the world. Tensions are growing, and becoming increasingly ethnically charged among Asians and Russians alike. And individual manifestations of nationalism are growing as well. The 1969 riots which occurred after a soccer match at the Pakhtokor stadium in Tashkent – in which some Asians carried placards reading 'Russians Go Home' – are already well-known. Since then, there have been similar incidents, occurring with apparently greater frequency in the late 1970s. In Chirchik (a small industrial town outside Tashkent) in 1978, a new chemical factory blew up only one day after its construction was completed. Although the incident was hushed up and the exact facts were hard to come by, rumour had it that it was 'not accidental'. During that same spring, part of the film theatre which had housed an Asian and African film festival blew up on closing night – again, 'not accidental'. And the trial of the Crimean Tatar Reshat Dzhemilev outside Tashkent in 1979 for the first time witnessed *listovshchiki*, or placards, pasted on the walls of buildings in certain regions of Tashkent.

Aside from overt demonstrations and bombings, subtle expressions of nationalism also occur. Native shopkeepers occasionally refuse to sell their wares to Russian shoppers and uncomplimentary ethnic jokes and derogatory names abound among Asians and Europeans alike. These incidents, however, are but isolated expressions of nationalism, and expressions of friendship and hospitality are also common among the nationality groups.

In the context of Soviet Central Asia, then, it is difficult to conclude that 'like the Empire that it succeeded, the Soviet state seems incapable of extricating itself from the nationality impasse'.[18] Pressures are growing in Central Asia; a lot of adjustments will soon have to be made in Soviet society at large. But for the time being, these pressures have been offset by two-sided economic and social policies and by ambiguities within Central Asian society itself. As in other areas, therefore, it seems that only a major catalyst – such as a sudden and large-scale shift in Soviet policy or a very severe erosion in Central Asia's economy – could raise tensions to such a pitch that they would seriously challenge the central authorities in Moscow. Without that catalyst, a balance appears to have been established, where competing currents will seemingly neutralise each other for some years to come. And by then, the Soviet Union as a whole may be quite a different place.

Appendix 1: Occupational Distribution by Nationality in Selected Organisations and Enterprises, Uzbekistan

TABLE A1.1   *The Chirchik Agricultural Machinery Plant (Chirchiksel' mash). Distribution of occupations by nationality, 1979*

Department and Position	Nationality
Director	Russian
Chief Engineer	Russian
Deputy, Chief Engineer	Russian
Department personnel: 19 people	Russian (19)
Chief Power Specialist	Jewish
Deputy, Chief Power Specialist	Russian
Department personnel: 15 people	Russian (14)
Director, Department of Capital Construction (OKS)	Uzbek (1)
	Russian
Deputy Director, OKS	Russian
Department personnel: 8 people	Russian (7)
	Uzbek (1)
Deputy Director for Supply	Jewish
Main bookkeeper	Russian
Accounting Department: 40 people	Russian (39)
	Uzbek (1)

Department Heads: 11 Departments   Russian (11)
Power specialists: 11 specialists   Russian (10)
   Uzbek (1)

Workers: Approximately 15 000 workers   Russian (98 per cent)

Guard personnel:
Director   Russian
Personnel: 20 people   Russian (10)
   Uzbek (10)

Construction and Repair Administration
Director   Jewish
Deputy Director   Jewish
Chief Engineer   Russian
Director, Production Technical Department (PTO)   Russian
Main bookkeeper   Russian
Administrative apparatus: 18 people   Russian (18)
   Uzbek (1)

Workers: 160   Russian (85 per cent)
   Uzbek (15 per cent)

SOURCE   Private communication to the author

TABLE A1.2   *Andizhan Sewing Factory, 1979. Distribution of Occupations by Sex and Nationality, 1979*

	Industrial Personnel	*Engineers and Technical Personnel*	*Employees*
Women	2554	140	49
of which,			
indigenous women	2264	58	15
Men	213	27	10
of which,			
indigenous men	170	24	8
Total	2767	167	59

SOURCE   Interview at the Andizhan sewing factory, 27 April 1979

Appendix 2: Locational Imbalances in Uzbekistan's Labour Force, 1975

In 1975, V. Mikheeva, a Soviet scholar of manpower questions in Soviet Central Asia, conducted a study on various aspects of labour utilisation in different types of urban areas in Uzbekistan. Because her results are so pertinent, part of her findings are presented here. Her study highlights many of the points in Chapter 3, in terms of growing locational imbalances in Uzbekistan's labour force and their implications for Uzbekistan's different nationality groups.

The following analysis focuses on thirty-three cities in Uzbekistan, and divides them into four groups based on population size and level of industrial development. Group I consists of four cities: Samarkand, Bukhara, Andizhan and Kokand, each with a population of 100–150 000 people, and each with 20–35 per cent of its employed population in industry. Group II consists of six cities: Chirchik and Fergana (with populations of 100–150 000 people); Navoi, Almalyk and Yangiul' (with populations of 50–100 000 people); and Akhangaron, with a population of under 50 000 people. In all of the cities in group II, more than 50 per cent of the employed population is in industry. Group III consists of nine cities: Nukus, Termez, Karshi and Urgench (with populations of 50–100 000 people) and Gulistan, Khodzheili, Denau, Kzhizak, and Takhiatash, with populations of less than 50 000 people. And group IV consists of fourteen cities, all with populations of less than 50 000 people: Shakhrisabz, Khiva, Turtkul', Kattakurgan, Chust, Leninsk, Beruni, Chimbai, Gazalkent, Uchkurgan, Pskent, Aktash, Muinak, Shakhrikhan. In all these cities except for three, the level of industrial employment is less than 35 per cent of the employed population, and in ten of these cities, the level is less than 20 per cent. (In Kattagurgan and Chust, industrial employment is

247

TABLE A2.1　*Level of employment and industrial development by type of city, 1975 (Uzbekistan)*

Type of city	Employment in social production	Gross production	Industrial production personnel	Labour productivity	Fixed industrial productive Stock
I	1.00	0.99	0.96	1.03	0.65
II	1.05	1.56	1.79	1.13	2.25
III	0.99	0.71	0.56	0.91	0.55
IV	0.95	0.77	0.51	0.80	0.45

NOTE　1.00 equals the average for all cities in Uzbekistan.

SOURCE　Mikheeva, V. 'Trudovye resursy malykh i srednikh gorodov Uzbekistana i perspektivy ikh ispol'zovaniia', unpublished doctoral dissertation (Tashkent, 1975) p. 80.

between 35 and 50 per cent of total employment; in Muinak, the level is 50–65 per cent of the employed population.) More than four out of five cities in Uzbekistan are classified as small or medium, containing one third of Uzbekistan's total urban population. In terms of nationality composition, the first two groups had largely European populations; the latter two, largely indigenous. Tashkent is not included in this analysis.

As Tables A2.1 and A2.2 illustrate, higher levels of 'unemployment' and

TABLE A2.2　*Employment by type of city, Uzbekistan, selected indicators, 1959–70*

Type of city	% labour resources employed in social production		% labour resources in household/ private subsidiary employment*		Growth rate labour resources 1959–70 (%)	Growth rate population employed in social prod. 1959–70 (%)
	1959	1970	1959	1970		
I	75.4	90.1	24.6	9.9	129.6	143.3
II	78.8	94.3	21.2	5.7	166.5	193.3
III	72.5	89.6	27.5	10.4	147.7	170.7
IV	68.5	85.4	31.5	14.6	131.6	160.7

* As discussed in Chapter 2, much of the decline in each case was due to definitional and other changes. Significant here are the relative proportions among the different types of cities and rates of decline, assuming that definitional changes were uniform in all of Uzbekistan's cities and towns.

SOURCE　V. Mikheeva, 'Trudovye resursy malykh i srednykh gorodov ...', unpublished doctoral dissertation, (Tashkent, 1975). Columns 1–4, p. 72. Columns 5–6, p. 69.

lower levels of labour productivity characterised the latter two groups, while levels of employment, of production, of labour productivity, of assets, and the number of industrial production personnel were all highest in the new industrial cities.

In all the small local centres (both type III and IV), levels of overall employment were low, both absolutely and relative to the new industrial cities (small, medium and large), especially among industrial production personnel. As Table A2.1 illustrates, if new industrial cities had a level of employment approximately 5 per cent higher than the average for about forty-five selected 'representative' cities in Uzbekistan, 1970, old small and medium local centres (group IV) had a level about 5 per cent below the same average. Similarly, levels of gross production in old small and medium size centres were less than half that of the industrial centres; the average number of industrial production personnel, less than one third that of industrial cities; and capital assets installed in enterprises, less than one fourth that in industrial cities. As Table A2.2 indicates, in 1970, 85–90 per cent of the labour resources in the small, predominantly Uzbek centres were employed in social production, while 10–15 per cent were employed in the household and private subsidiary economy; in the new, industrial and mainly European centres, these proportions were 94.3 and 5.7 per cent respectively.

As Table A2.2 also illustrates, growth rates of labour resources employed in social production in the smaller local centres have also lagged behind those of the industrial centres. Between 1959 and 1970, employment in social production grew by an average of 93 per cent in the cities of group II, against 61 and 71 per cent in groups III and IV respectively. In certain industrial cities, the able-bodied employed population in 1970 was as high as 392 per cent (in Navoi) and 233 per cent (in Almalyk) its 1959 level, with similarly high rates of growth illustrated in Chirchik and Fergana. 'From the grouping of cities carried out it is clear that the population of cities of type II, with great industrial potential, differ from the others by their high level of economic activity. In such cities, such as Chirchik, Navoi and Almalyk, every second inhabitant is employed in social production, at the same time that in almost all the cities of groups III and IV, only three out of every ten inhabitants are working.'[1]

Data on natural growth and migration by type of city, moreover, suggest that rapid growth of both the working-age population and of the employed population in new cities – cities where employment and economic growth are high – has been due largely to European in-migration rather than to the local nationalities. Growth in the mainly indigenous old small and medium size towns – where growth of the working-age population is higher, but where levels of employment and economic growth are lower than in the more industrial cities – is due almost entirely to natural increase. As Tables A2.3 and A2.4 illustrate, the number of people entering working age in small local centres grew by almost half from 1959–1970, but only by about 36 per cent in industrial centres. In the large cities and new industrial centres, however, close to 80 per cent of this growth of the able-bodied population was due to in-migration (against an average of 51 per cent for the republic's urban population as a whole) and mainly of Europeans from other republics. In Almalyk, 82.6 per cent of the growth of the able-bodied population was due to

TABLE A2.3   *Factors influencing the growth of the able-bodied population, Uzbekistan, 1959–70 (percentages)*

Type of city	People entering working age	People leaving working age	People dying in working age	Natural growth	Mechanical growth	General growth
I	39.7	19.6	5.5	14.6	12.8	27.4
II	35.9	16.7	5.5	13.7	50.9	64.6
III	48.2	13.3	5.9	19.0	34.4	53.4
IV	47.4	19.3	6.6	21.5	7.2	28.7
Republican average	40.8	18.5	5.5	16.8	19.8	36.6

SOURCE   Mikheeva, V. 'Trudovye resursy malykh i srednikh gorodov ...', unpublished doctoral dissertation, Tashkent, 1975, p. 55.

in-migration; in Chirchik, Termez, Karshi, Gulistan and Kagan, the proportions were between 74 and 82 per cent; and in Navoi, the proportion of population growth due to in-migration was as high as 94.3 per cent.[2]

In the old, mainly indigenous small and medium cities and towns, on the other hand, an average of about 75 per cent of the growth in the able-bodied population was due to natural increase and there was little migrationary movement, particularly in cities of type IV. In certain cities, such as Muinak, Akhangarad, Chust, Pskent and Yangiar, 100 per cent of the growth of the able-bodied population was due to natural increase.[3]

Barring any dramatic diversion of investment towards the old small and medium cities or a dramatic increase in mobility among the indigenous populations, present demographic trends suggest that the disparities among these types of cities, and thus among the levels of employment in them, will grow. Because of their predominantly indigenous character, old small/medium cities, like rural areas, are characterised by high birth rates and rates of natural

TABLE A2.4   *Level of migration by type of city*

Type of city	Intensity of migration (average for cities) In-migrants	Out-migrants	Out-migrants per 100 in-migrants 1959–70	1970–73
I	83.3	85.5	124	127
II	161.3	144.2	142	128
III	98.8	104.2	120	120
IV	56.3	72.4	99	83

SOURCE   Mikheeva, V. 'Trudovye resursy malykh i srednikh gorodov ...', doctoral dissertation, Tashkent, 1975, p. 59.

growth. Industrial cities, where Europeans form the majority of inhabitants, display lower birth rates: 'In industrially developed centres' Mikheeva writes 'where more than 50 per cent of the population is comprised of people of the European nationalities, the birth rate is lower, while in small cities, with an insignificantly-developed industry and where only 11–20 per cent of the populations are of European nationalities, the birth rate is higher, reaching up to 33–34 per thousand.'[4] In 1973, the average birth rate in the fourth group of cities – small local centres – at 34 per thousand was more than one and a half times that in group II (i.e. in industrial cities).

TABLE A2.5 *Birth rate by type of city*

| | Births per 1000 Population | | | |
Type of city	1960	1965	1970	1973
I	33.5	23.2	24.2	25.1
II	31.1	23.5	20.7	21.5
III	42.2	37.3	32.0	34.3
IV	41.1	38.6	37.6	33.3
Total for Uzbekistan	39.8	34.7	33.6	34.1

SOURCE Mikheeva, V. 'Trudovye resursy malykh i srednikh gorodov ...', unpublished doctoral dissertation, Tashkent, 1975, p. 46.

As Table A2.5 illustrates, between 1960 and 1973 the birth rate in small local centres declined more slowly than in cities of group II. The average birth rate for Uzbekistan's industrial cities declined by about 31 per cent; in small local centres, the decline was only 20 per cent. From 1939–59, the population of old small and medium cities with low levels of employment (type IV) grew by 38.3 per cent; between 1959 and 1970, it grew by 51.8 per cent.

The resulting younger age structures in the small local centres also imply a greater number of people, particularly of the indigenous nationalities, who will be entering the working ages than in the industrial cities in the near future. In 1970, about 47 per cent of the population of small local centres (IV), and 43 per cent of the population of Va were under fifteeen years of age, against about 33 per cent of the populations of industrial cities (type II) and of large urban centres (type I).

Problems of employment and population growth are only compounded by the levels of education in the different types of cities, especially among the populations working outside of social production in the household and private subsidiary economy. In cities of type IV, more than 50 per cent of the working-age population occupied in the household and private subsidiary economy has no higher than an elementary education (Table A2.6). The lower level of activity of the able-bodied population in large cities, according to Mikheeva, is explained by the higher number of 20–24-year-olds studying in

TABLE A2.6 Distribution of the working-age population occupied in the household and private subsidiary economy by level of education, as percentages

Type of City	Higher and specialised secondary[a]	Complete secondary	Incomplete secondary	Elementary	Without elementary education
I	5.5	17.3	32.5	25.0	18.8
II	4.9	15.7	30.0	24.9	20.5
III	4.4	15.3	33.3	24.8	21.2
IV	2.7	17.4	28.6	24.8	25.4

[a] complete and incomplete

SOURCE Mikheeva, V. 'Trudovye resursy malykh i srednikh gorodov . . .', doctoral dissertation, Tashkent, 1975, pp. 114–115.

TABLE A2.7   *Rates of growth of the able-bodied population, by type of city, estimates, (without migration), 1959–85*

Type of City	1970 as % 1959	1975 as % 1970	1980 as % 1975	1985 as % 1980
I	129.6	106.5	109.7	105.2
II	166.5	105.3	104.3	99.0
III	147.7	110.8	112.5	110.2
IV	131.6	112.8	116.0	110.9

SOURCE   Mikheeva, V. 'Trudovye resursy malykh i srednikh gorodov . . .', unpublished doctoral dissertation, Tashkent, 1975, p. 131.

institutes of higher learning and in secondary educational establishments, but this is not as true in the smaller cities and towns. Thus educational levels further compound problems of employment in the smaller cities to a greater extent than in the cities of types I and II.

Thus, the population of the able-bodied ages has grown more rapidly in small local centres than in industrial cities. Because of slowing rates of inter-republican migration and continued high rates of natural growth in these centres, moreover, dynamics in the growth of the able-bodied population are expected to remain relatively unchanged in coming years (Table A2.7).

In summary, the results of Mikheeva's study tend to confirm the conclusions of Chapter 3. They tend to support the notion that present levels of development and employment, demographic factors and prospects for demographic change all imply that labour surpluses in small and medium-size towns – where the indigenous nationalities are concentrated – might grow, at the same time that labour shortages remain in the new, industrial and mainly European cities and urban settlements. Table A2.8 illustrates that, barring any dramatic change in investment patterns or demographic policies, large labour shortages have been projected for new, mainly European industrial cities in Uzbekistan, while surpluses are projected for the indigenous small and medium size local centres (Table A2.8). As noted in Chapter 3, this supports Mikheeva's

TABLE A2.8   *Growth of shortages in the labour force and of the able-bodied population due to natural growth, Uzbekistan, 1970–90 (thousands)*

Type of city	Able-bodied population		Need for labour		Surplus/shortage	
I	362.3	454.8	264.5	430.0	97.8	24.8
II	265.2	287.5	227.7	405.8	37.5	118.3
III	204.6	302.6	157.2	347.9	47.4	−45.3
IV	137.6	218.4	96.8	203.2	40.8	15.2

SOURCE   Mikheeva, V. 'Trudovye resursy malykh i srednikh gorodov . . .', unpublished doctoral dissertation, Tashkent, 1975, p. 132.

assertation that 'there is a growing need for labour in the industrially developed cities, and in local economic centres with a level of employment at the republican average', while 'the other groups of cities have a sharply expressed opposite tendency, where the growth of the able-bodied population considerably exceeds the growth of the need for them in the labour force'.[5] Her projections only underscore the importance of this problem, and the challenges which will face planners in Uzbekistan in the near future.

Notes and References

PREFACE

1. See, for example, Iu. Bromlei, *K Probleme tipologizatsii etnicheskikh obshchnostei* (Moscow: Nauka, 1973) *passim*; Iu. Bromelei, *Sovremennye etnicheskie protsessy v SSSR* (Moscow: Nauka, 1977) pp. 4–12; and L. I. Gumilev, 'Etnos kak iavlenie', *Doklady geograficheskogo obshchestvas SSR*, no. 3, 1967. Bromlei, for example, has distinguished mainly between the 'nation', 'nationality', 'a people' and the '*ethnos*', and has divided societies into three major types: those based on the tribe and blood relations, those based on a people and those based on the nation ('for the era of capitalism and socialism'). Another Soviet ethnographer, Gumilev, cites four fundamental ethnic subdivisions: the superethnos ('a group of close ethnoses'); the ethnos ('a large, exclusive system with a dynamic stereotype of behaviour'), the subethnos ('the element of structure of the ethnos') and the consortium ('a group of people united by a single-characteristic way of life and family connections and a member of the ethnos'). Since the purpose of this book is more to draw political implications from the ethnic situation in Central Asia than to present a detailed analysis of the ethnographies themselves, the subdivisions noted by these and other authors will remain secondary to the broader and more politically salient distinction between European outsiders and Asian indigenes.
2. Rupert Emerson. *From Empire to Nation* (Cambridge, Mass: Harvard University Press, 1960) p. 102. See also Boyd C. Shafer, *Faces of Nationalism* (New York: Harcourt Brace Jovanovich, 1972): 'The nation for nationalists is larger than the sum of its parts, becomes a mystical system and organism, a being.' He suggests like other sentiments that nationalism is a composite of many interests, hopes and fears 'a soul, a spiritual principle', p. 14). For a more general discussion, see Isaiah Berlin, 'The Bent Twig': A Note on Nationalism', *Foreign Affairs*, 7 October 1972.
3. A. S. Chamkin, 'Motivy k trudu v sfere obshchestvennogo proizvodstva', doctoral dissertation, Tashkent, 1976, p. 96. See also Walker Connor, 'Nation Building or Destroying?' *World Politics*, vol. XXIV, April 1972

p. 71. With regard to the Ukrainian and Belorussian inmigrant to other republics, Connor writes 'Removed from his ethnic preserve, wherein all non-members of the nationality tend to be viewed as alien invaders, the émigré will now tend to stress that which he has in common with his fellow Slav. . . .' As a result of native perceptions of him ('There is little to distinguish a Ukrainian from any other Slav, all of whom he [the Central Asian] perceives as Russians') the Ukrainian or Belorussian is 'all the more encouraged to realise his common ties to the Russians'. (p. 72).

4. The system used for transliterating Uzbek to English is described in E. Allworth. *Nationalities of the Soviet East: Publications and Writing Systems* (New York: Columbia University Press, 1971).

INTRODUCTION

1. Between 1970 and 1979 the Uzbeks grew at an average annual rate of 3.43 per cent; the Turkmen, 3.22 per cent, the Kirgiz, 3.07 per cent and the Tadzhiks, 3.45 per cent. Ethnic Russians grew at an average rate of 0.7 per cent per year, and the Slavic populations as a whole, at 0.62 per cent per year. See S. Rapawy and G. Baldwin, 'Demographic Trends in the Soviet Union: 1950–2000', *The Soviet Economy in the 1980s; Problems and Prospects*. Selected Papers submitted to the Joint Economic Committee, US Congress, 31 December 1982, Washington, DC: Government Printing Office, 1983, p. 279.

2. 'USSR: Ethnic Composition of the Conscript Pool'. Intelligence Appraisal (unclassified), Defense Intelligence Agency, 1979, pp. 1–2. See also M. Feshbach, 'Population and the Labour Force', unpublished paper prepared for the conference on *The Soviet Economy: Toward the Year 2000*, Airlie House, Virginia, 24–25 October 1980, esp. pp. 17–23; 'Trends in Soviet Muslim Populations', Paper prepared for the *Symposium on the USSR and the Muslim World*, Tel Aviv University, 28–30 December 1980, *passim*; and 'Population and Manpower Trends in the USSR', unpublished paper, p. 16, Table 6.

3. See, for example, J. P. Stern, 'Soviet Natural Gas in the World Economy'. Discussion paper for the Association of American Geographers, Project on Soviet Natural Resources in the World Economy, sponsored by the National Science Foundation, Washington, DC, no. 11, June 1979, esp. p. 7–9.

4. C. Glynn, *Gold 1979*. Annual gold-market study conducted by Consolidated Gold Fields Ltd, London, June 1979, p. 49.

5. Although I recognise that many Western scholars include Kazakhstan among the Central Asian republics, this study, based largely on Soviet sources, follows the pattern of treating the region as comprised of four republics: Uzbekistan, Tadzhikistan, Turkmenistan and Kirgizia.

6. See M. Rywkin, 'Code Words and Catchwords of Brezhnev's Nationality Policy', *Survey*, Summer, 1979, pp. 83–90. and A. Brown, 'Political Developments, 1975–1977', in *The Soviet Union Since the Fall of Khrushchev*, 2nd edn, A. Brown and M. Kaser (eds) (London: Macmillan, 2nd edn, 1978).

7. See for example, A. Bennigsen, 'Several Nations or One People?' *Survey*, vol. 24, no. 3, Summer 1979, pp. 54–6.

8. Fozil Ergashev, 'Problemy predotvrashcheniia vosproizvodstva religii sredi molodogo pokoleniia v usloviakh razvitogo sotsialisma', dissertation submitted for the degree of *Kandidat Nauk*, Tashkent, 1975.

9. 'Naselenie SSSR.' (Preliminary Results of the 1979 Census) 'Moscow: Politizdat, 1980) p. 23. It should be noted that these figures are generally regarded with some suspicion among Western analysts of Soviet affairs.

10. During 1978–9, for example, a joint filming of *Ali Baba and the Forty Thieves* was in progress with the Uzbek Film Studio and the Eagle-Films Company of India. At the same time, an agreement was reached with the Ministry of Information in Afghanistan to begin work on a joint documentary film about Afghanistan. The work was projected to be conducted by the Uzbek Documentary and Popular Scientific Film Studio and the Afghan Film Studio. A film on World War Two made jointly by the US and Moscow – with Burt Lancaster narrating – played for several weeks in Tashkent. Television and radio stations throughout Soviet Central Asia are divided fairly evenly between broadcasts in Russian and in the local languages.

11. See W. Fierman, 'Uzbek Feelings of Ethnicity: A Study of Attitudes Expressed in Recent Soviet Literature', paper prepared for the US Department of State, Bureau of Intelligence and Research, 1978, esp. pp. 54–7.

12. Ibid, p. 11. See also J. Soper 'Uzbek Writers Look to the Past for Inspiration', Radio Free Europe/Radio Liberty report, RL 129/79, 24 April 1979.

13. F. W. Carpenter, W. K. Medlin and W. M. Cave. *Educational Development in Central Asia* (Leiden: Brill, 1971). (See Chapter 3 of this book).

14. Data from the Ministry of Higher and Specialised Secondary Education, UzSSR, Tashkent, 1979. See Chapter 4 of this book.

15. For a discussion of these questions particularly as they apply to Uzbekistan's national élites, see Irwin Selnick, 'The Ethno-Political Determinants of Elite Recruitment in the Soviet Republics: The Case of Uzbekistan'. PhD dissertation, Department of Political Science, Columbia University, expected date of completion, 1984.

16. For a more in-depth or comprehensive discussion of general developmental issues in Uzbekistan, see J. Gillula, 'The Economic Interdependence of Soviet Republics', *The Soviet Economy in a Time of Change*, Compendium of papers submitted to the Joint Economic Committee, US Congress, Washington, DC, 1979, and G. Schroeder, 'Regional Differences in Income in the USSR', *Regional Development in the USSR*, NATO Colloquium, 25–7 April 1979 (Newtonville, Massachusetts: Oriental Research Papers, 1979).

17. V. A. Osmimin. *Planirovanie v respublike* (Tashkent: Uzbekistan, 1979) p. 8.

18. Ibid, p. 80, and Table, pp. 81–2.

19. See, for example, W. Fierman. 'Uzbek Feelings of Ethnicity', p. 1 and Murray Feshbach, 'Trends in the Soviet Muslim Population – Demographic Aspects', *Soviet Economy in the 1980s: Problems and Prospects*,

Part 2, Selected Papers submitted to the Joint Economic Committee, Congress of the United States, December 31, 1983 (Washington, DC: US Government Printing Office, 1983) p. 299.

20. Walker Connor, 'The Politics of Ethnonationalism', *Journal of International Affairs*, vol. 27, no. 1, 1973, pp. 1–21.

1 DEMOGRAPHY AND ECONOMICS

1. The population of Uzbekistan grew at a mid-year rate of growth of 3.5 per cent per year from 1956–60; 3.6 per cent per year, 1961–5; 3.1 per cent per year, 1966–70; and 3.0 per cent per year from 1971–5 and from 1976–9. See Tsentral'noe Statisticheskoe Upravlenie (hereafter TsSU) *Itogi vsesoiuznei perepisi naselenie 1970 goda*, vol. I (Moscow: Statistika, 1972) p.7 and *Itogi. . . 1959 goda* (Moscow: Gosstatizdat, 1962) for 1959 and 1970; see 'Naseleniie SSSR', (Results of the 1979 Census) (Moscow: Politizdat, 1980) for 1979 census data. Growth rates computed from data of the 1959, 1970 and 1979 census, and from the TsSU, *Narodnoe Khoziaistvo Uzbekskoi SSR* (Tashkent: Uzbekistan) for appropriate years.

2. The Uzbek population grew by 110 per cent, while the Russian grew by only 53 per cent (see *Itogi. . .*, 1959 and 1970).

3. Uzbekistan's death rate declined from 13.2 per thousand in 1940 to 5.5 per thousand in 1970, before climbing to 7.4 in 1980; total fertility declined only from 5.0 in 1958–9 to 4.9 in 1979–80. Total fertility indicates the average number of children women would have altogether if the age-specific fertility rates of a given year remained constant. The birth rate for the USSR as a whole fell from 17.0 per thousand in 1950 to 8 per thousand in 1979. Fertility rates taken from R. Crisostomo, unpublished tables prepared for the Foreign Demographic Analysis Division, US Bureau of the Census, Washington, DC, and from M. Feshbach, 'The Soviet Union: Population Trends and Dilemmas', *Population Bulletin*, Washington, DC: Population Reference Bureau, Inc., vol. 37, no. 3, August 1982. USSR data from Godfrey Baldwin, 'Population Projections by Age and Sex: for the Republics and Major Economic Regions of the USSR 1970 to 2000', *International Population Reports*, Series P. 91, no. 26, Washington, DC: Foreign Demographic Analysis Division, Bureau of the Census, US Department of Commerce, 1979, p. 5.

4. See M. Feshbach, 'Trends in the Soviet Muslim population – Demographic Aspects', *The Soviet Economy in the 1980s: Problems and Prospects* Part 2, Selected Papers submitted to the Joint Economic Committee, US Congress, 31 December 1982. Washington, DC: US Government Printing Office, 1983, pp. 303–4.

5. TsSU, *Itogi. . . 1959 goda* and *Itogi. . . 1970 goda*. In Uzbekistan's rural areas, average family size was 6.2; in urban, 4.6. For family size by nationality, see 'Vsesoiuznaia perepis' naseleniia', *Vestnik Statistiki*, no. 11, 1981, p. 57. It should be noted that these data refer to families jointly residing together and apply to the nationalities on the territory of the USSR as a whole.

6. In 1958–9, the total fertility rate for Uzbekistan was 5.0. In 1971–2, it reached 5.8. By 1979–80, it had declined to its 1959 level – more than twice the all-Union average, and more than two and a half times the rate of the Russian republic. Expectations of continued high fertility among natives in Uzbekistan were confirmed in O. B. Ata Mirzaev and B. Gol'dfarb, 'Naselenie Uzbekistana' (*v pomoshch' lektoru*), 1978, p. 29, and in interviews, Obshchestvo Zhaniie, UzSSR, Tashkent, 1978–9. See also A. Orynbekov, and A. M. Kazakov, 'K voprosu modelirovaniia vosproizvodstva naseleniia Uzbekistana', *Regional'nye osobennosti vosproizvodstva naseleniia trudovykh resursov v Uzbekskoi SSR*, 1975, p. 83.

7. See R. Crisostomo, 'The Demographic Dilemma of the Soviet Union', unpublished paper prepared for the Foreign Demographic Analysis Division, US Bureau of the Census, Washington, DC: June, 1982, pp. 10–11. For the US–USSR comparisons and discussion of infant mortality generally in the USSR, see M. Feshbach, 'The Soviet Union: Population Trends and Dilemmas', p. 32. While some of this rise is due to improved statistical reporting, it apparently represents a real rise in infant mortality as well. For a fuller discussion of infant mortality in the USSR see C. Davis and M. Feshbach, *Rising Infant Mortality in the USSR in the 1970s*, International Population Reports, Series P.95 No. 74, US Dept of Commerce, Bureau of the Census, June 1980.

8. See V. Perevedentsev, 'The Population and the Party's Demographic Policy', *Politicheskoie samoobrazovaniie*, no. 8, August, 1981, pp. 45–53. Translated in Joint Publication Research Service, *USSR Report: Human Resources*, no. 41, 19 October 1981, p. 54.

9. A. Ia. Kvasha, 'Nekotorye problemy regional'nogo demograficheskogo Analiza', *Regional'nye Demograficheskie Issledovaniia* (compilation of scientific works no. 548) Tashkent: Ministry of Higher and Secondary Specialised Education (hereafter Minvuz), 1978) pp. 14–15.

10 See A. S. Chamkin, 'Motivy k trudu v sfere obshchestvennogo proizvodstva', doctoral dissertation, Tashkent, 1976.

11. See T. Shabad, 'Some Aspects of Central Asian Manpower and Urbanisation', *Soviet Geography*, vol. xx, no. 2, February, 1979, pp. 115–16. A city in Uzbekistan is defined as a population point wherein the population is equal to or exceeds 7000 people, and where at least three quarters of the population are workers, employees or members of their families. According to an interview with Ata Mirzaev, the definition also includes population points 'of administrative significance', even if all the above conditions are not met. Urban settlements are population points with between 2000 and 7000 inhabitants, at least three quarters of whom are workers or employees. These definitions differ somewhat from some other parts of the USSR.

12. T. Shabad, 'Central Asia and the Soviet Economy: Implications for Policy' paper delivered at a conference on Soviet Central Asia, US International Communications Agency, December 1978. See also M. Feshbach, 'Prospects for Outmigration. . . .', p. 670. According to Feshbach, in 1970, rural migrants comprised less than 17 per cent of the new arrivals to cities in Uzbekistan. For a discussion of the persistence of this situation in the 1970s, see, for example, T. Shabad, 'Economic Realities

and Dynamics of Central Asia', Paper presented at the Conference on the Study of Central Asia, the Wilson Center, 1983, p. 47; Murray Feshbach 'Prospects for Outmigration from Central Asia and Kazakhstan in the Next Decade', *Soviet Economy in a Time of Change*, Compendium of Papers submitted to the Joint Economic Committee, US Congress, 10 October 1979, Washington, DC: US Government Printing Office, 1979, p. 670.

13. V. Perevedentsev, 'Some Statistics on Migration', *Literaturnaia Gazeta*, 1975, p. 27.

14. A recent study conducted by J. Berliner attempts to quantify the extent to which high fertility in Soviet Central Asia may be due to cultural factors, and the extent to which it is due to more concrete factors such as age of mother, urban or rural residence, income, and female educational levels and labour force participation rates. While the study recognises the problems in positing a precise measurement of the contribution of each variable to reproductive behaviour, it illustrates the importance of considering culture as one important variable in fertility behaviour among the Soviet Central Asians. See J. Berliner, 'Research Report on the Family', monograph prepared for the National Council for Soviet and East European Research, May 1981.

15. O. B. Ata Mirzaev, and B. Gol'dfarb, 'Naselenie Uzbekistana', (V pomoshch' lektoru) p. 11.

16. See I. I. Kashtanenkova, 'Sotsial'no-demograficheskii analiz mnogodetnykh zhenshchin g. Tashkenta', *Regional'nye demograficheskie issledovaniia*, (Tashkent: Minvuz, 1978) see also V. A. Belova, *et al. Skol'ko detei budet v sovetskoi sem'ie* (Moscow: Statistika, 1977). According to this national survey, conducted among Russian and Uzbek women in 1972, close to 60 per cent of all Uzbeks surveyed desired six or more children, against 1 per cent of the Russians. 77 per cent of all Russians desired only one or two children, against less than 7 per cent of the Uzbeks. The survey was conducted among 347 314 women aged 18 to 59 by the USSR Central Statistical Administration.

17. For specific examples, see A. Orynbekov and A. Kazakov, 'K voprosu modelirovaniia naseleniia Uzbekistana', *Regional'nye osobennosti vosproizvodstva naseleniia i trudovykh resursov v Uzbekskoi SSR* (Tashkent: manuscript prepared by Gosplan, Council of Ministers, Uzbek SSR and the Scientific Research Economic Institute (NIEI), 1975) p. 83. As Orynbekov notes 'women of the local nationalities still have early marriages, exceeding the average all-Union indicator by almost two times'.

18. See R. Crisostomo, unpublished tables prepared for the Foreign Demographic Analysis Division, US Bureau of the Census, Washington, DC. Fertility in Uzbekistan in 1978–9 was 277.3 among 20–24year-old women, and 281.7 among 25–29year-old women.

19. See V. A. Belova, *Skol'ko detei...*, (Moscow Statistika, 1977) pp. 34–5.

20. See V. Perevedentsev, 'The Population and the Party's Demographic Policy,' *Politicheskoye samoobrazovaniie* in JPRS, p. 56.

21. A. G. Stankov, *Chto nado znat' do braka i v brake* (Tashkent: Meditsina, 1979) p.7. The first edition of this book appeared in 1971, the second, in 1973. Two other books of this type have been published in Uzbekistan by the same author: *Marriage Without Children* and *Artificial Sterility*, both

in Tashkent in 1969.

22. Ibid, p. 8.

23. Among European women in Uzbekistan in 1978, about 8 per cent of all first pregnancies and 40–50 per cent of all second pregnancies were terminated in abortion; with the third pregnancy, the number of abortions exceeded the number of births, and 'the higher the order of pregnancy, the greater the proportion of those which were terminated by abortion'. Among Asian women, however, the incidence of abortion was, and remains, exceedingly low. In the same year, among Asian women, 85–95 per cent of all pregnancies ended in birth, and of the remaining 5–15 per cent, most were miscarriages. As Aliakberova writes, 'Actual births among women of the local nationalities throughout the entire period of reproductive activity is exceptionally high, almost on the level of physiological possibilities.' See N. M. Aliakberova, 'Analiz sovremennykh tendentsii rozhdaemosti v Srednei Azii', *Regional'nye Demograficheskii Issledovaniia*, (Tashkent: Minvuz, 1978) pp. 23–4. For a discussion of the limited effectiveness of family planning services, see, for example, Orynbekov and A. Kazakov, 'K voprosu modelirovaniia...', p. 83.

24. See, for example, T. Maqsudov, 'Embodiment of Unity of Moral, Hygiene and Sex Education', *Sovet Maktabi*, no. 9, 1982, pp. 44–5, as translated in *USSR Report: Central Asian Press Surveys*, Foreign Broadcast Information Service, 23 August 1983, pp. 54–5.

25. T. Riabushkin, 'Demograficheskaia politika v svete reshenii XXVI s''ezda KPSS,' *Vestnik Statistiki*, no. 2, 1982, p.7. In recent years, Soviet planners have increasingly addressed the idea of formulating a differential population policy for the USSR as a whole. On the side of formulating a differential policy are such leading economists and demographers as Urlanis, Kvasha, Perevedentsev, Litvinova and Riabushkin. Against such a policy are Manevich, Katkova, Tatimov and almost all the Central Asian demographers whom I interviewed in the Asian republics. So far, however, these discussions have only referred to policies on an overall, all-Union level. There have been no explicit calls for differential policies with regard to the different nationalities within Uzbekistan or within any of the individual Central Asian republics. For further discussion, see M. Feshbach, 'Demography and Soviet Society: Social and Cultural Aspects', paper delivered at the Kennan Institute for Advanced Russian Studies, The Wilson Center, Washington, DC, February 1981, pp. 2 and 38–40.

26. In 1968–9, for example, out of a total of 270 000 people who moved their place of residence from one location to another, only 127 500 were Uzbeks (or only about 1 per cent of Uzbekistan's total population). Of those, only about 24 per cent (about 30 000 people) migrated to or from another republic, and among those, all movement involved another Central Asian republic. On the other side of the coin, of a total net migration of 32 211 people to Uzbekistan in 1970, 17 255, (54 per cent) were from the RSFSR. Only 3972, or 12 per cent from the other three Central Asian republics; their nationalities have not been published. See V. Perevedentsev, 'Some Statistics on Migration', p. 27; S. Alimov, 'Vlianie rosta mnogonatsional'nosti sovetskikh respublik na sblizhenie sotsialisticheskikh natsii', unpublished doctoral dissertation, Tashkent,

1971, p. 52. and I. Mulliadzhanov, *Naselenie Uzbekskoi SSR*, (Tashkent: Uzbekistan, 1973) p. 22.

27. See S. E. Wimbush and D. Ponomareff, *Alternatives for Mobilizing Soviet Central Asian Labour: Outmigration and Regional Development* (Santa Monica: The Rand Corporation, 1979) *passim* and various issues of *Komsomolets Uzbekistana, Partinaia Zhizn', Guliston, Yosh Leninchi, Sovet Ozbekistoni, Pravda Vostoka,* and other newspapers and journals in both Russian and Uzbek (for example, I. Dzhurabekov, 'Uzbekistan – Nechernozem', *Partinaia Zhizn',* no. 8, August 1982, pp. 43–7, and S. Saydaliyev, 'The Feeling of a Single Family', *Guliston,* no. 1, 1983, as translated in JPRS, *USSR Report: Central Asian Press Surveys,* 23 August 1983, p. 39). The non-black earth zone refers to a major agricultural land reclamation scheme begun in 1974 in lands located in the environs of Moscow and Novgorod, extending north through the Murmansk region and east to include some territories east of the Urals. It is a programme which was conceived in the hope of greatly increasing the USSR's food supply. In general, articles in Uzbekistan's republican newspapers commonly show photographs of Uzbeks relaxing in Asian-style *chaikhonas* (teahouses) after working happily in the fields with representatives of hundreds of other nationalities. For a discussion of these issues, see also R. Lewis, 'Regional Manpower Resources and Resource Development in the USSR, 1970–1990', discussion paper no. 18, prepared for the Association of American Geographers, December 1979, and M. Feshbach, 'Prospects for Outmigration from Central Asia and Kazakhstan During the Next Decade', *Soviet Economy in a Time of Change,* Compendium of Papers submitted to the Joint Economic Committee, US Congress, 1979, pp. 656–709.

28. See S. N. Zhelezko, *Sotsial'no-demograficheskiie problemy v zone BAMa* (Moscow: Statistika, 1980) p. 107, cited in R. M. Crisostomo, *Russian Language Fluency in the USSR's Southern Tier* (Center for International Research, US Bureau of the Census, May 1982) pp. 4–5.

29. M. Feshbach, 'Trends in the Soviet Muslim Population – Demographic Aspects', p. 314.

30. See the summary report of the CPSU Central Committee to the 26th Party Congress, and V. Perevedentsev, 'The Population and the Party's Demographic Policy p. 48. These views were confirmed in interviews I conducted in Moscow, August 1981.

31. Uzbek officials and scholars tend to agree that large-scale movement among the native population is highly unlikely in the near future. As late as 1978, Ata Mirzaev, Chief of the Population Laboratory of Tashkent University, noted that migratory movement largely depends on 'the particularities characteristic of representatives of the indigenous nationalities (Uzbeks, Karakalpaks). . . . Representatives of the indigenous nationalities' he added 'move mainly within the borders of the republic itself'. See O. B. Ata Mirzaev, 'Naseleniie Uzbekistana' (V pomoshch' lektoru) Tashkent: Obshchestvo 'Znanie' UzSSR, November 1978, p. 13. This was confirmed in interviews I held at the Institute of Ethnography, Moscow in 1979 and 1981.

32. On the first point, see, for example, A. McAuley, *Women's Work and Wages in the Soviet Union* (London: Allen & Unwin, 1981) p. 42 and conversations with the author, May, 1980; on the second point, see R. Lewis, and R. Rowland, 'East is West and West is East . . . Population Redistribution in the USSR and Its Impact on Society', *International Migration Review*, vol. 2, no. 1, Spring, 1977, pp. 3–29 and R. Lewis, and R. Rowland, *Population Redistribution in the USSR* (New York: Praeger, 1979). For arguments on the other side, see M. Feshbach, 'Prospects for Outmigration . . ., *passim*.

33. O. B. Ata Mirzaev, 'Aktual'nye zadachi kompleksnogo issledovaniia regional'nykh problem narodonaseleniia Srednei Azii', *Regional'nye demograficheskie issledovaniia* (Tashkent: Minvuz, 1978) p. 5. According to his projections, the level of urbanisation in Central Asia towards the end of the century will be just slightly over 50 per cent.

34. M. Feshbach, 'Between the Lines of the 1979 Census', *Problems of Communism*, vol. XXXI, Jan–Feb 1982, p. 32.

35. For the past twenty years, Uzbekistan has been characterised by a more equal distribution between the sexes than has the USSR as a whole, at about 48 per cent male and 51 per cent female in 1970. That favourable balance, however, conceals disparities among the different nationalities living within Uzbekistan. While the proportion of males and females in the total population of Uzbekistan has remained fairly constant for the last forty years, the 1970 census data indicate that the sex balance has been more even among the Uzbeks than among the Russians. While women comprised about 50 per cent of the republic's total Uzbek population, they comprised 56 per cent of the republic's Russian population. The only other nationality group with a disparity as large as the Russian was the Tatars.

36. See A. Orunbekov, and A. Kazakov, 'K voprosu modelirovaniia . . .', p. 83: referring to the early marriage age of indigenous women, they write: 'This circumstance, all things being equal – and also in the light of the existence of a high percentage of marriages and a low level of divorce – is raising the level of their birth rate'.

37. See J. Gillula, 'The Economic Interdependence of Soviet Republics', *Soviet Economy in a Time of Change*, Compendium of papers submitted to the Joint Economic Committee, Congress of the United States, (Washington, DC: US Government Printing Office; 1979) p. 626 and 634. The ratio of used to produced national income for Uzbekistan in 1966 was 1.10, in 1969, 1.18 and in 1974, 1.04 *v*. .90, .95, and .94 for the Latvian SSR and similar ratios for the Ukraine and the other Baltic republics. In 1966, Uzbekistan's import surplus (the difference between produced and used national income) was about four times greater than the USSR average. (Ibid, p. 631).

38. Ibid, p. 624. In the two five-year plans, 1966–1970 and 1971–1975, 99 per cent and 98 per cent of total turnover tax collections in Uzbekistan were retained within the republican budget, against 30 per cent and 39 per cent in the RSFSR and an average of 41 per cent and 46 per cent for all USSR republics. It should be stressed, that there is some discrepancy in

views as to just how committed the Soviet government in fact is to a policy of *equalising* economic growth among the republics. The point here, however, is not to suggest that Moscow's policy has in fact led to equality. Instead – whether through compensation to the lesser-developed republics, equal funding among all of the republics, or simply redistribution – there is evidence that Soviet subsidies or redistribution to the Central Asian republics have stimulated greater economic growth than these republics' contribution to the total Soviet economy might have merited. For a discussion of some of these arguments, see Donna Bahry and Carol Nechemias, 'Half Full or Half Empty?: The Debate Over Soviet Regional Equality', *Slavic Review*, vol. 40, No. 3, Autumn 1981, pp. 366–83.

39. Ibid, pp. 627 and 639; 1975 estimate from M. Feshbach, 'Prospects for Outmigration ...', p. 695. Because of the differences in family size, these indicators ideally should be examined by household rather than by per capita measures; those data, however, are presently unavailable. Per capita measures are therefore used as a revealing, but none the less poor substitute, simply to illustrate the general effects of population growth on economic change. Further difficulties in determining the relative deprivation or priority ranking of the different republics depend not only on population dynamics, but on climate, natural resources, pricing, etc. See A. Nove, 'The Economics of Nationality Policy', unpublished paper delivered at the annual convention of the American Association for the Advancement of Slavic Studies (AAASS), November 1980.

40. G. Schroeder, 'Soviet Regional Development Policies and Perspectives', *The USSR in the 1980s*, (series no. 7) (Brussels: NATO Directorate of Economic Affairs, 1978) p. 126.

41. See J. Gillula, 'The Economic Interdependence ...' p. 620. As Gillula notes, 'Clearly a major factor underlying the increasing coefficients of variation for measures of the level of development of republics in per capita terms is the much higher than average rates of population growth in most of the less-developed republics. The most obvious conclusion is that the increased levels of investment made possible by the redistribution of national income to these republics were just not sufficient to spur rates of economic growth that could keep pace with the growth of population.'

42. G. Schroeder, 'Soviet Regional Development Policies ...', p. 125.

43. See R. A. Ubaidullaeva, 'Regional'nye problemy razmeshcheniia i effektivnosti ispol'zovaniia trudovykh resursov v Uzbekskoi SSR', unpublished doctoral dissertation (Tashkent, 1974) and interviews.

44. See, for example, A. Nove, 'The Economics of Nationality Policy', paper delivered at the annual convention of the American Association for the Advancement of Slavic Studies, November 1980, pp. 5 and 16, and G. Schroeder, 'Soviet Regional Development Policies', p. 125.

45. See G. Schroeder, 'Soviet Regional Development Policies ...', p. 133.

2 THE LABOUR FORCE

1. If the total population of Uzbekistan grew by 90 per cent between 1959 and 1979, the working-age population grew by 83 per cent, from about

4.0 million to 7.3 million people (computed from *Itogi vsesoiuznoi perepisi naseleniia* . . . for 1959 and 1970, and 'Naseleniie SSR', [Moscow: Politizdat, 1980] for 1979.) The working-age population is defined as males 16–59 years of age and females aged 16–54.

2. See Godfrey Baldwin, 'Population Projections by Age and Sex: For the Republics and Major Economic Regions of the USSR: 1970 to 2000', *International Population Reports*, Series P. 91, no. 26 (Washington, DC: Foreign Demographic Analysis Division, US Bureau of the Census, 1979) pp. 128–9. Estimates from Soviet demographers in Tashkent, such as Ubaidullaeva and Mulliadzhanov, are uniformly higher than Baldwin's.

3. Unlike other regions of the USSR, Uzbekistan's population will retain its young age-structure through the turn of the century. For example, while the proportion of the USSR's total population aged 0–15 is projected to decline from 30 per cent in 1959 to 27 per cent in 1990, that same proportion in Uzbekistan is expected to rise from 39 per cent of Uzbekistan's total population to 42 per cent over the same period.

4. See M. Feshbach, 'The Soviet Union: Population Trends and Dilemmas', *Population Bulletin* (Washington, DC: Population Reference Bureau, Inc. vol. 37, no. 3, August 1982).

5. These figures were calculated as the sum of Baldwin's estimates for natural growth of Uzbekistan's labour force and Ubaidullaeva's projections for migration in the able-bodied ages. If Ubaidullaeva's projections for natural growth are substituted for Baldwin's, the projected growth of the working-age population becomes significantly higher. It should be noted that migratory movements are particularly difficult to project, and Ubaidullaeva's estimates may be disputed by other experts.

6. R. A. Ubaidullaeva, 'Regional'nye problemy razmeshcheniia i effektivnost' ispol'zovaniia trudovykh resursov', doctoral dissertation, (Tashkent, 1974).

7. See R. Lewis, *Regional Manpower Resources and Resource Development in the USSR: 1970–1990*, Discussion Paper no. 18, prepared for the Association of American Geographers, December 1979, pp. 51–60. Quoted in M. Rywkin, 'Central Asia and Soviet Manpower', *Problems of Communism*, January–February, 1979, vol. xxviii, p. 5.

8. A. McAuley, and A. Hegelson, 'Soviet Labour Supply and Manpower Utilization 1960–2000', paper presented at the Joint Whitehall-Academic Conference, The London School of Economics, 15 December 1978, pp. 20–21. See also R. Lewis, ibid: 'The expansion of the rural economy cannot absorb more than half of the surplus unless the Soviet leadership abandons further mechanisation in favour of more labour-intensive culture or drastically enlarges the acreage of land under cultivation'. Lewis regards both alternatives as unlikely.

9. As Massell writes, 'Two growing streams of people are arriving simultaneously to fill the new system of roles and opportunities . . . . Barring fundamental changes in present arrangements, the pressure of the two massive human streams may soon outstrip the system's capacity to absorb them, resulting in a saturation of role opportunities and status positions in Central Asia.' See G. Massell, 'Ethnicity and Nationalism', *IREX Occasional Paper*, vol. 1, no. 3, 1980, pp. 19–20.

10. R. A. Ubaidullaeva, 'Regional'nye problemy razmeshcheniia . . .', doctoral dissertation, Tashkent, 1974, p. 321. See also S. Ziadullaev, quoted in RFE/RL report, 27 October 1980: 'In view of the low mobility of the Asians . . . the complexity of the problem of how to make rational use of these rapidly growing labour resources is becoming evident'.

11. N. S. Esipov, 'Vazhneishei cherta narodonaselenia i voprosy ispol'zovaniia trudovykh resursov', *Materialy Mezhvuzovskoi Nauchnoi Konferentsii po Problemam Narodonaselenii Srednei Azii* (Tashkent: Tashkent State University, September 1965) p. 5.

12. These numbers might actually be higher, since a significant proportion of the employed population each year was not, and is not, in the able-bodied ages. According to census data, 8 per cent of the labour force in 1959 was either above or below working age. In 1970, 2.9 per cent of the employed population was 60 years or older, and 10.2 per cent was under twenty years of age; no breakdown was given, however, as to how many of the latter group were under sixteen years of age. Since there are no consistent data on the age and sex of the employed population for each of these years – thus making any attempt to determine the proportion of employed personnel who are above or below working age extremely difficult – the reported labour force is treated here as being comprised entirely of working-age people.

13. The difference between the ratios of the total labour force to the able-bodied population in the RSFSR and in Uzbekistan was only about three percentage points in 1970. When these same ratios were computed using annual average employment, the difference between these two republics was almost nine percentage points, or almost three times as great. It should be noted that the reported labour force includes the military, while annual average employment does not. Therefore, as Rapawy has pointed out, these differences in the growth rate of average annual employment and of the reported labour force may overstate the problem to some degree. Women on maternity leave are also not included in average annual employment.

14. H. P. Babamukhammedov, 'Muslims of our Country Today,' *Muslims of the Soviet East*, no. 1, 1980, p. 12.

15. R. A. Ubaidullaeva, 'Regional'nye problemy . . .', doctoral dissertation, Tashkent 1974.

16. In 1959, 139 000 people of working age in rural areas alone were employed in private subsidiary agriculture, or 5.7 per cent of the total number of rural people in the able-bodied ages; in 1970, Egamberdyev wrote, 38 100 people of working age were so employed, or 1.3 per cent. In 1959, 164 600 people of working age, or 6.7 per cent of the total number, were employed in household work, as opposed to 106 800 in 1970, or 3.8 per cent. Numerically, taken together, that would mean a decline of more than 50 per cent. See A. E. Egamberdyev (ed.) *Regional'nye problemy vosproizvodstva rabochei sily v Uzbekistane* (Tashkent: Fan, 1976) pp. 46–48.

17. See S. Rapawy, 'Estimates and Projections of the Labor Force and Civilian Employment in the USSR: 1950–1990', *Foreign Economic Report no. 10* (Washington, DC: Foreign Demographic Analysis Division,

US Bureau of the Census, September 1976) pp. 9–10.

18. See V. Mikheeva, 'Trudovye resursy malykh i srednikh gorodov Uzbekistana i perspektivy ikh ispol'zovaniia', doctoral dissertation, Tashkent, 1975, p. 107.

19. R. A. Ubaidullaeva, 'Regional'ny problemy . . .', dissertation, Tashkent, 1974.

20. R. A. Ubaidullaeva, ibid, appendix. All three variants used as their base the proportion of labour resources occupied in household and private subsidiary work on 1 January and 1 October 1970, and all were based on the same projections for number of women in the able-bodied ages ('since 95 per cent of those in household and private subsidiary work are women'). The first variant assumed 'maximum labour mobility' among the able-bodied population not employed in social production. The second variant assumed a minimal level of mobility. The third variant assumed a 'normative level', projecting that every woman giving birth will not participate in social production for one to two years.

21. A. A. Abduganiev, (ed.) *Trudovye resursy Uzbekistana* (Tashkent: Fan, 1970).

22. In 1974, one Uzbek scholar cited surpluses on ten state farms in Samarkand *oblast'* of about 9970 people of the able-bodied ages. Among the state farms with 'an especially large labour surplus' were the *sovkhoz* Koshrabad 1, the V. I. Lenin *sovkhoz*, and the *sovkhoz* Mastbulak, with surpluses of 2598, 1624 and 1244 people respectively. All three, allegedly, are mainly Uzbek in composition.

23. W. Mandel, 'Urban Ethnic Minorities in the Soviet Union', paper delivered at the annual convention of the American Association for the Advancement of Slavic Studies, Dallas, Texas, 1972, pp. 10–11.

24. A. S. Chamkin, 'Motivy k trudu v sfere obshchestvennogo proizvodstva', dissertation submitted for the degree of *Kandidat Nauk*, Tashkent, 1976.

25. V. Mikheeva, 'Trudovye resursy malykh i srednikh gorodov . . .', dissertation, p. 117. See also R. A. Ubaidullaeva, 'Regional'nye problemy . . .', dissertation, p. 53.

26. D. A. Khodzhaeva, 'O strukturnykh sdvigakh konservnoi promyshlennosti UzSSR', *Obschchestvennye nauki v Uzlekistane*, no. 5, 1979, p. 41.

27. For a discussion of the contemporary role of women in Uzbekistan, see N. Lubin, 'Women in Soviet Central Asia: Progress and Contradictions', *Soviet Studies*, April 1981, pp. 182–203.

28. R. A. Ubaidullaeva, 'Regional'nye problemy . . .', appendix.

29. Ibid, p. 48.

30. K. Makhmudov, 'O roli sferu obsluzhivanniia v obshchestvennom proizvodstve'. *Obshchestvennye nauki v Uzbekistane*, no. 1, 1971.

31. R. A. Ubaidullaeva, 'Regional'nye problemy . . .', dissertation, p. 252.

32. Ibid, p. 252. In 1971, full-day absences from work and wasted time per industrial worker in Uzbekistan on the average amounted to 17.1 days, as opposed to 14.9 days in the Ukraine and 13.7 days in Lithuania. While losses of working-time in industry because of sickness remained at about the same level in Uzbekistan from 1963 to 1973, absenteeism rose. This contrasts with the average for the USSR as a whole, where the total losses of working time in all categories declined.

33. See, for example, A. McAuley, 'Soviet Labour Supply ...', p. 39.
34. Ibid, p. 39.
35. Quoted in R. Solchanyk, 'New Turn in Soviet Nationalities Policy', *Soviet Analyst*, vol. 10, no. 8, 15 April, 1981, p. 5.

3 THE USE LABOUR BY SECTOR AND LOCATION

1. See E. Bacon, *Central Asians Under Russian Rule* (New York: Cornell University Press, 1966) p. 106. For a description of pre-Revolutionary Central Asia, see also O. Caroe, *The Soviet Empire* (New York: St Martin's Press, 1967) *passim* and Iu. Bromlei, *Sovremennye etnicheskiie protsessy v SSSR*, (Moscow: Nauka, 1977) p. 127.
2. R. A. Pierce, *Russian Central Asia: 1867–1917* (Berkeley: University of California Press, 1960) p. 102. Quote taken from Curzon, *Russia in Central Asia in 1889* (London: Longmans, Green & Co., 1889).
3. For an excellent discussion of the place of women in pre-Revolutionary and immediately post-Revolutionary Uzbekistan, see G. Massell, *The Surrogate Proletariat* (Princeton: Princeton University Press, 1974). passim.
4. O. Caroe, *The Soviet Empire*, p. 175.
5. These statistics refer to the 1926 administrative boundaries of Uzbekistan.
6. R. A. Ubaidullaeva, 'Regional'nye problemy razmeshcheniia i effektivnost' ispol'zovaniia trudovykh resursov v Uzbekskoi SSR', doctoral dissertation, Tashkent, 1974, p. 183.
7. From 1928 to 1935, fifty new industrial enterprises were brought into production in Uzbekistan, with a total staff of about 20 900 people. From 1933 to 1935 alone, however, more than 10 500 of these workers had been sent to Uzbekistan from the RSFSR. See I. E. Egamberdyev, *Regional'nye problemy vosproizvodstva rabochei sily v Uzbekistane* (Tashkent: Fan, 1976) p. 155.
8. In the non-agricultural sectors, the growth rate, too, in the number of Russian workers in Uzbekistan was higher than that of native workers. See Iu. Bromlei, *Sovremennye etnicheskiie protsessy ...*, p. 126.
9. By the 1949–50 school year, for example, almost half the 44 000 teachers in Uzbekistan were Uzbek. See *Handbook of Central Asia*, monograph prepared for the Bureau of Social Science Research, American University, Washington, DC, 1956, pp. 494–7.
10. Between 1929–1933, the number and proportion of natives in Uzbekistan's Communist Party increased rapidly, reaching a peak of 70 per cent of total membership in 1934. Between 1934 and 1938, the number and proportion of natives in the Party declined equally rapidly, as did the size of the Party as a whole. See D. Carlisle, 'Modernization, Generations and the Uzbek Soviet Intelligentsia', *The Dynamics of Soviet Politics* (Cambridge, Mass.: Harvard University Press, 1976) p. 258.
11. See TsSU *Narodnoe khoziaistvo Uzbekistana za 60 let* (Tashkent: Uzbekistan, 1977) p. 205.
12. The labour force employed in construction grew by 338 000 people,

against a growth of 461 000 people in state agriculture (see Table 3.3).

13. In 1970, the latter was only 274 per cent its 1950 level, while the former all had employment levels in 1975 at least 440 per cent of their 1950 levels. (Table 3.3.)

14. See S. Rapawy, 'Regional Employment Trends in the USSR: 1950–1975', *The Soviet Economy in a Time of Change*, compendium of papers submitted to the Joint Economic Committee, US Congress, (Washington, DC: Government Printing Office, 1979), vol. 1. Computed from his tables, pp. 604–13.

15. See Irwin Selnick, 'The Ethno-Political Determinants of Elite Recruitment in the Soviet Republics: The Case of Uzbekistan, 1952–1981', PhD dissertation, Department of Political Science, Columbia University, expected date of completion, 1984.

16. Ibid, *passim.*

17. See, for example, J. H. Miller, 'Cadres Policy in Nationality Areas,' *Soviet Studies*, vol. xxix, no. 1, January 1977, *passim.* This pattern is true for almost all the republics in the USSR. See also S. Paczolt, 'Soviet Nationalities Policy and Oblast' Political Elites in Soviet Kazakhstan, Transcaucasia and Central Asia', doctoral dissertation, Maryland, 1975, *passim.* In 1981, of the two *oblast'* first secretaries who were European, each had a native second secretary. See I. Selnick, 'The Ethno-Political Determinants . . .', *passim.*

18. Irwin Selnick, 'The Ethno-Political Determinants . . .,' *passim.*

19. The two Uzbek directors were the heads of the Department of Material and Technical Supply and of the Motor Pool Department. The first department was staffed entirely by Europeans, that is, by ten Russians and one Jew. The second, consisting mainly of chauffeurs, was comprised of two Uzbek deputies, one Russian deputy director, twenty-five Uzbek and twenty-five Russian drivers.

20. The figure of 35 per cent compares to 6–10 per cent in the Central and Northwest regions of the RSFSR, in the Urals and in Siberia. For estimates of the proportion of Uzbeks, see, for example, Iu. Bromlei, *Sovremennye etnicheskie protsessy . . .*, p. 131. It should be noted, moreover, while the proportion of the workforce employed in agriculture has declined, the number of agricultural personnel continues to rise. From 1971 to 1974, for example, it rose from 1 383 000 to 1 503 000 people, or by 120 000 people over that three-year period.

21. 'Book Publishing in the Soviet Union', pamphlet prepared by the Uzbek Friendship Society, Tashkent, 1978, p. 8.

22. See R. Kh. Aminova, 'Protiv burzhuaznoi fal'sifikatsii industrial'nogo razvitiia sovetskogo Uzbekistana', *Obshchestvennye nauki v Uzbekistane*, no. 9, 1975, p. 17.

23. Among women, the rise was from 9.4 to 13.5 per cent; among men, the proportion working in industry rose only 0.2 per cent, from 21.8 to 22.0 per cent. See G. A. Shister, *Promyshlennye rabochie Uzbekistana* (Tashkent: Uzbekistan, 1975) p. 80.

24. O. B. Ata Mirzaev, 'Voprosy vzaimodeistviia urbanizatsii i migratsii naseleniia', *Voprosy geografii respublik Srednei Azii* (Tashkent: Minvuz, 1975) p. 39.

25. As Egamberdyev writes, 'the creation of national cadres in industry still remains one of the little-solved and at the same time particularly important problems in reproducing the total labour force in the republics of Central Asia and Kazakhstan'. See A. Egamberdyev, *Vosproizvodstva trudovykh resursov sel'skoi mestnosti Uzbekistana i osnovnye puti uluchsheniia ikh ispol'zovaniia* (Tashkent: Fan, 1972) p. 14.
26. Interview with P. V. Semenov, Director, Tashmetrostroi, October 1978.
27. Lecture by R. A. Ubaidullaeva, Tashkent, November 1978.
28. See V. G. Kostakov, *Trudovye resursy: Sotsial'no-ekonomicheskii analiz* (Moscow: Ekonomika, 1976) p. 156.
29. G. A. Shister, *Promyshlennye rabochie Uzbekistana*, p. 79.
30. See A. S. Chamkin, 'Motivy k trudu v sfere obshchestvennogo proizvodstva', doctoral dissertation, Tashkent 1976, p. 49, and S. Tursunmukhamedov, 'Sovetskaiia inzhenerno-tekhnicheskaiia intelligentsiia', *Ekonomika i Zhizn'*, no. 1, 1978, p. 50. The number of specialists employed in Uzbekistan's economy grew from 354 000 in 1965 to 746 900 in 1975, or more than doubled in ten years. The number of Uzbek specialists, however, with higher education grew from 40 700 people in 1960 to 165 500 in 1974, or by more than four times, against a growth of only about three times for the republic as a whole. Among other local nationalities in Uzbekistan the growth of specialists in higher education was equally impressive, rising from 2800 to 10 400 among the Kazakhs in Uzbekistan, and from 2000 to 7200 among the Karakalpaks over the same time period, or by almost four times as well. Between 1941 and 1970, the growth in the number of specialists employed in the economy of the USSR as a whole multiplied seven times. In Uzbekistan, the total number grew by 9.7 times, and among the Uzbeks, the growth was by 27 times.
31. See Irwin Selnick, 'The Ethno-Political Determinants ...', *passim*.
32. For a fuller description, see M. Feshbach, *The Soviet Statistical System: Labor Force Recordkeeping and Reporting*, International Population Statistics Reports, series P. 90, no. 12, US Department of Commerce, Bureau of the Census, (Washington, DC: US Government Printing Office, 1960) pp. 43–64; and S. Rapawy, *Estimates and Projections of the Labor Force and Civilian Employment in the USSR: 1950 to 1990* Foreign Economic Report no. 10, US Department of Commerce, Bureau of Economic Analysis (Washington, DC, September 1976) pp. 26–30. In the early 1970s, approximately 63 per cent of all Russians on the territory of the USSR were workers, as were 63 per cent of the Kazakhs, 59 per cent of all Armenians and 51 per cent of all Azerbaijanis. Among Uzbeks, the exact proportion was only 39.9 per cent. See R. A. Ubaidullaeva, 'Regional'nye problemy razmeshcheniia ...', doctoral dissertation (Tashkent, 1974) p. 175.
33. See R. S. Tashkulova, 'Rabochii klass Uzbekistana na sovremennom etape', dissertation for the degree of Kandidat Nauk' (Tashkent, 1977) p. 71. As Ubaidullaeva writes 'the growth of the number of workers of the indigenous nationalities, despite rapid rates ... remains insufficient for opening new industrial capabilities. Attracting representatives of other nationalities, especially Russians, to the economic and cultural construc-

tion in these republics has answered the needs of the development of production, culture and the well-being of the local population.' See R. A. Ubaidullaeva, 'Regional'nye problemy razmeshcheniia . . .', p. 175.

34. See Table 3.9. In 1973, Uzbeks comprised 44.9 per cent of all employed specialists with higher and secondary education in Uzbekistan, as opposed to 26.9 per cent for Russians. See *Ekonomiki i Zhizn'*, p. 50, and Iu. Bromlei, *Sovremennye etnicheskie protsessy* . . ., p. 130.

35. L. Maksakova, 'Problemy ratsional'nogo ispol'zovaniia trudovykh resursov Uzbekistana', *Aktual'nye problemy povysheniia kachestva produktsii, proizvoditel'nosti truda i effektivnosti proizvodstva*, (materialy nauchno-prakticheskoi konferentsii), (Tashkent: 'Fan' 1976), p. 64. Taken from a sociological study of new industrial enterprises carried out by the planning sector for the use of labour resources, NIEI, Gosplan UzSSR in 1976, under the direction of Maksakova.

36. For a discussion of women in Central Asia, see N. Lubin, 'Women in Soviet Central Asia: Progress and Contradictions', *Soviet Studies*, vol. 33, no. 2, April 1981.

37. See L. Chizhova, 'Regional'nye aspekty . . .', *Narodonaselenie*, p. 24.

38. In 1975, women in Uzbekistan comprised only 16.5 per cent of all workers and employees in construction-installation work, and only 15.4 per cent of those in transport.

39. In 1977, women comprised about half the 466 800 specialists with specialised secondary education employed in Uzbekistan's economy. Of those, however, they comprised about 85 per cent of the medical workers with specialised secondary education, against less than 30 per cent of the technicians and less than 17 per cent of the agronomists, livestock specialists and veterinarians. (Table 3.9). In the light of the total number of specialists in each occupation, moreover, the number of women in the latter sectors is very small: While the vast majority of female specialists are medical workers, librarians or teachers, less than 2 per cent of all women specialists with higher and specialised secondary education are agronomists, livestock specialists and veterinarians, and less than 5 per cent are engineers, see TsSU *Narodnoe khoziaistvo Uzbekskoi SSR v 1977 godu*, pp. 218–19, and A. Egamberdyev, *Vosproizvodstvo* . . ., p. 65.

40. A. Egamberdyev, ibid, p. 65.

41. According to one source, in the early 1970s, about 52 per cent of all women working in industry in Uzbekistan were employed in manual labour, of whom about 25 per cent were employed in heavy manual labour. According to Ubaidullaeva, in the mid-1970s, 50 per cent of all women in ferrous metallurgy; 59 per cent of all women in the coal industry; 46 per cent of all women in oil extraction, 64 per cent of women in the industrial building materials industry and 49 per cent of the women employed in the china and glass industry were employed in heavy manual labour. See R. A. Ubaidullaeva, 'Regional'nye problemy razmeshcheniia . . .', pp. 229–30.

42. Ibid, p. 7.

43. See V. Mikheeva, 'Trudovye resursy malykh i srednikh gorodov Uzbekistana i perspektivy ikh ispol'zovaniia', doctoral dissertation, Tashkent, 1975, pp. 12–13. See also R. A. Ubaidullaeva, 'Regional'nye problemy

razmeshcheniia ...', p. 323 and A. V. Khisamov, *Ekonomicheskaia geografia Uzbekskoi SSR* (Tashkent: Ukituvchi, 1978) pp. 13–15.

44. R. A. Ubaidullaeva, 'Regional'nye problemy ...', p. 176.

45. B. Satvaldyev, 'Voprosy sovershenstvovaniia otraslevoi struktury zaniatosti naseleniia v Uzbekistane', *Razvitie i razmeshchenie proizvoditel'nykh sil i ispol'zovaniie trudovykh resursov* (Tashkent: monograph prepared by Gosplan, UzSSR and NIEI, 1977) p. 39. Confirmed in interview in 1979 with Y. T. Zakirov, Deputy Chairman, State Committee on Labour and Social Problems, UzSSR, who told me that the disproportion in the choice of profession by nationality 'is mainly due to the location of different industries'.

46. See R. Lewis, *Regional Manpower Resources and Resource Development in the USSR: 1970–1990*, discussion paper no. 18 (Washington, DC: Association of American Geographers, December 1979) p. 52.

47. B. Satvaldyev, 'Voprosy sovershenstvovaniia ...', p. 15.

48. R. A. Ubaidullaeva, 'Regional'nye problemy ...', p. 86.

49. See A. Egamberdyev, *Vosproizvodstva ...*, p. 165.

50. As Maksakova notes 'Computations conducted in the planning sector for labour resources, [Gosplan], show that potential reserves of working-time are not being fully used on collective farms in all regions of the republic'.

51. See K. M. Bulusheva, *Materialy zasedaniia mezhvedomstvennogo problemnogo soveta sotsial'no-ekonomicheskie problemy sela i povyshenie proizvoditel'nosti truda*, minutes from a conference held in the Fergana Valley, 7–9 September 1976. In 1975, the number of man-days worked per able-bodied collective farmer was as low as 195 per year in Surkhandar'ia *oblast'*; 202 per year in Andizhan *oblast'*; and 207 per year in Samarkand *oblast'*, (Bulusheva, p. 69). In the same year, another local scholar, Mirsagatov cited several collective farms in Kashkadar'inskaia *oblast'* where the average number of man-days worked per collective farmer was as low as 187 per year. (Mannat Mirsagatov, 'Vosproizvodstvo i problemy povysheniia effektivnosti izpol'zovaniia trudovykh resursov v sel'skom khoziaistve', dissertation abstract, Tashkent, 1975, p. 22). As but one example of the possible magnitude of agricultural labour surpluses in Uzbekistan due to loss of working-time alone, Ubaidullaeva estimated that in 1970 'the excess of unused working-time' of collective farmers in the collective farmers of Namangan *oblast'* was the 'colossal figure' of more than 101 000 man-days, and the 'general loss of working time' in Namangan's collective farmers was 'the equivalent of about 38 000 full-time personnel', (R. A. Ubaidullaeva, 'Regional'nye problemy razmeshcheniia ...', p. 79). As she added: 'In actuality, in recent years, there is a tendency towards a worsening use of the yearly fund of working-time in the agriculture of Uzbekistan, especially in collective farms.'

   In the mid-1970s, a report came out in Samarkand which showed that the working time of unskilled collective farmers there comprised about 4–4½ hours/day. More than ¼ of that time was spent on absences and on breaks – i.e., comprised an 'unproductive loss'. In Samarkand *oblast*, labour reserves due specifically to the 'incomplete use of working time' were estimated at about 52,300 ablebodied people. 67.7 per cent of these losses in Namangan *oblast*, moreover, were attributed to ablebodied collective farmers who 'didn't take part in social production actively enough', and 30.7 per cent, to ablebodied collective farmers who simply did not work at all; only 1.6 per cent were attributed to the non-ablebodied category of workers.

52. 'Studies confirm that if the foundations for freeing and rational use of labour resources are not laid out in perspective plans, then the growth rate of labour productivity in agriculture, especially in densely-populated areas, will stabilise and decline. This most crucial problem, evolving from regional particularities of the republic, calls for particular attention and positive resolution.' See K. Iakubov, *Materialy zasedaniia* . . ., conference minutes, Fergana Valley, 7–9 September 1976, and Usmanov, in the same volume. See also A. Egamberdyev, *Vosproizvodstvo* . . ., p. 165.

53. In other words, as Ubaidullaeva notes, 'In the winter months of 1970, approximately 700 000 collective farmers did not work at all in [Uzbekistan's] collective farms.' See R. A. Ubaiduallaeva, 'Regional'nye problemy . . .', p. 88. While no data are available for later years, I was told in several interviews that the situation has not significantly changed.

54. L. Maksakova, 'Regional'nye osobennosti . . .', 1975, p. 7–8.

55. See M. Mirzagatov, 'Vosproizvodstvo i problemy . . .' in *Materialy zasedaniia mezhvedomstvennogo problemnogo soveta* . . ., Fergana Valley Conference, 7–9 September 1976, p. 122.

56. For example, in the early 1970s, the average number of man-days worked per able-bodied collective farmer in Uzbekistan was 214.3 man-days per year. Among men, however, the number was 237.5 man-days per year, while among women, the average was only 192 man-days per year. See R. A. Ubaidullaeva, 'Regional'nye problemy . . .', p. 74.

57. A. Egamberdyev, *Vosproizvodstvo* . . ., p. 130.

58. U. Umurzakov, 'Vosproizvodstvo rabochei sily i obespechenie ee zaniatosti', dissertation abstract, Tashkent, 1973, p. 28.

59. R. A. Ubaidullaeva, 'Regional'nye problemy . . .', p. 85. Reconfirmed in a lecture, Tashkent, 1979.

60. A. E. Egamberdyev, *Regional'nye problemy* . . . 1976, p. 96.

61. L. Maksakova, 'Problemy ratsional'nogo ispol'zovaniia . . .', 1976, p. 62.

62. A. B. Fedorova, 'Tekhnicheskii progress i kachestvennyi sostav rabochikh kadrov', *Iangi Tekhnika*, 1975.

63. R. A. Ubaidullaeva, in *Materialy zasedaniia mezhvedomstvennogo problemnogo soveta* . . ., Fergana Valley Conference, 7–9 September 1976, p. 69. Regarding labour productivity, if the growth rate of labour productivity in Soviet industry as a whole, for example, declined in the second half of the 1970s – rising by 17 per cent in 1976–80, as opposed to twice that amount in the previous five-year plan – the rise in Uzbekistan was only 11 per cent. See T. Shabad, 'Economic Realities and Dynamics', p. 43.

64. A. Egamberdyev, *Regional'nye problemy* . . . 1976, p. 33.

65. V. Mikheeva, 'Trudovye resursy malykh . . .', dissertation, p. 3: 'In the republic's cities (basically in small and medium cities), because of particularities of the sectoral structure of the economy, the relatively low

professional-educational level of people working, the high proportion of people working in the household and private subsidiary economy, the insufficient development of the service sphere and other reasons, there is a considerable lag in the use of labour resources not only by comparison with all-Union indicators as a whole, but also by comparison with other Union-republics.'

66. Ibid, p. 133.
67. R. A. Ubaidullaeva, 'Regional'nye problemy . . .', dissertation, p. 267.
68. Ibid, p. 250.
69. A. E. Egamberdyev, *Regional'nye Problemy* . . . 1976, p. 156.
70. R. A. Ubaidullaeva, 'Regional'nye problemy . . .', pp. 199, 211. Ubaidullaeva estimated that about 75 per cent of all breakdowns in machine construction and up to 30 per cent of broken equipment and instruments in Uzbekistan 'is due to the low skills of the workers, who do not possess the essential knowledge and habits for work with new technology'.
71. V. Mikheeva, 'Trudovye resursy malykh . . .', p. 137.
72. Iu. Voronovskii, 'Ismenenie kharaktera i soderzhaniia truda i novye trebovanniia k podgotovke rabochikh kadrov', *Regional'nye osobennosti vosproizvodstva naseleniia i trudovykh resursov v Uzbekskoi SSR*. (Tashkent: monograph prepared by Gosplan UzSSR and NIEI, 1975) p. 21.
73. A. E. Egamberdyev, *Regional'nye problemy* . . ., 1976, p. 31.
74. Ibid, p. 31. In 1973, of the total number of workers in Uzbekistan's industrial enterprises, 0.7 per cent had completed higher education; 1.0 per cent had an incomplete higher education; 5.0 per cent had completed specialised secondary education; 28.7 per cent had completed only general secondary education; 61.3 per cent had not received a secondary education; and 3.3 per cent had not received even an elementary education. See Voronovskii, 'Ismenenie kharaktura . . .' 1975, p. 21.
75. A. E. Egamberdyev, ibid, p. 31.
76. R. A. Ubaiduallaeva, 'Regional'nye problemy . . .', dissertation, p. 267.
77. Ibid, p. 267.
78. O. B. Ata-Mirzaev, 'Voprosy vzaimodeistviia urbanizatsii . . .', *Voprosy geografii respublik Srednei Azii* (Tashkent: Minvuz, 1975) p. 39 and Ata Mirzaev, Naselenie Uzbekistana' (Tashkent, k pomoshch' lektoru November 1978).
79. See V. Mikheeva, 'Trudovye resursy malykh . . .', p. 138. In Dzhizak, for example, in 1975, of 1129 vacancies in industry and construction, more than 100 occupations demanded higher or specialised secondary education, and the remainder, a high level of skill and special preparation.

4 LABOUR POLICIES

1. See, for example, M. Orazgel'dyev, 'Training Personnel from the Local Population of the Central Asian Republics', *Voprosy Ekonomiki*, no. 5, May 1979, pp. 84–91 (translated in *USSR Report: Trade & Services*, JPRS L/8606, 3 August 1979) pp. 32–43 and p. 26; R. A. Ubaidullaeva, 'Regional'nye problemy . . .', dissertation, pp. 197–8; and S. Alimov, 'Vlianie rosta mnogonatsional'nosti Sovetskikh respublik na sblizhenie

sotsialisticheskikh natsii', doctoral dissertation, Tashkent, 1971, p. 95.

2. A. E. Egamberdyev, *Regional'nye problemy vosproizvodstva rabochei sily v Uzbekistane* (Tashkent: Fan, 1976) p. 152.

3. See *Handbook of Central Asia*, monograph prepared for the Bureau of Social Science Research, American University, Washington, DC, 1956, pp. 488–90.

4. R. A. Ubaiduallaeva, 'Regional'nye problemy . . .', op. cit., p. 209.

5. See TsSU, *Narodnoe Khoziaistvo Uzbekskoi SSR v 1977 godu* (Tashkent: Uzbekistan, 1978) pp. 207, 265. See also A. E. Egamberdyev, *Regional'nye problemy* . . ., 1976, p. 152–4.

6. TsSU, *Narodnoe khoziaistvo SSSR v 1968 godu* (Moscow: Statistika 1969) p. 694.

7. Data from the Ministry of Higher and Specialised Secondary Education, UzSSR, May 1979.

8. G. Shister, 'Sovershentsvovat' podgotovki rabochikh kadrov', *Kommunist Uzbekistana*, no. 8, August 1979, pp. 62–69.

9. See R. A. Ubaidullaeva, 'Regional'nye problemy razmeshcheniia i effektivnost' ispol'zovaniia trudovykh resursov v Uzbekskoi SSR', unpublished doctoral dissertation (Tashkent 1974) p. 182. See also Iu. Voronovskii, 'Ismenenie kharaktera i soderzhaniia truda i novye trebovaniia k podgotovke rabochikh kadrov,' *Regional'nye Osobennosti* . . ., 1975, p. 28.

10. M. Orazgel'dyev, 'Training Personnel . . .', p. 30.

11. It should be noted that in order to assess how successfully graduates are able to enter higher education, the ideal calculation would be as a percentage of those of the appropriate age group (17–21); no such data, however, are available. The working-age population has therefore been used as a poor, but none the less revealing substitute.

12. The number and proportion of students enrolled in daytime PTUs relative to the total working-age population grew more rapidly, but from a very low starting point. In 1970, only 43.6 thousand people, or less than 1 per cent of the working-age population was enrolled in full-time vocational training; by 1978, that number had quadrupled, to 176 000 students, but still comprised only about 2 per cent of the working-age population.

13. Iu. Voronovskii, 'Izmenenie kharaktera . . .', p. 17.

14. R. A. Ubaidullaeva, 'Regional'nye problemy . . .', p. 218.

15. In 1970, in the RSFSR, the Ukraine, Belorussia and Latvia, for example, fifteen or sixteen out of every 100 students of the able-bodied ages were studying in PTUs (all subjects); in Uzbekistan, only five out of every 100 were studying in PTUs. See R. A. Ubaidullaeva, 'Regional'nye problemy . . .', p. 216.

16. See G. Shister, 'Sovershentsvovat' podgotouvki . . .', pp. 62–69, op. cit.

17. TsSU, *Narodnoe khoziaistvo Uzbekskoi SSR v 1978 godu* (Tashkent: Uzbekistan, 1979) p. 276.

18. Ibid, pp. 277–8.

19. Interview with R. Kh. Dzhuraev, Deputy Chairman of the State Committee, UzSSR on Professional Technical Education, May 1979.

20. Data from the Ministry of Higher and Specialised Secondary Education, May 1979. Not surprisingly, the only pedagogical institute under the

Ministry of Education in which Uzbeks comprised less than 70 per cent of the entering class and student body was in the Republican Institute of Russian Language and Literature.

21. See L. Maksakova, 'Sotsial'no-ekonomicheskie problemy zaniatosti trudovykh resursov Uzbekskoi SSR', *Regional'nye osobennosti* ... 1975, p. 12.
22. See A. E. Egamberdyev, *Trudovye resursy v sel'skoi mestnosti*, p. 80.
23. L. Maksakova, 'Sotsial'no-ekonomicheskie problemy ...', p. 12.
24. G. Shister, 'Sovershentsvovat' podgotovki ...', pp. 62–9.
25. A. E. Egamberdyev, *Trudovye resursy* ...', 1972, p. 81.
26. Ibid, p. 80.
27. In the 1978–9 school year, the Bukhara Polytechnic – designed to become an important light and food industrial institute in Uzbekistan – was comprised of 3071 students, of whom 85 per cent were indigenous. On the other hand, the indigenous nationalities comprised only 45 per cent of the 2844 students at the Tashkent Electrotechnical Institute of Communications, and only 42 per cent of the 3534 students at the Tashkent Institute of Engineers of Railroad Transport (see Table 4.4). At the Bukhara Polytechnic, Uzbeks comprised 85 per cent of the full-time students, 86 per cent of the evening students, and one of the twenty-five correspondence students (twenty-three of whom were Ukrainian). Interviews at the Bukhara Polytechnic, 1979.
28. See N. Lubin, 'Women in Soviet Central Asia', *Soviet Studies, passim.*
29. See R. A. Ubaidullaeva, 'Regional'nye problemy ...', p. 215 and p. 71.
30. 'Report of the Central Committee of the Komsomol of Uzbekistan', speech presented by B. A. Allamuradov, First Secretary of the Komsomol Central Committee, UzSSR, in Tashkent, 30 March 1982, reported in *Pravda Vostoka*, 31 March 1982, p. 2. Translated in *JPRS: USSR Report*, 13 May 1982, p. 89.
31. Ibid: speech presented by Sh. R. Rashidov.
32. M. Orazgel'dyyev, 'Training Personnel from the Local Population of the Central Asian Republics', *Voprosy Ekonomiki*, no. 5, May 1979, pp. 84–91, translated in JPRS, *USSR Report: Trade and Services*, 3 August 1979, pp. 32–43.
33. See, for example, *CPSU Central Committee Draft Guidelines for 1981–85*, translated in FBIS, 4 December 1980, p. 35, and 'Sixty Years of the USSR: Yuriy Andropov's Report at the Kremlin Meeting' (Moscow: TASS, 21 December 1982) translated in FBIS, 23 December 1982, p. P5.
34. Interview R. Kh. Dzhuraev, Deputy Chairman of the Uzbek Committee on Professional Technical Education, May 1979.
35. B. A. Allamuradov, 'Report of the Central Committee of the Komsomol of Uzbekistan', p. 2.
36. Sh. Abdullaev, 'Nekotorye voprosy professional'noi orientatsii molodezhi', *Regional'nye demograficheskie issledovaniia*, monograph prepared by the Ministry of Higher and Specialised Secondary Education, UzSSR and Tashkent State University, Tashkent, 1978, pp. 99–100 and 105. According to this report, in 1974, only 4.7 per cent of all secondary school graduates who went on to work in Kashkadar'ya *oblast'* went to work in industrial enterprises. In Surkhandar'ya, Dzhizak and Khorezm

oblasts, the proportion was also less than 5 per cent. At the same time, in the Andizhan, Samarkand, Bukhara, Khorezm and Syrdar'ya *oblasts*, about 70 per cent started work in collective and state farms and other agricultural enterprises. In the Fergana *oblast'*, the proportion entering agricultural organisations was 72.3 per cent; in Kashkadar'ya *oblast'*, 74.2 per cent; in Surkhandar'ya and Dzhizak *oblasts*, almost 80 per cent (p. 100).

37. A. E. Egamberdyev, *Trudovye resursy v sel'skoi mest'nosti*, op. cit., p. 114. Ubaidullaeva has projected that the number of people in the able-bodied ages studying in higher educational establishments and *technikums* in Uzbekistan may reach as high as 450 000 people in 1980, and 800 000 people in 1990. The total number of people in the ablebodied population in educational establishments, she projected, would reach 885 000 people in 1980, 992 000 in 1985 and 1 200 000 in 1990. This means that the number of students in each of these categories as a proportion of the total working age population will remain unchanged through 1990. It also means that the working age population without skills or professional training will continue to grow. See R. A. Ubaidullaeva, 'Regional'nye problemy . . .', op. cit.

38. Interview with Y. T. Zakirov, First Deputy Chairman, and Merkulova, Director of the Department of Labour Resources, Committee on Labour and Social Problems, UzSSR, 19 May 1979.

39. Interviews with professors at Samarkand University, November 1978.

40. Four of these conferences were all-Union: 1962, 1967, 1976 and the most recent, 1979 conference held in Tbilisi. Four in Tashkent were specifically on Central Asia: in 1965, 1971, 1973 and 1975.

41. From *Zvezda Vostoka*, no. 8, 1980, p. 10, quoted in S. Voronitsyn, 'The Plan to Divert Siberian Rivers and Pressure from the Central Asian Lobby', Radio Free Europe/Radio Liberty dispatch, RL 400/80, 27 October 1980, pp. 3–4.

42. Objections range from environmental to financial concerns. The diversion scheme is expected to require a minimum investment of 14 billion roubles for building the basic hydraulic installations and canals, and another 17 billion for land improvement schemes connected with it. It is also expected to result in some environmental changes, although it is unclear whether these will be global or local in scope. Thus, while the Uzbek 'lobbies' have strongly argued their case, implementation of the scheme has been slowed due to wide-ranging debates in Moscow. For a discussion of the debates surrounding the scheme, see S. Voronitsyn, 'Will the Efforts of the Uzbek Lobby Speed up the Diversion of Siberia's Rivers?' Radio Free Europe/Radio Liberty dispatch, RL 76/81, 20 February 1981, p. 3. For an assessment of the potential, more global environmental effects of the water diversion schemes, see Philip P. Micklin, 'A Preliminary Systems Analysis of the Impacts of the Proposed Soviet River Diversions on Arctic Sea Ice', *EOS*, Transactions, American Geophysical Union, vol. 62, no. 19, 12 May 1981. For a discussion of how tenuous the project has been, see also Theodore Shabad, 'Soviet, After Studies, Shelves Plan to turn Siberia's Rivers', *New York Times*, 16 December 1983, pp. A.1, A.7.

43. See E. A. Akramov, 'Oroshenie Srednei Azii i problemy zaniatosti naseleniia', *Materialy mezhvusovskoi conferentsii* . . ., 1965, p. 50.
44. See *CPSU Central Committee Draft Guidelines for 1981–85*, p. 541.
45. M. Mirzagatov, 'Vosproizvodstvo i problemy povysheniia effektivnosti ispol'zovaniia trudovykh resursov v sel'skom khosiaistve', dissertation, Tashkent, 1975, p. 23. See also *CPSU Central Committee Draft Guidelines for 1981–85*, p. 24.
46. See, for example, A. E. Egamberdyev, *Trudovye resursy uzbekistana*, 1970, p. 39.
47. See A. E. Egamberdyev, 1970, *Trudovye resursy Uzbekistana*, 1970, p. 39 and p. 129. See also L. Maksakova, 'Sotsial'no-ekonomicheskie problemy . . .', 1976: 'in the republic's collective farms, the freeing of labour is occurring very slowly'.
48. Cited in M. Feshbach, 'Prospects for Outmigration . . .', p. 666.
49. L. Maksakova, 'Sotsial'nye-ekonomicheskie problemy . . .', 1975, p. 8.
50. See Chizhova, 'Regional'nye aspekty ispol'zovaniia trudovykh resursov,' *Narodonaselenie Uzbekistana*, Tashkent, 1973, pp. 25–6.
51. E. Tashbekov, 'Voprosy migratsionnykh sviazei naseleniia v krupnykh gorodakh Srednei Azii', *Materialy* . . ., 1965, p. 58.
52. Chizhova, 'Regional'nye aspekty . . .', p. 26. As O. B. Ata Mirzaev, Chief of the Population Laboratory, Tashkent University, noted in 1975, 'In the light of the "territorial inertia" characteristic of the local population which will be retained for many years to come, and due to the objective necessity for a noticeable acceleration of the republic's urbanisation, the problem of national industrial cadres at the given stage must be solved on the basis of locating industrial enterprises in densely populated and labour surplus rural areas. Attracting the surplus rural population to industrial production without changing the location of inhabitants is a very real and rational path for developing urbanisation processes in the conditions of Uzbekistan and for solving the series of social and economic problems connected with it.' See O. B. Ata Mirzaev, 'Voprosy vzaimodeistviia urbanizatsii i migratsii naseleniia', *Voprosy geografii respublik Srednei Azii*, Sbornik nauchnykh trudov no. 494, Tashkent State University, (Tashkent: Minvuz, 1975) p. 38.
53. See L. Maksakova, 'Sotsial'nye-ekonomicheskie problemy . . .', 1975, p. 8. See also the *CPSU Central Committee Draft Guidelines for 1981–85* . . ., p. 5.
54. Quoted in V. Mikheeva, 'Trudovye resursy malykh i srednykh gorodov Uzbekistana i perspektivy ikh ispol'zovaniia', doctoral dissertation, 1975, pp. 2–3.
55. *CPSU Central Committee Draft Guidelines for 1981–85*, p. 5. See also O. B. Ata Mirzaev 'Voprosy vzaimodeistviia . . .', 1975, p. 38.
56. Interview, S. Ziiadullaev, Chairman of the Council for the Study of the Productive Forces of the Uzbek Academy of Sciences, October 1978.
57. N. Mechikova, 'Nekotorye voprosy sovershenstvovaniia struktury kapital'noi vlozhenii v promyshlennosti Uzbekistana', *Aktual'nye problemy* . . ., 1976, pp. 182–4. One must be wary, of course, of using capital investment alone as a measure of priorities since, by definition, less capital is demanded to expand labour-intensive sectors – such as light industry,

the food industries or the service sectors – than to expand heavy industry, or capital intensive sectors. None the less, priorities have not changed dramatically over time to accommodate the more dramatic shifts in population dynamics which have taken place in Soviet Central Asia.

58. Examples of old small cities where not one enterprise was constructed are Biruni, Turtkul' and Khiva. Examples where only one was being constructed are Shakhrisabz and Leninsk. As noted in Table 3.10, at that time, new cities accounted for 22 per cent of all cities and 21 per cent of the republic's urban population. Large old cities represented about 15 per cent of the general number of the republic's cities, and 62 per cent of the urban population. Old cities accounted for 63 per cent of the total number of Uzbekistan's cities and 17 per cent of the urban population.

59. Two of the enterprises surveyed were textile enterprises; four were construction material plants; and departments of a silk factory, fertiliser plant, mechanical engineering plant, hydrolysis plant, furniture factory and canning factory were also included. Although Uzbeks comprised 45 per cent of the total sample, they comprised 51 per cent of the men and 44 per cent of the women. Russians, on the other hand, while comprising 37 per cent of the sample, accounted for 33 per cent of the men and 37 per cent of the women. R. A. Ubaidullaeva, 'Regional'nye problemy ...', dissertation, p. 189.

60. L. Maksakova, 'Problemy ratsional'nogo ispol'zovaniia trudovykh resursov Uzbekistana', *Aktual'nye problemy povysheniia kachestva produktsii proizvoditel'nosti truda i effektivnosti proizvodstva*, monograph prepared by Tashkent State University, 1976, p. 66.

61. R. A. Ubaidullaeva, 'Regional'nye problemy ...', p. 54.

62. Ibid, pp. 54 and 71.

63. O. B. Ata Mirzaev, 'Voprosy vzaimodeistvia ...', *Voprosy Geografii ...*, 1975, pp. 38–9.

64. Ibid, p. 38.

65. See A. S. Chamkin, 'Motivy k trudu ...', dissertation, p. 75.

66. R. A. Ubaidullaeva, 'Regional'nye problemy ...', Appendix.

67. Ibid, p. 193.

68. Among Western writers who have addressed this problem, see G. Hodnett, 'Technology and Social Change in Soviet Central Asia: The Politics of Cotton Growing', H. W. Morton and R. Tokes (eds) *Soviet Politics and Society in the 1970s*, (New York: The Free Press, 1974).

69. See R. A. Ubaidullaeva, 'Regional'nye problemy ...', dissertation, p. 71.

70. Ibid, p. 71.

71. Ibid, pp. 253, 255, 256, and pp. 71–2. Ubaidullaeva also referred to a possible surplus of administrative personnel on Uzbekistan's collective farms. According to the data in her dissertation, in the early 1970s, 9–12 per cent of the annual number of collective farm personnel were in administration or services – a proportion which, she writes, 'should be lowered, as [should] the proportion of personnel in subsidiary enterprises.' (p. 67).

72. M. Mirsagatov, 'Vosproizvodstvo i problemy povysheniia effektivnosti ispol'zovaniia trudovykh resursov v sel'skom khoziaistve', unpublished doctoral dissertation, Tashkent 1975, p. 25.

73. As one scholar noted, 'in Uzbekistan's collective and state farms ..., in 32 000 occupations which must be filled by specialists, there are apprentices who have not received specialised education. Yet about 12 000 agronomists, veterinarians and hydro-technicians work in enterprises and organisations in specialties which do not demand an agricultural education'. See A. Turaev 'Prevrashchenie sel'skogo khoziaistvennogo truda v raznovidnost' truda industrial'nogo v usloviiakh nauchno-tekhnicheskoi revoliutsii', unpublished doctoral dissertation, Tashkent, 1975, p. 118–19. For similar problems in Uzbekistan's industrial sector, see S. A. Bolotov 'Aktual'nye voprosy ispol'zovaniia spetsialistov v promyshlennosti', dissertation abstract, Tashkent, 1974, p. 7.
74. Ibid, p. 8.
75. S. A. Bolotov, 'Aktual'nye voprosy ...', p. 9.
76. Ibid, p. 9.
77. 'Rech' tovarishcha L. I. Brezhneva', text of L. I. Brezhnev's speech, in *Pravda*, 25 March 1982, p. 1.
78. See R. A. Ubaidullaeva, 'Regional'nye problemy ...', pp. 257–60.
79. Ibid, p. 260.
80. Ibid, p. 289.
81. See R. S. Tashkulova, 'Rabochii klass Uzbekistana na sovremennom etape (1966–75 gg)' unpublished doctoral dissertation, Tashkent, 1977, pp. 47 and 50–4.
82. See *CPSU Central Committee Draft Guidelines for 1981–85*, p. 31. 'Meeting more fully the population's demand for various goods and services must be considered a major task. ... The demand for consumer durables, household wares and other non-food goods must be met more fully. ... The range of foods must be expanded and their quality must be raised.'
83. Interviews with O. B. Ata Mirzaev, Chief of the Population Laboratory, Tashkent University, and members of the Population Laboratory, 1978–9. The Draft Guidelines of the XXVI Party Congress and subsequent legislation also mentions the importance of allowing for part-time work for mothers with young children in the USSR as a whole.
84. See R. A. Ubaidullaeva, 'Regional'nye problemy ...', dissertation, Appendix.
85. Ibid, p. 273.
86. 'Rech' tovarishcha L. I. Brezhneva', *Pravda*, 25 March 1982, p. 1.

INTRODUCTION TO PART II

1. H. Carrère d'Encausse, *Decline of an Empire* (New York: Newsweek, 1981) pp. 46 and 275.

5 WHO GETS HIRED FOR WHAT?

1. For example, see R. Lewis, R. H. Rowland and R. S. Clem, 'Modernization, Population Change and Nationality in Soviet Central Asia and

Kazakhstan', *Canadian Slavonic Papers*, Ottawa, no. 2–3, 1975, p. 295, and M. Shorish, 'Soviet Development Strategies in Central Asia', *Canadian Slavonic Papers*, p. 2. See also A. Bennigsen, *Islam in the Soviet Union* (New York: Praeger, 1967) p. 210.

2. A. Bennigsen, *Islam in the Soviet Union*, p. 212. See also G. Schroeder, 'Regional Differences in Incomes and Levels of Living in the USSR', in V. N. Bandera and Z. L. Melnyk (eds), *The Soviet Economy in a Regional Perspective* (New York: Praeger, 1973) p. 297. As Schroeder writes, 'the crucial fact is that within Central Asia ... the indigenous nationalities are deprived relative to outsiders'.

3. G. Massell, 'Ethnicity and Nationalism in the USSR', *Ethnicity and Nationalism*, IREX Occasional Paper, vol. 1, no. 3 (New York: International Research and Exchanges Board, 1979) p. 20.

4. Ibid, p. 26.

5. V. Zaslavskii, and Y. Luryi, 'The Passport System in the USSR', *Soviet Union/Union Sovietique*, vol. 6, Part 2, 1979, p. 148.

6. Data received from the Bukhara Pedagogical Institute, October 1979. Unless otherwise specified, the following data on education in establishments under Minvuz and Minpros were acquired from the Ministry of Higher and Specialised Secondary Education, Uzbekistan, in May 1979.

7. In 1978, in the Dzhizak Pedagogical Institute, representatives of the indigenous nationalities comprised 75 per cent of the applicants and 91 per cent of the entering class; in the Samarkand Pedagogical Institute, they comprised 83 per cent of the applicants, and 90 per cent of the entering class; in the Tashkent *Oblast'* Pedagogical Institute, they comprised 78 per cent of the applicants, and 87 per cent of those admitted.

8. In the Bukhara Technological Institute of Light and Food Industry, Central Asians accounted for only 60 per cent of the total of 1705 applicants, and 87 per cent of the 385 new entrants (Table 5.1).

9. In 1979, the population of the Karakalpak ASSR was 2 per cent Russian; in Dzhizak *oblast'*, 6 per cent; in Namangan *oblast'*, 3 per cent; and in Surkhandar'ya *oblast'*, the population was 4 per cent Russian. On the other hand, in Tashkent and Bukhara *oblasts*, the proportion of Russians and Europeans was between two and six times greater: Russians comprised 17 per cent of the total population in Tashkent *oblast'*, and Russians and Ukrainians comprised 12 per cent of the population of Bukhara *oblast'* (computed from 'Vsesoiuznaia perepis' naseleniia', *Vestnik Statistiki*, 1980, pp. 61–4).

10. Computed from data from the Ministry of Higher and Specialised Secondary Education, May 1979.

11. Interview with Prorektor Zakidov, Tashkent Institute of Communication, 1978–9 school year.

12. See N. Lubin, 'Women in Soviet Central Asia: Progress and Contradictions', *Soviet Studies*, April 1981. While I was unable to acquire data on female versus male qualifications, officials at every one of the more than twelve secondary and higher educational establishments where I conducted interviews consistently noted the fact that indigenous women, particularly from the outlying regions of Uzbekistan, were the least-qualified applicants.

13. See also M. Rywkin, 'Dissent in Soviet Central Asia', paper delivered at the Second World Congress for Soviet and East European Studies, Garmisch, West Germany, 1980, pp. 11–12: 'Simply speaking, the Russian manager is restricted by a kind of 'affirmative action', while the native manager has no other restriction than approximate job qualifications, and such can be somehow bent for the desired individual.'
14. *Handbook of Soviet Central Asia*, 1956, p. 402.
15. See A. Bennigsen, 'Several Nations or One People?' *Survey*, 1979, p. 52.
16. *Handbook on Soviet Central Asia*, p. 402.
17. Ibid. p. 402.
18. A. S. Chamkin, 'Motivy k trudu v sfere obshchestvennogo proizvodstva' unpublished doctoral dissertation, Tashkent 1976. See Chapter 7 for a fuller discussion.
19. Interview with K. I. Afanasiev, First Deputy Minister of Higher and Specialised Secondary Education, UzSSR, May 1979. For the USSR as a whole, see Sergei Voronitsyn, 'Entrance Exams Taking Place for Institutes of Higher Education', RFE/RL report, 25 August 1980 (RL 298/80).
20. Speech by Sh. R. Rashidov at the 22nd Komsomol Congress on 30 March 1982, in Tashkent. Reported in *Pravda Vostoka*, 31 March 1982, pp. 1–3 Translated in *JPRS: USSR Report*, 13 May 1982, pp. 87–9.
21. See, for example, T. Shabad, 'Some Aspects of Central Asian Manpower and Urbanisation', *Soviet Geography*, February 1979, p. 117.

6 THE STRUCTURE OF INCOMES

1. A. McAuley, *Economic Welfare in the Soviet Union* (Wisconsin: University of Wisconsin Press, 1979) p. 9.
2. Lack of data precludes a discussion of the effects of other factors such as taxes on the income of Soviet citizens. But since taxes are small in absolute magnitude and for the most part are scheduled proportionally, there is no reason to suspect that these factors would greatly affect comparisons in living standards among the nationalities within Uzbekistan or among Uzbekistan's employed and non-working populations. See ibid, passim.
3. For an excellent discussion of the second economy, see G. Grossman, 'The Second Economy of the USSR', *Problems of Communism*, September–October 1977, p. 26.
4. The Constitution of the USSR states that 'No one can rightly use socialist property for the aims of personal profit and for other mercenary ends', (see *Constitution of the USSR* [Tashkent: Fan, 1977] pp. 17–18). For fuller discussions of the second economy in the USSR, see G. Grossman, 'The Second Economy ...' *passim* and G. Feiffer, 'Russia's Disorders', *Harpers*, vol. 262, no. 1569, February 1981, *passim*.
5. G. Grossman, 'The Second Economy ...' p. 26. 'Although in principle the private plot and *kolkhoz* market are legal,' Grossman writes 'they are quite frequently associated with illegalities'.

6. A. Grigoriev, 'Basic Principles of the Organisation of Labour in the USSR', *Lectures on Labour and Economic Development* (Geneva: International Institute for Labour Studies, 1963) p. 25.
7. A. McAuley, *'Economic Welfare . . .'* p. 44. When the amount of time worked is taken into consideration, moreover, the income disparity among sectors may widen. Often, for example, a collective farmer in Uzbekistan may work fewer man-days than the average industrial worker, thus leading to further disparities in yearly income. Similarly, average family-size tends to be larger among collective farmers and personnel in light industries and the service sphere than among industrial personnel; this also affects household incomes by sector. In 1970, for example, the proportion of children under 16 years old in collective farm families in Uzbekistan was 1.4 times greater, and the total number of family members, twice those of the families of Uzbekistan's industrial workers. In 1968, collective farmers earned approximately 63 per cent of the average wage for industry; calculated per family member, they received about 36 per cent of the industrial average (calculated from K. Popadiuk, 'O sootnoshenii urovnei dokhodov i potrebleniia sotsial'nykh grupp naseleniia UzSSR', *Obshchestvennye nauki v Uzbekistane*, no. 7, 1970, p. 21).
8. See G. Schroeder, 'Regional Differences in Income in the USSR in the 1970s', *Regional Development in the USSR*, NATO Colloquium, April 1979, *passim*.
9. A. Nove, and J. A. Newth, *The Soviet Middle East* (London: Allen & Unwin, 1967) p. 102.
10. G. Schroeder, 'Regional Differences . . .', p. 297.
11. V. Zhivaev, 'Lichnoe podsobnoe khoziaistvo v sisteme sotsialisticheskikh proizvoditel'nykh otnoshenii', *Kommunist Uzbekistana*, no. 9, 1980, p. 41.
12. A. Nove, 'The Economics of Nationality Policy', paper delivered at the annual convention of the AAASS, Philadelphia, Pennsylvania, November 1981, p. 5. 'In the USSR' Nove writes 'it is not enough to know that beef costs two roubles per kilo, or sandals 15 roubles a pair. They may be only occasionally obtainable in one town, much more regularly available in others' (p. 5).
13. See R. A. Ubaidullaeva, 'Regional'nye problemy razmeshcheniia . . .', and interviews, 1979.
14. In making these comparisons, absence of data precludes taking into account the type of consumer goods bought by individual populations. As consumption patterns differ widely by region in the USSR – due to climate, tradition, etc. – the comparisons here are intended to provide insight into a broad situation only. Central Asians, for example, tend to buy less furniture, fewer household amenities and less winter clothing than the Russians in the north; and the higher proportion of children in Central Asia who consume less food than adults also makes comparisons with other parts of the USSR difficult unless measured in terms of households. None the less, during the 1978–9 school year, the availability of consumer goods and food at retail prices was reported by Soviet scholars as being in shorter supply in Uzbekistan, including Tashkent,

than either in Moscow or Leningrad and than the all-Union average. In 1974, Ubaidullaeva noted that the availability of underwear in Uzbekistan at retail prices was 40 per cent the USSR average, and of shoes, about 62–63 per cent. I never saw cheese or fresh meat available in a state store, only twice did I find eggs available, and, as elsewhere in the USSR, the limited selection of fruits and vegetables which could be purchased at state prices was generally already spoiled by the time it had reached the shelves of Uzbekistan's stores.

15. V. Zhivaev, 'Lichnoe podsobnoe khoziaistvo . . .' p. 44. According to this article, the private economy plays a significant role for urban and rural populations alike: 'The provision of collective farmers with agricultural products' Zhivaev writes 'occurs mainly due to subsidiary agriculture, since the socialised economy is still not in a state to produce the entire assortment of products necessary for the life of the people.' As another local scholar noted 'A significant part of the needs of the urban population are also satisfied by production of the private subsidiary economy of toilers of the countryside, through the *kolkhoz* markets and consumer co-operatives'. (See K. Saidov, 'Ekonomicheskaia rol' lichnogo podsobnogo khoziaistvo na sovremennom etape', *Kommunist Uzbekistana*, no. 5, May 1979, p. 42.)

16. K. Saidov, 'Ekonomicheskaia rol' lichnogo podsobnogo khoziaistva na sovremennom etape', *Kommunist Uzbekistana*, no. 5, May 1979, p. 28. Several Westerners feel that even these figures are severely underestimated.

17. V. Zhivaev, 'Lichnoe podsobnoe khoziaistvo . . .', 1980, p. 44.

18. K. Saidov, 'Ekonomichesaia rol' . . .', p. 28.

19. Ibid, p. 28, and V. Zhivaev, 'Lichnoe podsobnoe khoziaistvo . . .', *passim*. The high level of production in private subsidiary agriculture in Uzbekistan is particularly important with regard to meat and animal products. In 1977, 62.5 per cent of the gross agricultural product from private subsidiary activity in Uzbekistan was from animal husbandry, as against 37.5 per cent from farming. In the beginning of 1978, 53 per cent of all long-horned cattle (including 77 per cent of all cows); 27 per cent of Uzbekistan's sheep and goats; 37 per cent of all fowl; and 60 per cent of all rabbits were in the private subsidiary economy of collective farmers and of workers and employees of Uzbekistan's state farms, accounting for more than half the total beef production in Uzbekistan. Today, only the production of poultry is declining in the private sector, although this level, too, is still much higher than the average for the USSR as a whole. This scarcity of meat is often explained by the fact that animal husbandry comprises only 25 per cent of the gross *kolkhoz/sovkhoz* production, while crop cultivation comprises 75 per cent. The scarcity of meat for the USSR as a whole is illustrated particularly graphically by A. R. Khan and D. Ghai, *Collective Agriculture and Rural Development in Soviet Central Asia* (London: The Macmillan Press Ltd, 1979) p. 24. 'The really dramatic change occurred for meat. By 1976, it had become a very heavily protected item; its procurement price was more than twice as high as that in the world market', (p. 32).

20. F. Ovechkin, 'Idem na rynok', *Pravda Vostoka*, 1 July 1980, p. 3.

21. K. Saidov, 'Ekonomicheskaia rol' . . .', p. 28.

22. Calculated from TsSU, *Narodnoe khoziaistvo Uzbekskoi SSR 1974 goda*, pp. 162, 164, 136 and 300.

23. See M. Rywkin, 'Housing in Central Asia: The Uzbek Example', in Steven A. Grant (ed.) *Soviet Housing and Urban Design* (US Department of Housing and Urban Development, September 1980) p. 40. In 1977, Uzbekistan had an average of 3.17 square metres of per capita private housing, as against 2.30 in the RSFSR.

24. G. Feiffer, 'Russia's Disorders', pp. 29 and 31.

25. G. Grossman, 'The Second Economy of the USSR', p. 34. See also J. M. Kramer, 'Political Corruption in the USSR', *The Western Political Quarterly*, June 1977, p. 14.

26. Alex Pravda, conversation with the author, 1980.

27. See, for example, 'O Marksistsko – Leninskoi uchebe i ekonomicheskom obrazovanii rukovodiashchikh kadrov v Tashkentskoi gorodskoi partiinoi organizatsii', Decree of the Central Committee of the CPSU, 8 August 1972, and 'Ob organizatorskoi i politicheskoi rabote Tbilisskogo gorkoma kompartii Gruzii po vypolnenniiu reshennii XXIV s"ezda KPSS', Decree of the Central Committee of the CPSU, 29 February 1972.

28. See, for example, A. D. Davletov, *Predvaritel'noe rassledovanie i preduprezhdenie khishchenii sotsialisticheskogo imushchestva* (Tashkent: Fan,1978). Several new films have come out in Moscow, such as *Foam* (1979), satirising the second economy but with a strong moral message (see the *New York Times*, 2 December 1979, p. 93).

29. A. D. Davletov, *Predvaiitel'noe*, p. 192.

30. See I. Birman, *Secret Incomes of the Soviet State Budget* (The Netherlands: Sijthoff and Noordhoff, 1980) *passim*.

31. V. Zhivaev, 'Lichnoe podsobnoe khoziaistvo. . .', p. 45.

32. For example, see G. Grossman, 'The Second Economy. . .', p. 30: 'Generally speaking, in an economy with pervasive goods shortages such as exist in the Soviet Union, physical or administrative control over goods often confers both the power and the opportunity for economic gain to the individual, be he or she ever so humble in the formal hierarchy', and J. Berliner, *Factory and Manager in the USSR*, pp. 191–2: 'Everybody who has some power over goods has a supplementary income based on *blat*'. As Grossman adds, 'Given the plethora of administrative superiors, controllers, inspectors, auditors, law-enforcers, party authorities, expediters and just plain snoopers that beset every economic activity, legal or illegal, in the Soviet Union, anything done out of line requires buying off some, and often many people'.

33. For example, see A. S. Chamkin, 'Motivy k trudu v sfere obshchestvennogo proizvodstva', unpublished doctoral dissertation, Tashkent, 1976, p. 101: 'The prevalence of Uzbeks in the orientation towards the household economy is explained by the existence in their midst of large families. Employment in the household economy allows them to diminish significantly expenditures on food from the family budget.'

34. F. Ovechkin, 'Idem na rynok', p. 3.

35. For official figures, see TsSU *Narodnoe khoziaistvo Uzbekskoi SSR 1978 goda*. These statistics are similar to the estimates made by Khan and Ghai,

of an average of 900 roubles per year, or about 29 per cent of an average collective farm household income. (See A. R. Khan, and D. Ghai, *Collective Agriculture and Rural Development in Soviet Central Asia* [London: Macmillan, 1979]). On the basis of a study of five Central Asian collective farms, they conclude 'If the data about the five *kolkhozy* are anything to go by, the contribution of personal plots to family income is by no means small. Income from a personal plot, including self-consumption, varies rather widely – from 18 to 40 per cent of the total household income defined to include income from the following sources; collective *kolkhoz* labour, outside employment and personal plot.' Estimates made by other Western analysts, however, suggest that even these figures are too low. For example, see A. McAuley, *Economic Welfare . . ., passim.*

36. See K. Saidov, 'Ekonomicheskaia rol'. . .', p. 30, and A. R. Khan and D. Ghai, *Collective Agriculture . . .*, p. 93.

37. In other words, not only do the Georgians have a reputation for amassing great amounts of wealth from activities outside the socialised economy; the Central Asians must be accorded this honour as well. As one scholar put it, a high level of private initiative is often described, in so many words, as 'something a visitor to Uzbekistan or Georgia almost feels in the air', (M. Rywkin, 'Housing in Central Asia. . .', p. 4).

38. A. D. Davletov, *Predvaritel'noe . . .*, p. 191.

39. Ibid, p. 179. For a general discussion of different opportunities for corruption and embezzlement by economic sector, see M. Marrese, 'The Evolution of Wage Regulation in Hungary', Discussion Paper no. 111, October 1979, *passim.*

40. 'Depending on these factors, plunderers in industrial enterprises apply various methods of embezzlement, either of finances, of raw materials and half-finished or finished goods, or of "black" production', (ibid, p. 191).

41. See G. Grossman, 'The Second Economy . . .', p. 34. As he notes, for example, conversions of bank money into cash 'is crucial for underground operations which derive revenue from the state sector, because state-owned entities as a rule dispose of very little currency'. See also A. D. Davletov, *Predvaritel'noe . . .* p. 56. On the purely legal side, moreover, it is interesting to note that incomes among collective farmers in Uzbekistan are substantially higher than those in other parts of the USSR, despite the often lower productivity.

42. A. D. Davletov, *Predirvaitel'noe . . .*, p. 188. Indeed, as a Western observer writes 'It is safe to suggest that virtually everyone who holds a managerial position in the Soviet retail-trade network breaks the law almost daily.' In 1979, the deputy director of a clothing store was arrested; according to several accounts, he had been selling finished products on the black market, and according to rumour had amassed four twenty-gallon canisters of Tsarist gold coins! The directorship of a Tashkent market apparently is one of the most 'highly paid' jobs in Uzbekistan.

43. See, for example, P. Wiles, 'Anti-Systemic Economic Behaviour in the USSR (ASB): Definitions, Volume, Ethnicity', Unpublished paper, March 1980. As Wiles points out, transport in all countries is 'the backbone of anti-systemic behaviour in retail trade'. In the USSR, transportation is apparently the source of a considerable amount of

building material that enters illegal channels and makes possible much private, *kolkhoz* and at times even state-enterprise construction. It is also an essential ingredient of other forms of private activity.

44. For several examples, see A. D. Davletov, *Predvaritel'noe . . .*, p. 207.
45. Again, for a broad comparison, see C. Geertz, *Peddlers and Princes* (Chicago: University of Chicago, 1968). As he notes with regards to Indonesia, an arrangement where political and professional ties are personally rather than territorially organised tends to 'breed intrigue' anywhere in the world.
46. A. D. Davletov, *Predvaritel'noe . . .*, pp. 192 and 195.
47. Ibid, p. 195. Davletov notes that black production is often carried out 'by agreement with the guard personnel'.
48. See J. M. Kramer, 'Political corruption . . .', *passim*. As Kramer notes, the head of a wholesale consumer goods trust in Tashkent 'started the bidding' for position of warehouse chief at 5000 roubles. See also I. Zemtsov, *La Corruption en Union Sovietique* (Paris: Les Editeurs Reunis, 1976) *passim*. While this book focuses on Azerbaijan, Zemtsov cites the most 'expensive' occupations in Azerbaijan – that is, those which require the largest bribes – as the First and Second Secretaries; directors of *kolkhozes, sovkhozes*, plants, factories, institutes and theatres; government and party officials; the police and control commissions; legal work; professors; hospital personnel; Party posts, and some other service personnel. In Uzbekistan, most of these posts are dominated by the indigenous nationalities.
49. For a description of the elaborate amounts of money traditionally spent on births, marriages and deaths, for example, see Arminius Vambery, *Russia Observed* (New York: Amo Press and the New York Times, 1970) pp. 98–100. As Vambery notes, these festivals and celebrations are characterised by a 'considerable number of guests' who must be feasted 'as sumptuously as possible' (p. 100). Much the same emphasis on elaborate and expensive rituals and rites holds true today.
50. I. Birman, *Secret Incomes . . .*, p. 150.
51. L. Dupree, *Afghanistan* (Princeton: Princeton University Press, 1980). See also P. Wiles, 'Anti-Systemic Economic Behaviour . . .', pp. 21 and 48b. As Wiles notes, it appears that 'Uzbeks have an immense liquidity preference. They hoard gold, where Slavs buy durables. Part, but only part, of these hoards goes eventually in wedding feasts, which tourists may easily miss. So the tourist ascribes lower incomes to them'.
52. I. Birman, *Secret Incomes . . .*, p. 150.

7   THE ROLE OF CULTURE

1. D. Moynihan, and N. Glazer, *Ethnicity* (Cambridge, Mass.: Harvard University Press, 1975), pp. 12, 14 and 17.
2. See Louis Schneider and C. M. Bonjean, *The Idea of Culture in the Social Sciences* (Cambridge: Cambridge University Press, 1973) Introduction.

Culture is defined as 'that complex whole which includes knowledge, belief, art, morals, law, custom and any other capabilities and habits acquired by man as a member of society', (p. vi). As Talcott Parsons notes in the same volume, all human societies are interpenetrated with culture. The task is to systematically analyse the structure of culture systems and the way they are expressed in different societies. See also D. Moynihan, and N. Glazer, *Ethnicity*, p. 56 and p. 8, and A. Brown, Introduction in A. Brown and J. Gray (eds) *Political Culture and Political Change in Communist States* (New York: Holmes & Meier Publishers, Inc., 1979).

3. C. Geertz, *The Interpretation of Cultures* (New York: Basic Books, 1973) p. 10.

4. J. Berliner, *Research Report on the Family*, monograph prepared for the National Council, Washington, DC, May 1981. For the different types of arguments proposed, see A. Brown, Introduction, ibid, pp. 1–10. See also Daniel Bell, 'Ethnicity and Social Change', in D. Moynihan and N. Glazer (eds) *Ethnicity*, pp. 141–74.

5. K. Boulding, 'Towards the Development of a Cultural Economics', *The Idea of Culture in the Social Sciences*, pp. 47–65 and p. 53.

6. Ibid, p. 51. 'As far as economic theory is concerned', Boulding writes 'abstraction has completely conquered the field. One can look in vain, for instance, through issue after issue of the *American Economic Review* to try to find anything which even remotely suggests a cultural context'.

7. Ibid, p. 53.

8. Lucian Pye, 'Culture and Political Science: Problems in the Evaluation of the Concept of Political Culture', *The Idea of Culture in the Social Sciences*, p. 65.

9. Quoted in L. K. Shek, *Vospitanie ubezhdennogo internatsionalista* (Tashkent: Uzbekistan, 1974) p. 100.

10. See translation of TASS report on speech delivered by Iurii Andropov: 'Sixty Years of the USSR: Iurii Andropov's Report at the Kremlin Meeting', Moscow, 21 December 1982, translated in FBIS, 21 December 1982, pp. P4–6 and L. I. Brezhnev, *O kommunisticheskom vospitanii trudiashchikhsia. Stat'i i rechi* (Moscow: Isdatel'stvo Politicheskoi Literatury 1974) pp. 481–2, quoted in A. S. Chamkin, 'Motivy k trudu v sfere obshchestvennogo proizvodstva', dissertation, Tashkent, 1976, p. 6. As Brezhnev writes 'Nationalistic prejudices, the exaggeration or distorted manifestation of national feelings is an extraordinarily tenacious phenomenon, tenaciously keeping itself in the psychology of people insufficiently mature in a political sense. These prejudices continue to be retained even in conditions when the objective pre-conditions for some kind of antagonisms in the relations between nations has already long since ceased to exist.' As a contemporary social scientist, writing in Tashkent, noted more than six decades after Lenin's death, 'Socialist social consciousness at its foundation is the same for all social groups of our society, since it represents the common character of their interests, the commonality of ideology (our society has one ideology: Marxist Leninism); the commonality of feelings (for the absolute majority of members of our society, the feelings of patriotism, internationalism, collectivism,

etc. are characteristic); the commonality of goals and tasks arising from the programme of Communist construction. . . . However, the existence of political and ideological unity does not totally erase the differences in consciousness of the working class, the *kolkhoz* peasantry and the intelligentsia. At the same time, for some part of the members of socialist society, survivals of the old consciousness are retained. This is explained by the fact that changes in social relations cannot call forth an instantaneous, automatic change in the social consciousness, in the consciousness of the individual personality, since the significant power of inertia is in the nature of the spiritual ideas of people. In such a way, in the conditions of socialism, social consciousness is uniform; but simultaneously, the consciousness of individual personalities can differ from the consciousness of other personalities and from the basic norms of social consciousness.' See M. Soldatov, *Trudovoe vospitanie mass* (Tashkent: Uzbekistan, 1972), pp. 91–92.

11. Quoted in M. F. Soldatov, *Trudovoe vospitanie mass* (Tashkent: Uzbekistan, 1972) p. 93.
12. M. I. Kulichenko, *Natsional'nye otnosheniia v rasvitom sotsialisticheskom obshchestve* (Moscow: Mysl', 1977) p. 53. See also M. I. Kulichenko, *Rastsvet i sblizhenie natsii v SSSR* (Moscow: Mysl', 1981) *passim*.
13. M. F. Soldatov, *Trudovoe vospitanie . . .*, pp. 97–98.
14. Ibid, p. 91.
15. Olaf Caroe, *Soviet Empire: The Turks of Central Asia and Stalinism* (New York: St. Martin's Press, 1967) p. 215.
16. Ibid, p. 47.
17. Sh. Muzaparov, 'Kul'tura i byt Uzbekov-neftianikov Ferganskoi doliny', unpublished doctoral dissertation, Tashkent, 1967, p. 46.
18. E. Bacon, *Central Asians under Russian Rule* (New York: Cornell University Press, 1966) p. 187.
19. Speech presented by S. R. Rashidov at the 22nd Komsomol Congress, Tashkent, 30 March 1982, and printed in *Pravda Vostoka*, 31 March 1982, pp. 1–3. Translated in *Joint Publications Research Service: USSR Report*, 13 May 1982, pp. 87–9. See also interview with Talib Saidbayev, *Moscow News*, no. 47, 28 November–5 December, 1982, p. 12. Translated in JPRS, USSR Report, pp. 78–80.
20. James C. Scott, *The Moral Economy of the Peasant* (New Haven: Yale University Press, 1976) pp. 35–7.
21. Ibid, p. 55.
22. C. Geertz, *Peddlers and Princes*, p. 59.
23. See, for example, J. S. Birks, and C. A. Sinclair, 'The Kingdom of Saudi Arabia and the Libyan Arab Jamehiriya: The Key Countries of Employment', Migration for Employment Project, Working Paper WEP 2-26/WP39 (Geneva: International Labour Organisation, 1979) especially pp. 21–26.
24. See Giuseppe Pennisi, *Development, Manpower and Migration in the Red Sea Region* (Hamburg: Deutsches Orient-Institut, 1981) and B. Hansen and S. Radwan, *Employment Opportunities and Equity in a Changing Economy: Egypt in the 1980s* (Geneva: International Labour Office,

1982). Hansen's study notes an aversion to manual work represents a 'social value which is affecting the education and training system. Technical education and vocational training are frowned upon by the population as a second class type of education'. As he adds with regard to Egypt 'social values may be the factor which has the strongest impact on the education and training system' today (p. 225).

25. See J. S. Birks and C. Sinclair 'The Kingdom of Saudi Arabia . . .', pp. 21–6.

26. J. S. Birks and C. Sinclair, 'Manpower in Saudi Arabia, 1980–85', in R. El Mallakh and D. El Mallakh (eds) *Saudi Arabia* (Toronto: Lexington Books, 1981) p. 163.

27. E. Bacon, *Central Asians Under Russian Rule*, p. 167.

28. Again parallels with the Middle East may be instructive. As Birks and Sinclair have noted, traditional occupations in rural areas of many parts of the Arab world are not strenuous; are not subject to 'rigorous disciplines associated with modern sector employment'; and are 'not ordered by impersonal authorities which the tribesman has little reason or inclination to respect'. For these reasons, they note, most of the rural population in the Arab world is disinclined to be formally employed. With regard to Saudi Arabia, for example, they note that the high value placed upon leisure, the disinclination to work in manual, or manually strenuous jobs, and the desire not to be subordinate to an impersonal outside authority comprise 'an important explanatory factor behind many Saudi Arabian's reluctance to enter a wide spectrum of employments in the modern sector'. See J. S. Birks and C. Sinclair, 'The Kingdom of Saudi Arabia . . .', p. 23, and J. S. Birks and C. Sinclair, 'Manpower in Saudi Arabia . . .', in *Saudi Arabia*, p. 163.

29. Quoted from T. Shabad, 'Some Aspects of Central Asian Manpower and Urbanization', *Soviet Geography*, February 1979, p. 114.

30. See D. Montgomery, 'Return to Tashkent', *Asian Affairs*, Part I: vol. x, June 1979 and Part II: vol. x, October 1979, pp. 300–1. See also M. I. Kulichenko, *Natsional'nye otnosheniia v razvitom sotsialisticheskom obshchestve* (Moscow: Mysl', 1977): 'The steadfastness of labour and family traditions in significant measure still orients the indigenous nationalities of Central Asia and Kazakhstan to a rural way of life.'

31. A. Vambery, *Russia Observed* (New York: Arno Press, 1970).

32. Eugene Schuyler, *Turkestan* (New York: Praeger, 1966) pp. 21–2.

33. A. S. Chamkin, 'Motivy k trudu v sfere obshchestvennogo proizvodstva', doctoral dissertation, Tashkent, 1976, p. 7.

34. V. Pokshishevskii, 'Etnicheskie protsessy v sovetskikh gorodakh i nekotorye problemy ikh izuchenii', *Sovetskaia Etnografiia*, no. 5, 1969.

35. In 1973, for example, Arutiunian echoed the necessity for research in this field by analysing, albeit quite generally, motivations towards work and value orientations of different nationality groups in the USSR (see I. V. Arutiunian, *Sotsial'naia i natsional'naia* (Moscow: Nauka, 1973) *passim.*) Other Soviet scholars addressed the issue more tangentially in the course of works on other topics. For example, see T. R. Abdushukurov, *Zakonomernosti i osobennosti kul'turno-tekhnicheskogo rosta rabochego klassa Uzbekistana,* (Tashkent: Fan 1971). Abdushukurov analyses

problems connected with labour activity, but not attitudes towards work *per se.*

36. A. S. Chamkin, 'Motivy k trudu ...'.

37. Research was carried out in construction combines in the cities of Dzhizak, Bekabad and Yangier, and in construction assembly trusts in Karshi, Obrucheva and Binokora, UzSSR and in Leninabad, Tadzhikistan. Over half (52 per cent) the total labour force studied had come from another republic; one quarter (25.8 per cent) had been drawn from the given city or region; one eighth (12.8 per cent), from another *oblast'* within Uzbekistan; and about one tenth (9.4 per cent), from another city or region within the same *oblast'*. As Table 7.1 illustrates, more than half had moved to the given city or region since 1960, and one quarter had been born there. The personnel from neighbouring regions, cities and *oblasts* of Uzbekistan were for the most part youth who had been sent to these enterprises by *komsomol* assignment. From the 1960s on, the in-migrants were mainly youths without families, as opposed to the late 1950s when migration to these areas was mainly among young married couples.

38. Women comprised 37.5 per cent of Chamkin's sample, of whom about 37 per cent were in unskilled work, about 42 per cent in semi-skilled work, and 21 per cent in skilled work. Of the men, 20 per cent were in unskilled work, 32 per cent in semi-skilled and almost half (48 per cent) in skilled work. Of all personnel surveyed, 12.3 per cent had received educational training in evening courses and *tekhnikums*, 0.5 per cent in higher educational establishments, 1.4 per cent in the network of political educational establishments and 85.8 per cent had not received higher than secondary education. The younger personnel were concentrated in the skilled work, the older, in unskilled work.

39. Ibid, p. 101.

40. Ibid, p. 102.

41. 'A much more complex object of internationalisation are those spheres of social life in which the indelible stamp of national distinctiveness exists. Thus, production in the contemporary stage does not have specific national features and is rapidly crossing national boundaries – which cannot be said about culture, domestic life and art, which have national-specific features ...' (ibid, p. 98).

42. Ibid, pp. 132 and 12.

43. Ibid, pp. 76–7.

44. Sh. Muzaparov, 'Kul'tura i byt Uzbekov-neftianikov Ferganskoi doliny', unpublished doctoral dissertation (Tashkent, 1967) *passim.*

45. M. F. Soldatov, *Trudovye vospitanie mass*, p. 5.

46. Ibid, p. 16.

47. L. K. Shek, *Vospitanie ubezhdennogo internatsionalista* (Tashkent: Uzbekistan, 1974) p. 185.

48. Ibid, p. 186.

49. For example, see E. Iu. Iusupov (ed.) *Iz opyta partiinoi propagandy v Uzbekistane* (Tashkent: Uzbekistan, 1976) p. 146. In 1973 alone, he notes, more than 6400 lectures were delivered in factory collectives in Uzbekistan on these themes.

50. See Christel Lane, *The Rites of Rulers: Ritual in Industrial Society – The Soviet Case* (Cambridge: Cambridge University Press, 1981).
51. L. K. Shek, *Vospitanie ubezhdennogo internatsionalista*, p. 99.
52. Ibid, p. 100.
53. Ibid, p. 100. See also M. Kh. Karimov, 'The Strengthening of the Friendship of the Peoples of the USSR and International Education', *Nauchnyi Kommunism*, November–December 1982, pp. 65–70. Translated in JPRS, *USSR Report*, 19 April 1983, pp. 46–47.
54. Speech delivered by Sh. R. Rashidov, at the 22nd Komsomol Congress, Tashkent, 30 March 1982, *Pravda Vostoka*, 31 March 1982, pp. 1–3.
55. L. K. Shek, *Vospitanie ubezhdennogo internatsionalista*, p. 105.
56. See *Turkmenskaia Iskra*, 24 April 1976, p. 1. The article's findings were upheld in factory interviews in Uzbekistan, 1978–9, suggesting they may be equally applicable to the Uzbek republic.
57. L. I. Brezhnev, *O kommunisticheskom vospitanii ...* Quoted in A. S. Chamkin, 'Motivy k trudu...', p. 6

8 LOOKING AHEAD

1. Quoted in D. Carlisle, 'Modernisation, Generations and the Uzbek Soviet Intelligentsia', in P. Cocks, R. Daniels and N. Heer (eds), *The Dynamics of Soviet Politics* (Cambridge, Mass.: Harvard University Press, 1976) p. 261. Fainsod's analysis of the attitudes of new governing élites applies to present-day Uzbekistan: 'The Bolshevik Revolution' he writes 'built its own network of revolutionary beneficiaries with vested interests in the perpetuation of the new order'. For a similar reaction regarding the present day Middle East, see also Malcolm Kerr, 'Arab Nationalism: Is it Obsolete?' *Middle East Insight*, vol. II, no. 3, 1982, p. 20.
2. William Fierman, 'Uzbek Feelings of Ethnicity', unpublished paper prepared for the Bureau of Intelligence and Research, US State Department, 1980, p. 3.
3. As M. Rywkin writes 'British or French settlers (except for the poorest among the *"petit francais"* of Algeria) have always regarded themselves as socially superior to the native masses. Indeed, their way of life, their manners, dressing-style, recreation and sports habits, became symbols of "the good life" for the élite of the colonised groups ... But this has not been the case with the Russians. While some higher class Russians, especially the officers of the victorious Imperial Army, impressed the awed natives, the much more numerous low-class Russian settlers failed to impress their Muslim neighbours ... While some native habits, like spitting tobacco, sitting on the floor and eating with their hands, seemed unhygienic to the Russians, low-class Russian rudeness seemed equally "uncultured" to the natives.' See M. Rywkin, 'Dissent in Soviet Central Asia', paper delivered at the Conference on the Soviet Union and Eastern Europe, Garmisch, West Germany, 1980, pp. 4–5.
4. See V. Zaslavskii and Iu. Luryi, 'The Passport System in the USSR', *Soviet Union/Union Sovietique*, vol. 6, part 2, 1979, p. 150.

5. H. Seton-Watson, 'The Last of the Empires', *Washington Quarterly,* vol. 3, no. 2, Spring, 1980, p. 42.
6. Cyril Black, 'The Dynamics of Modernization', in F. Tachau (ed.) *The Developing Nations: What path to Modernization?* (New York: Dodd, Mead & Co., 1972) p. 39.
7. C. Geertz, *Peddlers and Princes* (Chicago: University of Chicago, 1968) p. 150.
8. Walker Connor, 'The Politics of Ethnonationalism', *Journal of International Affairs,* vol. 27, no. 1, 1973, p. 20.
9. See J. F. Besemeres, *Socialist Population Politics* (New York: M. E. Sharpe, 1980) p. 68.
10. H. Carrère d'Encausse, *Decline of an Empire* (New York: Newsweek, 1981) p. 249.
11. For a description of the demonstrations which occurred in Georgia in April 1978 and other manifestations of dissent over language issues, see, for example, Elizabeth Fuller, 'Expressions of Official and Unofficial Concern over the Future of the Georgian Language', *RFE/RL Research Bulletin,* RL 149/81, 7 April 1981.
12. An acronym for the three major cities of the Fergana Valley: Fergana, Andizhan and Namangan.
13. D. Montgomery, 'Return to Tashkent', *Asian Affairs,* June and October 1979, p. 295.
14. See, for example, 'The Status of the Khorezm Turks in the Uzbek National Identity', *RFE/RL Background Report,* RL 61/77, 15 March 1977, and ibid, p. 301.
15. According to one estimate, less than 5 per cent of Ireland's population, or 150 000 people out of a total population of 3.3 million, today speaks Gaelic. See also W. Connor, 'The Politics of Ethnonationalism', pp. 37–8.
16. A. H. Brown, 'Political Developments: Some Conclusions and an Interpretation', in A. Brown and M. Kaser (eds) *The Soviet Union Since the Fall of Khrushchev* (London: Macmillan, 1975) p. 258.
17. Walker Connor, Lecture at the Ethnic and Race Relations Seminar, St Antony's College, Oxford University, Autumn, 1977.
18. H. Carrère d'Encausse, *Decline of an Empire,* p. 275.

APPENDIX 2

1. V. Mikheeva, 'Trudovye resursy malykh i srednykh gorodov Uzbekistana i perspektivy ikh ispol'zovaniia', unpublished doctoral dissertion (Tashkent, 1975), p. 73.
2. Ibid, p. 57.
3. Ibid, p. 57.
4. Ibid, p. 46.
5. Ibid, p. 133.

Index